Gandhi, Women and Sexuality
Reflections Through Letters

About the Author

Dr. Anil Dutta Mishra is a distinguished Gandhian scholar and writer. He started his career as Assistant Professor in the Department of Nonviolence and Peace Studies, Jain Vishva Bharati University, Ladnun, Rajasthan, became Deputy Director of National Gandhi Museum and Honorary Professor, Centre for Gandhian Philosophy and Human Development, Gayatri Vidya Parishad Degree College (Autonomous), Visakhapatnam.

Dr. Mishra has held the post of General Secretary of Indian Society of Gandhian Studies, Alliance for Sarvodaya, Member Board of Studies, Nagpur and Punjab Universities and is Member of Gandhian Studies Centre of different colleges and universities across India sponsored by UGC. He has authored/edited 30 books and published a number of research papers. His recent book Reading Gandhi is widely acclaimed. Presently, he is Treasurer, IIPA, Delhi Regional Branch, New Delhi.

Email: anilduttamishra@gmail.com

Gandhi, Women and Sexuality

Reflections Through Letters

Anil Dutta Mishra

CONCEPT PUBLISHING COMPANY PVT. LTD.
NEW DELHI - 110059

ISBN: 978-93-5594-650-8 (HB)
ISBN: 978-93-5594-651-5 (PB)

First Published 2023

Published and Printed by

Concept Since 1974

Concept Publishing Company Pvt. Ltd.
A/15-16, Commercial Block, Mohan Garden
New Delhi-110059 (India)
T: +91-11-41101460
E: publishing@conceptpub.com, *W*: www.conceptpub.com

Cataloging in Publication--Courtesy: D.K. Agencies (P) Ltd. <docinfo@dkagencies.com>

Mishra, Anil Dutta, 1965- **author.**
Gandhi, women and sexuality : reflections through letters / Anil Dutta Mishra.
pages cm
Includes bibliographical references and index.
ISBN 9789355946508 (HB)
ISBN 9789355946515 (PB)

1. Gandhi, Mahatma, 1869-1948--Relations with women. 2. Gandhi, Mahatma, 1869-1948--Correspondence. 3. Nationalists--India--Correspondence. 4. Statesman--India--Correspondence. I. Title.

LCC DS481.G3M57 2023 | DDC 954.035092 23

Acknowledgements

This work 'Gandhi, Women and Sexuality: Reflections Through Letters' is the result of more than two decades of my original research on Mahatma Gandhi, who always carried out experiments after experiments for the liberation of mother India from the yoke of colonial power. It is my pleasure to express my gratitude to a large number of people without whom this work would not have been possible. First and foremost, I would like to place my gratitude to Dr. Amrendra Kumar Dubey, IAS, for going through the preface and introduction minutely and making corrections and changes wherever necessary. I would also like to thank my teachers, Professor Susheela Kaushik, Professor Manoranjan Mohanty, Professor Neera Chandhoke, Professor R.B. Jain and Professor M.P. Singh, all from University of Delhi and Professor M.S. Verma, Professor Prabhakar Pathak and Professor Bharti Srivastava of L.N.M.U.

I cannot forget my friends, Mr. Prabhat Ranjan, IRTS, Mr. Atul Tiwari, IAS, Professor P.V. Sarma, Professor A.B.S.V. Ranga Rao and Professor Manohar Lal Sharma, who have always stood by me in all my academic endeavours.

I would like to thank Dr. Bindeshwar Pathak a great emancipator of women in contemporary world, who dedicated his life for social cause and upliftment of dalit and downtroden through Sulabh Movement, Dr. Pathak constantly encourage and blessed me in all my academic pursuits. I have no words to express my inner feelings for him.

Within the family I am grateful to my wife, Dr. Sweta Mishra, and my pretty daughters, Sanstuti and Sansriti, for providing me peaceful environment to complete this work.

Vaishali **Anil Dutta Mishra**
21 May, 2023 anilduttamishra@gmail.com

Preface

Mahatma Gandhi was a creative man, concurrently writing history for himself and rest of the world to follow. Being a constructive activist throughout his life, he was continuously experimenting with his ideas and actions in the face of ever evolving contemporary challenges. He experimented with truth in plurality rather than in singularity. His concept of truth was not a static phenomenon. It varied in perspectives, person to person, and hence became a relative concept. He was most simple in thought process but adduced the complexities of thinking in a unique way by combining theory with practice, words with deed and nonviolence with action. He was greatly admired both in India and abroad but this did not leave him from being misunderstood by his own people and colleagues. Gandhi became global necessity but perhaps increasingly less followed in India including in the Gandhian Institutions and the Institutions established by Gandhi himself or in his name.

Through his creativity Gandhi became a great man in diverse sense and in many ways. It is difficult to understand a great person. Bhavbhuti, a great scholar of Sanskrit, rightly said 'who indeed can claim to know and understand the mind of the great?' This is true in case of Gandhi.

Gandhi was a man of public. His approach was humane. He inspired masses and masses inspired him. Being a leader, he used to write and reply the letters everyday. These letters are treasure of information and functions like a light-house in the journey of thought in the ocean of knowledge. There is a lot of misconception about Gandhi. Neither his political mentor (Guru) Gopal Krishna Gokhle, nor his political heir, Pandit Jawaharlal Nehru could fully understand him. Gandhi's adherence to truth and pristine purity demonstrated by his own conduct is perhaps the most transparent way, may seem brahamanical to many. But apparently in this way, the supposedly brahamanical way led Gandhi to record every event of his life truthfully and honestly, that forms the single major source of knowledge about him. Hence, it is hardly surprising when Gandhi interacts with his followers, opponents, critics, fence sitters and detractors with equal ease.

Gandhi's relationship with whosoever came in contact with him was simple, honest and free from psychological and sociological encumbrances. He was at as much ease with the Viceroy as with other grassroots level party worker. He was as considerate to Raj Kumar Shukla, who invited him to Champaran in Bihar, as was he towards Albert Einstein or Romain Rolland, his great personal friends. There was something unique in him that enabled him to interact as confidently with Lord Irwin, as with Madeline Slade (Mira Behn) or Sarojini Naidu. However, in the pre-Independence era, his interaction with women was still a matter of great curiosity and enigma if not an outright stigma.

Gandhi was doing something fundamentally original and unique for aspiring women. Gandhi's relationship with women is well-known, but highly controversial and misunderstood due to various reasons. Lack of proper understanding of Gandhi and lack of knowledge of Indian culture and traditions were the main reasons for such misconception. Gandhi's understanding of women was based on Indian tradition of spirituality and concomitant four purusharthas-Dharma—Artha, Kama and Moksha. Such an understanding indeed formed the world view of Gandhi. If one misses this vantage point of Gandhi, one might end up trivializing his strong sense of gender equality and holding him responsible for his undue attraction towards women. In fact everything was open and transparent in Gandhi's life, and anybody could have ever put it to public scrutiny. In this sense Gandhi epitomises finer values of truth, dignity and integrity in public and private life. Gandhi's extraordinary experiment of celibacy and non-coercion towards women was misconstrued as his degeneration by both his mistaken friends and foes. However, it might be inconvenient to those women Gandhi shared his bed with. But hardly there is any evidence of such women ever raising any doubts on his intention. In fact the answer is simple and straight—Gandhi's relationship with women can be explained as one based on spiritual or platonic love where physical attraction and sex are not even a remote reference.

Therefore, Gandhi's relationship with women can be easily understood by keeping the Indian tradition in mind. As Vinoba says: "Gandhiji was a great man", nevertheless, he had laid bare his mind in its fullness before the world. For his part, he had permitted no secrecy. Even so, I must confess, the last chapter of his life, which I have called the "Swargarohan Parva", or the chapter of the "Ascent to Heaven", remains a mystery to me. Indeed, in my eyes, it stands equal to the last phase of Lord Krishna's Leela. To unravel its mystery, "it may become necessary for Gandhiji himself to be born again".

Gandhi continues to attract the attention of scholars and social scientists on question of his relationship with women and question of sexuality. On the one hand, Gandhi was influenced by his mother and a number of other women, on the other; he influenced a large number of women. Gandhi influenced women and women influenced Gandhi. It was a two way process. To understand Gandhi's relationship with women one must go through all letters which Gandhi himself wrote during his life time. In order to understand the truth, one must read and quote these letters not only inconvenient parts but the whole text in its entirety. Otherwise, the essence of these letters will never come out and people will keep on misunderstanding Gandhi and the mystery about Gandhi's relation with women and question of sexuality will get converted in a weird and distorted way.

The moot question before any scholar will be why Gandhi was comfortable in the company of women? Secondly, why he took naked bath with women or why he preferred body massage by women? And finally, why he slept with women in the last phase of his life? To answer these questions is not an easy task and any interpretation will attract controversy and hue and cry. It was in this background that I referred to most of the letters Gandhi wrote to women in original and have reproduced selected letters of selected women with whom his relationship was misunderstood, and placed them before the readers in this volume.

These letters will be an eye-opener for the readers as it will clear the myths about Gandhi's experimentation with women and question of sexuality. These letters will remove to a large extent, the misconceptions about Gandhi's relationship with women. While quoting Gandhi and his letters, one should invariably refer to the context in which he had written those letters. Never before, letters written by Gandhi to Women were placed at one place. These letters are reproduced here without any distortion and alteration so that the readers draw their own conclusions. I am sure that the book 'Gandhi,Women and Sexuality: Reflections Through Letters' will open new vistas of research and proper understanding of Gandhi on this issue.

Anil Dutta Mishra

Contents

List of Photos

Introduction

From the beginning of human history men and women were attracted towards each other. This attraction is natural and universal. In other words, it is the law of nature. Kanchan (gold) and Kamini (women) have always attracted women and men since the beginning of human civilization. The attraction may be due to love, sharing and caring, social security and desire for fulfilling sexual necessity. Fundamentally, men and women are one; their problems must be shouldered by both. Both are the beings of the same physical reality. The mutuality of each other is reflected through their age-old companionship. Their indispensability is reinforced in the popular chanting of hymns, like Sita-Ram, Gauri-Shankar and Radha-Krishna by the common men and women in India. However, the sublime aspect of it is aesthetically represented by Shivalings that symbolizes the oneness of man and woman and non-duality of their relationship.

The human world is incomprehensible without the complementarity of man and woman. The society is ordered in a way where the company of each other is naturally cherished and valued. Gandhi was not averse to this natural social order. Like any other human being, he too sought the company of women. In fact, Gandhi's concept of truth and nonviolence is based on this universal unity of both man and woman. Pertinently, many women played significant role in Gandhi's life, and commensurably Gandhi also thought that the world was inconceivable without their active participation in it. All the available standard literatures on Gandhi authenticate this proposition. Moreover, he always felt comfortable in the company of women. Though there were a number of women in and around him, he experimented with wife, private secretary or ashramites, who were intimately attached to Gandhi. His life was full of unique experiments, and the experiment of celibacy was one of them.

Gandhi was one of the greatest charismatic leaders, the twentieth century had ever produced. His personality was so mesmerizing that everyone longed to become his close aides and confidants. This is equally true in the case of women. The mere company of Gandhi catapulted a large number of women to name, fame and social recognition. Some of them became very close while working with him. Women under his tutelage were metamorphosed that ultimately accorded them an altogether a new identity and an enduring position in the society. It led them to a voyage to re-exploring their true self that was incongruence with their self-esteem. They were so much swayed by Gandhi that they willingly became the part of Gandhi's experiment of *brahmacharya*. Women, urban and rural, educated and uneducated, Indian and foreign, were attracted to his ideas, deeds and actions. While some like Sucheta Kripalani, Sarojini Naidu, Merabhen, Sushila Nayyar and Rajkumari Amrit Kaur rose to prominence, there were thousands of unsung and unnoticed heroines of India who learnt the meaning of liberation from him and contributed with all their energy to the struggle for independence. Women who came in contact with Gandhi got liberated and he allowed them to come out of the cocoon and develop their individual personality.

Gandhi's relationship with women must be seen in broader context of his worldview based on the harmony of four *purusharthas*—.*Dharma*, *Artha*, *Kama* and *Moksha*. The place and position of women crucially depend on striking a balance among these four cardinal principles as any imbalance will lead to partial understanding of the universe. Although the practice does not confirm absolute equality between man and woman, Indian legends, traditions, myths and mysticism and spirituality unambiguously underlie non-duality and bring unison between them. The riddle of Gandhi's association with women can only be unfolded with the proper understanding of non-duality of man and woman relationship. In other words, Gandhi's mission of life was to elevate women's position to that level of non-duality where merger rather than split rules the roost.

Gandhi was influenced by his mother Putlibai and other women throughout his life. Gandhi beautifully stated that "The outstanding impression my mother has left on my memory is that of saintliness. She was deeply religious. She would not think of taking her meals without daily prayer. She would take the hardest of vows and keep them without flinching. Illness was no excuse for relaxing them." He got his mother's permission to go to England for studies by taking an oath: "I vowed not to touch wine, women and meat." These three vows shielded him throughout his stay in England and later in the public life. Gandhi strictly adhered to these vows.

Gandhi married Kasturba, who was six months older than him, at the age of thirteen. Gandhi was very possessive of Kasturba. In the initial years, she was reluctant to agree with Gandhi on social issues and on the question of his association with women. As the years passed, she became his active partner and supporter in all his endeavours. Like any other Indian woman, she was a truly devoted wife. She had multi-dimensional personality and became "Ba", known as mother of all who took care of Bapu's "extended family". Kasturba was part of Gandhi's experiment on women and as such she provides vital clues to Gandhi's view on women. Gandhi stated honestly about Kasturba, "it is because of her that I am today what I am."

When Kasturba died in captivity due to illness in Aga Khan Palace, Gandhi said "I cannot imagine life without Ba. I had always wished her to go in my hands so I would not have to worry as to what will become of her when I am no more. But she was an indivisible part of me. Her passing away has left a vacuum which will never be filled."

Nobody has done as much as Gandhi had done to bring out mass of illiterate women from the four walls of their houses. A few talented women were spotted by him who worked shoulder to shoulder with him. Like Midas touch, anybody whom he touched, became vibrant and active soldier of movement and not a lifeless idol of adornment. Many of them happily embraced a new lifestyle corresponding to the pressing demand of the time.

Women's influence on Gandhi was not only limited to his mother and wife Kasturba. Gandhi was profoundly influenced by

Annie Besant, Sarojini Naidu, Kamaladevi Chattopadhyaya, Miss Pettit, Miss Slade, Millie Graham Polak, Sonja Schlesin, Sarala Devi Chowdharani, Mirabehn, Lilavati Asar, Premabehn Kantak, Sushila Nayyar, Bibi Amutussalam, Marget Spiegel, Nilla Croom Cook, Rajkumari Amrit Kaur, Prabhavati, Kanchan Shah and Manu Gandhi . These women were what Gandhi calls his "inner circle". Apart from Kasturba, thirteen women whose letters were selected for this volume were part of Gandhi's experiment on *brahmacharya.* A large number of scholars had criticized Gandhi on account of their intimate association with them. He was attacked time and again by these scholars because of his association with these thirteen women, who were part of his experiment. These women were well educated and devoted their live for emancipation of India and become social worker and what not. These women associated themselves with Gandhi for a cause. These letters give us the real picture about his engagement with them. Being educated themselves, they were conscious of their identity, individuality and self-esteem. They were from diverse social backgrounds—hailing from Western countries, princely states and also from humble background. It is the test of one's wisdom, after reading these letters, to find the answer of these women's willing participation in Gandhi's great experimentation on *brahmacharya.* It is naïve to assume that these enlightened women, master of their own persona, were uncritically swayed and persuaded by Gandhi to become a part of the so called unusual experiment. Besides, I leave the final judgment to the critical readers of these letters.

However, one can get answer from what Rajkumari Amrit Kaur, who was part of *brahmacharya* experiment, herself stated that "We found him (Gandhi) not a "Bapu"—wise father, but what is more precious, a mother, whose all embracing and understanding love all fear and restraint vanish." Gandhi gave motherly love, affection and care and security to women who were associated with him. Women were never afraid of Gandhi. Instead, they felt secured and unthreatened. Further in a letter written to Rajkumari Amrit Kaur on 20-10-1936, Gandhi writes, "If you women only realize your dignity and privilege, and make full sense of it for mankind, you will make it much better than it is. But man has delighted in enslaving you and you have proved willing slaves till the slave and holders have become one in the crime on degrading humanity. My special function from childhood, you might say, has been to make women realize her dignity. I was once slave holder myself but Ba proved an unwilling slave and thus "opened my eyes to my mission."

Since Gandhi believed in moral pluralism, he was opposed to any idea and practice of exclusion. He was keen to learn from any philosophical streams coming anywhere from the world but not at the cost of snapping ties between theory and practice suitable to one's own social and cultural reality. He asserted this view in an article in Young India, June 1, 1921: "I do not want my house to be walled on all sides and my windows to be stuffed. I want the cultures of all lands to be blown about my house as freely as possible. But I refuse to be blown off my feet by any. I refuse to live in other people's houses as an interloper, a beggar or a slave."

Gandhi holds his notion of sexuality quite differently where it is exclusively associated with men's or women's lust. Initially, sex for him signifies regeneration and reproduction that is subsequently followed by its total negation to bring both wife and husband much nearer to each other to elevate them, absolutely eliminating lust. Gandhi referring to his own life observed that he began to enjoy his married life only after he abandoned sex. For him, "the conquest of lust is the highest endeavour of a man's or a woman's existence whereas physical union for the sake of carnal satisfaction is reversion to animality which has to be avoided by both." In Gandhi's leadership, the women of India found a new identity and hope. That is why his words and deeds have inspired thousands of women, and will continue to do so, in their struggle against injustice and inequality.

Gandhi did not refrain from raising women issues through his extraordinary experiment with the idea of celibacy, and contrary to popular belief that was quiet liberating for women who came in contact with him. Women held him as a messiah descending on the earth to give utterances to the long subjugated women in India. Gandhi rearticulated a new idea of sexuality that is enjoyed more not through its abundance rather through its timely renunciation. Instead of trivializing his ideas of sexuality that he abandoned in 1906 and stuck to it till his death, one should appreciate its sublime and culture specific values. Moreover, Gandhi was quiet explicit and transparent in dealing with the issue of sexuality both with his wife and other women. He wrote and took open public position on it. He saw his experiments as important for testing the vow that would enable him to achieve moksha. Thus his views on sexuality have simultaneously evoked strong reaction and admiration as well that have become the part of unprecedented and unparalled in human history.

It is pertinent to mention that Gandhi not only valued experiment but he also intended to merge it with metaphysical worldview. The tangible aspect of it is reflected through his experiments and adoption of various other means. In line with this thinking, after twenty three years of happy marital life, Gandhi took a vow of lifelong celibacy in 1906. It is important here to mention that giving up sex is a renunciation and was a well-established practice of Hindu devotion, known as *brahmacharya*. Renunciation of sexuality was part of Gandhi's spiritual discipline and final journey towards *moksha*, that is salvation. It was also a part of his self-presentation as a holy man in the eyes of his followers, and certainly added to his prestige in the Indian society. In the course of time, this helped Gandhi to identify himself with Indian masses. Although it was difficult to adhere to such a difficult and challenging task, Gandhi succeeded not only in following it but he also convinced his co inhabitants in the Ashram to practice celibacy. However, Prabhavati adopted '*brahmacharya*', but Kanchan Shah objected and rebelled against it.

Gandhi's '*brahmacharya*' was different from the old Indian ascetic system that abjured all interactions with women. In Jain tradition, women cannot touch monk and *vice versa*. The underlying assumption behind this tradition is to maintain purity of highest order and spiritual discipline. Contrary to this, Gandhi presented a counter-view to man and woman relation where running from each other would not serve the cause of either of them. In fact, Gandhi had number of close women associates, many of whom he treated as daughter, sister, mother, and so on. Interestingly, he himself acknowledged Sarala Devi, as his 'spiritual wife'. In one of the letters, he explained in detail what he meant by 'spiritual wife'. In a letter written to Sarala Devi, in July 1920, Gandhi explained being "spiritually" married meant to him that the "physical must be wholly absent". However, he also admitted that he was "too physically attached to" her. His apparently ambivalent views on sexuality, reaffirm that renunciation will be achieved not only escaping from it but by passing through it. Gandhi's life must be seen as a journey from worldly *ashakti* (attachment) to anashakti (non-attachment) for final liberation.

There were several instances that reinforced Gandhi's views on inseparability of man and woman to ensure equality between them. His life and daily practices set such precedents. In the 1920s, Gandhi had started resting his hands on the shoulders of young women during his walks and affectionately called Manu and other girls his "walking sticks". There was absolutely no aspect of Gandhi's life that was veiled from the public gaze. Sometimes, this openness became the cause of hue and cry for those who could not understand Gandhi's worldview. Gandhi's daily massage was done by young women. Even he used to take bath in the presence of a woman attendant. Sushila Nayyar was one such woman. She would take her bath along with Gandhi. Gandhi countered unnecessary whisper around bathing gossip among the ashramites by himself giving them the graphic details of his bathing rituals.

Probably, Gandhi wanted to break the mystery surrounding women's body, and this was not possible unless he would have dealt head on with hidden reality of women's anatomy from where his idea of celibacy emanates. In that sense sleeping with women was part of his experiment. He had told a correspondent in March 1945, that "sleeping together came with my taking up of *brahmacharya* or even before that". Gandhi said he had experimented with his wife "but that was not enough". In a letter to Birla in April 1945, Gandhi referred to 'women or girls who have been naked with me'. He stated that, "this experiment is very dangerous indeed", but thought, "that it was capable of yielding great results".

Some of the practises of his *brahmacharya* experiment seemingly threw bizarre habits of Gandhi that attracted criticism. However, he never ever forced either his practices or ideas on anybody. Gandhi himself explained the reason for sharing his bed with young women for a number of years. He wrote that he did this for bodily warmth at night and termed his actions as "nature cure". Initially, Gandhi slept with his women associates in the same room at a distance but later on, he started sleeping with them on the same bed and finally, he started sleeping naked with them. These practises might appear to be atavistic for a while but he strongly restricted these practices to his novel experiment of celibacy.

Gandhi was an extraordinary human being who could have conflated existing practice with utmost ease. This shows Gandhi's daring experiment of sleeping with young women, to test and affirm his own sexual self-control. This was not acceptable in Indian tradition. Despite opposition he did so and explained the ideal he was trying to achieve. In a letter to Rajkumari Amrit Kaur, March17,1947, he explained his position, "One who never has any lustful intention, who by constant attendance upon God has become proof against conscious or unconscious emissions, who is capable of lying naked with naked women, however beautiful they may be, without being in any manner whatsoever sexually excited. Such a person should be incapable of lying, incapable of intending or doing harm to a single man or woman in the whole world, is free from anger and malice and detached. . . . Such a person is a full '*brahmachari*'." About his relations with Sushila Nayyar, Gandhi stated, "She has experienced everything I have in me. . . . She is more absorbed in me. Hence, I would even make her sleep by my side without fear." Sushila Nayyar told Ved Mehta that long before Manu came into the picture, I used to sleep with him just as I would with my mother. . . . In the early days there was no question of calling this a *brahmacharya* experiment. It was just a part of nature cure. Later on, when people started asking questions about his physical contact with women, the idea of *brahmacharya* experiments was evolved. In the twilight of his life, Gandhi's sleeping bare with women, attracted public attention during the winter of 1946-47 in Noakhali. It came out that Gandhi was sleeping with his 19-year-old grandniece, Manu. He was testing his vow of *brahmacharya,* or total chastity in thought and deed. If he could spend the night in a woman's embrace without feeling sexual stirrings, it would demonstrate that he had conquered his carnal impulses and become a true *brahmachari*. Thus he remained unyielding from his stated position despite being attacked time and again.

Gandhi's unusual experiment evoked sharp reaction from his own associates. His stenographer, R.P. Parasuram, resigned in huff when he saw Gandhi sleeping naked with Manu. Nirmal Kumar Bose, who served as Gandhi's interpreter in Noakhali, too parted company with him in April 1947, in protest. Despite resignations and protests Gandhi continued to sleep with women until his assassination in 1948. N.K. Bose, in his book, "*My Days with Gandhi*", gives a detailed account of Gandhi's relationship with women. Many considered N.K. Bose an apostate, while Sushila Nayyar, who was part of Gandhi's experiment of *brahmacharya*, believed that Bose had "a dirty mind". The fact remains that how you are interpreting the facts. The fact is that Gandhi had intimate relations with young women. He never confessed it rather defended it in the name of ongoing experiment of *brahmacharya*. Gandhi, used to say that his "relationships with women were, from beginning to end, as pure as mother's milk and also Gandhi insisted that he never felt aroused while he slept beside her, or with Sushila or Abha." Gandhi admitted that "all of them would strip reluctantly. . . and they did so at my prompting." So far as the reason for complete nakedness was concerned, Sushila Nayyar recalled Gandhi's explanation to Manu during his peace mission in Noakhali: "We both may be killed by the Muslims at any time. We must both put our purity to the ultimate test. . . and we should now both start sleeping naked." Gandhi described his sleeping with Manu as a bold and original experiment, one that required a practising *brahmachari* such as he was, and a woman such as Manu who was free from passion. Confessing as she even might have done with her own mother, Manu told Gandhi that she had not ever experienced sexual desire.

The fact that women felt no unease in his presence was proof to Gandhi that he was approaching perfection as a *brahmachari*. Indeed, Bose contended that Gandhi attempted to conquer sex was by becoming a woman. Gandhi told Pyarelal that he once tore the burning *sari* off a woman in his ashram, but "she felt no embarrassment, because she knew I was a *brahmachari* and so almost like a sister to her." Gandhi himself stated that his goal was to a achieve the state of "complete sexlessness" by prayer.

Gandhi himself said that, "The greater the temptation, the greater the renunciation". If you go through *The Collected Works of Mahatma Gandhi*, one can know that Gandhi shared his bed with young women as part of his experiments in *brahmacharya*. It is a Sanskrit word which means "celibacy," in thought, words and body. It is control over body and mind. It is the ultimate state of yogic self-control. But for Gandhi way to conquer desire was to face the temptation head-on with a naked female in his bed. Gandhi has his own definition of *brahmacharya*. He said "My meaning of *brahmacharya* is this: "One who never has any lustful intention, who . . . has become capable of lying naked with naked women . . . without being in any manner whatsoever sexually excited."

Gandhi's sexual experiments with young women suggest that he has his own brand of *brahmacharya*. He was influenced by Jainism where too, it was not allowed to touch women. One can argue rightly or wrongly that Gandhi's sexual experiments may have been an abuse of personal charismatic power, where questioning Gandhi's act does not arise. Abha Gandhi's husband, Kanu, once objected to his wife sleeping with Gandhi and instead offered himself as a "bed warmer" to him. Gandhi rejected his proposal by making it clear that *brahmacharya* tests required young women as bedmates. This was nothing but clear deviation from Indian tradition where even the grown-up daughters were not allowed to sleep with their fathers. Gandhi's experiment is replete with many such deviations. In his conversations with Margaret Sanger, Gandhi referred to a "woman with whom I almost fell," and "the thought of my wife kept me from going to perdition." Again, writing to Rajkumari Amrit Kaur, he admitted that, "with one solitary exception," had never "looked upon a woman with lustful eyes."

At their first meeting in November 1925, Mirabehn found Gandhi "divine," and she was able to confirm Rolland's claim that he was indeed the second Christ. They fell in love with one another. They did, however, keep in contact with weekly self-described "love letters," and Gandhi wrote that she haunted his dreams. Mirabehn agreed with Gandhi's depiction that their passion was like a "bed of hot ashes," a veritable ascetic—erotic rhapsody of yogic *tapas*. Gandhi also shared with Mirabehn agonies about his spontaneous erections, daytime ejaculations, and wet dreams, for which he castigated himself unmercifully, and they even discussed the causes and cures of constipation.

Gandhi takes the defiant stand and says that he cares nothing for what others think of his practice: "The whole world may forsake me but I dare not leave what I hold is the truth for me ?" Gandhi in a letter to Sushila Nayyar wrote, "I can hurt colleagues and the entire world for the sake of truth." Thus, Gandhi's experiments with truth were highly personalized and subjective.

Gandhi was honest about his relationships with women. Whatever we know about this relationship, it is because Gandhi himself wrote and spoke about it. His relationship with women is above sex. Gandhi's letters indicate these relationships to be humane in thoughts and not on body or fulfilment of sexual desire. These letters are not about the sex life of Gandhi. These letters are now placed at one place to enable the readers to appreciate them in totality and remove the misconceptions. In Gandhi's letters to women, one can find a number of issues such as poverty, inequality, socio-economic condition of the women etc. Some letters are long and deal with spiritual and philosophical aspects including *brahmacharya* or celibacy.

My own understanding is that Gandhi's relationship with women can be interpreted by the different interpreters in different ways due to their different ideologies, backgrounds, and time and space in which they interpret. I am sure that the work, "*Gandhi, Women and Sexuality: Reflections Through Letters*" will attract the attention of critics, admirers, researchers and general readers and provide them an opportunity to have a glance over these letters at one place to evolve their own perspectives.

Gandhi inspired women and women inspired Gandhi. The charismatic personality of Gandhi attracted a large number of women and some of them became part of Gandhi's experiment of *brahmacharya* directly or indirectly. These women constitute the inner circle of Gandhi. In this book only those women are selected who were part of Gandhi's experiment of *brahmacharya* and evoked sharp reactions. The trajectory of these women first began with Mohandas Karamchand Gandhi and continued it also with Mahatma Gandhi in all his activities—from bed to breakfast, bath to *satyagraha*, prison to final liberation, till the death of Gandhi. Gandhi became Mahatma also because of the role played by these women, and in turn these women got prominence because of their association with him. Gandhi gave them a place to come out from the cage and lead a dignified life with integrity and self-esteem. In the following pages a brief sketch of all the fourteen women is being presented to corroborate and accentuate his epistemological views on sexuality.

His own conscience keeper, Kasturba, was the first woman, after his mother, in his life who shaped the personality of Gandhi. It is a fact that we know about Kasturba because of Gandhi. But the reverse is also true that she played a crucial role in making Gandhi from Mohandas to Mahatma Gandhi. Gandhi himself has conceded this fact at several of his utterances and writings. His potent weapon like *satyagraha* owes its origin to her. The mutuality of each other's life manifested the day they tied the wedding knot in 1883. Since then Gandhi overcame his fearlessness solely at the behest of Kasturba. This great woman, Kasturbai Kapadia, was born on 11 April, 1869 at Porbandar in Gujarat to wealthy businessman Gopaldas Nanakji, a trader in food grains and cotton textiles in Saurahstra. She was not given formal education. Kasturba was few months older to Gandhi. She was beautiful, small in stature, satiny black hair, framed nose and immense eyes in a quiet lovely willful face. She was simple, straightforward, methodical, courageous, and bold and a deeply religious woman.

After her marriage, Gandhi taught her to read and write in their mother tongue, Gujarati and she picked up enough language to go through the daily newspapers. Kasturba gave birth to a male child in 1885, but he died soon. They had four sons – Hiralal (1896), Manilal (1897), Ramdas (1898), and Devadas (1900).

Kasturba's public life started after she joined her husband in South Africa in 1897. From 1904-14, she was the heart and soul of the 'Phoenix Settlement' and from Kasturbai she became Ba—mother to the inmates, a role she continued at Kochrab, Sabarmati, and Sevagram Ashrams in India. She became true companion to Gandhi and participated in all the experiments of her husband in South Africa and in India. She followed her husband in word and deed and took to austere and simple ashram life with ease. The fact is that, she identified herself with her great husband, but she did not accept his ideas unless she understood them and considered them right. Gandhi often had to work hard to convince her.

Working closely with her husband, Kasturba Gandhi became a political activist fighting for civil rights and India's independence from the British. During the 1913 protest against working conditions for Indians in South Africa, Kasturba was arrested and sentenced to three months in a hard labour prison. In 1915, on his return to India when Gandhi took up the cause of the indigo planters in Bihar, Kasturba joined her husband and taught cleanliness, hygiene, discipline, reading and writing to the village women and children.

In his nonviolent struggle for freedom, whenever Gandhi was arrested, Kasturba took up the reigns of the leadership. Hers was a life of love, devotion, sacrifice and silence. Gandhi said in his autobiography that she had worked with him voluntarily or otherwise, in all the great transformations of his life. He felt that her life was an extremely sacred one. In discharging her duty as a wife she had even sacrificed her conscience. She never stood in between him and his sacrifices. Everyone called her Ba in great respect.

When Gandhi set up the *satyagraha ashram* in Sabarmati, Ba was his chief assistant in running the ashram. When Gandhi started the *khadi* movement, Ba organized its propaganda. Whenever Gandhi went into a fast against what he thought was unjust, Ba was with him. She gave leadership to the women in the *satyagraha* movement and had been jailed many times. She actively participated in Quit India Movement.

Kasturba suffered from chronic bronchitis due to complications at birth. Stress from the Quit India Movement's arrests and hard life at Sabarmati Ashram caused her to fall ill. Kasturba fell ill with bronchitis which was subsequently complicated by pneumonia.

The frequent fasting that Gandhi undertook ate into her health also and her own internment in prisons added fuel to this malady. More than sixty years of life led together, on 22 February, 1944, this great lady, breathed her last, lying in the lap of her beloved husband in prison in Aga Khan Palace, Pune. On her death, Gandhi mourned: "I can't imagine a life without Ba. She went away to freedom, imprinting on the heart to work or to die." Gandhi's letters to Kasturba was not a letter between husband and wife but letters that discussed all the contemporary issues confronting them and the country.

Apart from his wife Kasturba, the other woman, Millie came to Gandhi's contact in South Africa. Beautiful and charming, Millie Graham Downs was born in 1880 in London, Britain in a Christian family. At the age of 18 she began work in connection with the Christian Socialist movement. In December 1905, she travelled to Johannesburg, South Africa, by boat, to marry her fiancé, Henry Polak, a Jew by faith, who had become active in Gandhi's campaign for the rights of Indians living in South Africa. She reached South Africa on 30 December, 1905. At six o'clock in the morning of December 30th, 1905, Millie arrived at Jeppe Station, Johannesburg, where Mr. Gandhi and Mr. Polak were waiting for her on the platform.

Same day on 30th December, 1905, marriage took place and Millie and Polak became wife and husband. Gandhi was present on this occasion. After marrying Henry Polak, Millie Downs became Millie Graham Polak. An informal reception for the couple was hosted at the residence of M.K. Gandhi, which was attended by a large number of friends and well-wishers. A small notice under the headline 'Congratulations' was published in the Durban weekly, *Indian Opinion,* on January 5th, 1906. As she later wrote, it had been clear from the moment of her arrival in South Africa that in marrying Henry Polak she was also marrying Gandhi's cause.

Henry Polak was Gandhi's right-hand man. He was like a younger brother to Gandhi. He was articled to M.K. Gandhi while at the Inner Temple. Millie and Henry lived over the next nine years in the same Johannesburg house with Gandhi and his family. Millie soon discovered that the middle class comforts of London, to which, she had been accustomed, had no place in the Gandhi household. They started each day together grinding corn for the household's bread, and they ended each day with a communal vegetarian meal. Within months, the whole extended family moved to the Phoenix Settlement established by Gandhi outside Durban, which was to be the base for his political campaign, and where the paper, *Indian Opinion*, was produced. The paper had established itself as the mouthpiece of Gandhi's campaign for the rights of Indians living in South Africa. But Phoenix wasn't just about a group of like-minded people experimenting with living together as simply as possible. They also had a political job to do: and everyone in the community, male and female, adults and children, were expected to pull their weight to bring out the weekly editions of the newspaper, *Indian Opinion*. Subsequently, Millie became a part of Gandhi's life and participated in each and every activity of his.

Gandhi acknowledged that Millie Polak's arrival in January 1906, was a significant, and potentially vibrant moment for the household, .especially, his wife, Kasturba. It could only have been difficult for Kasturba Gandhi, who was still illiterate, to experience her husband's close intellectual relationship with such untouchables—both male and female. From what she wrote later, Millie Polak, seemed well aware of the delicacy of the situation.

Millie herself, well-educated, curious, and usually self-confident, eventually felt that she could challenge Gandhi even on the most sensitive things, like how to treat his wife in the house. Millie Polak along with Gandhi played an important role for the cause of Indians in South Africa. Millie Polak couldn't resist a particularly difficult request Gandhi made to her just before he finally left South Africa to return to India in 1914. She was anxious, after more than eight years away, to get back to England with her husband and the two young sons they now had.

But Gandhi needed people he could trust to stay and continue his work at Phoenix; and when he asked the Polaks, they agreed. So it would have been with a heavy heart that Millie travelled down to the Cape to say goodbye to the brilliantly strange Indian man with whom she had shared so much over the previous years.

Millie was proud women for Indians. To both Millie and Henry, life was a battle in the cause of *dharma*. Hardship, sacrifice and skepticism were their lifelong companions.

Millie spent twp years in India. She and her two children stayed with her sister at Conoor during their stay in India. She fell victim to an attack of influenza epidemic along with her children. After the end of Second World War she returned to England.

Gandhi and Millie Polak conversed frequently, about every subject under the African sun, and in the evenings she would jot down what they had said to each other in her notebook. Nearly three decades later, in 1931, she published a small volume of reminiscences (Mr. Gandhi, the Man) about her time as part of the Gandhi household in South Africa. The great women died in 1962, leaving behind the historical legacy. Undeniably, Millie also left her imprint on the life of Mahatma.

Sonja was the third woman who came in contact with Gandhi in South Africa. Kallenbach, Millie and Sonja were the backbone of Satyagraha in South Africa. Mohan became Mahatma in South Africa where he spent twenty one years for the cause of Indian's in South Africa. Sonja was born on 6 June, 1888 in Moscow, Russia. Her father was Isidor Schlesin and her mother Helena Dorothy. She was Jewish. Her family migrated to South Africa in June 1892. Sonja matriculated from the University of the Cape of Good Hope in 1903 at the age of 15.

Gandhi enrolled as an attorney in the Supreme Court of the Transvaal in 1903 and opened an office in Johannesburg. He required the services of a clerical assistant. So, Herman Kallenbach introduced Sonja Schlesin to Gandhi. She had exceptional speed and accuracy at shorthand. Gandhi was prepared to pay her up to £20 for her clerical work, but Schlesin was perfectly satisfied with the amount of £6, which Kallenbach had suggested to Gandhi. Her response to Gandhi's offer of more than £6 was, "I am not here to draw a salary from you. I am here because I like to work with you and I like your ideals." Sonja was Gandhi's secretary, who, in course of time took complete charge of Gandhi, his office and his movement in South Africa. Her role was crucial in making Gandhi successful in his early days. She performed her role beautifully, honestly and Gandhi achieved everything. She became a confidante of Gandhi that she drafted letters for him that he merely signed. Because of her increasing role in Gandhi's life and her autonomous and inflexible thought made Robert Payne to call Sonja a Russian anarchist.

Schlesin participated in *satyagraha* movement in South Africa. For her dedication to the cause, the Indian community expressed their appreciation and she was symbolically rewarded. Appreciating her work, Gandhi also wrote about Schlesin, "Miss Schlesin . . . taxed herself to her utmost by labouring day and night." Gandhi engaged himself in the political struggles of the community and was arrested and detained several times. In Gandhi's absence, Schlesin managed the office efficiently. Schlesin wanted to study law, so she was indentured as a clerk on 24 February, 1909.The Articles of Clerkship training was to last three years. But High Court, Pretoria, denied her admission as attorney in April 1909. The refusal was based on the premise that " . . . the articling of women is entirely without precedent in South Africa and never was contemplated by the law. . . ." The Transvaal Indian

Women's Association (TIWA) was formed in March 1909 and Schlesin was appointed secretary.

In 1909, Gandhi left for London to influence British politicians. While Gandhi was in London, Schlesin was in charge of his affairs and she was kept informed of the developments. To overcome the financial difficulties at The Phoenix Settlement, Schlesin was appointed as one of its trustees.

Schlesin passed an Intermediate Arts Examination at the University of the Cape of Good Hope in January 1911, and started teaching at a government school in Mayfair. When Gopal Krishna Gokhale was in South Africa, during his stay he was able to observe Schlesin at work and paid this tribute to her: "I have rarely come across such purity, single-minded devotion to work and great determination as I have seen in Miss Schlesin. I was simply astonished how she had sacrificed her all for the Indian cause without expecting any reward whatsoever...."

She actively participated in *Satyagraha*. When Gandhi led the Great March, which was a strike staged in opposition to a £3 poll tax for indentured labourers, the march began in Charlestown and led to the incarceration of 300 *satyagrahis*. While the march took place, Schlesin remained in Charlestown to take care of the remaining women, children and the elderly. She was also involved in the social aspects of *Satyagrahi*'s life.

In 1914, Gandhi left for India. Before departure, Gandhi along with his wife attended the farewell dinner where Schlesin was presented with books. Gandhi paid a glowing tribute to Schlesin for her work in the Indian cause. He entrusted her with a pair of sandals, made in prison, to be given to Smuts. Sonja began life as Gandhi's secretary and ended up as the leader of Indian Community in South Africa and died on 6 January, 1956 in Johannesburg. Gandhi's correspondence with Sonja in the formative years of her career needs to be researched.

Sarala Devi Chaudhurani was the spiritual wife of Gandhi. She was born to Janakinath Ghosal and Swarnakumari Devi in the old Tagore house at Jorasanko in Calcutta on 9 September, 1872 in a well-known and well-to-do Bengali intellectual family. Her father was one of the earliest secretaries of the Bengal Congress and mother (Swarnakumari Devi was the daughter of Debendranath Tagore and elder sister of legendary poet Rabindranath Tagore) was the first successful noted woman novelist of Bengali literature. She spent there some of the most impressionable years of her childhood, when her father was in England. Her natural talents for music, literature and art, as well as her passionate patriotism were nurtured by her relatives.

Sarala Devi was first taught by a private tutor at home. Later she was admitted into the Bethune School, and after passing her Entrance examination in 1886, continued her studies in the Bethune College. She took her B.A. degree with Honours in English in 1890 from Calcutta University and received the *Padmavati Gold Medal.* She later studied French and Persian and prepared herself for the M.A. examination in Sanskrit. She was also one of the few women graduates of her time, and the first woman political leader from Bengal in the Indian independence movement.

In 1905, she was married to Pandit Rambhuj Dutt Chaudhary (1866-1923), a Punjabi Brahmin, lawyer by profession, living at Lahore. He was an ardent patriot and editor of an Urdu paper called *Hindusthan* and member of Arya Samaj and Congress. She believed in physical culture and instituted the 'Virashtami Utsava' with exhibition of physical feats. During the 1903 Congress, she proposed a display of Indian games. She tried to popularise 'Udayadiya Utsava' accompanied by physical feats. In 1904 she opened a Swadeshi shop called Lakshmir Bhandar. She collected and sent Swadeshi goods to the Bombay Congress and was awarded a gold medal for her endeavours. A spirited mind cannot be that easily quelled. Sarala Debi's nationalistic commitment led her to set up an *akhara* (gymnasium) for training young men in the martial arts.

She was born and grown up in the ambience of luxury and had every opportunity to imbibe national and Western culture. However, she was never in favour of Western education and could be easily converted to Gandhiji's ideals. In her mature years she gave up her militant patriotism and turned to nonviolence, non-cooperation and *Khadi* movement. She came into close contact with the great personalities of the social and political world of the day—Lala Lajpat Rai, Tilak, Gokhale and Mahatma Gandhi.

Sarala Devi was a born teacher. Even at early stage she taught music to many young girls. She shortly took the bold step of going to Mysore as a teacher in the Maharani School. She also acted as the Maharani's secretary for some time.

She worked for women's education in the villages around Lahore and had larger plans for the education of *purdah* women. This led to the foundation of the Bharat-Stri-Mahamandal in Allahabad in 1910, with branches in many Indian cities and villages. She was the founder of the first women's organization. The primary goals of the organisation were to promote female education, which at that time was not well developed. The organisation opened several offices in Lahore, Allahabad, Delhi, Karachi, Amritsar, Hyderabad, Kanpur, Bankura, Hazaribagh, Midnapore and Calcutta to improve the situation of women all over India. In 1930 she opened the Bharat-Stri-Shiksha-Sadan, a school for girls, in Calcutta. Sarala Devi's whole life was one of hard work.

Due to the displeasure of the British Government, Rambhaj's patriotic work annoyed the British Government and as a result, he had to suffer harassment and was later even arrested. After the arrest, Sarala Devi took over the editorship and even published English versions of the paper. Her excellent management drew the praise of Englishmen like Ramsay Macdonald.

She edited the journal called Bharati with the help of her elder sister, Hiranmoyee Devi, for a shortwhile. After the death of her husband in 1923, she returned to Calcutta. In 1935, she accepted Howrah's Acharya Bijoy Krishna Deb Sharma, as her guru and spent the last ten years of her life in reading spiritual texts, reflecting and writing, much of her autobiography. She died in 1945. The memoirs of Sarala Devi's early life were serialized in the weekly, *Desh* magazine. Later, they were put together as *Jibaner Jhara Pata* (Life's Fallen Leaves). The relationship between Sarala Devi and Gandhi was spiritual and based on platonic love. Gandhi's letters to Sarala Devi is a wonderful record of honest and pristine purity in private and public life of a man, who later became a great leader of the humankind.

Another great woman, Madeline Slade, was greatly fascinated with Gandhi and his ideas. The level of her attraction to the cause, espoused by Gandhi, was so great that she had dispensed with her aristocratic background and readily joined Bapu in his Ashram. Mira was the new name given to her by Gandhi himself. She was a beautiful and charming girl. She was born on 22 November, 1892 in an aristocratic, highly cultured English family and was brought up in a luxurious environment. Her father, Edmond Slade, an officer in the British Navy, later became the Commander-in-Chief of the East Indies Squadron in Bombay. In early childhood she spent two years in India. She learned German and Egyptian languages and developed a deep fascination for Western classical music, Beethoven. Beethoven's music was a spiritual experience for her. She loved nature and liked simple living. Madeline was a sensitive and willful child who grew up as a pretty woman. However, she was not interested in marriage and many highly eligible suitors were politely put off by her.

She read the English translation of Jean Christopher of Romain Rolland which cast such a magic spell on her that she wanted to read the original. She went to Paris to learn French. She wanted to meet Rolland, who gave her an appointment for which she travelled to Switzerland in 1922. It was from him that she came to know about Gandhi for the first time. She wanted to go to India to meet Gandhi, and so she wrote to him. Once she decided to go to India, she consciously adopted Indian ways of life, like eating vegetarian food, and sitting and sleeping on the floor and entirely gave up hunting. Such was the influence of Gandhi over her even before she met him. In 1925 she reached Bombay and the same day boarded the train for Ahmedabad. The train reached Ahmedabad Station in the morning of 7 November, 1925. Gandhi's three close associates, Mahadev Desai, Vallabhbhai Patel and Swami Anand were waiting on the platform to receive her. They brought her to the Ashram. As she entered, a brown figure rose up and came forward. Madeline was conscious of nothing else but a sense of light. She fell on her knees. Two hands gently raised her up, and a voice said, "You shall be my daughter." On hearing these words, her consciousness of the physical world began to return and she saw a face smiling, with eyes full of love and a gentle twinkle of amusement. He was Bapu.

In all their mutual relationship, Gandhi always remained a father figure and she a loving daughter to him. The tall, beautiful Madeline, shaved off her head and adopted *brahmacharya* as Gandhi, and became a true disciple of the great man. She wore *khadi*, learned spinning and weaving and taught the villagers what she had learned. This transformation made her an admirer and follower of Gandhi, and a servant of India. She accompanied Gandhi when he went to London for the Second Round Table Conference, and she functioned as a bridge between the Indian leaders and the Britishers. She undertook the propaganda and publicity for Gandhi's ideals and programmes. She reported to foreign press about the repressive measures the British regime adopted against the Congress and thus the news came to light and she was promptly arrested. After her release, she was prohibited from entering Bombay, but she violated the order and was arrested again. On being released, she accompanied Gandhi in his tour of India, and went abroad to speak on Gandhi's ideals and to seek support for the Indian cause.

Whenever she was with Mahatma Gandhi she looked after him in minutest detail. At times she went to the Viceroy as a personal emissary of Mahatma Gandhi and at other times to the Congress President and the members of the Working Committee. To plead the case of India, she went abroad and met Lloyd George, Lord Halifax, General Smuts, Sir Samuel Hoare and Winston Churchill. She also visited United States and went to New York, Philadelphia, West Chester, Boston, Harvard and Washington, delivered a lecture at the Harvard University and met Mrs. Roosevelt at the White House in Washington. Mirabehn took keen interest in the formation of Sevagram Ashram and organised cleanliness campaigns in the surrounding villages. She was always unfailing in her service to Bapu and longed to be with him as long as possible. For such longing, she earned reprimands more than once from Gandhi. Gradually she undertook independent activities with the help and blessings of Bapu.

Mirabehn lived in India during the most eventful period in which she saw the Simon Commission facing black flags everywhere in 1927, the resolve of the people for complete independence in 1929, the Dandi March and the Civil Disobedience movement in 1930-31 and the Gandhi-Irwin Pact in 1931. She was not only a witness to the most tumultuous period of India's Freedom Struggle but also suffered herself like any other Indian, of the brutalities unleashed by the callous British regime. She was in detention together with Bapu in the Aga Khan Palace during the Quit India Movement. When the leaf was turned in the series of India's crucial negotiations with the British, she was herself a witness to these like Shimla Conference, the Cabinet Mission, the Interim Government and the formation of the Constituent Assembly.

Gandhi had transformed her anthropocentric ideas that she learnt through her modern upbringing. This reflected in her love not only for the human beings but also for plants and animals. That is why Mira started Ashram Pashulok near Hrishikesh in 1947, and a settlement, named Bapu Gram. When Gandhi returned to Delhi after his peace mission in the riot-stricken areas, immediately after the dawn of freedom, Mira was there to receive him. She stayed with him for three months at the Birla House and returned to her ashram on December 18, 1947. As the Providence so desired, that was her last meeting with her mentor, the beloved Bapu.

She continued teaching and spreading Gandhi's ideals and messages in ashrams. She left India for Germany in 1959. She set up her perch in Vienna, Austria, in the Indian style and was known in the locality as the Indian lady. She was not alone but her lifelong love for music, Beethoven always stayed with her. To keep the memory of her wonderful journey alive, she wrote her autobiography, '*The Spirit's Pilgrimage*', and '*Bapu's Letters to Mira*'.

This great lady from Europe, who spent her life in the service of Gandhi and India, breathed her last on July 20, 1982. India honoured her Padma Vibhushan in 1982, and also released a postal stamp, named after her.

The remarkable thing about Gandhi does not only lie in the apparent visibility of the things and his ordinary deeds but there is something transcendental that creates an altogether new meaning which could only be comprehended by linking it with the human cause. The women from the West understood the universal message upheld by Gandhi in the service of humanity, which readily turned them towards Gandhi to make their own contribution in his extraordinary endeavours. Some of them even found the glimpse of Jesus in him. Hence, the letters should be read, critiqued and comprehended in the light of this very concern.

Lilavati Asar, the long time associate of Gandhi, from 1929 to1948, lived in and studied at the Ashram. Gandhi used to tutor her personally and called her by a nickname, 'Limpet'. Gandhi was her mentor. She was quarrelsome and a lonely person by nature. Due to this nature, nobody loved her. So, Gandhi was quite concerned about her. She used to accompany Gandhi and subsequently she also played an important role in Gandhi's experiment with *brahmacharya*. She was always at the beck and call of Gandhi. All her pursuits, programmes and activities fully merged with Gandhi's chosen cause of India's liberation from the foreign rule. She had a conspicuous presence in all the major movements including Quit India Movement of 1942 launched by Gandhi.

Prema Kantak, an ardent patriot, a scholar, a revolutionary and a beautiful woman, was born at Kanwar in 1905, in a Brahmin family. She was a brilliant and charming student with a creative mind. She was a student of Wilson College and passed the B.A. examination of the Bombay University in 1928. She was very active in student movement and participated in public demonstrations against Simon Commission. She was elected to the Executive Council of the Bombay Presidency Youth League.

Like other women, Prema's life was also full of ups and downs. When she was only ten months old baby, her mother passed away. She was brought up by her maternal grandmother. She stayed there with her for ten years. Her father had already married twice. She was the only daughter out of the five brothers. Being the only girl in the family, she invited the attraction of every member of the family. When she reached the marriageable age, her father and brother pressurized her to get married. But she revolted against her father and decided not to marry.

She saw Mahatma Gandhi for the first time when she was in school. The first sight of Gandhi cast magic spell on the mind of young Prema and with the passage of time, her attraction towards Gandhi grew. She again got an opportunity to see Gandhi in 1924. She passed M.A. examination in April 1929 and after that she wrote a letter to Mahatma Gandhi. On 25 May, 1929 she met Gandhi in Bombay and the next day she left for Sabarmati Ashram with him. On 26 May,

1929 she travelled together with Gandhi to the Ashram from railway station in the same car. Gandhi assigned her the charge of managing the Ashram which she did efficiently from 1929 to 1933.

Prema actively participated in Salt Satyagraha and was arrested twice. After her release, she shifted from Ahmedabad to Pune and became actively associated with the Constructive Programme. She devoted her life in the propagation of *Khadi* and Swadeshi, and emancipation and empowerment of women. She was one of the prominent women *Satyagrahis* during the Individual Satyagraha started by Gandhi for resisting the war-effort of the British Government. Prema was arrested four times and sentenced to three months imprisonment each time. For some time she also worked for Congress Seva Dal.

Gandhi had a high respect and affection for Prema Kantak because of her courage, commitment and devotion. She was a scholar par excellence and was a reputed literary figure in Maharashtra. Her correspondence with Gandhi on *brahmacharya* was published in a book, 'Prasad Diksha', in Marathi in 1938. This was followed by her next book, '*Kama and Kamini*'.

She participated in the Quit India Movement of 1942 and was jailed for one and half years. While in jail, she realized that the young women detainees were attracted more by the militants. After her release she joined Shankarerrao Deo's Ashram at Saswad. Prema worked for Women Committee for Constructive Work till 1952. When she realized that women preferred active politics to constructive work, she observed a fast for seven days, blaming herself for this change in the attitude of women, and went to Himalayas, detaching herself from the worldly things for the peace of mind.

After her return from Himalaya, she went to Pune and took the responsibility of Kasturba ashram at Saswad. She successfully organized a movement for prohibition and succeeded in getting four months declared as dry-months in a year. She led Matkabandi movement and was actively involved in bringing about an awakening among the women in the rural areas and helped them to become self-reliant. Prema left her legacy behind after her death in 1985.

Dr. Sushila Nayyar, born on 26th December, 1914, in Kunjah, Gujarat (now in Pakistan), was the younger sister of Pyarelal Nayyar, who was the personal secretary to Mahatma Gandhi. She graduated from erstwhile Punjab University. From Punjab she came to Delhi to study medicine at Lady Hardinge Medical College. Later on she joined her alma mater first as Registrar and then as Assistant Professor.

Meanwhile, she visited Sevagram to join her brother, where she came in contact with Gandhi in 1939 and became his close associate. Shortly after her arrival, cholera broke out in Wardha, and being a young doctor, she tackled the outbreak singlehandedly with dedication to serve the needy people. Gandhi got impressed with her dedication to service and appointed her as a personal physician. She was one of the important parts of her young peer group serving Gandhi day in and day out and was deeply impressed by his charisma and personality. She was so much preoccupied with her work in the ashram that she hardly ever thought of getting ever married. Moreover, she earned her MD degree in 1942. She took part in the Quit India Movement and was imprisoned along with others at the Aga Khan Palace in Poona.

In 1944 she set up a dispensary at Sevagram, but soon turned into a big medical centre that caused a lot of commotion and disturbed the peace and serenity of the ashram. Consequently, it was shifted to a guesthouse, donated by the Birlas, in Wardha. In 1945 this centre formally became the Kasturba Hospital and later on in 1969 it became the famous Mahatma Gandhi Institute of Medical Sciences, where she was Professor of Community Medicine.

Since she was a medical professional and personal physician of Mahatma Gandhi, Gandhi unhesitatingly discussed his experiment on *brahmacharya* and wanted to make her part of his experiment, to which she consented. Also Gandhi was a man of action, and unless something concrete was achieved through this process, he would not form his opinion about it. In fact, he wanted to overcome his carnal desire through the practice of *brahmacharya*. Sushila was part and parcel of such an outstanding experiment for an extraordinary result. It was so embarrassing for her brother Pyarelal, private secretary to Mahatma Gandhi that he resigned in protest. Even after this Gandhi's experiment remained righteous in her eyes and she continued with it.

After the demise of Gandhi, his values and service towards humanity were uninterruptedly carried by her first as a doctor and then as an important functionary of the state. Her works continued till her death on 3rd January, 2001. Thus, Gandhi's woman followers immortalized his ideals and works.

Bibi Amutussalaam who hailed from a prominent Muslim family, was born in Zamindar Pathan family of Patiala, Punjab in 1907. She too was greatly influenced by Gandhi. In 1930-31, she visited him for the spiritual guidance. She worked with Gandhi for Hindu-Muslim unity. She epitomized the synthetic culture of India. As such, she was well versed with the Sikh religious scripture and could recite Guru Granth Sahib. She was closely associated with Gandhi from 1931 to 1948. She was a nationalist par excellence from the core of her heart, and was with Mahatma Gandhi in Noakhali in 1946, when the worst riots took place in Bengal. Gandhi treated her like her own daughter and affectionately called her 'the crazy daughter'. She was not only the part of Gandhi's political programmes but also a willing participant in his liberatory experiment of *brahmacharya*.

Gandhi was concerned about her because she (Amutussalaam) suffered from poor health. She was thin, pale and sick, suffering from Tuberculosis, piles, asthama, pleurisy, tonsillitis, pneumonia, migraine and other diseases. Despite these diseases, she actively participated in the freedom struggle and was bold enough to tackle the communal riots in Sind.

When her brothers and other family members left for Pakistan, she was enraged and expressed her disappointment to Gandhi, who had arranged for the safe journey of her brothers to West Pakistan. She wanted to return to Patiala (from Noakhali where she was coordinating Gandhi's work of re-establishing communal harmony) from where the Muslims, including her family, had migrated to Pakistan. She wanted to demonstrate her indomitable spirit by living there, all by herself as a young Muslim woman, that she could dare the worst, perhaps even die, by way of exemplifying her absolute commitment to the cause of peace and communal harmony. Despite all her efforts with Gandhi to avert partition, it became inevitable that left agonizing effect on her. Gandhi wrote to her on August 26, 1947: "You are needlessly finding fault with your brothers. When all others lost courage there, they too decided not to risk their life. It is enough if we ourselves stand firm. Let us not sit in judgment on others though they may be our own relatives." He further wrote, "You are fickle-minded in wanting to go to Patiala. It is one and the same, whether you are in Noakhali or in Punjab. It is not that your place is only in Punjab. Your place is everywhere."

She was undergoing great agony at the divide between Hindus and Muslims. To assuage her feelings, Gandhi wrote to her, "I have never felt that you are a Muslim and that I am a Hindu. The only feeling I have is that you are A.S. and I am Gandhi, where our *atmans* are concerned, we are one. In my view, you are the moving spirit behind whatever peace has been achieved in Noakhali. It was and still is your most significant work. Only you can sustain it. Wherever you stand, you stand in the capacity of my daughter, do you not ? What can be done if you hold a different view, despite my opinion that you should forget all about Patiala ? ..."

Despite that Bibi did not forget Patiala, her native place. Between 1947 and 1948, she along with Lajjawati Hooja (a prominent Congress worker of All-India Women's Congress), evacuated thousands of kidnapped Hindu and Muslim women from their respective homes in India and Pakistan. Lajjawati Hooja, who was very active in Jalandhar and associated with K.M.V. College, worked in three districts of Pakistan, including her native place Dera Ghazi Khan, while Bibi worked in Bahawalpur district. Both worked under the guidance of Rameshwari Nehru, a close relative of Jawaharlal Nehru, to mitigate the sufferings of thousands of innocent women.

Son of the soil, Amutussalaam worked at the grassroots level and set up many institutions to serve the people and country. She had her maternal relations near Rajpura. So, she established the Kasturba Seva Mandir and other institutions in Rajpura, where she helped Hindu migrants from Bahawalpur, Pakistan, to settle down. A dedicated, self-sacrificing and a quiet worker who never sought the limelight died on September 29, 1985. Thus, the Gandhi's dream of secular India was kept alive during and after his life time by Bibi Amutussalaam. She set remarkable example for the posterity.

Another woman from Europe, Margarete Spiegel, became a part of history for her mere association with Gandhi. She was interested in India since a very young age. Living in Germany during the First World War, she realized the futility of war and was drawn towards pacifism. She read Rabindranath Tagore and came to know about Gandhi through Romain Rolland's book. As a result, she turned towards this great soul, Mahatma Gandhi.

She got an opportunity to visit India for two months to study Gandhi's movement in1932. After travelling over several parts of India, she stayed as a guest at the Sabarmati Ashram and took part in all the activities of the ashram from morning to night. In December 1932, she saw Gandhi for the first time sitting under a mango tree in the Yeravda jail. Gandhi's remarkable personality cast a magic spell on her. Under his influence she opted for vegetarianism.

After her return to Germany, she was in constant touch with Gandhi through letters, and Gandhi used to reply her promptly. She embraced the idea of nonviolence because of her association with Gandhi. On 1st April, 1933, her Jewish identity cost her job from the Government College in Berlin. Not only that her passport was expounded, but she was also forced to leave Germany for Venice on 2nd April, 1933 where she waited for twelve days for the next boat to India. From Venice she wrote to Bapu of her coming, and she straightaway went to Yeravda jail after reaching Bombay. This made her to stay in Poona and got an opportunity to see Gandhi almost daily in the prison.

In May1933 Gandhi began a fast for 21 days. To understand the science of satyagraha, she also emulated him by observing fast but after two days, she was persuaded by Gandhi to give up fasting. On the same day (10th May), she got the following little note from Gandhi: "I am glad you have broken your fast. You were too decent to persist in your folly. Now be good. You are forgiven. You should come and see me when you feel like it. Love." Gandhi then sent her to the Ashram at Sabarmati, and named her Amla. Thus, she internalized Gandhi as her spiritual guru. Commensurably, Gandhi told her, "I shall love you in spite of your faults."

After his release from prison in August 1933, Gandhi went from Poona to Wardha in the last week of September, and she had the good fortune to stay with him till he embarked upon the Harijan tour. Her connection with India also figured as a teacher at Shantiniketan.

Another great woman who became the part of Mahatma Gandhi's ideas and experiments, Rajkumari Amrit Kaur, an eminent Gandhian, a freedom fighter, and a social activist, was born on 2nd February, 1889 in Lucknow. She had a royal lineage as she was scion of Kapurthala royal family. Rajkumari had her early education in Sherborne School for Girls in Dorset, England, and had her college education at Oxford University. After completing her education in England, she returned to India.

Amrit Kaur's father was associated with Gopal Krishna Gokhale and many other party leaders of Indian National Congress. She had great opportunity to see, meet and interact with the leading leaders of India's freedom struggle who came at her home to meet her father. Again because of her father, she got a chance to meet both Gokhale and Gandhi. This was a turning point in her life that led her to freedom struggle. During the course of struggle, she became one of the close associates of Gandhi. She participated in Dandi March in 1930 and was imprisoned by the British authorities. Rajkumari went to live at Gandhi's ashram in 1934, and took up the austere life there, despite her royal family background. She served as one of Gandhi's secretaries for sixteen years. During this period, her bond with Gandhi and ashram life became intense. There was hardly any activity, programme and experiment of which she was not a part. She did a lot of commendable job that Gandhi picked her for his experiment of celibacy. Like other women, she had divine experience of Gandhi's experiment. Therefore, it gives rise to skepticism on the different conclusions drawn from the experiences of the women in the experiment after going through these letters.

If one delves deep into her public life, apart from her holding important positions and creating institutions, she had the rarest distinction of becoming the first woman Cabinet Minister of Independent India. She spent most of her time for the upliftment of women and the eradication of social evils. She was a strong champion of women education and was equally concerned with the elevation of the Harijans. She dispensed her ancestral property and donated it to the nation. Her untiring work came to an end with her death in 1964. However, she successfully lit the flame of Gandhian idealism during and after her life time.

Kanchan Shah was another woman who also occupied an important place in Gandhi's life and his works. She was married to Munnalal G. Shah, who was a lawyer by profession. Munnalal as manager of the ashram, looked after its various activities as it was the hub of the political activities of the country. Kanchan was staying in the ashram with her husband. Under the influence of Gandhi, both

Kanchan and her husband took the vow of observing *brahmacharya* as a married couple. Kanchan and her husband were the role models for other married couples to emulate them. She commanded the trust of Gandhi and accompanied him during the tours. However, Kanchan did not stick to the vow and, as a result, she was blessed with a daughter. Nevertheless, she remained loyal to Gandhi and his experiment.

Prabhavati, yet another women coming from a decent educated family of Bihar, played a significant role in the life and mission of Gandhi. She was born in June 1906 in the then Saran district of Bihar. Her father was a prominent lawyer and a renowned Congress leader of Bihar who gave up his lucrative legal practice for the sake of the country. He was the President of the Bihar Provincial Congress Committee for several years. When Gandhi reached Bihar to lead the Champaran movement, Prabhavati's father joined Gandhi in his campaign. During this campaign, Gandhi stayed at her father's residence. That gave her a chance to meet Gandhi, when Gandhi requested her father to send Prabhavati to his ashram as his adopted daughter. Since her husband, Jayaprakash Narayan, had already left for USA for higher studies in 1922, Prabhavati was curious to join Gandhi in his work in the ashram. This was the beginning of her association with Gandhi. At ashram she devoted herself completely to Mahatma Gandhi and Kasturba. Both Gandhi and Kasturba treated her like their own daughter. Gandhi became her father, teacher, guide and guru. She, on her part, took keen interest in the ashram life. Bapu gave her regular lessons in Sanskrit, Gujarati, English, Mathematics, Health and Food Sciences. She studied the *Ramayan* and the *Gita* and tried to acquire knowledge of English.

After studying seven years in USA, her husband Jayaprakash returned to India in 1929 and went straight to Gandhi's Ashram at Sabarmati, where his wife was staying. Gandhi discussed with Jayaprakash about Prabhavati's vow of *brahmacharya* and advised him to remarry. This unsolicited advice annoyed him. But Jayaprakash respected Prabhavati's vow and both decided not to have any child until the country was free from the foreign rule.

At ashram Jayaprakash met Jawaharlal Nehru. Both travelled together to Lahore, where Nehru presided over the historic Congress session. Jayaprakash helped Nehru with the party work at Allahabad and was given the charge of the Labour Research Department. Prabhavati accompanied her husband to Allahabad.

Prabhavati actively entered in the Freedom Movement in 1932. At the annual Congress session at Ramgarh in Bihar, she was made the leader of women volunteers. She was appreciated for the role she played in 1942. She was imprisoned and spent time in gaol on several occasions.

Jayaprakash was a revolutionary and this led to several differences with her because of her Gandhian orientation. It was under her influence that her husband by now a cult figure in India, joined the Sarvodaya movement.

After independence she established two institutions, Mahila Charkha Samiti and 'Kamala Nehru Shishu Vihar' to involve deserted and abandoned women in the charkha or the spinning wheel movement on the Gandhian model.

One can easily discern Gandhi's impact on J.P.'s articulation of total revolution that he launched against the government's unaccountability and moral degeneration of politics and society. In this endeavour Prabhavati stood behind him like a rock. Though, she departed in 1973, her Gandhian legacy always came to the rescue of J.P. It is not out of place to mention that Prabhavati played a crucial role in turning J.P. from a hardcore Marxist to a sombre, nonviolent sarvodaya leader of India, which J.P. conceded publically.

Manu, grandniece of Gandhi, born in 1928 was the daughter of Jaisukhlal Gandhi. Manu was a lonely child. She lost her mother when she was only twelve years old. At the age of fourteen, she came to live with Gandhi. She was very close to Kasturba. Manu actively participated in the Quit India Movement of 1942. She was arrested and placed in Nagpur Jail. At that time, Gandhi and Kasturba were in detention in Aga Khan Palace. Kasturba was seriously ill. So, Manu was transferred to Aga Khan Palace to look after Kasturba. Kasturba called Manu's father and advised him to take Manu to his residence in Karachi for studies.

Manu became Mahatma Gandhi's closest associate during 1946-48. She was with Gandhi in Noakhali, touring bare foot in a riot affected area for establishing communal harmony and peace. When Gandhi returned to Delhi she was with him. Gandhi was her mentor and she was with Gandhi till he was shot dead on 30th January, 1948 at Birla House, New Delhi.

Manu never married and sacrificed her life for the cause of Gandhi and his ideals. She was a part of Gandhi's experiment of *brahmacharya*. Gandhi's death left deep impact on her life. She had left a graphic account of her days with Gandhi in books and diaries. She wrote two books, '*The Lonely Pilgrim*' (1962) and '*Last Glimpses of Gandhi*' (1964). She died in 1969 at the age of forty one, leaving behind the legacy, unknown, unwept and unsung, without honour and recognition.

An account of these letters presented so far, is a modest attempt to understand the extraordinary persona of Gandhi. It is important to mention that these letters may lead to misunderstand him and misconstrue his ideas that may provide some readers of these letters to make wild speculations, reaching a horrendous conclusion not in conformity with Gandhi's international repute and actual historical evaluation. However, the personality of the man is immune from all allegations and labelling, as he commands almost universal allegiance to solve even the ills of our time and society. Any objective analysis of his association with women, would remain partial and subjective if they are not made in the light of the reactions and opinions of those women who were parts of his *brahmacharya* experiment and lived many more decades after Gandhi's death. Though they were all women, they represented different spatial, cross-cultural background to assign validity to Gandhi's findings on *brahmacharya*.

In short, there was unanimity among them about their feelings of sublimity and divinity after going through this great experiment of human liberation. However, I do not want to pre-empt any reader to make their own conclusions. These observations are based on my own readings, they may be contingent, and however, they are drawn on the evidences and deeper understanding provided by these letters. In fact, the Gandhian perception of the world is epistemologically different from the ancient tradition of philosophy, emanating from the West. The former emerges out of the rigours of mundane affairs to arrive at metaphysics, whereas the latter begins with the metaphysics to prescribe a particular view to be followed by the human society, sometimes, it stretches it to even decry human affairs. One should keep these differing perceptions at the back of mind, while discerning the true contents of the letters as Gandhi's life, thinking and action were inseparable.

Chapter 1
Kasturba Gandhi (1869-1944)

Kasturbai Kapadia was born on 11 April, 1869 at Porbandar in Gujarat to wealthy businessman Gopaldas Nanakji, a trader in food grains and cotton textiles in Saurashtra. She was not given formal education.Kasturbai betrothed to Moniya (Mohandas Karamchand Gandhi) in 1876, the younger son of Karamchand Gandhi, the dewan of Porbandar. After six years of engagement she married with Gandhi in 1883. Kasturba was older than Gandhi. Kasturba was beautiful, small in stature, satiny black hair, framed nose and immense eyes in a quiet lovely willful face. She was simple, straightforward, methodical, courageous, and bold and a deeply religious woman.

After the marriage her husband taught her to read and write in their mother tongue, Gujarati and she picked up enough language to go through the daily newspapers. Kasturba gave birth to a male child in 1885, but it died soon. They had four more sons—Hiralal (1896), Manilal (1897), Ramdas (1898), and Devadas (1900).

Kasturba public life started after she joined her husband in South Africa in 1897. From 1904-14, she was the heart and soul of the 'Phoenix Settlement' and from Kasturbai she became Ba—mother to the inmates, a role she continued at Kochnab, Sabarmati, and Sevagram Ashrams in India. She became true companion to Gandhi and she participated in all the experiments of his husband in South Africa and in India. She followed her husband in word and deed and took to austere and simple ashram life with ease. The fact is that, she identified herself with her great husband, but she did not accept his ideas unless she understood them and considered them right. Gandhi often had to work hard to convince her.

Working closely with her husband, Kasturba Gandhi became a political activist fighting for civil rights and Indian independence from the British. During the 1913 protest against working conditions for Indians in South Africa, Kasturba was arrested and sentenced to three months in a hard labour prison. In 1915, on his return to India when Gandhi took up the cause of the indigo planters in Bihar, Kasturba joined her husband and taught cleanliness, hygiene, discipline, reading and writing to the village women and children.

In his nonviolent struggle for freedom whenever Gandhi was arrested Kasturba took up the reigns of the leadership. In the transformation of Mohandas Gandhi into Mahatma Gandhi, there was one person who played a very prominent but silent role was his wife, Kasturba. Gandhi, has admitted more than once that he learned the art and science of satyagraha from Kasturba. Her was a life of love, devotion, sacrifice and silence. Gandhi said in his autobiography that she had worked with him voluntarily or otherwise, in all the great transformations of his life. He felt that her life was an extremely sacred one. In discharging her duty as a wife she had even sacrificed her conscience. She never stood in between him and his sacrifices. Everyone called her Ba in great respect.

When Gandhi set up the satyagrah ashram in Sabarmati, Ba was his chief assistant in running the ashram. When Gandhi started the *khadi* movement, Ba organized its propaganda. Whenever Gandhi went into a fast against what he thought was unjust, Ba was with him. She gave leadership to the women in the satyagraha movement and had been jailed many times. She actively participated in Quit India Movement.

Kasturba suffered from chronic bronchitis due to complications at birth. Stress from the Quit India Movement's arrests and hard life at

Sabarmati Ashram caused her to fall ill. Kasturbai fell ill with bronchitis which was subsequently complicated by pneumonia.

The frequent fastings that Gandhi undertook ate into her health also and her own internment in prisons added fuel to this malady. More than sixty years of life together, on 22 February, 1944, this great lady, breathed her last, lying on the lap of her beloved husband in prison in Aga Khan Palace, Pune. On her death Gandhi mourned: "I can't imagine a life without Ba. She went away to freedom, imprinting on the heart to work or to die."

1. Letter to Mrs. Kasturba Gandhi

Volkrust Gaol,
November 9, 1908

Beloved Kastur,

I have received Mr. West's telegram today about your illness. It cuts my heart. I am very much grieved but I am not in a position to go there to nurse you. I have offered my all to the satyagraha struggle. My coming there is out of the question. I can come only if I pay the fine, which I must not. If you keep courage and take the necessary nutrition, you will recover. If, however, my ill luck so has it that you pass away, I should only say that there would be nothing wrong in your doing so in your separation from me while I am still alive. I love you so dearly that even if you are dead, you will be alive to me. Your soul is deathless. I repeat what I have frequently told you and assure you that if you do succumb to your illness, I will not marry again. Time and again I have told you that you may quietly breathe your last with faith in God. If you die, even that death of yours will be a sacrifice to the cause of satyagraha. My struggle is not merely political. It is religious and therefore quite pure. It does not matter much whether one dies in it or lives. I hope and expect that you will also think likewise and not be unhappy. I ask this of you.

Mohandas

2. Letter to Kasturba Gandhi

Nadiad,
July 29, 1918

Beloved Kastur,

I know you are pining to stay with me. I feel, though, that we must go on with our tasks. At present, it is right that you remain where you are. If you but look upon all the children there as your own, quite soon you will cease to feel the absence of the latter. This is the least one can do as one gets older. As you come to love others and serve them, you will have a joy welling up from within. You should make it a point to visit early in the morning all those who may be sick, and nurse them. Special food should be prepared or kept apart for anyone who needs such food. You should visit the Maharashtrian ladies, amuse their children or take them out for a walk. You should make them feel that they are no strangers. Their health should improve. You should converse with Nirmala on useful subjects, that is, on religious matters and the like. You may ask her to read out the *Bhagavat* to you. She will even find the thing interesting. If you thus keep yourself busy in the service of others, believe me the mind will always be full of joy. And you must not omit to look after Punjabhai's meals and other requirements.

Mohandas

3. Letter to Kasturba Gandhi[1]

On or after May 12, 1930

Take this letter as meant for all. How good it was that I met you all on Sunday evening and accompanied you back as far as your camp ? I was very happy that I did so. God is showering His grace on me. Let all the women write to me. All the letters should be put in one envelope. Most likely I shall get those letters. If I don't get them, it will not matter. Do not feel nervous, any of you. All the verses in the section of women's prayer were purposely selected. The very first verse teaches us a great deal. The last three verses of the *Gita* which have been included sum up the whole prayer. They are like the *kalasha* on the top of a temple which adds lustre to the temple and completes its beauty. I hope the verses in this prayer are recited every morning with careful attention to their meaning.

Blessings from
Bapu

4. Letter to Kasturba Gandhi

December 19, 1933

BA,

I got your letter today. The letter addressed to Sabarmati must have been received. I will continue to write to you regularly. I will write every Monday or Tuesday, for on those two days I get some free time. Take care of your health. I will send the slivers. If I don't have any extra stock with me, I will get them from some source and send you. I have been having some blood pressure. I was examined by Dr. Ansari in Delhi. Do not at all worry about me. I will surely write to Manilal and Sushila every fortnight. I wrote to them long letters. I will send your blessings to everyone. Do not worry about anybody. I have written to Manu also regarding Kusum. The latter is really ill and may or may not survive. Kishorelal has been having fever intermittently. He is in bed. Brijkrishna also has been bed-ridden for a long time. Devdas is well, and so also Rajaji. Give my blessings to all the women there. I hope all of them are doing physical work and maintaining good health. Ramanama is an unfailing remedy. I had prepared an abridged *Gita* for Ramdas. It is being printed. When it is ready, I will send a few copies there. If you want anything else, write to me. Address your letters always to Wardha. I hope you are supplied newspapers.You have asked for a discourse from me. I will not send one this time. I will see if I can do so next week. It is certainly very good that you read the *Gita* regularly. Who teaches you to read it ? What food do you get there ? You remember don't you, that you can write to Premlilabehn or Trivedi for anything that you may want. You will have fewer visitors there and so the best course will be that you should write one letter to me and receive one from me every week. However, you may do as you like. Om is all right. Premabehn's friend, Kisan, has joined me recently. You remember her, don't you ? She is very hard-working and has been well educated.

Blessings from
Bapu

5. Letter to Kasturba Gandhi

December 25, 1933

BA,

You must have got the long letter which I wrote to you last Monday. This Monday we are in Sitanagaram. It is situated on the banks of the Godavari. It is a small village, in Andhradesha, and has an ashram in it. Being a village, it is completely peaceful. We came here in a boat. The river is quite big and, therefore, small steamers can sail on it. We visited Madras and spent three days there. Sastri was, of course, there. I met Jethalal. Gangabhabhi lives in the city itself. I met Jethalal's wife, too. Both are in good health. Jethalal gets a pay of Rs. 150 and is, therefore, quite happy. I met Urmiladevi's son also. There was a large number of visitors. Lakshmi is quite well. Papa also is in Madras. Lakshmi stayed with me all the three days. She was happy in the company of Mirabehn, Kisan and Om. We shall be meeting once again, for my tour of that part is incomplete. My health is all right. I was again examined by two doctors. There is, therefore, no reason at all for you to worry about me. Have Dahibhen's teeth improved ? Do you get the *Jam-e-Jamshed* ? You asked for something like a discourse. I think I must give you one today.

The chapters of the *Gita* recited today were IX, X, XI and XII. In Chapter IX, the Lord says that those who worship Him attain to Him.[2] In Chapter XII, He explains who should be called a *bhakta.*[3] The beauty of the description is that it does not contain any quality which even the most ignorant person cannot cultivate. Any man or woman who strives unaided by another can become a *bhakta* and be one with the Lord. The qualities mentioned are these. The *bhakta* has ill will for nobody but is a friend of all and has compassion for all; he has no feeling of personal attachment towards anything or anybody, is devoid of ego, is equal-minded to happiness and unhappiness and is of a forgiving nature. He is ever contented, is self-controlled and keeps his vows; he has dedicated his mind and reason to God. He causes pain to none and has no fears and worries, desires nothing, is pure in mind and heart and skilful in work, has renounced everything and treats friend and enemy with equal regard, is indifferent to respect and disrespect, bears heat and cold, is unmoved by praise or censure, looks upon wherever he happens to be as his home, that is, has no home of his own, doesn't speak unnecessarily and has a steady mind. Such a person (says the Lord) may be described as my *bhakta*. If all of you reflect over this deeply, you will realize that anybody who wants can become a *bhakta* without help from any other person.

Blessings to all from
Bapu

6. Letter to Kasturba Gandhi

Cuddapah Station,
January 1, 1934

BA,

Send me a copy of the discourse I sent you last time.[4] I got your letter only today. I am writing this letter on my silence day. Do not worry about Manilal. I am sending your letter to him. You need not get alarmed by what Pragji said. Both are mature persons. If they have made a mistake they will correct it. Arrangement has already been made for *jame-e-jamshed.* Mathuradas informs me that this has been done, and so I have done nothing further about it. I hope you get it now. All the same, I am inquiring again. I will try about the *Ramayana* and the *Bhagavata.* Don't feel the slightest hesitation in writing to Premlilabehn for anything you want. After all, what are you likely to want ? What few things you want she will send with great love. But about anything which you do not require immediately, it will be enough if you write to me. I will then make the necessary arrangements. Can you use your dentures ? Do you gargle with potassium permanganate water ?

Thakkar Bapa is not in the party with me this time. He will meet me on the 15th. Just now Malkani is with me. He also is working very hard, along with the others. Chandrashankar keeps fairly good health. Om and Kisan are taking good care of their health. Om works as hard as she can. She is a simple-hearted and straightforward girl. And so is Kisan. Surendra has regained his strength.

The Andhra tour ends on the 3rd. After that we shall go to Mysore. Wherever I go, there is bound to be a lot of activity and some hardships too. But I am carefully protected by everybody and so don't feel the hardships much. As Mirabehn looks after the smallest detail, I don't feel the discomfort of travelling at all. You will be permitted to receive a letter from me every week only if you forgo your right of receiving visitors. I for one will go on sending a discourse every week. Be satisfied with visitors who come to see the other women. However, do as you wish. If you are keen on having visitors, there would be many ready to go. They would even wish to go. We have deliberately made it a practice to receive the fewest possible visitors. But let me know your wish without any hesitation. Janakibehn is all right. I think I have already written to you about her son Ramakrishna's tonsils being removed. Kamala has now resumed solid foods. Kishorelal is still not free from fever. But there is no cause for worry. These days my silence commences on Sunday night. I, therefore, don't speak till Monday night. The silence will be broken today at ten minutes past nine. Hence, I shall hardly have to speak to anybody, since soon after it will be time to go to bed. I have to get up at three in the morning. Brijkrishna's fever has come down. But he has yet to regain strength. Hemibehn is no more. Now the discourse. Last time I wrote about the attributes of a *bhakta.* I also explained that there could be no *bhakti* without service. This time I will write about how one can serve, since people frequently ask me that question. Some say that service is possible only under certain conditions. Some others that it is possible only after certain studies. I explained last week that these were wrong notions. One can serve under any conditions. If we offer up to Shri Krishna all our gifts and possessions, we shall get full marks. Anybody who can give one crore but gives only half a crore, will not get more than 50 marks. But he who has only one pie and gives it will get 100 marks. If, therefore, you and the other women prisoners behave in this manner towards the women with whom you come into contact or towards the officials, you are fufilling the dharma of service. Behaving towards the officials in the spirit of service means never wishing them ill, showing them due respect and not deceiving them. All the rules should be obeyed and the women undergoing imprisonment for criminal offences should be treated as if they were your blood-sisters. If you let them feel your love and see your purity of heart, that also will mean practising the dharma of service. In both cases one's motives must be clean. If a person behaves in a good way with a selfish motive or through fear, his actions cannot be reckoned as service. We often see one person doing a thing with a selfish motive and another doing the same thing with a benevolent motive. There can be no room for self-interest in anything done as an offering to the Lord. One who serves in this manner daily gains more strength. His studies and his work, both are inspired by the motive of service. Even the laughing or playing, eating or drinking of a person who is thus dedicated to service are informed with the spirit of service. All his actions, therefore, will be innocent. The Lord always gives to such *bhaktas* the strength they need. You probably remember the three verses in the women's prayer which have a bearing on this. They are as follows:

> As for those who worship Me, thinking on Me alone and nothing else, ever attached to me, I bear the burden of getting them what they need. With Me in their thoughts, their whole soul devoted to Me, teaching one another, with Me ever on their lips, they live in contentment and joy. To these, ever in tune with Me, worshipping Me with affectionate devotion, I give the power of selfless action, whereby they come to Me !

Refer to the *Anasaktiyog* for the meaning of these verses. You will find them in Chapters 9 and 10. Remember that we read the *Gita* to put its teaching into practice. All that I have said above is, you should know, on the basis of the *Gita.*

Blessings to all from
Bapu

7. Letter to Kasturba Gandhi

Bangalore,
January 8, 1934

BA,

I have still not received your letter, but I believe it will reach me after some wandering. I hope you are getting the newspaper now. You must have received the *Bhagavat* and the *Ramayana*. Write for anything else you may wish to have. I had a letter from Manilal, as also one from Sushila. They are both well. Manilal is unperturbed and asks you not to worry about him. Sita is growing up fast. She is always playing about. Devdas has been released earlier than expected. He has gone to Ahmedabad. I had a wire from him. Perhaps he will visit you.

There were letters from Ramdas and Nimu too. I keep on writing to Manu, but again there has been no letter from her. Kishorelal's fever has come down a little and so it can be hoped that he will have fully recovered in a few days. There is nothing but good news about Mani. Om, Kisan, Chandrashankar etc., are all well. I am in Bangalore today. Everyone has been inquiring after you. Shankerlal and Gulzarilal have come here. There is to be a meeting of the *Panch* regarding the workers' wages. Tomorrow is Tuesday, and so it will meet tomorrow. Afterwards I have to go to Malabar. I will be going to the area which you once visited. Urmila Devi's[5] son has a job in Madras now. I keep good health. There is no cause at all for worry. At every place people come in large crowds and give me purses, jewellery etc. Kanti is better now. I see that Bal will be seeing me in a few days. His health also is quite good. I hope all of you there are well. What progress have Shanta and Lalita made in their studies ? And now the discourse. Today I will write something about what the *Gita* says concerning *yajna*. The subject is introduced in Chapter III. In that chapter the Lord says that he who eats without performing *yajna* eats stolen food[6]. This is a very serious statement indeed, for eating stolen food is like swallowing raw mercury. Nobody can digest it and, if anyone eats it, he will get eruptions all over the body. Hence, Akho Bhagat has said: "Eating stolen food is like swallowing raw mercury." If, therefore, a person stops performing *yajna* even for a while, he becomes a thief. All of us should know that this *yajna* means. Fortunately for us, it is easy for all whose heart is in the right place. It requires no wealth, no intellect nor education. *Yajna* means any act of service. Only about a person whose whole life is a ceaseless *yajna* can it be said that he does not eat stolen food. Hence, those who do just a little work as *yajna* may be said to be not guilty of theft to that extent. Looking at the matter from this point of view, we see that all of us are guilty of theft more or less. Our *yajna* can be said to be perfect only when we have shed all selfishness. To do this means to give up the sense of 'I' and 'mine', to cease feeling that this belongs to me and that to somebody else, that this is my son and that somebody else's. There should not be even a trace of such a feeling in one's heart. He alone can do this who offers up his all to Shri Krishna. He who has done that does everything with God as witness, as His servant and in a spirit of service. Such a person is always happy and peaceful in mind. Happiness and sufferring are the same to him. He uses his body, mind, intellect, possessions—all that is his—for the service of others. All of us cannot do such perfect *yajna*. If, however, we have the aspiration in our heart to serve the whole world, what work is there which most people can do and which would include service to the whole world ? Asking this question, we found that the answer was spinning, which is the work that countless people can do in the spirit of service. One who spins will have done that much labour for the service of the world. But I mention this only as an example. What I wished to explain was the meaning and importance of *yajna*. I shall be satisfied if I have been able to explain it.

Blessings to all sisters from
Bapu

8. Letter to Kasturba Gandhi

Kumarika, Travancore,
January 22, 1934

BA,

We are in Kumarika today. I got your letter. You have visited this place once in Urmila Devi's company. This is the farthest end of India.

The Himalayas represent her head. We may, therefore, call this place Mother India's feet, which are daily washed by the sea. Since nobody lives here, perfect silence reigns. I bathed in the sea, and so did Om, Kisan and Chandrashankar[7]. There is no danger of cold here. Devdas and Lakshmi will most probably have gone to Delhi now. They went and met Rajaji. There has been no change in my diet and I keep very good health. I have secured a typist from Madras. He has been loaned to me by Anna[8]. He is good. As Thakkar Bapa has come now, Malkani has gone to Delhi. I have just received a letter from Ramdas and one from Nimu. At present they all seem to be well. Ramdas takes care of Sumitra's eyes. He has not yet recovered his peace of mind, but I think he will do so. There is no cause for anxiety.

I understand about Dahibehn's health. Let us all remember that the mind has a powerful effect on the body. In jail one is a prey to too many thoughts, which one should learn to control. If one can preserve one's equanimity in all conditions, one can be happy. Shanta should by now have grown very wise. Tell her I want her to live for eighty years more and do service. I hope Lalita also is quite happy. Do not hesitate to request Premlilabehn[8] for any article of food you may require in the interest of your health. Kanti is better now and keeps cheerful. He has lost some weight, though. I will write to Jamnabehn. I have at present no news of Madhavdas[9]. There was a letter from him some days ago. Now that you have specially inquired about him, I will write to him in your name. I have received a letter from Manilal and one from Sushila. There is nothing special in them. Both keep good health. Manilal is perfectly calm now. Surendra is still in Wardha. He is helping Jamnalalji there. All the women prisoners are expected to be released today. I have written a few words to each of them. And now the discourse.

The *Bhagavad Gita* says that the Lord's *bhakta* should cultivate solitude. This requires to be carefully grasped. We came into the world alone and shall leave it alone; why, then, should we yearn for anybody's companionship during the uncertain interval between birth and death ? However, though we come alone we also see that we are not altogether alone. We have the company of our parents. Were it not for that, we would not be able to live even for a moment. When we grow up, we generally get married. That also gives us similar company. Then we get the company of friends too. For spiritual progress also we require company to some extent. Why, then, does the *Gita* advise cultivating solitude ? Let us try to understand this point. Think of any companions and you will see that the bond is a sign of our dependence. Father, mother, husband, wife, friend, everybody makes us dependent on him or her to some extent. But one who is a *bhakt* of the Lord is full of compassion. He is dependent on God alone. He is the only true friend and, besides, He is our charioteer too.... What else can he want who has His company ? Mother *Gita*, therefore, advises us to seek solitude. This does not mean that we should shun the company of fellow beings. It only means that we should not desire it. We should not lose heart when we do not have it and, on the other hand, even in the midst of crores of people, should feel mental solitude and nearness to God. I hope you remember the *bhajan*: "Friends of the body are selfish, one and all; they will refuse to accompany one at the end." One who cultivates solitude will never be unhappy anywhere, for he sees only Vishnu in all places. Prahlad, the *bhakta*, saw Vishnu even in a red-hot pillar. With some effort, everybody can cultivate such love of solitude. All of you have got, unsought, an opportunity to do so. Try and cultivate it.

Blessings from
Bapu

9. Letter to Kasturba Gandhi

Coonoor,
February 5, 1934

BA,

I have your letter. What you say about Bihar is correct. Large numbers were killed and now in this cold thousands have become homeless. Much help is being sent from all parts of the country. From among the Ashram inmates, Panditji, Parnerkar, Raojibhai, Soman, Bal, Swami and Dhotre have gone there. Dhotre is the gentleman from Wardha. If more workers are required, I will send some others. I have had letters from all the women. All except Velanbehn are well. Velanbehn has gone to Baroda, taking Anandi and Mani with her If necessary, she will go and consult a doctor in Bombay. She has lost weight considerably. It will take her some months to be restored. Durga has gone to Bulsar. From there she will go to Belgaum. I also will be there on March 6. Lilavati was having fever, but she has returned to jail along with Premabehn. Devdas has not gone to Patna. There is no need, even, for him to do-so. Tara is fairly seriously ill. She is in Ahmedabad at present. Mani Parikh is at her maternal uncle's. Afterwards she will go to Kathlal. I shall meet Rajaji tomorrow. Amutussalaam is here. She has taken ill, but is better today. It seems she will go to Kashi and stay with Krishnakumari. Muriel Lester, in whose Ashram I stayed in England, will meet me tomorrow—Gangabehn has gone to Wardha to see Surendra. He is working there with Jamnalalji. Mahalakshmi is in Bombay with her children. I had letters from Manilal and Sushila. Both say that you should not worry about him. Sita is happy. Kallenbach was on a visit to Phoenix for two days. There has been frost in Gujarat and other parts of the country and most of the crops have been completely destroyed. The frost was severe and lasted many days. We must submit to God's will. Vallabhbhai is fairly well. There was a letter from Mridula. She also is well. I have inquired about Madhavdas.[10] I will most certainly let you know. I have not forgotten about it. There was a long letter from Ramdas. He and Nimu and the children are in good health. Keshu and Krishna are still in Wardha and are quite well.

There have been no letters from Radha recently. Brijkrishna is fairly well. He is slowly regaining strength. There is a well-known paper named *The Hindu* published from Madras. There was a wire today saying that its Editor had died. I have sent a wire of condolence.[11] Prabhavati is well. She is still in Patna. I hope you and the other women are in good health. I will start from here tomorrow morning and go to see Raja. And now the discourse.

There is a saying among us: "One road, two purposes." What road is that following which will always serve "two purposes" ? "Two purposes" should not, either, be understood to mean only two. Here "two" means more than one. One may, therefore, also say: "One road and a hundred purposes." In Bihar thousands of people were buried alive in the matter of a minute. This cannot but make us think that one should not waste a single moment. "Make the best of today, for who has seen tomorrow ?" —sang Mira. We don't know what will happen even after a minute or a second. One may pass away even in the act of yawning. What, then, is that golden road following which would serve all purposes ? There is only one, viz. helping others. That means service of the neighbour. Another name for it is *paramartha*. The word means 'supreme purpose'. A third name for it is *Haribhakti*[12]. We sing in the *prabhatiyan*[13] of Narasinh Mehta that such *bhakti* is not practised by telling beads or putting marks on the forehead or bathing in the Ganga. *Bhaktas* tell us that it means pledging one's head. We should, therefore, always wish the world's good all the hours of the day whether in jail or outside, and do whatever service may fall to our lot in order to advance it. I hope this will be enough for today's discourse.

Blessings to all from
Bapu

10. Letter to Kasturba Gandhi

Mysore,
February 22, 1934

BA,

I am writing this letter in a train. I got your letter. I had so much work to do that I could not write on Tuesday. Today is Thursday. You can ask me to do anything for you or put me any question that you may wish. I will attend to it or reply to it. At least I will try. You have asked me about Harilal. He had gone to Pondicherry. There also he begged for money and indulged in drinking. He even got some money. I do not know where he is now. I think he will now remain what he is. We must wait till God gives him wisdom. Will not our good and evil actions, too, have their effect in this ? How sunk in passion I was when he was conceived ! You and I must reap as we sowed. Parents are in this way undoubtedly responsible for the character of their offspring. Now there is only one thing we can do, namely purify ourselves. Let us be content with the effort that we are making for that. Our purification is bound to have a conscious or unconscious effect on Harilal. There has been no letter from Manu recently, but Jamnadas gave me news about her. I will write to Sushila. Purushottam has been betrothed to Harakhchand's daughter. His health cannot yet be considered as good. The wife of Ranchhodbhai's brother has died, and Motibehn remains depressed because of that. Her responsibility has increased now. Ambalalbhai and Mridula came and saw me. He and Saralabehn are going to England. They will stay there for three or four months. Devdas-Lakshmi are all right. Lakshmi does feel the burden of the pregnancy. Ramdas-Nimu are well. I am sending a copy of your letter to them. The original letter I am sending to Manilal. I have sent a copy to Vallabhbhai too. He also worries about you. There has been no reply yet from Madhavdas. Mathuradas is with me. He will stay for a day or two more and then return to Bombay. Esther Menon has returned from England. She came and saw me. Miss Lester has gone to Ceylon. Rajaji parted from us yesterday at the end of the Madras tour. It seems he will go to Delhi. Amutussalaam is still weak, and so I have kept her in Madras. Rajaji will look after her. You must have received the slivers. Write to me again when they are exhausted. I will send some more. Kusum has been very much affected by the death of her brother in Zanzibar. Pyarelal was released yesterday. Kishorelal is at Deolali. He is somewhat better now. Lakshmi will have her baby at Bardoli. Manjukesha will look after her. Moti or Lakshmi also will be there at that time. Nanibehn Jhaveri has been operated upon for the trouble in her joints. I think I have given sufficient news. I will leave Hyderabad on the 9th and go to Patna. Rajendrababu has called me there. Prabhavati also is there. It seems I shall have to stay in Bihar for quite a while. And now the discourse.

If you do not remember the *bhajan* "The Name is my support, Your Name is my support", look it up. These days I keep thinking about the idea. Tulsidasji has sung a great deal of the power of the Name. The Name means Ramanama or any name of God. Tulsidas has said that the name Rama is more powerful than Rama himself. In other words, the man called Rama who lived in the past was subject to limitations. His body was perishable but his name is immortal. The qualities of the man who bore that name had limitations, but the attributes of God signified by Ramanama have no limit. We may imagine in Him any attributes that we like. Because His attributes are infinite, God transcends all attributes. That is, He is above all attributes. Since we cannot exhaust the attributes of God by any enumeration of them, cannot we say that He is above attributes ? If we inscribe in our hearts the name of God which has such power, there can be no doubt that we shall cross this sea of life and reach the other shore. Repeating that name will drive away all miseries. That is, we shall endure whatever suffering falls to our lot. If such repetition becomes automatic with us, we would need nothing else. That is why the poet wrote and sang that song: "My only support is Rama's name," all else is false. "All friends of the body are selfish and will refuse to accompany us at the end." If we have learnt to repeat Ramanama, it alone will go with us.

Blessings to all women from
Bapu

11. Letter to Kasturba Gandhi

February 27, 1934

BA,

I have not yet received your letter this time. I also am wandering about in a part where the post is very irregular, because there is no railway. I am touring small villages on the coast and there are so many streams and rivulets that building a railway would be too expensive. At the foot of the hills is the sea. The rivers flowing from the hills form a big estuary which can be crossed only in a boat. In a region like this, it is not possible to travel fast and, therefore, letters take very long to reach. This morning we boarded a steamer at a place called Kundapur, and it will bring us to Karwar at night. We shall be on the sea for twelve hours. You have been to Mangalore. We were there yesterday. From there we reached Kundapur at night, crossing many rivers on the way, and at that place we boarded the steamer. The people here speak Kannada. All these places are in the region from where Gangadharrao hails. The province is called Karnataka. On the 5th and the 6th I shall be in Belgaum. Since we are on the sea-coast, the air is cool. It has been decided that, after completing Karnataka, I should go to Patna. I shall be in Hyderabad on the 9th, from where I will board a train for Patna. I will most probably meet Sarojini devi in Hyderabad. Padma at any rate is there. In Wardha, which is on the way to Patna, Pyarelal is likely to meet me. He has just been released and after his release he has gone to Wardha. Most probably Jamnalaji also will go to Patna. Thakkar Bapa will not come with me to Patna but will go to Delhi instead. He will have to work there. Lakshmidas is in Patna. He is quite ill. He has got typhoid. There was a wire from Swami to that effect. Chandrashankar has taken leave for 15 days and gone to see his wife. I have written to him and asked him to call on Madhavdas. I have received no reply to my letter to Madhavdas. Narandas will be released on the 9th and Chhaganlal on the 3rd. There was news of Vasumati having been released. I have not heard from her. Prithuraj is still with me. At the moment he does not wish to go to Patna. Poor Velanbehn must be pining to see him. I have not received Manilal's letter as yet. Mahadev keeps good health. Durga has been to visit him. She was accompanied by Jivanji. Prabhavati and Jayaprakash are in Patna. They are doing relief work. And now the discourse.

Last week I wrote about the power of the Name. But the question arises: how should one repeat the Name ? What good does it do to keep repeating it when thousands of idle thoughts distract the mind ? Either one should repeat the Name from the heart, or not at all. This is partly right and partly not. If one repeats the Name for outward show, it has no meaning. On the contrary it is a sin to do so since it amounts to deception. But a person may wish sincerely to repeat the Name, and yet his mind may be continually distracted by other thoughts when he is repeating it. He should not lose heart, however. He should go on repeating the Name in spite of the distraction of thoughts. If he keeps up the practice, some day the Name will get inscribed in his heart. This is the reason why the power of the Name has been glorified. Even an illiterate or dull person can repeat the Lord's name. One can learn to do so in one second. After that one has merely to keep repeating it. By and by this becomes so much a habit that one does not feel happy unless one is going on with it. When the habit becomes so strong that one goes on repeating the Name at all hours of the day, whether eating or drinking or working or resting, then it may be said that the Name has sunk in one's heart. Such persons are rare, but they rise above all suffering. An interesting story about Hanuman illustrating this was told in the Ashram once by Panditji's guru. I will narrate it next week.

Blessings to all from
Bapu

12. Letter to Kasturba Gandhi

March 13/14, 1934

BA,

You must have received my letter of last week. It was dictated to Om. Today is Tuesday. I am writing this after brushing my teeth. It is not yet four. I am in Patna. The Relief Committee has rented a building. In the compound they have put up tents. Some persons are staying in these tents, too. Rajendrababu, his sister, Prabhavati and her husband, all of them are here. Jamnalal also is here. Bal, Maganbhai, Swami, Kripalani, Somanji and the others are here, too. Tomorrow I shall be visiting the part which has been worst hit. Lakshmidas is better now. He can even walk about a little. He is regaining strength. Velanbehn is trying hard to come, but has not come so far. I had letters from Manu, Bali and Rami this time. All of them had fallen ill together, so that none of them could write. Manu and Bali say that in their illness all of them forgot the grief of Kusum's death. They are all better now. Rami must have gone to Bombay or will go now. Manu has been able to make no progress in her study. She started eating pickles etc., as a result of which she got fever and also sore throat. They all send their *pranams* to you. In fact in every letter there are *pranams* for you. Kaka is happy in Hyderabad. Chhaganlal Joshi is in Dwarka and so Ramabehn also has gone there with Vishnu. Vasumati is in Borivli. Gangabehn had gone to Kutch, from where she has returned and gone to Ahmedabad. Krishnakumari is ill. Amutussalaam is still with Rajaji. Pyarelal is in Bombay. Kusum Desai had come to meet me at Wardha Station. The station was on the way when I came here. I came in Hyderabad. Sarojinidevi had come there. She also is quite happy. Thakkar Bapa has gone to Delhi and Mama has accompanied him for keeping accounts. We are, therefore, only seven now. Before that we were sixteen. Ramdas met me. He travelled with me for one or two stations. He is all right. And now the discourse:

As I wrote in my last letter, I will narrate the story told by Vishnu Digambar Shastri. It has been devised to explain the meaning of *bhakti*. When Rama returned with Sita to Ayodhya in the flying-chariot Pushpak, he was accompanied by Hanuman and others. It was time now to bid them farewell, and so a durbar was held. Rama embraced all and Sita blessed them by putting her hands on their heads. The eyes of all were moist with tears. Rewards were distributed to all. It was Hanuman's turn to receive his. Sita took off the necklace of precious jewels which she was wearing, put it round Hanuman's neck and embraced him. But what could Hanuman have to do with a necklace of jewels ? He snapped it into two and started opening up each bead with his teeth and, not seeing Ramanama inside, would throw it away. Everybody was stunned. The necklace which Sita had given from off her neck to be thus treated ! Sita asked Hanuman why he was acting in that manner. Hanuman replied: "Mother, what shall I do wearing a necklace consisting of jewels which do not contain Ramanama ? I want to have nothing but that." The reply increased their amazement. Somebody said: "If that is so, Ramanama cannot be seen in your body either; what about it ?" Hanuman burst out laughing and said: "All right. Look." He then tore open his chest and there flowed out a stream of blood in every drop of which they saw Ramanama. They all shouted: "Enough, enough. We have seen it. Please forgive us." Hanuman closed the cut and the court was filled with shouts of victory to him. Sita embraced him and bathed him in tears of joy.

This is an invented story. It is not found even in the *Ramayana.* There was no need for Hanuman to tear open his chest in order to show his *bhakti.* But we have to learn something from this story. Hanuman did not care for a reward. To him his service was its own reward. His *bhakti* was not for show. Nor did it require expression in words. Service itself constituted *bhakti* for him. Rama filled his whole being and accompanied every breath of his. He thought of nothing but Rama whether working or resting, eating or drinking, waking or asleep. He had put himself, mind, speech and body, in the hands of Rama. His heroism was dependent on his *bhakti.* It sprang from it. If we try, we can attain to *bhakti* like Hanuman's. If Ramanama is on our lips all the hours of the day, some day it will sink into our heart; and once it has sunk into the heart it is bound to fill the whole being. Prabhavati specially sends her *pranams* to you. She has inquired after everybody. I started writing this letter yesterday and have finished it today, Wednesday. It is still not four.

Blessings to you all from
Bapu

13. Letter to Kasturba Gandhi

Patna,
March 20/21, 1934

BA,

I have still not received your letter this time. I am writing this on Tuesday after morning prayer. I am in Patna. By my side is Satisbabu, spinning on the *takli.* There is Rajendrababu's sister. Prabhavati too. Om and Kisan are preparing to go to bed. Swami also is sitting near me. Mirabehn has gone to get the milk ready. Malaviyaji, Maulana Abul Kalam Azad, Dr. Mahmud etc., are here just now. There was a meeting of all of them on Sunday. At that meeting a new committee was appointed for relief work in Bihar. Jamnalalji also is a member of it. The work is progressing well. I visited Motihari and other places. Even big mansions have been reduced to heaps of bricks and mortar. Everywhere in the streets we saw heaps of bricks and ruins of buildings. The fields are covered with sand ejected with water from the bowels of the earth. Till this sand is removed, no crops can grow, and removing it is no easy work. For it is not only one or two *bighas* that are so covered. Thousands of *bighas* have been covered and in some places the layers are six inches thick or even thicker. The people's misery, therefore, is beyond measure. But even then life is so dear that people, dizzy with the thought of having escaped death, can forget their hardships and keep smiling faces. They have no food in their homes and no clothes to wear, but they do not seem to worry much about that. Such is the scene here. What can we do to help them ? Those who are working in the midst of the people may serve them humbly and unostentatiously. They may plead with the idle to start working, and teach sensualists self-control by their own example.

They may teach people *Ramadhun* and turn them Godward. There are such silent workers, too, at many places. God's ways are beyond our understanding. He erased the difference between birth and death in a matter of two minutes. Who was born and who is dead ? Whether human beings are born or die, His play goes on. Why then rejoice and grieve ? The Lord's name is the only truth. He who is aware of Him and serves Him, that is, His creation, as well as he may, lives. Those who do not do this are as good as dead, though living. Well, having started to write a letter I have given you this week's discourse. There may be a few words which you may not understand. But Dahibehn or Shanta or Lalita, one of them will surely be able to understand them. If, however, there is any word which none of you can understand, ask me its meaning.

After writing the above yesterday, I could not go on further. I have resumed the letter today, Wednesday, in the morning (8.45). I shall soon be called to a meeting. There was another letter from Madhavdas. His health has improved so much that he sees no need now to go to Porbandar. He will remain in Bombay and start some business. Devdas and Lakshmi are quite happy. Rajaji has still not gone to Delhi. Most probably he will come here and meet me before going there.

Blessings to you all from
Bapu

14. Letter to Kasturba Gandhi

March 29, 1934

BA,

It is 3.30 in the morning, and Thursday. I got your letter only yesterday evening. We are in Muzaffarpur today. Panditji, Swami and Kripalani are here. Madhavdas also is here. I shall meet Bal at 11. I am going to visit the place where Maganbhai, Raojibhai, Soman and others are working. I will ask Raojibhai to write to you. I will try to give you all the news that you want from me. But if anything is left out, ask me again. Prabhavati accompanies me these days wherever I go. Kunvarji is in Bombay. Rami also has gone there. Manu is better now. Madhavdas also is better. Vasumati has gone to Wardha. Chhaganlal and Rama have gone to Dwarka. Chhaganlal fasted for seven days just for self-purification. The fast ended on Monday. He is all right. Dudhibehn and Junior Kusum are in Bhavnagar. Kusum Desai has gone on a visit to Santiniketan. Her problem is not yet wholly solved. She is in search of suitable work. There was a letter from Manilal and Sushila. They are quite well. Chandrashankar will be returning in four days now. In Ahmedabad children get headaches, lose power of thinking, get fever and die. It is on the decline now. The disease is caused by going to cinemas etc. Bad air is the chief cause. Yes, they have started a hospital in the Vidyapith building. I do not know where Kanti will go or stay after his release. I am going to write to him. Anandi and the other children are with Anasuyabehn and are quite happy. Anandi had mild fever. She is better now. Lakshmidas also is better. He is in Patna. Parvati visited Pragji. The latter is quite well. Devdas and Lakshmi are still in Delhi. Rajagopalachari will go there in a few days' time. Manibehn seems to be doing fairly well. I have had no letter from her. Nagini has gone to America and Amala is quite happy at Sabarmati. Janakibehn, Madalasa and others are in Wardha. Raojibhai's Vidya is in Wardha. She has grown up and wishes to marry. They are in search of a suitable young man for her. Lakshmibehn Khare is looking after the work at Wardha. The number of girls has gone up very much. It has exceeded fifty. Dwarkanathji also is there. Brijkrishna is in Delhi. He is better now.

Pyarelal is with me.

The lady who was helping me in England is with me just now. It has not been decided what to do about the person who has come with her. It will be decided now. For the present she is here. Padmaja is all right. Mrs. Naidu did come to see me at Hyderabad. Panditji was not present on the Ramanavami day. The *bhajan "Jaya Rama Rama"* was sung by Somanji. We shall be leaving Bihar on the 10th to go to Assam. I will spend ten days in Assam and then return to Bihar. From there I will go to Orissa. I will reach that province in May. Yesterday I met Rajendrababu's wife and Vidyavati. I am not sending a discourse this time. It is nearing prayer time now.

Blessings to you all from
Bapu

15. Letter to Kasturba Gandhi

April 18, 1934

BA,

I got your letter, even though late. It is 3.15 just now. I have taken up your letter after cleaning my teeth. This place is called Jorhat. It is in Assam. Two days remain now for the tour here to end. After that I will spend a little more than a week in South Bihar and then I will go to Utkal, i.e. Orissa. I see that I shall be in Bengal when you are released. If the date of your release has been fixed, let me know it. There was a letter from Manilal specially meant for you. He writes in it about your inquiring after everybody. I have replied saying that I send your original letters to Phoenix, and copies to Ramdas, Devdas and Sardar. I have already written to you about Kanti having been released. He is all right. Since there is to be no jail-going now, it will shortly be decided where he will stay. He will come and meet me somewhere. Jamnalalji is now expected in Bihar. Satisbabu is all right. He is in Calcutta. Raojibhai, Panditji, Parnerkar and others are all working together in Bihar. Madhavdas also is with them. Bal and Prithuraj are with me. Narandas's nostrils bleed and so he is still at Rajkot. Perhaps he may come and see me at Ranchi. Chhaganlal is in Bhavnagar. He has almost regained the weight which he had lost. He visited Bhansali. There is something the matter with Bhansali's legs. He cannot move them or walk. He has got his lips stitched up. He drinks flour mixed with water through a tube. He also drinks gram or *mung* flour mixed with water. He drops me a postcard now and then. Despite the pain, he remains cheerful. Rajendrababu keeps excellent health. Prabhavati and Jayaprakash are better now. My weight is 108. Mirabehn doesn't make speeches. Sometimes she goes to open *khadi* exhibitions. I myself am not able to attend such functions. While opening the exhibitions, she says a few words. You see them reported in newspapers. I rarely get time to read newspapers. Ramdas's mother-in-law and Navanit have gone to Wardha. The epidemic in Ahmedabad has spread to other places too. I had written to Allahabad regarding Shyamlal Nehru. Umabehn has borne the separation from her husband with fortitude. Her daughter wrote a long letter to me. You must have received the slivers. Let me know when you want more. Where do you intend to break the semi-fast of the *Purushottam*[14] month ? I hope you get enough milk and fruit. Ranchhodbhai and others are in Ahmedabad, of course. They did not go out anywhere. Chimanlal has been having fever, and so he has gone to Veraval. Sharda has accompanied him. Mithubehn stays on in Bombay. Kalyanji and Kunvarji also are there. I did write a letter of condolence to Kunvarji on the death of his wife. Chandrashankar had returned, but he fell ill again and so went back.

I will write to Premlilabehn on your behalf. Kishorelal is still ill. He is at Deolali. Radha of course is there. Santok and Gomati also are there. Velanbehn is in Baroda. Om and Kisan go back to sleep after the morning prayer whenever they have no work. The constitutions of both need more sleep. I think this is enough for this time.

These days I am not able to send a discourse.

Blessings to all from
Bapu

16. Letter to Kasturba Gandhi

Chandanpur,
May 10, 1934

BA,

I have still not received your letter this time. The above place, where I am writing this, is ten miles from Puri. It is one o'clock after midnight just now. After cleaning my teeth, I wrote one postcard and have now taken up this letter for you. We decided the day before yesterday that from now on I should tour on foot. One cannot propagate dharma by travelling in trains or cars, nor in bullock-carts. That can be done only on foot. The local leaders and Thakkar Bapa finally agreed. We started the tour on foot the very same day. This has given me new strength. Yesterday we covered more than eight miles, but I felt no fatigue. I have got up quite fresh at this odd hour. People came in huge crowds, but there was complete peace. The pushing and jostling had stopped. Comparatively more work was done. The composition of the party remains the same. Among the women, Sushila, Prabhavati, Om and Mira are there of course. Besides them there are Purbai[15], Sonamani who was in the Ashram, and Ramabai, Gopabandhubabu's wife. Jivrambhai[16] also is in the party. And so also are Harakhchand, Purushottam's father-in-law. All of them will part form us at Cuttack. From there I shall have to go to Patna for three days. The All-India Congress Committee is meeting there. Personally I want to return from there to Orissa and complete the tour. But that will be finally decided when I meet the other co-workers.

Kusum Desai had met me in Puri. She has gone to her relations in Calcutta. She is likely to see me again in Patna. Vasumati is in Wardha. Ramdas, Nimu and the child are quite happy, as also Devdas, Lakshmi and her baby; also Hariji, Lakshmi and her baby. Pyarelal is still with Rajendrababu. Valjibhai, Bal and Prithuraj are with me. Chandrashankar is not in the party. He is still ill. I send with this a copy of the *Gita Praveshika* or *Ramagita*. You will have no difficulty in understanding it. If you want another copy, let me know. Leave this one behind you. I have already written to you suggesting what you should do after you are released. However, do what you like. There was a letter from Uttamchand. He has gone to Maroli. His wife too has gone with him.

Blessings to all from
Bapu

17. Letter to Kasturba Gandhi

November 2, 1938

BA,

Only nine days remain now, and God willing, we shall meet. We shall leave for Segaon the same day. I forgot to reply to one remark in your letter. You said that while leaving I did not even put my hand on your head. As the motor started I also felt that, but you were away from me. Do you require outward signs ? Why do you believe that because I do not show my love by outward signs, it has dried up ? I assure you that my love has increased and goes on increasing. Not that it was less before, but what was there is becoming purer day by day. I do not look upon you merely as a clay doll. What more need I say ? If you also, like . . . ask for outward signs, I will comply.

Blessings from
Bapu

18. Letter to Kasturba Gandhi

March 24, 1941

BA,

Either write or dictate a letter to me. A letter from Kanti is enclosed. On one side he has written to you and on the other to me. I get regular news about Manu. It looks as if she will have to be operated upon. I have written and suggested[17] that another doctor should be consulted and, if he also is of the same opinion, she should be operated upon. There is no risk at all in the operation. Do not worry. Now that you are there, go through the full treatment and get well.

Here it is quite hot. Do not worry about me. Things are all right. Lilavati[18] looks after my food etc.

Blessings to Lakshmi[19] and the children.

Blessings from
Bapu
(PS.)

A letter from Mani[20] is enclosed. Reply to her at length. Lakshmi or Sushila will write it for you.

NOTES

1. The source does not mention the addressee, but Mirabehn, writing *Young India*, 22-5-1930, says that this was addressed to Kasturba Gandhi.
2. IX. 29.
3. XII. 13 to 20.
4. *Vide* "Letter to Kasturba Gandhi", 25-12-1933.
5. Sister of C.R. Das.
6. III. 12.
7. The source has "Chandrashekhar".
8. Harihar Sharma.
9. Premlila Thackersey.
10. Brother of Kasturba Gandhi.
11. *Vide* the preceding item.
12. *Vide* "Telegram to K. Srinivasan", 5-2-1934.
13. Devotion to God.
14. Devotional hymns for early morning.
15. The intercalary month in the Hindu calendar occurring once in four years.
16. Co-worker of Jivram Kothari.
17. Jivram Kothari of Kutch.
18. *Vide* "Letter to Kunvarji K. Parekh", 23-3-1941.
19. Lilavati Asar.
20. Lakshmi Devdas Gandhi.
21. Manibehn Patel.

Chapter 2 Millie Graham Polak (1880- 1962)

Millie Graham Downs was born in 1880 in London, Britain in a Christian family. At the age of 18 she began work in connection with the Christian Socialistic movement. In December 1905 she travelled to Johannesburg, South Africa, by boat, to marry her fiance Henry Polak, a Jew by faith, who had become active in Gandhi's campaign for the rights of South Africa's Indians. She reached South Africa on 30 December, 1905. At six o'clock in the morning of December 30th, 1905, Millie arrived at Jeppe Station, Johannesburg, where Mr. Gandhi and Mr. Polak waiting on the platform for Millie.

Same day on 30th December, 1905 marriage took place and Millie and Polak became wife and husband. Gandhi was present on this occasion. After marrying with Henry Polak, Millie Downs became Millie Graham Polak. An informal reception for the couple was hosted at the residence of M.K. Gandhi, which was attended by a large number of friends and well-wishers. A small notice under the headline 'Congratulations' published in the Durban weekly *Indian Opinion* on January 5th, 1906. As she later wrote, it had been clear from the moment of her arrival in South Africa that in marrying Henry Polak she was also marrying Gandhi's cause.

Henry Polak was Gandhi's right-hand man. Henry Polak was like a younger brother. He was articled to M.K.Gandhi of the Inner Temple. Millie and Henry lived over the next nine years in the same Johannesburg house with Gandhi and his family. Millie soon discovered that the middle class comforts of London, to which, she has been accustomed, had no place in the Gandhi household. They started each day together grinding corn for the household's bread, and they ended each day with a communal vegetarian meal. Within months the whole extended family moved to the Phoenix Settlement established by Gandhi outside Durban, which was to be the base for his political campaign and where the paper *Indian Opinion* was produced. The paper had established itself as the mouthpiece of Gandhi's campaign for the rights of South Africa's Indians. But Phoenix wasn't just about a group of like-minded people experimenting with living together as simply as possible. They also had a political job to do; and everyone in the community, male and female, adults and children, were expected to pull their weight to bring out the weekly edition of the newspaper *Indian Opinion*. Gandhi, Millie Polak soon had to accept, wanted a broader canvas on which to work out his theories. Millie became a part of Gandhi's life and participated in each and every activity of Gandhi.

Gandhi acknowledges that Millie Polak's arrival in January 1906 was a significant, and potentially fraught, moment for the household—especially, he seems to recognise, for his wife, Kasturba. And it can only have been difficult for Kasturba Gandhi, who was still at this time illiterate, to experience her husband's close intellectual relationship with such untouchables—both male and female. From what she wrote later, Millie Polak seemed well aware of the delicacy of the situation.

Millie herself, well-educated, curious, and usually self-confident, evidently felt able to challenge Gandhi about even the most sensitive things—like how he treated his wife around the house. Millie Polak plays important role with Gandhi for the cause of Indians in South Africa. Millie Polak couldn't resist a particularly difficult request Gandhi made of her just before he finally left South Africa to return to India in 1914. She was anxious, after more than eight years away, to get back to England with her husband and the two young sons they now had.

But Gandhi needed people he could trust to stay and continue his work at Phoenix; and when he asked the Polaks, they agreed. So it would have been with a heavy heart that Millie travelled down to the Cape to say goodbye to the brilliantly strange Indian man with whom she had shared so much over the previous years.

Millie was proud woman for Indians. To both Polak and Henry, life was a battle in the cause of dharma. Hardship, sacrifice and skepticism were their life long companions.

Millie spent two years in India. She and her two children stayed with her sister at Conoor during their enforced stay in India. She fells victim to an attack of influenza epidemic along with her children. After the end of Second World War she returns back to England.

Gandhi himself and Millie Polak conversed frequently, about every subject under the African sun, and in the evenings she would jot down what they had said to each other in her notebook. Nearly three decades later, in 1931, she published a small volume of reminiscences (Mr. Gandhi, the Man) about her time as part of the Gandhi household in South Africa. The great woman died in 1962, leaving behind historical legacy.

1. Letter to Millie Graham Polak

Sunday, December 26, 1909

My Dear Millie,

I am writing this in Mr.Kallenbach's tent. It has been raining for the last two days. The tent is soaking wet, water dropping here and there. The wind is howling about me. Manilal is with us. He is a good boy. I notice that he is over-particular about his dress. He devoted nearly a(n) houlr to ironing his suit. He is pining to go to goal. I see you address me Brother in inverted commas and underlined thrice. We may well call ourselves brother and sister. Our conduct certainly justifies it. But will you give me a sister's confidence ? If you say 'yes', I shall try to be 'brother' to you. No real increase in my family can be cause of sorrow to me. Henry wants me to send you £ 17 now. His previous letter said £ 16. I think I wrote to you from 'on board' that I should like to be able to send you more. Now it is done by Henry which is the same thing. Henry wonders how you will take his prolonged stay in India. And yet he is there in his element. After a certain stage, my presence is a hindrance to friends' growth. Henry is doing much better independently of me. He has succeeded in captivating Dr. Mehta who wants me to print his address on industrialism and its evils for free distribution.

Your letter is full of epigrams in your best style. You could hardly be so sweet as you are if you never needed a friend's help and consolation. Though a brother could never replace a husband, I tried during my stay in London to replace Henry so far as I could. It was no more a wrench to you to separate from me than it was to me to separate from you. We certainly came nearer each other in London than ever before. It was natural.

You may well envy Maud and yet you cannot. Maud is a different type. Friends can make or mar her. You can be helped by friends and never marred. A trusting nature like Maud's is beautiful. It can under good auspices develop into a very strong nature. Her progress can be rapid but so can her retrogression. With you retrogression is impossible. And progress, shall I say, slow if not even difficult. You would be justified. I know, in saying the same of me. We are both strong natures. We may be nearest each other but never identical. I was tempted to analyse Henry. But I must not speculate any further. Your wonderful letter before me has given rise to these thoughts. That is the beauty of epigrams. You could say so much on each.

You are right in assuming that Lord Morley's reforms may be a piece of bone thrown to a hungry dog. And yet it is open to those who will be the leaders in the new Assembly to make much out of them. Lord Morley can do little for India unless Indians themselves are prepared to do something for themselves. Just now assassination is the order of the day. Lord Morely can stop it but he is too blind to see the way. I should like to be able to throw myself into the work but I cannot, and have no desire to force the pace.

I am glad Waldo and Baby are getting on. I hope Celia and Amy are keeping well.

Of myself, you will learn from elsewhere.

With love,
Yours sincerely,
Your 'Brother'

2. Letter to Millie Graham Polak

April 24, 1910

My Dear Millie,

Henry is a tender flower. The slightest breeze ruffles his spirits. You and I divide him. When he is in such a mood, you can make him happy and to a lesser degree I. But alas ! He can just now have neither you nor me. The publication and confiscation of the little book of mine have disconcerted him a bit.[1] There is no occasion for it. I have written to him at length. And then the wretched pecuniary business. He gives me the position of an elder brother and yet would not be content with my taking over the pecuniary burden. I wish you would not discuss money matters with him at all. You may do all that when you are together again. Let me alone have all your pecuniary needs. He has enough to occupy his attention besides worrying about money matters which he hates.

The farm idea is still progressing. Hosken has offered a portion of his farm. If this thing comes off, I may shift very soon. It promises to be a mighty thing if it comes off.

I was sorry to learn about Mater's and Celia's trouble. It seems useless to inquire after a lapse of a month as to how they are getting on.

From what you say, it is evident that winter has not in any way affected Waldo.

With love to you all,
Brother

3. Letter to Millie Graham Polak

May 8, 1910

My Dear Millie,

I can think of nothing to write to you about. I therefore give you the following beautiful thought:

"Therefore the means of deliverance from all those evils from which men suffer lies only in one thing, the inner work of each man upon himself.

"Martha ! Martha ! thou art anxious and troubled about many things, but one thing is needful."

I remain with love,

Yours,
Brother

4. Letter to Millie Graham Polak

February 17, 1912

My Dear Millie,

What a horrid thing that you should get chicken pox ! Henry says it was due to the sin of going to Delhi even after the event. Whatever the cause, I am sorry you were not able to attend the Congress sittings. It was quite like you to have turned your illness to good account by reading on things Indian. I hope that the illness has not left you weaker. These illnesses if properly treated invigorate patients in the end.

Waldo is evidently having a good time of it here. I hope you are not worrying about Amy. To worry where we cannot help if possible is to render us still more helpless for future service.

Of the bill and the prospects of the struggle, you will learn from my letter to Henry.

Manilal, Ramdas and Devdas are with me at present. They are all well. Manilal will be going to Phoenix shortly. Hoosen too has been paying a visit to the Transvaal. He proposes to leave for India shortly. I have now 25 boys on the Farm 8 Mahommedans, 2 Parsees and the balance Hindus. Of the latter, 5 are Tamils, one Calcuttan and the rest Gujaratis. They are divided into at least four standards. Medh, Pragji and Jamnadas assist me at school. Gujarati, Hindi and Tamil are being taught besides English. I shall find it somewhat difficult to manage the school if and when Desai and Medh go to India.[2]

I want to teach the boys sewing. Mrs. Vogl has been coming once a fortnight for the purpose. Poor woman. She has her old trouble coming on again and again. The doctor has now forbidden railway travelling. So the class may be interrupted. But I have learnt sufficient to continue the class for some time. Sandal-making is going on regularly. I make my own shirts now. Ramdas, Devdas and I wear shirts of my own make. Mrs. V. is quite proud of her new pupil. But I fear she conceals the true fact when she credits me with having turned out an excellent shirt. I have just finished Devdas's knickers too. During the past six months, we must have made nearly 50 pairs of sandals mostly for the Farm boys. Some have been made to order also. I sent one pair to Maud and if you give me the tracing of your right foot, holding the pen perpendicular I shall do myself the honour of making a pair for you. Mrs. Vogl and Miss Schlesin have theirs.

I think I gave you the school hours. Rise at 6 a.m., breakfast 6.45 a.m. home-made bread toasted or fried in ghee and cereal, coffee or milk (condensed I am sorry) and stewed peaches 7.15 manual work some hoeing, some in the kitchen, some wood-chopping and others sandal making and sewing 10 a.m. bell for bathing, 11 a.m. to 12 noon, dinner rice and curry and bread, fruits if any and some cereal preparation for those boys who are experimenting in saltless diet. 12 to 1 boys read for themselves. 1 to 4.30 schooling. 4.30 to 4.45 drill. 5.30 p.m. supper-wholemeal porridge, milk, stew and coffee and bread. 7 to 8 some religious reading and hymns Gujarati, Hindi and English. Religious reading from Mahommedan scriptural books, Parsee and Hindu. At 8 p.m. boys are fee to go to bed. I sleep with them on the open verandah. Mrs. Gandhi too sleeps on the open verandah with the boys who cannot be accommodated on the verandah where I sleep. Devdas shares Mrs. Gandhi's bed as of old. Boys do their own washing. On the Farm they wear nothing but the shirts and trousers. If it is cold, they wear jerseys and jackets too if they wish to. There is hardly any compulsion used. Appeal is always made to their good nature for making them do anything. All boys must be vegetarians and non-smokers at least on the Farm. No boys may come from outside to have tuition only. Parents pay 3 per month for board. They pay also £10 for books. The £10 should last six months. And now you have the whole picture of the school. They are taught English, arithmetic and their own mother tongue. History, geography etc., are taught incidentally.

With love,
Brother

5. Letter to Millie Graham Polak

Box 6522,
Thursday (July 10, 1913)[3]

My Dear Millie,

So Henry is on the waters on his way to London.[4] Such is the uncertainty of the life of those who are associated with me. It was very brave of you to have permitted Henry without a murmur to separate from you. I need hardly say that you will as before unreservedly fall back upon me for your wants. You will not leave me to anticipate your wants, will you ?

There is no reply yet from General Smuts. I am expecting one everyday. The strike has dislocated many things.[5]

How are you all getting on ? I am not likely to leave here, if at all, before Monday next.

With love to you all,

Yours,
Brother

(PS.)

The Bazaar was a social success but not a financial success that it might have been.

6. Letter to Millie Graham Polak

July 13, 1913

My Dear Millie,

Herewith a cheque for £12.

I had a wonderful meeting last night. Manilal insists on observing the same penance vow that I am. His fast too therefore starts from today. And yet I know that in spite of all that, there may be no change of heart. But I must continue to trust and believe. I take it that you will bank all the monies that may be received there and send me the deposit slips. Is Solomon keeping the books ?

Of course, you may come down during the fast week too. And if Voysey offers to come during the week, let him come. West will attend to him.

With love,
Brother

7. Letter to Millie Graham Polak

Dundee,
Wednesday (November 12, 1913)[6]

My Dear Millie,

You are brave. So I know you will consider yourself a proud and happy wife in having a husband who has dared to go to gaol for a cause he believes in. The £3 tax cause is the cause of the helpless and the dumb. And I ask you to work away in the shape of begging, advising and doing all you can. Do not wait for their call but call the workers. Seek them out even though they should insult you. Miss S. knows the struggle almost like Henry. Assist her. I have asked her to move forward and backward and assume full control. Draw upon West and

Maganlal for your needs. May you have strength of mind and body to go through the fire.

With love,
Yours,
Bhai

8. Letter to Millie Graham Polak

Ahmedabad,
September 5 (1916)[7]

My Dear Millie,

I have your letter today. Even if Henry comes, you will be there to receive this letter. I had Henry's long letter but I did not wish to interfere with his plans, so I said nothing. I quite share your feeling that if his stay there can only increase the bitterness of his soul, it is better that he should not be so near the fire. All the same it will be a calamity for South Africa, his permanent withdrawal. Both the races will lose a common friend. But at times, it is better to lose one's friends. We sometimes know them only after they are gone.

Yes, you will feel very lonely. I fear very much that you will never have a really settled life. You will, therefore, have to find peace in preparedness to move on when required. I do not share Henry's optimism about the London practice. Anyway I shall be perfectly useless in helping him in that direction. I know not a soul to whom I could appeal for such help. If however, he cannot find his way to settle in London, he will find little difficulty in doing so here. There is ample scope for his energy in India. But I will not anticipate the future. I do not fear the intimate issue. We have a common belief in the goodness of God. Though the path immediately in front of us may be full of darkness, as to the destination to be reached, there never would be any doubt.

Of course, I shall go to Bombay to meet Henry unless his coming synchronizes with the Provincial Conference meeting here. Morgan-Bush affair is a sad thing. Thambi never wrote again to me. I am ready to send the boys if he wants them. We are here a busy nine all engaged in hand-weaving. To me it appears as a great thing. But we shall see. Just now we expect that we shall be self-supporting in a year's time through this work.

With love to you all,

Yours,
Bhai

(PS.)

Manilal does not yet knew his own mind.

9. Letter to Millie Graham Polak

Bhettiah,
May 6 (1917)[8]

Dear Millie,

Your letter and wire were redirected here and come into my hands today. Henceforth, please write at the above address. Simply Bettiah, Champaran will do.

I am sorry to hear the news about Henry's illness. Somehow I do not share your gloomy forebodings. He has marvelous recuperative powers and I think he will quickly recover his original vigour. What I do feel, however, is that both of you should join Ceilia at Ooty. Mama too wrote saying that Ceilia was not keeping well. But I go further to say that even if she were well, she ought not alone to have charge of a child, especially a child so wonderful as Leon. Ooty will do Henry good and may do you also good. If the high altitude does not suit you all, you should go to Bangalore. It has perhaps the finest climate in India. Even Belgaum or Poona will be alright for you. But somehow or other, I prefer Banglore. Change to any such place will be the best tonic for Henry. And he must live on the plainest foods such as we have at the Ashram. Everything simply boiled. As for Waldo, I must differ from your views. It is because Waldo is a trust that you may not play with him. I would not mind your being vaccinated if you chose to be. But to add a weakness—causing operation to an already weak constitution is to do infinite harm to it. It is not obligatory on you to travel or to live in insanitary surroundings. By all means take all reasonable precautions that the science of hygiene may suggest. If the worst fear is realized and Waldo has smallpox, why should you consider yourself guilty ? It is *not* a dangerous disease. And natural smallpox if properly treated does not leave the patient debilitated. But the purest lymph is not as pure as you may imagine. By having him vaccinated, you will expose Waldo to an additional risk to his health. Pock marks, if you are afraid of them, are really nothing. By proper treatment, in course of time they disappear. Did you see Bala and Naransamy ? They had confluent smallpox of the most virulent type. The marks are growing or were growing fainter daily under the treatment of anointing with oil and rubbing thereafter. Pray read my plan for Waldo twice, then pray and then do as the voice within you bids you.

Do please write to me frequently if you cannot write to me daily about Henry's health. It is God's mercy that when every member of the family is down, you are keeping well. I do hope you won't have a nervous breakdown after Henry rises from his sick-bed which he will soon do, I am sure.

My work is steadily progressing. I have come in touch with many planters too and often meet the collector etc. I cannot leave this place for some months to come.

With love to you all,

Yours,
Bhai

(PS.)

Pray remember me to Dr. Sapru.[9]

10. Letter to Millie Graham Polak

Bankipore,
May 11 (1917)[10]

My Dear Millie,

Just a line before leaving for Bettiah. Your telegram of yesterday has frightened me. Immediately on receipt of your wire, I wrote to you a long letter about Henry and Ceilia. I do still hope that (you) have received it. The postal hours in Bettiah are most inconvenient. I have to trust to chance friends to post the letters and it is possible that the one who takes the letter might have missed the post for which my letter to you was intended.

It alarms me to find that fever has not yet left Henry and I have telegraphed to you to wire or write to me at Bettiah. I came in yesterday on the invitation of the Government to see Hon'ble Mr. Maude.[11] I had two hours' interview. I shall write more about this later. The matter is critical. I dare not gone down to you. Please use the wire freely if necessary. I shall expect at least a postcard from you daily.

With love,

Yours,
Bhai

11. Letter to Millie Graham Polak

Bettiah,
May 14 (1917)[12]

Dear Millie,

I have just received your letter. Matheran is not habitable in the month of June. And Bombay is likely to suit Ceilia best then. If you are not living with the Petits, a flat in Colaba will give you a splendid breeze.

It is difficult for me to believe that Henry can be so bad as you have described him. It is indeed a great relief that he is where he receives a brotherly attention and has best possible medical advice. I shall anxiously await a daily bulletin from you. If you do not give me a letter, give me only p.c. please.

Is Waldo alright now ? How do you find the weather there ? Does the doctor say that both Henry and Waldo will be entirely free from the poison ? You know what the doctors generally say. They say that once the poison has entered the system, it does not leave it for years. Of course, I do not believe it and Henry's body being so pure cannot be so shattered as to be liable to a recurrence of the attack. However, the greatest care has to be used during convalescence if complete cure is to be attained.

Is Leon keeping well ?

With love to you both,

Yours,
Bhai

12. Letter to Millie Graham Polak

Bettiah,
May 18 (1917)[13]

Dear Millie,

Your description of Henry still sounds unbelievable. The mind simply refuses to think that he can be so pulled down. I shall still retain my faith in the vitality of his system and believe that he will quickly regain his original strength.

My heart goes out to poor Waldo. It must be terrible for him to be without a companion.

I like Dr. Sapru's advice which does not apply to Henry at all. He has never dreamt impossible dreams, he has always settled down like a respectable man as a conscientious man can feel settled in this unsettled world and he has always been a practical man of affairs and as such won esteem. His life up to the present is unimpeachable evidence of all this. I have found that most people here and elsewhere are highly unpractical, and falsely believing themselves to be matter of—fact men, render themselves incapable of dreaming dreams impossible or otherwise and therefore remain totally dry as dust. Good dreams are to the soul what fresh air is to the body. I am pushing forward. Hundreds of men are being examined everyday. I have sent the papers bringing the position to date to Mr. Kunzru[14] and have asked him to show them to Henry when he wishes to and is allowed to see them.

With love to you all,

Yours,
Bhai

(PS.)

Mr. Andrews sends his love to you both.

13. Letter to Millie Graham Polak

Bettiah,
May 21 (1917)[15]

My Dear Millie,

I see that as your labours are about to finish (thank God) the heat is beginning to tell on you. It is ever thus. Somehow or other Providence is the kindest when it puts us through the sorest trials. Please tell Henry he ought to have sent me the speeches to which he has written his eloquent preface. But if the preface is eloquent it is not written from the depth of his heart. If he had, he would have shown the sham underlying it all without wounding anybody. The preface leaves on one the impression that there was no other side to the picture. And yet it obtrudes itself on one wherever we go. So, I shall charitably assume that Henry thought he might for once at least leave it alone.

With love,

Yours,
Bhai

(PS.)

Mr. Kunzru brings you the news from here.

14. Letter to Millie Graham Polak

May 26 (1917)[16]

My Dear Millie,

This illness of Henry's must have been the greatest trial of his life. He need not allow the illness to upset his belief in a guiding providence. Nala is said to have been bitten by a cobra. The cobra when asked by Nala, told him that he was bitten so as to transform his appearance and so enable him successfully to hide his identity during his banishment.[17] I do believe that our illnesses often comes to us as disciplinary measures.

After a long silence I received a letter from Natesan[18] today in which he says that he has been away in Ooty etc. This may account for his silence. But he is, I know, very careless about answering letters. I am not excusing him. I am describing his limitations.

You will be glad to read the enclosed letter.[19] I do hope that Kothagiri is near enough for Ceilia to meet Miss Faering. She is a most kind-hearted girl. Do write to her if you feel inclined. Miss Esther Faering, Spring Cottage, Kothagiri. Please send the letter to Ahmedabad after you have done with it.

With love,
Yours,
Bhai

15. Letter to Millie Graham Polak

Nadiad,
June 7 (1918)[20]

My Dear Millie,

I was glad to have your letter. I was looking forward to it. Pearson[21] has written a book which is undoubtedly seditious in the sense that he desires separation, not home rule within the Empire. I have not read the book but this is what I am told. The book is prohibited.[22] There is nothing wrong in Pearson's activity if he believes in it. And it must be conceded that there is nothing wrong in the Government trying to crush the rebellious spirit. P. was in China. This gave the Government an easy way of getting hold of P. They have got him and now he is probably on his way to England where I suppose he will be comparatively free to preach separation. From what I hear, he is quite happy and almost expected the result. Yes, the letter to the Viceroy cost many an anxious hour? I could not help writing the letter. The story of its creation is worth telling but I have not the time to reproduce it here. When we meet and have leisure you shall have it if it has not become too stale then. You will see my letter about S.A. You should write to Cachalia. I wonder why Anasuyabehn has not replied. I shall speak to her. She is by no means so lazy or discourteous.

I am going to Bombay on the 10th instant. I must then see about your trunk. Narandas is there now. He was away in Kathiawad. I will see to the proper labelling and have the carriage prepaid. I hope you are all keeping well. So the Kaira struggle has ended. You will see my final letter on it.

I have not had practically a single acknowledgement of my many letters. They have evidently been sunk or miscarried. Please pass this on to him. I have not heard from him otherwise either.

With love to you all,

Yours,
Bhai

(PS.)

Do you know that Manilal is now all alone in Phoenix ? Mr. West and Sam are in Durban doing commercial printing. Of course West is helping Manilal. *I.O.* is now truly independent. I understand Manilal is working day and night. West could not do otherwise than what he has done.

16. Letter to Millie Graham Polak

Nadiad,
July 22 (1918)

Dear Millie,

The enclosed is just to cheer you. I have been corresponding with Dr. Mehta too. Of course, I do not expect Henry will have to do war work.[23] And if he has, you know that you have no cause for anxiety. I am undergoing a revolution in my outlook upon life. As it seems to me some old cobwebs are falling away. But of these when I have more time.[24]

With love,
Yours,
Bhai

(PS.)

Do write to me please. Devdas is in Madras, do you know ? Write to him a line care Natesan. He is teaching Hindi.

17. Letter to Millie Polak[25]

August 31, 1918

As I am writing this, I am watching the glorious rain descending in torrents before me. It will gladden the hearts of millions of men and women. There was a great dread of a most severe famine overtaking Western India. In the twinkling of an eye, all that fear has gone. It has given place to boundless joy; this rain is a veritable deliverance for millions upon millions of cattle. There is probably no place on earth that is so dependent on rain as India. You will now understand what part this rain must have played in giving me health. I have suffered agonies—all due to my own follies. The punishment was adequate to the wrong done by me to the body. Through a faulty experiment, I was suffering from dysentery. Whilst I was getting over it, I ate when I should have refrained and that brought on the inevitable crisis. I am so reduced in body that I have now to build anew but there is no cause for anxiety. I am convalescent and regularly taking some nourishment and am daily increasing the quantity and I hope to be able to walk about in ten days' time. You ask me about nursing. Everything that human love can do has been done for me. It was my privilege and my pain to be on the sickbed— privilege to find so much love rained on me, pained that I should need it all through my weakness and folly. This rich experiencing of love makes an added call on such service as I may be capable of rendering to humanity. But service to humanity is service of self and service of self is self-purification. How shall I purify myself ? It is the question that has been agitating me throughout my sickness; Pray for me.

18. Letter to Mrs. M.G. POLAK

Post Andheri,
April 6, 1924

My Dear Mrs. Polak[26],

I was so delighted to have from you after so many years your handwriting, your language, your thoughts just the same as they were before. Your description of Waldo makes me think that I would not recognize him if I meet him without notice. I hope he will be successful in the examination and find a naval job to suit him. I am so sorry to hear about Mater[27] and Maud[28]. Let me hope that this will find them all in good health. I forgot to ask you about Amy, nor have you given any news about her. You may know that Andrews is still with me at this delightful retreat and that he is looking after me like a mother. Ramdas and Devdas are also here. This place has been turned into a cottage hospital. Radha, Maganlal's daughter, is here recovering from a severe attack of pleurisy. Another inmate is Vallabhbhai Patel's daughter whom you do not know. There is also Professor Kripalani's sister whom too you do not know. The fourth, though not laid up in bed, is Prabhudas, Chhaganlal's son. Radha's mother and sister are also here. So you see we are a fairly big family. Andrews tells me that Henry has grown fairly stout. I wonder if I can recognize him if he comes to me unawares. I am looking forward to his. . . .

I am getting on as well as it is possible. Andrews takes me for a walk in the evening by the seaside.

With love to you all,
Yours,
Mrs. M.G. Polak
33, Mowbray Road
Burnsbury
London, N.W.

19. Letter to Millie Graham Polak

Ahmedabad,
August 3 (1929)[29]

My Dear Millie,

I am writing this as I am watching the glorious rain descending in torrents before me. It will gladden the hearts of millions of men and women. There was a great dread of a most severe famine overtaking Western India. In the twinkling of an eye, all that fear has gone. It has given place to boundless joy. This rain is a veritable deliverance for millions upon millions of cattle. There is probably no place on earth that is so dependent on rain as India. You will now understand what part this rain must have played in giving me health. I have suffered agonies—all due to my own follies. The punishment was adequate to the wrong done by me to the body. Through a faulty experiment I was suffering from dysentery. Whilst I was getting over it, I ate when I should have refrained and that brought on the inevitable crisis. I am so reduced in body and I have now to build up anew but there is no cause of anxiety. I am convalescent and regularly taking some nourishment and daily increasing the quantity and I hope to be able to walk alone in ten days' time. You ask me about nursing. Everything that human love can do, has been done for me. It was my privilege and my pain to be on the sick-bed, privilege to find so much love rained on me, pain that I should need it all through my weakness and folly. This rich experiencing of love makes an added call on such service as I may be capable of rendering to humanity. But service to humanity is service of self and service of self is self-purification. How shall I purify myself ? It is the one question that has been agitating me throughout my sickness. Pray for me.

With love,
Yours,
Bhai

(PS.)

Please pass on this letter to Henry as I shall not be dictating a separate letter to him.

20. Letter to Millie Graham Polak

Monday

My Dear Millie,

I cannot undertake to answer your prose poem. You have at times flights which baffle me. I shall not comment. Let our hearts speak to each other.

Bapu has become the conventional name and that may remain without the signification attached to it. We are and must remain brother and sister, always confiding, always trusting, always loving and helping, but neither entirely leaning on the other. We have kept the fast splendidly. I do not feel it at all. All the boys and Chhaganlal's family are fasting today. Maganlal has been fasting 3 days, Ramdas and Revashankar 2 days. Miss Bush came in today. She will go away on Friday. You should try to come before then if you can.

I hope you received my letter. Suliman and that you were able to get Mr. Laughton to fix the matter up.

With love,
Yours,
Bapu

NOTES

1. Gandhiji's book *Hind Swaraj* had been declared seditious and proscribed in India; *vide* "Johannesburg", 13-3-1910, "Preface to "Indian Home Rule", 20-3-1910 and "Our Publications", 7-5-1910.
2. Pragji Desai and Surendrarai Medh left for India in the second week of March 1912, *vide* "Speech at Farewell Meeting", 9-3-1912.
3. H.S.L. Polak left for London on July 10, 1913 to assist Gokhale in representing South African Indians' case. From the contents it is evident that the letter was written on this day, a Thursday.
4. *Vide* "Letter to G.K. Gokhale", 12-7-1913 and "General Knowledge about Health (XXXII)", 9-8-1913.
5. *ibid.*
6. The addressee's husband H.S.L. Polak, along with Hermann Kallenbach, had courted arrest on November 10, 1913. Gandhiji was sentenced on November 4 and sent to Dundee. He was removed to Volksrust on November 13. This letter was evidently written on November 12, 1913, which was a Wednesday.
7. From the references to the Provincial Political Conference which was held in Ahmedabad in October 1916, and Polak's arrival; Gandhiji received him at Bombay on November 13, 1916; vide also the following item.
8. From the contents.
9. Tej Bahadur Sapru (1875-1949); lawyer and statesman.
10. From the contents.
11. W. Maude, Member of the Executive Council, Bihar and Orissa.
12. From the contents.
13. From the contents.
14. Hriday Nath Kunzru.
15. From the date-line and post-script; vide also the preceding item.

16. From the contents.
17. The story is told in the Mahabharata.
18. G.A. Natesan.
19. This was a letter from Esther Faering; *vide* "Letter to Esther Faering", 26-5- 1917.
20. From the contents; *ibid.*
21. W.W. Pearson.
22. *Vide* "Letter to C. F. Andrews", 23-5-1918.
23. *Vide* also "Fragment of Letter to Ambalal Sarabhai", 17-3-1918.
24. For an extract from this letter *vide* "Letter to Esther Faering", 22-7-1918.
25. Millie Graham Polak, wife of H.S.L. Polak; author of *Mr. Gandhi: The Man* (1930).
26. Millie Graham Polak, wife of H.S.L. Polak.
27. Polak's mother.
28. Polak's sister.
29. From the reference to dysentery caused by Gandhiji's experiment in uncooked food; Gandhiji began to suffer from dysentery in the first week of August 1929 and gave up taking uncooked food from August 15, 1929; *vide*, "Telegram to G.D. Birla", 17-8-1929, "Telegram to G.D. Birla", 19-8-1929 and "Unfired Food", 22-8-1929.

Chapter 3
Sonja Schlesin (1888-1956)

Sonja was born on 6 June, 1888 in Moscow, Russia. Her father was Isidor Schlesin and her mother Helena Dorothy. She was Jewish. Her family migrated to South Africa in June 1892. Sonja matriculated from the University of the Cape of Good Hope in 1903 at the age of 15.

Gandhi enrolled as an attorney in the Supreme Court of the Transvaal in 1903 and opened an office in Johannesburg. He required the services of a clerical assistant. So, Herman Kallenbach introduced Sonja Schlesin to Gandhi. She had exceptional speed and accuracy at shorthand. Gandhi was prepared to pay her up to £ 20 for her clerical work, but Schlesin was perfectly satisfied with the amount of £ 6, which Kallenbach had suggested to Gandhi. Her response to Gandhi's offer of more than £ 6 was, "I am not here to draw a salary from you. I am here because I like to work with you and I like your ideals." Sonja was Gandhi's secretary, who, in course of time took complete charge of Gandhi, his office and his movement in South Africa. Her role in making a success of Gandhi was crucial in the early days. She performed her role beautifully, honestly and Gandhi achieved everything. She become so confident of Gandhi that she drafted letters for him that he merely signed. Robert Payne called Sonja a Russian anarchist.

Schlesin participated in satyayagraha movement in South Africa. For her dedication to the cause the Indian community expressed their appreciation and she was given £10. Appreciating her work Gandhi wrote of Schlesin, "Miss Schlesin—taxed herself to her utmost by labouring day and night." At a dinner to celebrate her contribution to the cause, Schlesin was presented with a gold watch by the President of the Chinese Association.

Gandhi engaged himself in the political struggles of the community and was arrested and detained several times. In Gandhi's absence Schlesin managed the office efficiently. Schlesin wanted to study law, so she was indentured as a clerk on 24 February, 1909.The Articles of Clerkship training was to last three years. But High Court, Pretoria denied her admission as attorney in April 1909. The refusal was based on the premise that "...the articling of women is entirely without precedent in South Africa and never was contemplated by the law..." The Transvaal Indian Women's Association (TIWA) was formed in March 1909 and Schlesin was appointed secretary.

In 1909, Gandhi left for London to influence British politicians. While Gandhi was in London, Schlesin was in charge of his affairs and she was kept informed of developments. To overcome the financial difficulties at The Phoenix Settlement, Schlesin was appointed as one of its trustees.

Schlesin passed an Intermediate Arts Examination at the University of the Cape of Good Hope in January 1911, and started teaching at a government school in Mayfair. When Gopal Krishna Gokhale was in South Africa Schlesin during his stay he was able to observe Schlesin at work and paid this tribute to her: "I have rarely come across such purity, single-minded devotion to work and great determination as I have seen in Miss Schlesin. I was simply astonished how she had sacrificed her all for the Indian cause without expecting any reward whatsoever...."

She actively participated in Satyagraha. When Gandhi led the Great March, which was a strike staged in opposition to a £ 3 poll tax for indentured labourers. The march began in Charleston and lead to the incarceration of 300 *satyagrahis*. While the march took place, Schlesin remained in Charlestown to take care of the remaining women, children and the elderly. Schlesin was also involved in the social aspects of Satyagraha life.

In 1914, Gandhi left for India. Before departure Gandhi along with wife attended farewell dinners where Schlesin was presented with books. Gandhi paid a glowing tribute to Schlesin for her work in the Indian cause. He entrusted her with a pair of sandals, made in prison, to be given to Smuts.

In 1918, Schlesin registered at the University College of Johannesburg. In 1920, she became a teacher at the High School in Krugersdorp, where she remained for the next 23 years, teaching primarily Latin. Between 1921 and 1924, Schlesin passed B.A. and M.A. examination with First Class from the University of Witwatersrand. Her subjects were French, Latin, English, Logic and Philosophy. Between 1929 and 1931, from the same university she took on a Diploma in Afrikaans.

She lived alone in a house called 'The Hermitage' in Sievewright Street from which she could walk to school. In 1937, she acquired a donation of more than a thousand books for the school library. Schlesin put great emphasis on education and hard work. She retired from teaching at the age of 55 in June 1943. In 1953, at the age of 65 she enrolled at the University of Natal to study law. But could not completed due to ill health.

Sonja began life as Gandhi's secretary and ended up as the leader of Indian Community in South Africa and died on 6 January, 1956 in Johannesburg.

1. Letter to Sonja Schlesin[1]

Cape Town,
March 27, 1911

Here is roughly the purport of the conversation between J.C.S. and me:

Smuts: You see, Gandhi, I am giving you everything. I could have done so by regulation but now I am protecting wives and children in the Bill. I do not know why, but I know that everybody suspects me.

I am also recognising domicile. But you are very unreasonable. Your point is absolutely new.

Gandhiji: How can you say so, General Smuts ? Are you not creating a racial bar ?

S.: No, I am not. Can you show it to me ?

G.: Certainly. Will you admit that throughout the four years we have been simply fighting against the racial or colour bar ?

S.: Started and said after some hesitation, 'Yes'.

G.: You know that in the Transvaal Immigration Law there is no colour bar, but you read sub-section 4 and the Asiatic Act, and you have the bar.

S.: You are not stating it fairly.

G.: Then you shall state it in your own words.

S.: In the Transvaal we wanted total exclusion and that is brought about by the combined effect of the two laws.

G.: And now you want the same thing for the Free State. The combined effect of the Free State Law and the new Bill will be (to) shut out the Nizam of Hyderabad, and I assure you that the passive resisters will fight against it.

S.: There you are unreasonable.

G.: I must deny the charge. I am not at all anxious that a single Indian should actually enter the Free State. I am sincerely anxious to help you.

S.: You do not know my difficulties.

G.: I do. And because I do, I suggest that only so much of the Free State Law should be a basis for exemption as will enable a highly educated Indian to enter the Free State. If you send for the Law, I will show you what I mean.

S.: (Sends for the law): But the Free Staters will never consent.

G.: Then why did General Botha write to Lord Crewe that educated immigrants will be able to enter any province ?

S.: You do not know all the dispatches. We have not printed everything, you know. Lord Crewe knows that we never wanted to give the rights as to the Free State.

G.: But you repeated the same thing at the second reading.

S.: Yes. I was simply sounding the Free Staters, and I noticed that they were very much opposed.

G.: If they are, it is your duty to persuade them, and if they cannot be, you may simply amend the Transvaal Legislation.

S.: But I am bound to the Imperial Government to pass this Bill.

(Reads the Law and asks G. to go over to his side. G. points out the section from which the exemption is to be granted.) Yes, I now see what you mean.

G.: Yes, the educated Asiatics will be still prohibited from owning fixed property and from trading. I am not raising that issue at all. We have still to fight you on the question of Law 3 of 1885. But this has nothing to do with passive resistance. I for one do not wish to offer passive resistance for material gains, but the racial bar we can never accept.

S.: But you have no idea of my difficulties.

G.: I know that you are quite able to overcome greater difficulties.

S.: All right, I shall now talk to the Free State members. You should leave your address with Lane. I hope you will keep the Cape and the Natal Indians silent.

G.: They will certainly not remain silent. I have just got a wire from Natal. It is absolutely necessary to protect existing rights. The question of domicile is ticklish and section 25 requires amending. Certificates should be issued for the asking.

S.: But discretion is always reserved.

G.: Not in the existing statutes. But of this I shall talk later if you will let me.

S.: What are you doing in Jo'burg etc. ?

G.: Looking after the families of passive resisters etc.

S.: It has hurt me more than you to imprison these people. It has been the unpleasantness episode of my life to imprison men who suffer for their conscience. I should do the same thing for conscience' sake.

G.: And yet you are persecuting Mrs. Sodha.

* * *

Please let Sorabjee and those on the Farm read the interview. I have written it more for their sakes, and then you may send it to Mr. Polak.

The notes of the interview are not for publication. But they are not to be destroyed. I hope you received Mr. Hosken's permission to publish the correspondence.[2] Do please get Sorabjee to write daily to the people at the Farm.

Yours sincerely,
M.K. Gandhi

2. Letter to Sonja Schlesin[3]

Ahmedabad,
January 16, 1916

My Dear Daughter,

You have at last favoured me with a letter. Even six letters in a year you do not call a brilliant performance. Do you ? However, I must be content with what you may give me.

You might at least have given me the credit for uttering no such nonsense as Mrs. Besant's correspondent attributed to me. Natarajan apologised for reproducing the calumny. What I did say bore a totally different construction. I made use of a Gujarati proverb in defence of my proposition that man continually did an injustice to woman by using her for his lusts.

I have taken such vow as you attribute to me about anger. And if I had, I agree with you that it would lose all point by being disclosed.

I quite agree with you that Polak has done more during the past 18 months than what he did even in India. I would certainly feel delighted if Thambi[4] came. But it is not a nice thing to pay his debts out of the passive resistance funds.

Jeki[5] is with her father quite settled down to the humdrum life of the home.

3. Letter to Sonja Schlesin

Nadiad,
June 23, 1918

Dear Miss Schelsin[6],

The long expected letter has come. We have all been looking forward to a letter from you. Of course, Phoenix is not going to be sold. You can have 5 acres of ground in the centre. I like your dream specially as it includes a visit to India.

It delights me to find you getting tired of the typewriter....[7] I have not asked Ramdas to become a tailor; not that there is no poetry in tailoring. Ramdas may become a living *Sartor Resartus*. But he is a conscientious boy. He wants to gain all kinds of experiences. If he becomes a poet he will be one not of words and in words, but of actions and in actions. Ramdas is a visionary. And I like visionaries. I hope you will guide him, and befriend him. I wish you would live with Manilal for a while. You could carry on your studies there. How are the Vogls[8], the Phillipses[9] and the Dokes[10] ? Do you ever meet them ? Where is MacIntyre[11] ? What do you think of the community ? Do you meet Thumbi[12] ? What has come over him ? These are questions which I should expect discussed in your letters. But something is better than nothing.

My life has become very complex. You must have read at least my important public letters. Now I am entering upon a big recruiting campaign. My work has involved constant railway travelling. I am longing for solitude and rest. They may never be my lot. Mrs. Gandhi has developed remarkably. She has beautifully resigned herself to things she used to fight. But I must (not) describe things. You must see them for yourself.

With love

Yours,
M.K. Gandhi

4. Letter to Sonja Schlesin[13]

February 23, 1919

It was so good of you to give me credit if only for once for being business-like. My own opinion of myself is that I am the most business-like man upon the earth and, so long as no one can disillusion me, I shall continue to derive pleasure from the belief and to have a stray certificate from you only adds to the pleasure. I present you another illustration of my business-likeness. I know I would wound your vanity, self-esteem, glorious womanliness, whatever you like to call it, by making friend my carrier instead of a bank, for this very simple purpose of lending you money. Had I taken your impractical advice, it would have taken me much longer to send you the money because you must know that I am living in India where we do things in a fairly leisurely manner befitting the climate and the surroundings. Here bankers are not the servants of their clients but their masters except when the clients happen to belong to the ruling race and probably it would have cost you £ 15 to send £ 50. You with your poetic instinct set no value on money, whereas I, a simple prosaic business-like man, realize that it requires £ 150 to finish the education of someone. Therefore, if I spend away £15, I waste one-tenth of that sum if I can avoid having to spend it. Q.E.D.

You shall certainly treat what you have received as a loan. I believe I have already told Mr. Rustomji[14] as much but I cannot swear as I cannot keep copies of my correspondence as a rule and I shall accept repayment whenever you choose to send it, with compound interest if you will, provided that you do not borrow to pay me. You will infer from what has preceded that my health is better. I am still bed-ridden. My head is supposed to be weak and I may not undertake any great exertion. But the feel is all right and I am cheerful. Devibehn[15] writes to me regularly and tells me that you rarely (do so). That is not how people treat their goddesses, or had women the privilege of acting different ?

Yes, Harilal has been sorely stricken. Chanchi was far superior to me. I did not specially write to you as I felt my cable to Ramdas in reply to his was enough for all. At the time, moreover, I was too ill to think of writing to anybody. All Harilal's children are here and are playing about me while I am dictating this letter.

Passive resistance is on the topics regarding certain legislation that the Government of India are passing through the Council. The war council meets tomorrow at the Ashram. You may depend upon it that it won't be a bad copy of similar councils in which you were both an actor (or actress ?) and a fairly intelligent spectatress. You won't therefore need from me a description of the council meeting. I am surprised at your remark about Ashrams here prohibiting the entry of women. It betrays your lack of interest in the Ashram. We have so many women here at the Ashram. We are educating them all, including three girls.

The latter are no doubt our own girls. But that is not our limitation. It is due to the disinclination of the people to send their girls under the conditions that we impose. It will delight your heart to see the transformation that the women undergo here after a few days' stay. The *purdah* and all other unnatural restraints fall away as if by magic. I know you will hug most them when you come here. Only you will have to revive your knowledge of Gujarati. Imam Saheb is today here, and naturally also his daughter and his wife.

M.K. Gandhi

5. Letter to Sonja Schlesin

June 2, 1919

Dear Miss Schlesin,

Ramdas advises me that you have passed your teacher's examination with some distinction. You do not want me to congratulate you, I know. I am simply anxious that you should get through your final examination, because I expect you one of these days to take your place in India. The summer months are trying enough, but the winter months give you sufficient compensation. I hope you had all you wanted without any inconvenience. You will not hesitate to come to me for more, if necessary.

Satyagraha is going on merrily. Civil disobedience is expected to commence very soon. How I often wish you were here for more reasons than one ! But I must plough the lonely furrow. It often makes me sad when I think of all my helpers of South Africa. I have no Doke here. I have no Kallenbach. Don't know where he is at the present moment. Polak in England. No counterpart of Kachalia or Sorabji. Impossible to get the second edition of Rustomji. Strange as it may appear, I feel lonelier here than in South Africa. This does not mean that I am without co-workers. But between the majority of them and me, there is not that perfect correspondence which used to exist in South Africa. I do not enjoy the same sense of security which you all gave me there. I do not know the people here; nor they, me. This is all gloomy, if I were to brood over it. But I do not. I have not the time for it. I have a few moments of leisure just now. Ramdas' letter reminds me of your existence in South Africa, and I am giving myself the momentary pleasure of sharing my innermost thoughts with you. But now no more.

6. Letter to Sonja Schlesin

Sabarmati,
August 15, 1924

My Dear Miss Schlesin,

Though late in the day, your letter was most welcome. If you wanted to make it a model of neatness, you have failed badly. The same slovenliness, the same smudging. I can almost see your inky fingers in your letter. Here is the certificate[16] you want. You will be entitled to accuse me of untruthfulness in that I have not certified to your slovenliness. Let me hope the new 'master' will fare better. I must refuse to plead guilty to all the charges you have noted against me. Why should I care about giving you a 'business certificate' ? But how are the mighty fallen ! Regarding the £ 24, I thought the draft of £150 included the amount. However, I am writing to Parsee Rustomji to write off the whole of the balance, whatever it might be, of the £150. My health is fair. Now that you have commenced to write, will you continue ?

The rest I must leave to[17] Ramdas to deal with.

Yours,
M.K. Gandhi

Enclosure:
Satyagrahashram

Sabarmati,
August 15, 1924[18]

Miss Sonja Schlesin served me as confidential secretary in South Africa for nearly seven years and during a most important part of my public life. She was entrusted with heavy responsibilities including account-keeping, involving transactions extending to four figures at a time. She came in touch with hundreds of people belonging to different races and nationalities. During my last incarceration in South Africa, she was in sole charge of my affairs. I never once had reason to doubt her integrity or ability. Indeed, she did not work for the sake of pay but for the sake of the work itself which she loved. Her services were available to me at all times of the day. Her knowledge of shorthand and literary talents were of great assistance to me. I could not wish for a better secretary. I should like to hear that she was entrusted with a post requiring close attention, strictest honesty and ability.

7. Letter to Sonja Schlesin

February 2, 1930

Dear Miss Schlesin,

I have your letter. I do wish you will come in time to correct the many inaccuracies you have discovered in the volumes. It is highly likely that when your long leave is on I may be in one of the king's hotels. Even so, you will see my spirit incarnate in the Ashram. It certainly brings into prominence all my shortcomings and some of my good points.

Manilal, Sushila and Sita are here. Ramdas has also a baby[19]. I think I told you of the event. He is in Bardoli. Manilal is anxious to be with me during these times. He is waiting for a word from Sorabji.

Yours,
M.K. Gandhi

8. Letter to Sonja Schlesin

Ahmedabad,
August 18, 1931

Dear Miss Schlesin,

Well, I can't go to S. Africa since I am not even going to London.

Believe me there is nothing spectacular in the loin-cloth. It is a vital necessity. Was there anything spectacular in the change made in S. Africa ? Is the dress, i.e. the loin-cloth of the coolie in Natal spectacular ? And how if I do not feel anything better than he ? Do you know that millions in India do not wear anything more than a loin-cloth ? But I forget you are a superior woman. You cannot judge people by the ordinary standard.

My book is true, because it is a faithful reproduction of my recollections. It is open to all those who were associated with me to correct mistakes. And since it is not an advertising medium, what does it matter if some dear friends escaped my memory at the time ? But send me a list of all inaccuracies and omissions. And endeavour will be made to make the necessary corrections and additions when the second edition is called for.

My right hand is out of use. Hence the effort with the left hand.

Yours etc.

9. Letter to Sonja Schlesin

Sevagram,
January 20, 1945

Dear Miss Schlesin[20],

I do not think there is any chance of my coming to S(outh) Africa or going to America. But whether I do or not, of course I expect you one day to drop in here and pass the rest of your days in India. Of course it may be that the climate here does not suit you as it did neither Kallenbach nor Hannah[21].

I quite agree with you about Manilal and his wife. Sita is working hard for her examination.

Yours,
M.K. Gandhi

Miss S. Schlesin
P. O. Box 2234
Johanesburg, South Africa

10. Letter to Sonja Schlesin

May 13, 1945

Dear Miss Schlesin,

Your letter. I value it for its contents.

You did well to send me the ticket. There is no Khalifa family in Kathiawar requiring relief as far as I know.

Matriculation here is not simpler than yours. But for Sita it would be somewhat easier here. She is getting on well and gaining the experience she would never have got there. She wants to fit herself for service. There is no restraint upon her freedom. Manilal will shape himself at will. Of course he has come for a year only and that to serve me. There is not much for him to choose from.

I agree about Thambi Naidoo[22]. Anything can be named after him here. It will mean nothing. Something worthy should be done there. You must shape things there. Thambi must have many admirers besides you and me. I am glad about Mrs. Naidoo. What is she doing ? What about his children ? Could you send me a photo of the family with Thambi in it ?

So you see, San Fransisco was managed without you and me.1 But you are dropping in here one of these days. Yes, Kallenbach's niece did give me a long letter after K's death. A truly good man has left us.

I hope to write the story of 125 years. Hold yourself in patience till I write.

Love,
M.K. Gandhi

(PS.)
I am at a hill station. My address must be Sevagram, Wardha.

11. Letter to Sonja Schlesin

Poona,
March 11, 1946

Dear Miss Schlesin[23],

You never write for the sake of writing. But the letter before me is the first such.

A highly industrial system under capitalism and full employment are incompatible.

Your proposition about Manilal needs revision. But all such things when we meet, if we do.

The rest from the papers and Manilal.

Love,
M.K. Gandhi

NOTES

1. The addressee's name is not available, as the first two pages of the letter are missing; but from the instructions given in the last four paragraphs, it appears to have been written to Miss Sonja Schlesin, who looked after Gandhiji's Johannesburg office.
2. *Vide* appendix, "General Smuts Telegram to Hosken", 24-3-1911.
3. A Jewish girl, steno-typist and Private Secretary to Gandhiji for many years; made herself useful to *Indian Opinion*; was ardently interested in the Indian cause.
4. Naidoo, a leading passive resister during the South African struggle.
5. Jayakunvar, daughter of Dr. Pranjivan Mehta.
6. Sonja Schlesin joined Gandhiji as a steno-typist and later played an important role in the satyagraha struggle in South Africa ; *vide* "Johannesburg Letter", Before 10-1-1908.
7. Some words are missing here in the source.
8. Mrs. Vogl conducted classes for Indian women and organized Indian Bazaars in Johannesburg. She, as also her husband, a draper, took keen interest in the cause of Indians in South Africa.
9. Charles Phillips, congregational minister in the Transvaal.
10. Mrs. J.J. Doke and Olive Doke.
11. Thambi Naidoo, a passive resister.

12. *Vide* "Appeal for Enlistment", 22-6-1918.
13. A Jewish girl, steno-typist and Gandhiji's private secretary for many years in South Africa; made herself useful to *Indian Opinion*; was ardently interested in the Indian cause.
14. Parsi Rustomjee, Indian merchant of Natal; took prominent part in Gandhiji's satyagraha campaign in South Africa.
15. Ada West, sister of Gandhiji's friend and co-worker, A.H. West.
16. *Vide* the enclosure.
17. The source has "ideal with".
18. The source has "1914", a slip of the pen.
19. Sumitra Gandhi.
20. A Jewish woman; she worked as Gandhiji's steno-typist and private secretary in South Africa.
21. Niece of H. Kallenbach.
22. A Tamil cartage contractor from Mauritius whom Gandhiji described as "lion-like". He was one of the most eminent *satyagrahis* of the Transvaal.
23. Gandhiji's secretary in South Africa.

Chapter 4

Sarala Devi Chaudhurani (1872-1945)

Sarala Devi Chaudhurani was born to Janakinath Ghosal and Swarnakumari Devi in the old Tagore house at Jorasanko in Kolkata on 9 September, 1872 in a well known and well-to-do Bengali intellectual family. Her father was one of the earliest secretaries of the Bengal Congress and mother (Swarnakumari Devi was the daughter of Debendranath Tagore and elder sister of legendary poet Rabindranath Tagore) was the first successful noted woman novelist of Bengali literature. She spent there some of the most impressionable years of her childhood, when her father was in England. Her natural talents for music, literature and arts, as well as her passionate patriotism were nurtured by her relatives.

Sarala Devi was first taught by a private tutor at home. Later she was admitted into the Bethune School, and after passing her Entrance examination in 1886, continued her studies in the Bethune College. She took her B.A. degree with Honours in English in 1890 from Calcutta University and received the Padmavati Gold Medal. She later studied French and Persian and prepared herself for the M.A. examination in Sanskrit. She was also one of the few women graduates of her time, and the first woman political leader from Bengal in the Indian independence movement.

In 1905, she was married to Pandit Rambhuj Dutt Chaudhary (1866-1923), a Punjabi Brahmin, lawyer by profession, living at Lahore. He was an ardent patriot and editor of an Urdu paper called *Hindusthan* and member of Arya Samaj and Congress. Their son Dipak Dutt married Radha, granddaughter of Mahatma Gandhi.

She believed in physical culture and instituted the 'Virashtami Utsava' with exhibition of physical feats. During the 1903 Congress, she proposed a display of Indian games. She tried to popularise 'Udayadiya Utsava' accompanied by physical feats.

In 1904 she opened a Swadeshi shop called Lakshmir Bhandar. She collected and sent Swadeshi goods to the Bombay Congress and was awarded a gold medal for her endeavours.

A spirited mind cannot be that easily quelled. Sarala Debi's nationalistic commitment led her to set up an *akhara* (gymnasium) for training young men in the martial arts.

She had been born in the lap of luxury and had every opportunity in imbibe national and Western culture. She was never in favour of Western education and was easily converted to Gandhiji's ideals. In her mature years she gave up her militant patriotism and turned to nonviolence, non-cooperation and *Khadi* movement. She came into close contact with the great personalities of the social and political world of the day—Lala Lajpat Rai, Tilak, Gokhale and Mahatma Gandhi.

Sarala Devi was a born teacher. Even at early stage she taught music to many young girls. She shortly took the bold step of going to Mysore as a teacher in the Maharani School. She also acted as the Maharani's secretary for some time.

She worked for women's education in the villages around Lahore and had larger plans for the education of *purdah* women. This led to the foundation of the Bharat-Stri-Mahamandal in Allahabad in 1910, with branches in many Indian cities and villages. She was the founder of the first women's organization. The primary goals of the organisation was to promote female education, which at that time was not well developed. The organisation opened several offices in Lahore, Allahabad, Delhi, Karachi, Amritsar, Hyderabad, Kanpur, Bankura,

Hazaribagh, Midnapur and Calcutta to improve the situation of women all over India. In 1930 she opened the Bharat-Stri-Shiksha-Sadan, a school for girls, in Calcutta. Sarala Devi's whole life was one of hard work.

Due to the displeasure of the British Government, Rambhaj was a patriotic work displeased British Government had to suffer harassment and was later arrested. After the arrest Sarala Devi took over the editorship and even published English versions of the paper. Her excellent management drew the praise of Englishmen like Ramsay Macdonald.

She edited the journal called *Bharati* with the help of her elder sister, Hiranmoyee Devi, for a short while.

After death of her husband in 1923, she returned to Calcutta. In 1935, she accepted Howrah's Acharya Bijoy Krishna Deb Sharma as her guru and spent the last ten years of her life in reading spiritual texts, reflecting and writing, much of it autobiographical. She died in 1945.

The memoirs of Sarala Devi early life were serialized in the weekly *Desh* magazine. Later, they were put together as Jibaner Jhara Pata (Life's Fallen Leaves).

1. Letter to Sarala Devi Chowdhurani

April 29, 1920

As I write this I hear Dipak[1] singing to Balkrishna's sweet sitar. Balkrishna is a great gift of the gods to me. He (is) innocent as a flower. He looks after me like a mother. Did you read my message on the Khilafat to the A.P. [2] ? Lest you may not have got a copy of *Y.I.*, I am sending you a copy. Do please read the article on *khaddar*. Here is yesterday's *bhajan* [3]:

मोरी लागी लगन गुरुचरननकी
चरन बिना मुझे कछु नहीं भावे;
झूठ माया सब सपननकी। मोरी
भवसागर सब सूख गया है;
फिकर नहीं मुझे तरननकी। मोरी
मीरां कहे गिरधार नागर;
उलट भई मोरे नयननकी। मोरी[4]

2. Letter to Sarala Devi Chowdhurani

Sinhgadh,
April 30, 1920

I posted a pencil letter[5] just before leaving Poona for Sinhgadh. The doctor (told me that I) was too pulled down to attempt walking up. I in my infatuity thought I could do it. So Mahadev, Dipak and I began climbing-up. But you will be sorry to learn that I could not move up even half a furlong when I felt an unbearable strain on the left thigh and I had to give up the attempt. I felt humiliated and deeply cut up to find myself so much reduced in strength. But I must be cheerful even under reverses. I shall try to be.

I have just got up with two dreams, one about you and other about the Khilafat. To my great joy, you returned within two days. I asked 'How so quickly ?' You replied, "Oh it was Panditji's[6] trick to have me by him. Jagdish's[7] marriage is as far off as ever. I have therefore returned." I discovered that it was a dream. I fell off again to sleep in disgust to find myself there before a huge Mohammedan audience. One speaker who was speaking on the use of Hindustani as the common medium included the dialect spoken by the Bagdadis as Hindustani offshoot and therefore worthy of study. The others in the audience protested against this travelling outside India. Abdul Bari Saheb who was with me sided with the man. But he was speechless under the angry protest of the audience. Bari Saheb did not like this treatment of the man. I was explaining the pros and cons to them. The conversation drifted into the ways and means. I emphasized the necessity for adhering to truth at all costs when there was confusion and I got up. I commenced this (letter) immediately on getting up.

Dipak climbed up with Mahadev without any chair. He is none the worse for it. He had milk on starting and cake on reaching. He is now sleeping heavily. Prabhudas is looking much better and more active. Balkrishana had come half way to receive us. Revashankerbhai is coming tomorrow. The ice doctor too has just now turned up bringing two goats for me. I understand that Tilak Maharaj is coming this evening. His party is already in his bungalow. Here are goats coming in with their agreeable music. If the marriage is over or postponed I expect you to join the party and enliven it with your music and your laughter.

I can go on writing. But I must stop not from fear of wearying you but for the sake of taking up other work.

I am just reminded of L. Girdharilal's postcard asking for your bracelet which you had subscribed to the Bagh fund[8]. I think it was sent to you yesterday. In any case I put you in mind of it. I thought you had given the bracelet there and then.

You will not worry about my leg. The magnificent climate of this place should see me through. About Dipak you will not worry. We shall all look after him. Shankarlal[9] took him out for a drive round Colaba. He asked me whether he could take him to the cinema. I said I would not take the responsibility. I would send him some other time if you wished me to. I suggested instead a drive to Colaba or the Victoria Gardens. Hence the drive. Both Mahadev and Dipak dined with Shankarlal. Was I right about Dipak ?

With love,

Yours,
Law-Giver

3. Letter to Sarala Devi Chowdhurani

May 1, 1920

It is now nearly 5 p.m. I have hardly left my bed. I had a most torturing headache last night and I remained in a comatose condition up to 11 p.m. I slept fairly well after. I am free from the headache but I cannot walk even a furlong. I ask you however not to worry about me. I thought you should know my condition, if only to keep you to the fortnight's limit if Jagdish's marriage is then over[10] or if it is postponed. If you would persuade Panditji, too, to come so much the better. He must see and live the Ashram life. Tilak Maharaj paid us a visit in the morning. He came in with his son and son-in-law. The conversation was purely formal. Dipak is getting on. He seems to like the place. His tastes are clean. He is easily led. I shall put in[11] with this what I succeed in getting from him.

Revashankerbhai came in this morning. He brought some luscious mangoes. I fretted to find that you were not here to share them. This morning I got (up) at our usual time but turned in again. I did not watch the sunrise. Had you been here I know you would have dragged me to watch His Majesty coming in. Padshah has been writing in the *East and West*. Perhaps the cutting came in whilst we were yet together. I have dictated an article based on it. It is rather good. You shall certify.

And now for a boon. I know you have granted many. The appetite has grown with the receiving. You said you were shy over working at the Ashram. Will you not get rid of your shyness by commencing household work there ? This I do not mind having for my sake. It is not a matter of changing our viewpoint. It is merely a matter of getting rid of one's disinclination. Great and good though you are, you are not a complete woman without achieving the ability to do household work. You have preached it to others. Your preaching will be more effective when people know that even at your time of life and in your station you do not mind doing it.

With love,

Yours,
Law-Giver

4. Letter to Sarala Devi Chowdhurani

May 1, 1920

मुक्तिमिच्छसि चेत्तात विषयान् विषवत्त्यज।
क्षमार्जवदयातोषसत्यं पीयूषवद्भज।।२।।
यदि देहं पृथक्वकृत्य चिति विश्राम्य तिष्ठसि।
अधुनैव खी शान्तो बन्धमुक्तो भविष्यसि।।४।।
मुक्ताभिमानी मुक्तो हि बद्धो बद्धाभिमान्यपि।
किवंदन्तीह सत्येयं या मतिः सा गतिर्भवेत्।।१।।1[12]

I have culled the most powerful verses from the twenty I read yesterday. I remembered you once said the *Bhagavad Gita* did not appeal to you so much as some other things from other poets. These verses, too, may therefore fall flat on you. But I could not help sharing with you what seemed at the moment ennobling to me. Moreover they are my solace in my enforced idleness[13]. For I have not been able to leave my bed.

5. Letter to Sarala Devi Chowdhurani

May 2, 1920

Yesterday I gave you selections from the first chapter of the *Ashtavakra Gita*[14]. In it Janaka learnt that the remedy for his deliverance lay with himself, and that was to be free from the snare of the senses. In the second chapter he expresses his joy at the revelation. Here are some of the verses:

अहो निरंजनः शान्तो बोधोऽहं प्रकृतेः परः।
एतावन्तमहं कालं मोहेनैव विडंबितः।।१।।
तन्तुमात्रो भवदेव पटो यद्वद्विचारितः।
आत्मतन्मात्रमेवेदं तद्वद्विष्वं विचारितम्।।५।।
आत्माज्ञानाज्ज्गाद्भाति आत्मज्ञानात्र भासते।
रज्ज्वज्ञानादहिर्भाति तज्ज्ञानाद्भासते न हि।।७।।
मत्तो कुम्भो जले वीचिः कनके कटक यथा।।१०।।
अहो जनसमहेऽपि न द्वैंत पश्यतो मम।
अरण्यमिव संवृत्त क्वषतिं करवाण्यह्म।।२१।।

I have selected five out of twenty-five. May I again charge you to copy them out and send them to Devdas ? I should love to finish for you an abridged edition of this beautiful work of art.

I am no better today. I must still confine myself to bed. You still continue to haunt me even in my sleep. No wonder Panditji[15] calls you the greatest *shakti*[16] of India. You may have cast that spell over him. You are performing the trick over me now. But even two swallows cannot make a summer. If you are the greatest *shakti*, you will enslave India by becoming her slave in thought, word and deed. I cannot get Dipak to write both to you and Panditji. You must therefore be satisfied with one letter to Panditji alone. He says, "Why should I write daily to Mataji, if she will not write ?" I hung on this the lesson of good for evil. I told him too that probably you had written but the post had not yet been delivered. I was certain of a letter from you yesterday. But none came. Today too there is a blank. I wonder however. I know you have not failed me. It is the wretched post. I enclose herewith two cuttings from *The Times of India* on Indian music. They may interest you. Or get rid of your inertia and you can give your music to India. It is not enough that you sing for her. You can make her sing even as you do. But that requires application and study, a determination to give your musical talent to India. If you are taking the trouble of copying the verses for Devdas I take it you will copy the *bhajan* too for the boy.

We had a visit from Tilak Maharaj yesterday also. He frankly said he had not my forbearance and he believed in giving tit for tat. This was in answer to my gentle remonstrance over his trenchant criticism of Mrs. Besant. Probably you have not read it. I read it only here. He has even defended Mr. Khaparde's description of her as aunt Putna[17]. He was refreshingly frank in his remark. Miss Faering has not yet arrived. I have invited her to come to Sinhgadh if she need not be in Bombay for her passage. The last hope of hearing from you today is gone. For the post-boy has arrived bringing some newspapers only. Devdas writes saying Panditji— pardon me, I mean Malaviyaji—again thinks I should go to England. I am afraid he is too late now, and perhaps it is as well. Without perfect organization here our going would be worse than useless.

6. Letter to Sarala Devi Chowdhurani

May 3, 1920

My Dear Sarala,

Finding Janaka exulting in the discovery that he was the changeless Brahma, Ashtavakra challenges his position in the 3rd chapter and says:

> अविनाशिनमात्मानमेकं विजाय तत्वतः ।
> तवात्मज्ञस्य धीरस्य कथमर्थार्जने रतिः ।।1।।
> आत्माज्ञानादतो प्रीतिः विषयभ्रमगोचरे ।
> शुक्तेरज्ञानतो लोभो यथा रजतविभ्रमें ।।2।।
> विश्वं स्फुरति यत्रेदं तरड़गा इव सागरे ।
> सोऽहमस्मीति विज्ञाय किं दीन इन धावसि ।।3।।

श्रुत्वापि शुद्धचैतन्यमात्मानमतिसुन्दरम् ।
उपस्थेऽत्यन्तंससक्तो मालिन्यमधिगच्छति । ।4 । ।
सर्वभूतेषु चात्मानं सर्वभूतानि चात्माने ।
मुनेजनित आष्चर्यम् ममत्वभनुवर्तते । ।5 । ।
अस्थितः परमौद्धंत मोक्षार्थेऽपि व्यवस्थितः ।
आष्चर्य कामवषगो विकलः केलिषिक्षया । ।6 । ।
उद्भूतं ज्ञानदुर्मित्रीभवधार्यातिदुर्बलः ।
आष्चर्य काममाकांक्षेत्कालमन्तमवुश्रितः । ।7 । ।
इहामुत्र विरवतस्य नित्यानित्यविवेकिनः ।
आश्चर्यं मोक्षकामस्य मोक्षादेव विभिषिका । ।8 । ।
धीरस्तु भोज्यमानोऽपि पीड्यमानोपि सर्वदा ।
आत्मांन केवलं पश्यन् न तुष्यति न कुप्यति । ।9 । ।
चेष्टमानं शरीरं स्वं पष्यत्यन्यषरीरवत् ।
संस्तवे चापि निन्दांया कंथक्षुष्चेन्महाषयः । ।10 । ।
मायामात्रमिदं विष्वं पश्यन् विगतकौतुकः ।
अपि सन्निहिते मृत्यौ कथम् त्रस्यति धीरधीः । ।11 । ।
निस्पृहं मानसं यस्य नैराष्येऽपि महात्मनः ।
तस्यात्मज्ञानतृप्तस्य तुलना केन जायते । ।12 । ।
स्वभावादेव जानानो दृष्यमेतत्र किंचन । .
इदं ग्राह्ममिदं त्याज्यं स कि पष्यति धीरधीः । ।13 । ।
अन्तस्त्यक्तकषायस्य निर्द्वन्द्वस्य निराषिषः ।
यदृच्छयागतो भोगो न दुःखाय न तुष्टये । ।14 । ।[18]

The challenged Janaka, retaining the same exultant mood, replies in the fourth chapter:

हन्तात्मज्ञानस्य धीरस्य खेलतो भोगलीलया ।
न ही संसारवाहिकैर्मूढैः सह समानता । ।1 । ।
यत्पदं प्रेप्सवो दीनाः शक्राद्याः सर्वदेवताः ।
अहो तत्र स्थितो योगी न हर्षमुदगच्छति । ।2 । ।
तज्ज्ञस्य पुण्यपापाभ्यां स्पर्षो ह्यान्तर्न जायते ।
नह्याकाषस्य धूमेन ’दृष्यमानाऽपि संगतिः । ।3 । ।

आत्मैमैनेदं जगत्सर्वं ज्ञातं येन महात्मना।
यदृच्छया वर्तमानं तं निषेद्धुंक्षमेतकः।।4।।
आब्रह्मस्तम्बपर्यन्ते भूतग्रामे चतुर्विधे
विसायैव हि सामर्थ्यमिच्छानिच्छविवर्जने।।5।।
आत्मानमद्वयं कष्चिज्जानाति जगदीष्वरम्
यद्वेत्तितत्स कुरुते न भयं तस्य कुत्रचित।।6।।[19]

You will note that the verses in the fourth chapter are somewhat dangerous. It is strong food for a delicate stomach. All the chapters are not of equal length. The third for instance has 14 verses and the fourth only six.

7. Letter to Sarala Devi Chowdhurani

Bezwada,
August 23, 1920

Either the night or the day has been passed each day in the train. The nights have been always disturbed by crowds. Thank God we have nearly finished this exhausting tour. Considering everything I have kept remarkably fit and strong. Your letters have your usual self. Some of them decidedly despondent and sceptical and suspicious. You still do not understand Mathuradas[20]. He and the others who surround me are superior to us, if you will allow me to include you. They are certainly superior to me. And it is as should be. It is my claim that I have selected as my companions my superiors in character, superiors, that is to say, in their possibility. My progress can only be little. Theirs is still illimitable. They are jealous of their ideal which is my character. I and (if you are mine in the purest sense of the term) you must give everything to retain or deserve their love and affection. There can be no yielding only on principle. For that we must forsake all and everything. But I would surrender all the world to deserve love so pure and unselfish. Their love uplifts me and keeps me on the square. They are my sheet-anchor as I am theirs. You should be proud of their jealousy and watchfulness. They want to run no risks and they are right. You and I are in duty bound to satisfy every lawful requirement. And we shall have well met.

Yes, if you remain at your post in Lahore it would be quite all right. You can gain little by coming to Calcutta during the week of turmoil and stress. The pilgrimage to your mother may take place in quieter time and after you have perfected your spinning-wheel and Hindi and put our Lahore work on a sound footing. You see I say Lahore in preference to the Punjab. I want you to lay the surest foundation and therefore I want intensity rather than extent. You ask for a reward of your great surrender. Well, it is its own reward.

With deep love,

Yours,
L.G.[21]

8. Letter to Sarala Devi Chaudhurani

On the Way to Manmad for Bombay,
August 24, 1920

My Dearest S.,

Your letters have caused me distress. You do not like my sermons. And yet so long as you remain a school girl, what should I do except giving you sermons ? If my love is true it must express itself in sermons so long as you do not realize the ideal accepted by you as worthy. I do not at all like your doubting the necessity of the life adopted by you or the life you are trying to adopt. What can be the reward of always speaking and doing Truth even at the peril of one's life ? What can be the reward of dying for one's country ? What is the reward of your having given years to acquiring perfection in piano-playing ? You give all for the cause you represent because you cannot do otherwise. Your satisfaction must depend upon complete surrender. A surrender that gives not satisfaction is compulsory surrender, unworthy of a self-respecting person. And if your association with me does not teach you this simple truth, I must be unworthy of your love. For, if my life has not taught you this much, I am a worthless being. There is no worth in me except the capacity for unlimited self-surrender and truthfulness. All have noticed these two qualities in me and there must be something wrong in me if you who have penetrated my life so deeply have failed to notice them. And what can I give you to share except my richest possessions ? And so, you must not resent my giving you sermons but receive them in the same loving manner in which they are delivered. If I am your Law-giver and if I do not always lay down the law, surely I must at least reason with you on things of eternity or supreme importance for the country for which we live and which we love so well.

But this does not mean that you must not write nasty things if you think them. My plea is that you must cease to think nasty thoughts.

With love,

Yours,
L.G.

9. Letter to Sarala Devi Chowdhurani

November 28, 1920

Dipak[22] asks for being relieved from English studies for the time being. I honour the boy for it. If you do not even mentally resist I would like to let Dipak have his way. I will see to it that some day he learns English. But I assure you he will lose nothing by omitting English for the time being. Do you know that when a boy has acquired linguistic talent and has mastered the science of language it is an easy thing for him to learn a new language. Thus did Max Muller learn sixteen languages. When you have mastered the science, you have only to memorize a few hundred root words and you know your language. Do therefore please give me your willing consent. Dipak is a great and noble boy. I would not force him in the matter of learning or anything else so long as he remains busy and trains himself to think. Please tax yourself and give me your true decision. Remember it is ever safe to trust one's children's teachers. Take all the precautions you like about your choice; but having made it leave the training to the teacher. I had a nice time in Benares.[23] What the outcome will be I do not know. The atmosphere is certainly clear and Malaviyaji is calmer if not entirely calm.

10. Letter to Sarala Devi Chowdhurani

On Way to Bhagalpur,
December 11, 1920

I had two letters from you, one a scrap, the other a longish letter which shows that you do not understand my language or my thoughts. I have certainly not betrayed any annoyance over your complex nature, but I have remarked upon it. If a person is born with a deformation (*sic*) one may not quarrel with nature for it, but one may pardonably take note of it and try to remove it. And that is what I have done. I refuse to call an indefinable complexity a piece of art. All art yields to patient analysis and shows a unity of design behind the diversity on the canvas. You are hugging your defects even when they are pointed out by a friend in a friendly manner. I do not feel vexed but it makes my task of helping difficult. What art can there be in moods, in fits and starts ? The simplest natures are certainly complex in a sense. But they are easily analysed. But they are called simple because they are easily understandable and readily yield to treatment. But I do not want to quarrel with you. In you I have an enigma to solve. I shall not be impatient. Only bear with me whenever I try to point (out) what to me appear to be your obvious limitations.

We all have them. It is the privilege of friendship to lay the gentle finger on the weak spots. Friendship becomes a divine institution only when it educates friends. Let us try to elevate each other. I await with interest your letter on *shuddhi*[24].

11. Letter to Sarala Devi Chowdhurani

Calcutta,
December 14, 1920

My love for you is not a task. It is one of the keenest pleasures of my life. It is based on faith in you, i.e. in your ultimate goodness. It will go only if I find you to be bad. My love is nothing if it does not draw the best out of you and make you better and purer than you are. And you must bear with me if in the process of helping you sometimes I seem to be rubbing you up the wrong way. Anyway, I am studying you and shall endeavour not to do so.

12. Letter to Sarala Devi Chowdhurani

December 17, 1920

I love you more (for) loving me less for any hate you may see in me. And you would be right in your regret over my being engaged in N(on)-C(o-)O(peration), if it was a matter of politics with me. As it is, with me it is my religion. *I am gathering together all the forces of hate and directing them in a proper channel.* Hatred is a sign of weakness as contempt of insolent power. If I could but show our countrymen that we need not fear the English, we will cease to hate them. A brave man or woman never hates. Hatred is essentially the vice of cowards. N(on-)C(o-)O(peration) is self-purification. Even as the dirt comes to the surface when you are purifying sugar, so does our weakness come to the surface whilst we are purifying ourselves. But what I like about your letter is your clear position. Your love for me is based on your belief in my purity and gentleness. I am worth nothing if I have not these and I should hold myself unfit for all the renunciation of yours described in your previous letter. I have been analysing my love for you. I have reached a definite meaning of spiritual wife. It is a partnership between two persons of the opposite sex where the physical is wholly absent. It is therefore possible between brother and sister, father and daughter. It is possible only between two *brahmacharis* in thought, word and deed. I have felt drawn to you, because I have recognized in you an identity of ideals and aspirations and a complete self-surrender. You have been 'wife' because you have recognized in me a fuller fruition of the common ideal than in yourself. For this spiritual partnership to subsist, there must be complete coincidence not from faith, but from knowledge. It is a meeting between two kindred spirits. This partnership can take place whilst either party is physically married to another, but only if they are living as celibates. Spiritual partnership is possible even between husband and wife. It transcends physical relations and persists beyond the grave. It follows from what I have stated that spiritual partners can never be physically wedded either in this life or a future, for it is possible only if there is no carnality, latent or patent. Are you spiritual wife to me of that description ? Have we that exquisite purity, that perfect coincidence, that perfect merging, that identity of ideals, that self-forgetfulness, that fixity of purpose, that trustfulness ? For me I can answer plainly that it is only an aspiration. I am unworthy to have that companionship with you. I require in me an infinitely higher purity than I possess in thought. I am too physically attached to you to be worthy of enjoying that sacred association with you. By physical attachment I here mean I am too much affected by your weaknesses. I must not be teacher to you, if I am your spiritual husband, if coincidence or merging is felt. On the contrary there are sharp differences between you and me so often. So far as I can see our relationship, it is one of brother and sister. I must lay down the law for you, and thus ruffle you. I must plead gently like a brother ever taking care to use the right word even as I do to my oldest sister. I must not be father, husband, friend, teacher all rolled in one. This is the big letter I promised. With dearest love I still subscribe myself,

Yours,
Law-Giver

13. Letter to Sarala Devi Chowdhurani

Delhi,
September 22, 1924

I have your pathetic appeal. I do want to live. I was imposing on myself 40 days. But on deeper scrutiny I saw I must impose the minimum consistent with the situation. If God wants more service through this body He will surely spare it.

The Tribune, 27-9-1924

14. Letter to Sarala Devi Chowdhurani

Delhi,
September 24, 1924

My penance is not vicarious. It is for the possible mistake I might have committed . . . .Why do you suppose that I have drawn inspiration from Christian examples ? I should not be ashamed, only this has nothing to do with it.

The Tribune, 27-9-1924

15. Letter to Sarala Devi[26] Chowdhurani

Yeravda Mandir,
May 25, 1930

Dear Sister,

I have received the fruit sent by you. I am asked to write to you not to send them hereafter. Any fruit I require is given to me here. Mangoes and oranges are given to the Jailor to eat. When there has been conflagration on all sides how can I eat mangoes ? I took oranges for two or four days and (then) gave them up. I do not see any necessity for them. (If) I require I shall indeed take them. I shall ever cherish the love behind the idea of sending fruit. I hope the children are all right.

Vandemataram from

Mohandas

16. Letter to Sarala Devi Chowdhurani

July 5, 1932

Dear Sister,

I was grieved to note from the papers that your mother was no more. My sympathies go out to you and Deepak[27] in your sorrow. Sardar and Mahadev join me in sending you condolences.

Yours sincerely,
M.K. Gandhi

Smt. Sarala Devi Chowdhurani
Calcutta
Bombay Secret Abstracts, Home Department, Special Branch, File No. 800 (40) (3), Pt. II, p. 159.

17. Letter to Sarala Devi Chowdhurani

September 16, 1932

I have your letter overflowing with love. That the children also have joined you in expressing their love made the letter as dear to me as a sacred gift. I took this step only when I was convinced that it was my duty to do so. I have taken it in God's name and for His work. I have faith in Him that He will protect my honour and, therefore, do not worry. All of you should rejoice that one of your own family has got such a holy opportunity.

(From Gujarati)
Mahadevbhaini Diary, Vol. II, p. 28.

18. Letter to Subhadra, Sarala and Jayadevi

April 13, 1933

Chi. Subhadra, Sarala and Jayadevi,

How can I say to you, you will reap as you sow ? The sanatanists say: "The Harijans reap as they sow. How can we commit the sin of helping them to improve their condition in disregard of that law ?" If I were to apply the Sanatanists' logic to you, I would have to demolish the little nest I have built for the Harijans. Since I can't do that, you are safe. According to the Sanatanists' idea of justice, since you wrote your letter with a lead pencil, I should reply with a pencil made of stone, shouldn't I ? But our aim is to win over even the sanatanists. But you have shown that you deserve Nandubehn's description of you.[29] As soon as you were out, you showed your nature. You started straight away drinking leaf-water. And dry leaves at that ![30] I must say Chinese bullocks are better than Kathiawari bullocks. They also drink leaf-water but the leaves are green. If you again run away to the cattle-pen in a huff, Sardar is generous and will forgive your getting angry and so you need not be afraid.

In one sense the description given by Nandubehn seems to be perfectly apt. Has anybody ever heard of cows, bullocks, horses and other animals worrying ? If animals had knowledge, they would be no less than yogis. It is said that yoga is extremely difficult for men to practise, but that it is part of women's nature. If a woman gives up ignorant attachment, she could easily be a *yogini*. But all of you are only learned animals !!! Remember that if you squander away the health cultivated in the yoga school by eating all kinds of sweets, you will deserve to be punished for that.

In your next letter describe some other doings of yours, namely what you read etc.

I am helpless about Manibehn. I write to her, but she does not get my letters. After all there must be some indications that one is a prisoner.

Kevalrambhai and my elder brother were of the same age. Both were liberal and extravagant. They both loved luxuries and comforts. In their old age, both of them lost interest in worldly pleasures and pursuits. They wrote to me, independently of each other, that they wished to join me in South Africa and spend the rest of their life there and hand over their children to my care. I gladly welcomed their desire and made preparations to receive them. But fate was unkind to me. They left me. I never got my elder brother's children under my care, though I tried hard to get them. But I got all of you without trying. Shall we attribute this to fate ruling human relations, or to the ripening of the fruit of our deeds in past lives ? Now that you have come, do not leave me. Everybody who wishes may have a share in what I have to give. Secure as much of it as you can and wish good name for yourself in life. Where has that Chandrahasa hidden himself ?

Blessings from
Bapu

(PS.)
Where is Nirmala ? How is she ?

19. Letter to Sarala Devi Chowdhurani

February 13, 1937

Chi. Sarla,

I had got your letter. I am late in replying. Won't you forgive me for it ? In fact there is nothing in your letter which calls for a reply. But I think I ought to reply. Since you yourself have become a devi[31], need I suffix 'devi' to your name ? How old are you ? How do you spend your time, or waste it ? Don't be shocked to see this sheet ragged (at the edges). Such paper is made by the poor now-a-days. It is not made with machines. Do you keep the poor in your thoughts ?

Blessings from
Bapu

NOTES

1. Son of Sarala Devi Chowdhurani.
2. Associated Press. Here Gandhiji presumably refers to the statement to the Press published on April 29, 1920, the preceding item.
3. Devotional song.
4. Mira Bai:
   My heart longs for the Master's feet
   Nothing pleases me while the longing remains unsatisfied
   All else is illusion, a play of dreams.
   The ocean of life is all dried up,
   Crossing it does not worry me.
   Mira says, O Lord Giridhar Nagar,
   My eyes see all things in a new light.
5. Gandhiji presumably refers to "Letter to Sarala Devi Chowdhurani", 29-4-1920; he left Poona for Sinhgadh on April 29, 1920.
6. Pandit Rambhuj Dutt Chowdhari.
7. Eldest son of Sarala Devi Chowdhurani.
8. Jallianwala Bagh Memorial Fund.
9. Shankarlal Banker.
10. His marriage was solemnized on May 19, 1920.
11. The source, however, has "up".
12. If you aspire after deliverance, my child, give up sense pleasures like poison and enjoy forgiveness, straight forwardness, compassion, contentment and truthfulness as you would *amrit. Ashtavakra Gita*, I, 2.

    If, no longer identifying yourself with your body, you abide on the plane of *chilt*, this very day you will find happiness and peace, free from your bonds. I, 4. He who believes himself free is free; he who believes himself bound is bound; truly do they say: "As you think, so you are." I, 11.
13. The letter was written from Sinhgadh where Gandhiji was resting as he had some leg trouble.
14. A dialogue between King Janaka of Videha and Raikva, the low-born, ugly-looking philosopher.
15. Pandit Rambhuj Dutt Chowdhari.
16. Embodiment of life-force.
17. A female demon, daughter of Bali. She attempted to kill the infant Lord Krishna by suckling him, but was herself sucked to death by the child.
18. Having known the *atman* to be in truth the Imperishable One without a second, how is it that you, enlightened about the *atman* and ever firm in mind, take pleasure in acquiring possessions ? *Ashtavaktra Gita*, III, 1.

Just as, not knowing a sea-shell, one covets it under the delusion that it is a piece of silver, so through ignorance of the *atman* one sees it as the delusive world of sense objects and takes pleasure in them. III, 2.

Having known yourself to be that One from Whom emanates this universe waves rise in an ocean, why do you run about like a weak, miserable wretch ? III, 3.

Having learnt that the *atman* is the living spirit, absolute and unconditioned, supremely beautiful, if one remains attached to the gross pleasure of sense, one gets defiled. III, 4.

It is strange that even a wise one, knowing himself present in all creatures and all creatures present in himself, should be dominated by the sense of "I" and "Mine". III, 5.

It is strange that even a man abiding in the Supreme Oneness and set on attaining *moksha* should get distraught with passion, yielding to its overmastering urge through experience of the pleasure it brings. III, 6.

It is strange that a man who knows for certain that the desire which has possessed him is an enemy of knowledge should yet long for pleasure even though extremely enfeebled and nearing death. III, 7.

19. It is strange that a man unattached both to this world and the other, able to discriminate between the transient and the eternal and aspiring after *moksha*, should be afraid of *moksha* itself. III, 8.

The steadfast man when consuming things which please, or when made to suffer, is neither happy nor angry, ever seeing the one *atman* everywhere. III, 9.

The high-souled man, looking upon the ever-active body of his as not his, how should such a one be affected by praise or blame ? III, 10.

The man of steady intellect, who the entire universe as *maya* and is no more interested in its shows, how will he have fear even when death is near ? III, 11.

The high-souled one whose mind is free from desire even when things look hopeless, who, self-realized, rests supremely content in himself, with whom may such a one be compared ? III, 12.

The man of steady intellect who knows that all this, in very truth, is appearance and no more, will he feel drawn by one thing and repelled by another ? III, 13.

He who has inwardly renounced attachment, who is unaffected by the pairs of opposites and who hopes for nothing—to him chance-brought things of enjoyment occasion neither happiness nor suffering. III, 14.

There can be no comparison, indeed, between the man, self-realized and steady or intellect, who enjoys things as sport, and the beclouded man carrying on his back, the burden of this world. IV, 1.

The yogi, firmly established on that plane, which Indra and the other gods weakly yearn to attain, is never moved to joy. IV, 2.

Neither good deeds nor sins touch the man who knows That : the sky and smoke do not touch each other in fact, though seem to. IV, 3.

The high-souled man who knows that this whole universe is but the *atman* itself, who can forbid him from living as he will spontaneously? IV, 4.

None but the man of perfect knowledge has the strength to end all desire and aversion, in all the four planes of existence, from *Brahma* to a blade of grass. IV, 5.

Rare is the man who knows the identity of his self and the Lord of the Universe; such a one does what he may and knows fear from no quarter. IV, 6.

20. Mathuradas Trikumji (1894-1951); grandson of Gandhiji's sister, occasionally his secretary; secretary, Bombay Congress Committee, 1922-23; Mayor, Bombay Municipal Corporation.
21. Law-giver.
22. Sarala Devi's son. He was studying in the Ashram School, Sabarmati.
23. Gandhiji was in Benaras on November 25, 26 and 27.
24. Literally, purification.
25. This was written in reply to a letter in which Sarala Devi had expressed her regret over Gandhiji's being engaged in non-co-operation which, in her opinion, was based upon hatred. She had stated that she could have loved him more if he had got rid of hatred.
26. This is a translation. The original letter is not available.
27. Son of the addressee.
28. *Mahadevbhaini Diary*, Vol. II, p. 28.
29. As bullocks.
30. Gandhiji means "tea".
31. Goddess.

Chapter 5
Mira Behn (1892-1982)

Mira Behn devoted her life to the service of Mahatma Gandhi. Her original name was Madeline Slade. She was a beautiful and charming girl. She was born on 22 November, 1892 in an aristocratic, highly cultured English family and was brought up in the lap of luxury. Her father, Edmond Slade, an officer in the British Navy later became the Commander-in-Chief of the East Indies Squadron in Bombay. In early childhood she spent two years in India. She learned German and Egyptian languages and developed a deep fascination for Beethoven. Beethoven's music was a spiritual experience for her. She loved nature and liked simple living. Madeline was a sensitive and willful child and grew up to be a beautiful woman. She was not interested in marriage and many highly eligible suitors were politely put off by her.

She read the English translation of Jean Christopher of Romain Rolland which cast such a magic spell on her that she wanted to read the original. She went to Paris to learn French. She wanted to meet Rolland, who gave her an appointment for which she travelled to Switzerland in 1922. It was from him that she came to know about Gandhi for the first time. She wanted to go to India to meet Gandhi and so she wrote to him. She prepared herself to go to India .She gave up hunting, took a vegetarian food, and learned to sit and sleep on the floor. In 1925 she reached Bombay and same day boarded the train for Ahmedabad. The train steamed into the Ahmedabad Station on the morning of 7 November, 1925, three persons were waiting on the platform to receive her. They were Mahadev Desai, Vallabhbhai Patel and Swami Anand. Vallabhbhai brought her to the Ashram and ushered her into a room. As she entered, a brown figure rose up and came forward. Madeleine was conscious of nothing else but a sense of light. She fell on her knees. Two hands gently raised her up, and a voice said, "You shall be my daughter." On hearing these words her consciousness of the physical world began to return and she saw a face smiling, with eyes full of love and a gentle twinkle of amusement. He was Bapu. In all their mutual relationship he was to remain Bapu and she his daughter, Mira. The tall, beautiful Madeline, shaved off her head and adopted *brahmacharya* as Gandhi, and became a true disciple of the great man. She wore *khadi*, learned spinning and weaving and taught the villagers what she had learned. It was Gandhi who renamed her as Mira. This transformation made her an admirer and follower of Gandhi, and a servant of India. She accompanied Gandhi when he went to London for the Second Round Table Conference and she functioned as a bridge between the Indian Leader and the Britishers. She undertook the propaganda and publicity for Gandhi's ideals and programmes. She reported to foreign press about the repressive measures the British regime adopted against the Congress and thus the news came to light and she was promptly arrested. After her release, she was prohibited from entering Bombay but she violated the order and was arrested again. On being released, she accompanied Gandhi in his tour of India, and went abroad to speak on Gandhi's ideals and to seek support for the Indian cause (1934).

Whenever she was with Mahatma Gandhi she looked after him in minutest detail. At times she went to the Viceroy as a personal emissary of Mahatma Gandhi and at other times to the Congress President and the members of the Working Committee. To plead the case of India she went abroad—met Lloyd George, Lord Halifax, General Smuts, Sir Samuel Hoare and Winston Churchill, visited United States and went to New York, Philadelphia, West Chester, Boston, Harvard and

Washington, delivered a lecture at the Harvard University and met Mrs. Roosevelt at the White House in Washington. Mirabehn took keen interest in the formation of Sevagram Ashram and organised cleanliness campaigns in the surrounding villages. She was always unflinching in her service to Bapu and longed to be with him as long as possible. For such longing she earned reprimands more than once from Gandhi, Gradually she undertook independent activities with the help and blessings of Bapu.

Mirabehn lived in India during a most eventful period in which she saw in 1927 the Simon Commission facing black flags everywhere, the resolve of the people for complete independence in 1929, the Dandi March and the Civil Disobedience movement in 1930-31 and the Gandhi-Irwin Pact in 1931; she accompanied Gandhi and others to the Round Table Conference in London in the autumn of 1931; prepared the people of Orissa to resist Japanese invasion nonviolently in the beginning of 1942, and was arrested and kept in detention with Gandhi in the Aga Khan Palace. She was a witness to the Simla Conference and the Cabinet Mission, the Interim Government and the Constituent Assembly.

During the Quit India Movement days she was arrested along with Gandhi and brought to jail. After, Mira started Ashram Pashulok near Hrishikesh in 1947 and a settlement named Bapu Gram. When Gandhi returned to Delhi after his peace mission in the riot-stricken areas, immediately after the dawn of freedom, Mira was there to receive him. She stayed with him for three months at the Birla House and returned to her ashram on December 18, 1947. And that was her last meeting with the great man.

She continued teaching and spreading Gandhi's ideals and messages in ashrams. She left India for Germany in 1959. She set up her perch in Vienna, Austria, in her Indian style and was known in the locality as the Indian Lady. Her only companion was the music of Beethoven. She wrote 'The spirits Pilgrimage', her autobiography, and Bapu's Letters to Mira.

This great lady from Europe, who spent her life in the service of Gandhi and India, breathed her last on July 20, 1982. India offered respects to her by conferring on her the Padma Vibhushan in 1982, and also by releasing a postal stamp marked for her.

1. Letter to Madeleine Slade[1]

148 Russa Road,
Calcutta
July 24, 1925

Dear Friend,

I was pleased to receive your letter which has touched me deeply. The samples of wool you have sent are excellent. You are welcome whenever you choose to come. If I have advice of the steamer that brings you, there will be someone receiving you at the steamer, and guiding you to the train that will take you to Sabarmati. Only please remember that the life at the Ashram is not all rosy. It is strenuous. Bodily labour is given by every inmate. The climate of this country is also not a small consideration. I mention these things not to frighten you, but merely to warn you.

Yours sincerely,
M.K. Gandhi

(PS.)
As my right hand requires rest, I am dictating my correspondence.

2. Letter to Mirabehn

Saturday, December 11, 1926[3]

Chi. Mira,

I have your 4 letters. Two I have acknowledged already. I suppose you know the meaning of *chi*[4]. It stands for *chiranjivi*[5] meaning 'long-lived'. That is the blessing which an elder prefixes to the names of the younger members of his family. I like all your letters. I am glad you had an early opportunity of going to the Mussalman friend. Miss Grover's[6] name I had forgotten altogether. I was delighted that you went there. She is a good earnest soul, much devoted to her work.

You should give me your day's doings, and describe the prayers, the studies and the meals. Tell me what you are eating. How are your bowels acting ? What is the quantity of milk you are taking ? What are the times of your meals ? Are mosquitoes there ? Do you take your walks regularly ? Do you write any Hindi ? Does anyone teach you ? What fruit are you getting ?

I duly got the corrected chapter.[7] You should find out the posting time leave Wardha on 21st inst. Motilalji[8] insists on my going to Gauhati. I hope you will be getting your *Y.I.* regularly. If you do not, you should ask Swami and write to Mrityunjay to attend. I take it you will be getting Hindi *Navajivan* also.

You will not forget the Urdu script please. The American friends, mother and daughter, are still here. I think I told you about their arrival. The daughter is a teacher in an important school. They are leaving tomorrow. Jamnalalji has over 40 guests on my account. Poor Jankibehn[9] !

I am keeping exceptionally good health. Exercise regularly morning and evening.

You can't complain of any brevity about this letter.

With love,
Bapu

Saturday

I was uncertain about the correctness of the passage in Rolland's letter which you have now corrected. It reads perfectly intelligible now. Please do not return the original. File it among your papers.

3. Letter to Mirabehn

December 27, 1926[10]

Chi. Mira,

I have all your love letters. The one about the repugnance against Mussalmans is disturbing. It is the fear of conversion that has caused this repugnance.

You are doing the right thing there. Watch everything. Mend where you can. Be still, where you are helpless. You have gone there only as a learner. Your *business* is to finish your Hindi. You will teach and reform only by the way. You will not therefore become a participator in anything that goes on in your school which the Gurukul is for you, even as I cannot be a participator in the sins of a drunkard who may teach me how to shave. But this is not to criticize anything you have hitherto done. This is merely to assure you that you are doing quite well.

Why apologize about the expenses ? We do want to be stingy. But we do not want to deny ourselves the things we need for keeping us fit for service. You know that you can get what funds you need from Mr. Gadodia. *Rita* is *aritha* the soap-nut.

You will see many more Miss Rams. May your contact open their eyes. Raisina is all you describe it to be and much worse. It is built with blood money. Instead of the blood circulating down to the feet, it is all being sucked by the head. Presently there will be meningitis and— !

Here the scenery is beautiful. Our hut is on the edge of the bank of the mighty Brahmaputra. It is damp and cold; very windy. But the weather is most bracing if one would take vigorous exercise. I generally walk to the Congress tent—one mile and a little over. I leave tomorrow for Calcutta where I expect to be for four days.

With love,
Bapu

4. Letter to Mirabehn

Unrevised March 4, 1929

Chi. Mira,

This sheet tells you where I am writing from. Tomorrow takes me away from you for a fair distance. My third-class travelling is becoming a fraud in a way. From Delhi I had a whole compartment given to me and the party. There was thus greater freedom than in the 2nd class and I had the satisfaction of having the whole company with me. The separation pained me. The being together gives me joy.

The Mandir is making visible progress, so I fancy. The joint kitchen is becoming more and more popular, and I do not think, at the end of the year, anybody would want to break it up. But let us see. Do not be anxious about me. There are three services from Rangoon per week. I hope to write to you therefore three times a week. The sailings from Calcutta to Rangoon are Sundays, Tuesdays and Fridays. So you too need not write more than three times per week. The steamer always leaves in the morning. You will not forget to give me a summary of your work after some time now. I want your informed opinion on the soft spindles and a description of your improvements on the bow, also your digest of comparison between the results of well carded slivers and what they used to have before. I hope you are keeping a diary of these bare experiences. I want you to treat your experiment scientifically. I want you also to tell me from time to time all about the morning and the evening prayers and what you sing there. And give me also your final changes about food. I am attaching more and more importance to your experiment, for I know you are accurate about these things, and will not easily deceive yourself.

I have a curious party with me this time. It includes a mad girl graduate. She is the daughter of a well-known Tamil leader—Rajaji's friend. Last time I was in Delhi, she and her cousin came in to see me. I suggested their coming to the Ashram for a change. The father jumped at the idea. And there they are. In order to be able to look after her more easily, I have cropped her hair. Now she and the cousin are going with me to Burma. She will listen, if at all, to me and no one else. It is a serious responsibility. But it is God's, not mine. Then there is Champa with her two babies—Dr. Mehta's daughter-in-law whom you know. Dr. M. wanted me to take her with me. I expect she will be left in Rangoon. The rest are Pyarelal, Girdhari, Subbiah, Mahadev and Purushottam. Mahadev arrives this morning. As Purushottam was still somewhat constipated, I suggested his joining me. He being with me, I am able to avoid the lights for the prayers. He recites the *Gita* without any assistance.

I am more and more reverting to uncooked food. During the journey I had raw vegetable, chopped up with bread. So bread was the only cooked preparation. Fruit is now becoming a superfluity. Raw green vegetable is proving a perfect and cheap substitute. Cabbage, cauliflower or any *bhaji* serves the purpose. And one needs such a small quantity when you eat the vegetable in a raw state.

Love,
Bapu

5. Letter to Mirabehn

June 24, 1929

Chi. Mira,[11]

It is well you do not want me to speak to you tomorrow on the incident. But I did want, after witnessing the exhibition, to reduce to writing my thoughts. I do that now.

The exhibition is proof of the correctness of my statement. None else would have felt like committing suicide over a simple innocent remark of mine. You want to be with me in my tours occasionally, it is true; you want to come to the Ashram leaving your work at least every four months. You recognize these desires as limitations. I make allowance for them. But why feel disturbed when I tell you what I feel to be the truth that they are not themselves the been touched. If you were not what I have described you to be, you would disease, but they are symptoms of a deep-seated disease which has not rejoice over my drawing attention to the disease and courageously strive to overcome it. Instead, you simply collapsed, much to my grief and anxiety.

This disease is idolatry. If it is not, why hanker after my company ! Why touch or kiss the feet that must one day be dead cold ? There is nothing in the body. The truth I represent is before you. Experience and effort will unravel it before you, never my association in the manner you wish. When it comes in the course of business you will, like others, gain from it and more because of your devotion. Why so helplessly rely on me ? Why do everything to please me ? Why not independently of me and even in spite of me ? I have put no restrictions on your liberty, save those you have welcomed. Break the idol to pieces if you can and will. If you cannot, I am prepared to suffer with you. But you must give me the liberty to issue warnings. My diagnosis may be wrong. If so, it is well. Strive with me cheerfully instead of being nerve-broken. Everyone but you takes my blows without being unstrung.

If your effort has hitherto failed, what does it matter ? You have hitherto dealt mechanically with symptoms. There you have had considerable success. But if I say you have not been able to touch the root, why weep over it ? I do not mind your failures. They are but stepping-stones to success. You must rise from this torpor never to fall into it again.

I have done. May God be with you.

Love,
Bapu

6. Letter to Mirabehn

Vejalpur,
April 17, 1930

Chi. Mira,

I have your two letters.

I can understand how the mishap occurred as to the yarn. I understand too your natural desire to come. But I am (sure) restraint was better. It is a fine saying "there is no remission of sin except by being born again."

You know however that you are at liberty to come if you cannot help it. But then you must come plainly to satisfy the natural desire. If you can suppress the desire, so much the better.

Calcutta and Karachi have broken the spell. Somehow I am unmoved. But there is no suspending even if moving violence takes place.

Love,
Bapu

6. Letter to Mirabehn

Unrevised Banda,
November 20, 1929

Chi. Mira,[12]

Our train being two hours late, the whole of the programme was upset. It was somewhat set right by my forgoing the afternoon rest and putting off the bath for the night station. I finished spinning at 9.30. It is now nearly 10 p.m. But I may not retire before writing this. The foregoing preface is to show you I have been thinking of you the whole day long. Now that you are away from me, my grief over having grieved you is greater.[13] No tyrant has yet lived who has not paid for the suffering he has caused. No lover has ever given pain without being more pained. Such is my state. What I have done was inevitable. Only I wish I did not lose temper. But such is my brutality towards those I love most. But now that you are away from me, I can think of nothing but your extraordinary devotion. May God remove what I consider is your *moha*[14] or may He open the eyes of my understanding and let me see my error. You are to keep well.

Love,
Bapu

8. Letter to Mirabehn

Yeravda Mandir,
November 13, 1930

Chi. Mira,

Your letter. The arrangement about translating my remarks on the *Gita* chapters is quite good. I shall look forward to the joint handiwork. I want to pour myself out into those chapters. This means additional work for you and will take up a great deal of your time. However, I know you won't feel the strain of it, as you love that work.

Here is a letter from Andrews, this time, for me to send you. He could not restrain himself from writing to me directly. I have at last given him a few lines. Don't give any time to the Gandiv till Keshu has obtained mastery over it and gives you a machine in working order. For me it continues to provide further delights. The original *mal* for the motor wheel at last had to be discarded, as I could not cut it any further for tightening it. It has to be fairly stout and thick. I had nothing with me in the hand-spun *mals* of the required thickness. As you know, I criminally neglected to learn how to make these little odds and ends. And I was bent on having only the hand-spun stuff. I had to give full two hours to the first attempt. It was successful and was possible only because only a short length was required. My second attempt took me barely half an hour. I had to make another for emergency, which occurred at once, for the original threads from which I made the *mal* were weak. I have now thought of a device of quickly twisting to the required strength practically any number of threads. My third attempt will therefore mean still less time. And meantime I am having now an accumulation of little bits of stout hand-spun chords which I can use for watchguards and the like. All this gives me delight and comfort, for it means greater mastery over the wheel. And this has become so easily possible because of the incredible simplicity of the Gandiv. But I am not going to regard my opinion as final or authoritative till I have corroboration from someone who knows much more than I do of the mechanism of the *charkha*. But I warn you against regarding this detailed description as any incentive for you to tackle the Gandiv. I know if I was outside, I could not have given all this time, thought and attention to the thing. It might not have even been desirable if it was to exclude other urgent matters. I have given you the details merely to share my joy with you. The *charkha*, the *takli* and the bow have become a fascination with me. I do not seem to get tired of them. Daily I wish I had more time to give to these things. I want to secure greater output on all the three. But I am so clumsy and so stupid and slow. Somehow or other I feel that it is not the rigidity of old age that prevents from gaining a greater output. I have not the proper knack I fear. However I find satisfaction from the knowledge that God will accept this little offering as the best possible for me in the circumstances. If you can stand the cold bath in winter, nothing can be more bracing. You will not strive against nature. If there is no instantaneous warm reaction, you must revert to the warm bath. The condition of reaction is vigorous rubbing with the bare hands. I had sorrowfully to give up cold baths only after that wretched attack of pleurisy in London in 1914. Your food is quite good. It may be necessary to take more ghee. Experience has shown that you need a fair measure to keep strength, heat and weight. Gangadevi may walk a little. She must take measured steps and begin with a few minutes only at a time. All risk of a setback should be avoided. She will get rid of the urinary trouble by taking a hip-bath. If the water is chilly a little hot water may be added to take the chill off. This hip-bath is almost an infallible remedy. Is not this uncle, who has married, somewhat elderly and who vies with you in indifferent spellings, though very learned ? So according to your birthdate, you are only a babe a few months old !! You have therefore many a summer to look forward to.

Love,
Bapu

9. Letter to Mirabehn

September 20, 1932

Chi. Mira,

I got up at 2.30 today to write to Gurudev, then to Sastri and then to you. I have your tearing letter. At first I thought I would send it to the Governor. But I rejected the thought as soon as it came. You have chosen to enter the furnace. You must remain in it. My society is no easy job as you have seen all these years. Drink then the poison to the last dregs.

As I wrote that first letter conveying my vow, I thought of you and of Ba. And for a time I became giddy. How would you two bear the thing ? But the voice within said, 'If you will enter in, you must give up thought of all attachment.' And the letter went. No anguish will be too terrible to wash out the sin of untouchability. You must therefore rejoice in this suffering and bear it bravely. I know how difficult all this is to do. Yet that is exactly what you have to try to do. Just think and realize that there is no meaning in having the last look. The spirit which you love is always with you. The body through which you learnt to love the spirit is no longer necessary for sustaining that love. It is well that it lasts whilst there is use for it. It is equally well that it perishes when there is no use for it. And since we don't know when it will outlast its use, we conclude that death through whatever cause means that there was no longer any use for it. If it is any comfort, know that Vallabhbhai, Mahadev, Ramdas, Surendra, Devdas, whom I have met are all bearing the thing wonderfully well. Love to your companions. I am glad Kisen is with you. She is a good and brave girl. May God sustain you.

Love,
Bapu

Shri Mirabai (Slade)
Arthur Road Prison
Bombay

10. Letter to Mirabehn

March 11, 1933

Chi. Mira,

It is 3.15 a.m., 11th, Saturday now. The day of my writing to you has become upset owing to the uncertainty of the arrival of your weekly letter. This week I had two from you. Last week's was received only on Tuesday and this week's on Wednesday. But yesterday morning I thought I had still to hear from you and I devoted the morning to writing other important letters. And then when it dawned upon me that there was nothing more to come from you, I would not write to you during what you may call office hours. I love to write this letter and such others in the early morning.

I see that you are once more enjoying the company of birds and animals. Frogs have somehow or other appeared to me helpless creatures. They can't run, they can't fly and thus become an easy prey to the wily cat. And they seem to look at you so appealingly in their helplessness. The monkey on the other hand never excites my pity. He is a most resourceful and mischievous fellow and takes delight in overreaching you. He has no such thing as thankfulness in him. And yet I suppose all this is imagination or ignorance ! If we thrive on knowledge, we seem somehow to do so on ignorance and imagination too. 'It is folly to be wise when ignorance is bliss.' And the shortest and the oldest Upanishad[15] says, "He overcomes death through ignorance and mounts to immortality through knowledge." The original words are and, meaning also respectively activity and inactivity, body and spirit, attachment and detachment. They can be made to mean several other things without doing violence to the text. It is a very simple and lofty Upanishad and is also abstruse. It is an epitome of all knowledge like the *Gita.* The latter is perhaps a commentary on the former. An old commentator or rather the devotee of the *Gita* compares the Upanishads to cows, the *Gita* to milk and Krishna to the cowboy who milks them. But no more of this now.

I hope your progress continues and will not be interrupted by the hot weather which is on us now. Make use of the earth bandage on the forehead or a mere wet rag. It has a wonderfully cooling effect.

What cools the head cools the whole body. I came across a potent sentence yesterday in an American book on the eyesight, a book received from Gregg. It says that a lie heats the body and injures the eyesight. It is true if you would give an extended meaning to 'lie'. Any departure conscious or unconscious from the laws of nature is a lie. A conscious departure from the known laws is a lie that hurts our moral fibre, not so, or not to the same extent an unconscious departure. But the body is injured in every case. Writers on *pranayama* claim that the ability to regulate and control breath, enables one to defy changes of climate. The *Gita* seems to lend support to the belief. This is a field that needs reinvestigation in the light of modern knowledge Kuvalayananda of Lonavala is doing it. Form your lips as you would when whistling and slowly breathe the outside air and you will have an immediate sensation of cooling. When lying flat on the back, remember that the muscles of the back do not expand. Hence your breathing must be extra gentle. It is intended to create a soothing effect on the system and relax it and rest it. There is nothing apart from sleep to relieve tension of the mind and body. Therefore the deep breathing should be taken whilst sitting cross-legged with the body erect like a straight board. All these exercises have to be gentle, deliberate and rhythmic, always on an empty stomach. Here the writing was interrupted for prayer and is now resumed after a break of 25 minutes at 4.35.

I have always found Arnold's to be on the whole a more helpful translation than any other. "Abstemious" is a wrong word. "Spare diet" is a good expression. Yi means less than enough. What is enough is a matter of conjecture, therefore our own mental picture. The man of truth knowing that man is always indulgent to the body, said, in order to counteract the indulgence, that he should take less food than what he would think was enough; then there was likelihood of his taking what in fact was enough. So what we often think is spare or meagre is likely even to be more than enough. More people are weak through overfeeding or wrong feeding than through underfeeding. It is wonderful, if we chose the right diet, what an extraordinarily small quantity would suffice.

I am glad Ba is prospering with you and learns Hindi and makes you sing *bhajans*. Does Mridula sing ? She ought to if she does not. She must shed her shyness if she has any still left. How otherwise does she pass the day ? She should now be Ba's secretary or letter-writer. My weight now registers at 104. The food still remains fruit and milk (raw). I am taking just now less than one lb. of milk. It is the fruit that keeps up my weight. The elbows remain as they are. No cause for anxiety. I have reduced the spinning to a minimum—no fixed quantity. The count just now is anything round 55 and 60. This from *devakapas* carded on Keshu's little invention.

Love from us all.
Bapu

11. Letter to Mirabehn

April 6, 1933

Chi. Mira,

Your letter came in only yesterday. I am beginning this before prayer 3.45. I overslept myself. Being the fasting day it does not much matter perhaps.

You have done well in writing as you have done. The difficulty about the execution is threefold: (1) The Ashram site has to be removed or the other activities have to be. (2) There is no one in the Ashram who would stay on the condition you name, save perhaps Narandas. (3) The Ashram has not been conceived in the manner suggested by you. The last is perhaps the fatal difficulty. Mine is a novel experiment, dangerous and, it may be, even impossible of achieving. The idea is to have a place where people can train themselves to lead the celibate life in the midst of ordinary temptations. . . [16] and . . .[17] fell not because they could not overcome animal passion. They have not gone so far. But they suppressed truth. Now truth can only be cultivated in the midst of men and women of different temperaments and subtle temptations. It is easy enough for a few people of similar habits not to deceive one another or be found out. That is no truth. It has to be lived in the natural surroundings. Exception has been taken even to the Ashram life as being not natural.

I wonder if you have followed me so far. If you have, you must at once perceive that the first two difficulties are the natural consequence of the deliberate creation of the third. Having constituted the Ashram as it is we have the men and women and the activities that we have.

And out of these men and women and the activities we cannot create what you have contemplated. What you suggest can only be done by withdrawing two or three men and women and sending them to another place to live their own life and draw some kindred spirits in due time. But that would be to admit failure. I should not mind it if it became inevitable. I am not at all convinced that it is. If out of the present experiment a few of us lived of whom it could be said that they fairly satisfied the test, I should be quite satisfied that the experiment had succeeded. In an experiment such as we are making failures must be the order of the day. Each will be a stepping-stone to success. The . . . incident has disturbed me but not baffled me at all. Prompt measures have been taken after the discovery and are still being taken. You should know also my diagnosis. The fault lay in my over-confidence in both these young people. The earlier fault lay in their parents. . . . had the notion that his children will better conform to the Ashram ideal if they were brought up in isolation. . . . nursed the thought. And so the children grew to be selfish, and exclusive and self-centred. The motive behind . . . was good. And so I carried out the tradition after . . .'s death. I was bound to as his heir to test its efficacy. The result we know. I am not sorry. . . . had every right to do what he thought was good for the Ashram. As for . . . the way with . . . was reverse. But . . . did not quite assist her husband. She had no policy of her own but she herself could not follow out the Ashram ideal and so . . . grew anyhow as the pet of the Ashram. The natural thing is likely to happen now. The proud family of . . . will cut themselves from the Ashram and live their natural life. That will not be bad. . . . has learnt her lesson. She will for . . .'s sake more and more conform to the ideal. . . . was the dupe, . . . was the villain (used not in its quite ugly sense). The whole Ashram knows that truth at any cost will alone save it. Things will tighten themselves along these lines. Several other things will be gradually done. No violent changes will be made. There is not the slightest cause for alarm. You are perhaps unnecessarily harsh on Prema. She has her grave blemishes but she has contributed nothing to the incident. Her physical *brahmacharya* appears to me to be above suspicion and she is truthful to the point of bluntness. She is meticulous in the observance of the outward rules. She has a vile tongue. She is trying to control it. Anyway there is no one who can conduct the Ashram better than Narandas. He must be left to manage it to the best of his ability. Now I want you to work at this exhaustive letter and give me your criticism, ideas and suggestions unhesitatingly and without reserve. You have plenty of time for hard thinking. I am unperturbed, I am taking things easy, meeting each situation as it arises. Narandas will faithfully carry out instructions. And if I felt the call I am quite capable of disbanding the whole Ashram in so far as I have the power which legally I have not. But that is nothing. The moral authority is there. You may therefore make any drastic suggestions you like. All well here otherwise. You will explain to Ba whatever is said here in so far as it may be necessary.

Love from us all,
Bapu

12. Letter to Mirabehn

April 11, 1933

Chi. Mira,

Your long letter came yesterday. Your argument appeals to me. Women themselves have resisted the argument that you have advanced. I have believed it always that man is the aggressor. He is more sensual than woman. I have therefore no difficulty in following your argument. But the corollary you draw defies experience. It has been happy where it has worked. But they are rare cases and will always be so—nor is it unfortunate. The usual condition is marriage and procreation. That means breach of *brahmacharya* as we know it. That does not mean that we should not aim at it. We must aim at it even though there may be only one case of perfect *brahmacharya* out of the experiment. Many attempts, only a few will attain salvation. Therefore generally we shall have to be satisfied with married people growing to *brahmacharya* and a few only being life *brahmacharis*. If I am right, the Ashram will have to be what it is, always rising higher after every failure. . .[18] and . . . are infinitely better for having lived in the Ashram nor is the Ashram any the worse for their having lived in it. They would easily have been much better if I had been less imperfect and more wise and for that matter the other elders. But I was their foot-rule, so imperfect and untrue. Yet I do not consider myself an unsafe guide because I am not consciously untruthful and always attempt to discover and throw away my imperfections. All I say is that failures there must be so long as we have not in our midst a perfect man or woman. But we need not lose hope nor become unnerved on discovering instances like . . .'s; they are attempts of the system to throw off impurities. I rejoice at the discovery, while I deplore . . .'s error, even as I would rejoice at the discovery of a disease in my own body, though I may deplore it. Further than this I cannot carry this tremendous problem—'one step enough for me, I do not ask to see the distant scene'. We know the fundamental truth we want to reach, we know also the way. The details we do not know, we shall never know them all, because we are but very humble instruments among millions of such moving consciously or unconsciously towards the divine event. We shall reach the Absolute Truth, if we will faithfully and steadfastly work out the relative truth as each one of us knows it. Ba wants her letter separately because of the separate delivery. According to the date of the delivery of my letter to her, the fortnight is not yet complete. I do not understand this intricate working of the jail regulations. It differs in every jail evidently. But that ought not to cause any worry. The philosophy of prison life is that the body belongs to the keeper, i. e. the State. Therefore, generally speaking it may be said that a prisoner is foolish who worries about exterior wants the supply of which depends wholly upon the keeper's will. Thus everything given to a prisoner is a concession which may be withdrawn at the will of the State. Domestic letters fall under that category. We may thankfully receive and write them so long as they are allowed but we may not foam or fret or curse, if we are not allowed to do so. Regularity of delivery we may prize but irregularity ought not to unhinge us. Those who are prisoners for conscience' sake should at least grasp this very simple but not generally understood truth. If you can explain it to Ba, you should do so. I shall see about the delivery of Hindi *Harijan*. My weight is steady at 104.

Love from us all,
Bapu

(PS.)

Sacred cards going in a separate packet. The slip containing your copy of the vows is too precious a possession to be with me. I therefore return it for you to keep.

13. Letter to Mirabehn

April 27, 1933

Chi. Mira,

This is Thursday morning before prayer. Your letter came in yesterday with Ba's.

A book on Astronomy is being sent to you. I enclose also a map for the month. You will find herewith so Dr. Saunders's[19] letter. It is satisfactory on the whole.

Letter for Ba will also accompany this.

You may pursue the conduct of the Ashram as much as you like. It won't tire me. It will assist me. It will enable you to understand my viewpoint better. You must not accuse yourself of want of faith in me or my wisdom because you do not see a point of mine at once or because having seen it you cannot agree with me. I am not a perfect being. Why should you see eye to eye with me in my errors ? That would be blind faith. Your faith in me should enable you to detect my true error much quicker than a fault-finder. What I would like your faith to do is that when you cannot convince me of my error you should think that it is likely that I see more clearly than you do in matters where I have thought and experienced more. That would give you peace of mind. Therefore you should not paralyse your thought by suppressing your doubts and torturing yourself that you do not agree with my view in particular things. You should therefore pursue the discussion of the Ashram till you have the clearest possible grasp of all my ideas about it.

You need not have argued about the man being the worse sinner of the two. I have always held that view against most, if not all, of my male friends who have expressed their opinion on the point of course I agree with you also that man's superiority, if it is that, over the brute creation, consists in his capacity for observing *brahmacharya.* It must therefore be an Ashram ideal to be attained immediately if that were possible.

There is therefore complete agreement between us so far as the fundamental thing is concerned. The difficulty or the difference comes in when we begin to devise ways and means of encompassing the ideal.

I am becoming more and more confirmed in the view that it must go on as it is now doing, with ample liberty to the manager to regulate fresh admissions. Our life should become daily simpler and not more complex. We should be progressively more self-restrained. But we should remain a composite family that we now are. The present composition is not the hindrance. The hindrance is that we have so few real complete *brahmacharis.* All were broken vessels, all had their own individual passions to conquer. But I hold that most of them were and are sincere strivers. Therefore we are blind leaders of the blind and ever stumbling. When some of us have, by constant striving, become at least matriculates in the effort, we shall certainly do better. Therefore the problem resolves itself into each one of us striving to the utmost to approach the ideal. Remember my definition of *brahmacharya.* It means not suppression of one or more senses but complete mastery over them all. The two states are fundamentally different. I can suppress all my senses today but it may take aeons to conquer them. Conquest means using them as my willing slaves. I can prick the ear-drum and suppress the sense of hearing by a simple, painless operation. This is worthless. I must train the ear so that it refuses to hear gossip, lewd talk, blasphemy, but it. Is open to the celestial music, it will hear the most distant cry for succour from thousands of miles. Saint Ramdas is said to have done so. Then how (to) use the organs of generation ? By transmuting the most creative energy that we possess from creating counterparts of our flesh into creating constructive work for the whole of life i.e., for the soul. We have to rein in the animal passion and change it into celestial passion. Read here Chapter II, Verse 64, of the *Gita.* The burden of the Divine Song is not "fly from the battle but face it without attachment". Therefore you and I and everyone of us have to stand unmoved in the midst of all kinds of men and women. There is no physical seclusion except temporarily for some. The Ashram is all right where it is but we must branch out for larger growth. But that would be a natural evolution coming in its own time.

Love from us all,
Bapu

14. Letter to Mirabehn

May 8, 1933

Chi. Mira,

It is now 3.10 a.m. and I have finished my first letter. That is to Andrews. Not only I but we are all thinking of you. People write to me or speak to me about you suggesting that I should abandon the fast for your sake. It is a great tribute to your love for me but also an unintended reflection. I want myself and everyone who knows you to feel that your love is so deeply true and knowing that it can stand the strain of physical separation no matter of what duration. I know that this will come, is coming. It cannot come through reason. It will come through the heart. Essential love depends wholly on the spiritual part, though it at first comes through the sense perception. I want you to feel with me. That this fast is a gift greater than God has ever made to me. That I approach it in fear and trembling is a sign of my weak faith. But this time there is in me a joy which I have not known before. I want you to share that joy with *me.*

Do not therefore deprive yourself of any food. Eat your food thankfully and keep yourself fit for service. Time for you may come when you might have to take up a similar fast. Under certain circumstances it is the one weapon which God has given us for use in times of utter helplessness. We do not know its use or fancy that it begins and ends with mere deprivation of physical food. It is nothing of the kind. Absence of food is an indispensable but not the largest part of it. The largest part is the prayer—communion with God. It more than adequately replaces physical food. Mahadev will drop you a line, as far as possible, daily.

May God give you strength.

Love,
Bapu

(PS.)

Letter for Ba herewith.

(PPS.)

I hope you got my letter written on Saturday. One was sent to Ba also.

15. Letter to Mirabehn

Parnakuti, Poona 6,
June 7, 1933

Chi. Mira,

I must not write. The last letter that I wrote to you caused much strain upon the hand. I am, therefore, dictating this letter, in reply to yours of the 5th instant.

You say that the brief sentence[20] I wrote at the end of the letter written by Mahadev, gave you pangs. It is wonderful how we create misery for ourselves where there is not even the slightest cause. My sentence had reference to your fever, which you yourself had said was due to over-anxiety on your part. You had explicitly mentioned that you were ill able to bear the separation. It was in answer to this that I wrote that sentence. It had reference only to enforced separation. There was no thought whatsoever that you should live out of sight even when it was possible for you to be with me, that is, if we were both not imprisoned. Of course, in that case, you would be most naturally with me. But to be out of prison is not my natural life. My natural life is that of a prisoner and therefore I suggest that you should learn to do without my physical presence. Is not this as clear as daylight ?

I do not like this loss of weight by you. There is something radically wrong in your carrying this load of anxiety on your shoulders. It is incompatible with a living faith in a living God. As days pass I feel this living presence in every fibre of my vein. Without that feeling I should be demented. There are so many things that are calculated to disturb my peace of mind. So many events happened that would, without the realization of that presence, shake me to the very foundation. But they pass me by leaving me practically untouched. I want you to share that reality with me. Then you would not be disturbed because you cannot be physically near me. Remember that no heroic effort is necessary in order to be able to bear such enforced separation, as you and I have to put up with. Millions of human beings do so without any effort. Do not make the mistake of thinking that they bear such separation because their nature is not sensitive to such things. If we would examine them we would find that they are just as sensitive as you and I are likely to be. Only they have a natural faith in God of which they have not even the knowledge. Ours is, beside theirs, a laboured faith. Hence we have to put forth a Herculean effort to bear separation. Anyway that is my analysis of your mentality. If it is not true you will make your own analysis and somehow or other cure yourself of the terrible anxiety. Carefully ponder over Krishna's discourses in the second chapter of the *Gita.* Then go to the twelfth chapter, and see whether you cannot find real peace and calmness of mind. Do not try to give me a detailed reply to this argument of mine. I do not want you to go through that strain. I have advanced the argument simply to soothe you, if at all I can. I know that argument is vain when one's whole being is in rebellion against itself. Perhaps the painful process through which you are passing is preliminary to the coming realization of the living presence of God. May it be so. Anyway do not again allow the thought to cross your mind that there is any question whatsoever of your having to live in separation from me when we both find ourselves out of prison.

Now about myself. I am flourishing. Rebuilding the body at the age of 64 must be a slow process, and I see that it will be slower than I had expected. Yet recovery is steady. I am taking easily 24 oz. of milk. I am trying to go to 2 lb. and may, under Dr. Dinshaw Mehta's care, do even better. I am entirely satisfied with the way I am progressing. Besides milk I take oranges and juice of three to four pomegranate(s). I am taking also a fair quantity of honey, perhaps 4 oz. Up to yesterday, I was taking vegetable soup. Dr. Mehta has stopped it from today in order to increase the quantity of milk. So you see that there is nothing to grumble about my food, and the way I am progressing.

You complain of sultry weather there. Here we have delicious cool weather. Of course, Poona is ideal in the rainy season. Devdas will be married to Lakshmi on the 16th; that is the date when the religious ceremony will be gone through. But as this will be a marriage in breach of the present Hindu usage, there will be also a civil registration on the 21st. Jamnalalji is trying to fix up a match for Prabhudas also. If it comes off, he too would be married about the same date. Ramdas is here; not at all keeping well. His body largely depends upon his mental state and he has not yet found his peace of mind. Jamnalalji is going to mother him. Probably that will pull him through. He will be living in Wardha with his wife. N. seems to be shaping well. Margarete Spiegel, who is named Amala, is as mad as a mad-hatter. But what was one to do ? She simply came and one had to take her. She is a good woman. But it remains to be seen how she shapes. Both N. and Amala are to do Harijan work. I think I have now given you enough for the week.

Love,
Bapu

16. Letter to Mirabehn

May 3, 1938

I like your letter for its transparent love. It tells me nothing new, but it comes at a moment when I am most receptive. The problem however is not so simple as you have put it. If complete *brahmacharya* under the conditions I am trying is like an attempt to climb the craters in the moon. What is the value of the species that requires the nine fortifications ?[21] You are quite right in describing my experiment as new. So is my experiment in *ahimsa*. The two hang together. Remember that my experiment has natural limitations. I may neither tempt God nor the Devil. I have not the time to prolong the argument. In your next letter you must tell me in concrete terms what definite changes I should make so as to fit in with your idea. Should I deny myself the service rendered by Sushila ? Should I refuse to have *malish*[22] by Lilavati or Amtul Salaam for instance ? Or do you want to say that I should never lean on girls' shoulders ? Needless to say you won't pain me at all by telling me frankly whatever you think I should do to get out of the terrible despondency. Just now I am most in need of support from those who surround me with service and affection, undeserved as it seems to me, for the time being. In guiding me remember that what I am doing I have done all my life you may say. And my *brahmacharya* has become firmer and more enlightened. Of course, I have been far away from perfection. But I felt I was progressing. That degrading, dirty, torturing experience of 14th April shook me to bits and made me feel as if I was hurled by God from an imaginary paradise where I had no right to be in my uncleanliness.

Well, I shall feel pride in my being parent to so many children, if any of them will give a lifting hand and pull me out of the well of despair. My faith in myself and my experiment will revive and will burn all the brighter.

Love,
Bapu

17. Letter to Mirabehn

May 12, 1938

Your letter is most helpful. I would have called it perfect if there had not been the usual exaltation. But I have no time to dissect your letter. Your own experience settles me. I must change my manners. There will be considerable response to your suggestions. I have been daily taxing myself about my course of action. I am not yet certain what shape the change will take.

About Lilavati I can't recall anything of what you say. But once I felt that I had put my arm around her neck. I asked her in the morning. She said she had no knowledge of any touch. Nevertheless from that day I asked her to sleep at a proper distance. Give me more details about the incident you relate.

You will continue to make whatever suggestions may occur to you. I must not interrupt the experiment, but there is room for revision. My problem is: "Had the awful experience of the 14th April anything to do with the contacts or has it any other meaning ?"

Love (in great haste),
Bapu

18. Letter to Mirabehn

July 3, 1941

Chi. Mira,

Your note. I missed you last night and yet was I wishing that you would not come. When I learnt that Undhru was sent to you, I thought you were being attended (to). On inquiry just now, I find that only Undhru was sent. I hear just now that Undhru was sent with full instructions. Nevertheless I am sending Puri to see how you are faring, You will break your silence to speak to him.[23]

Love,
Bapu

19. Letter to Mirabehn

Sunder Bun, Juhu,
June 12, 1944

Dear Miss Slade,

There is nothing wrong about being formal. "Familiarity breeds contempt." The letters will not be destroyed. I have nothing to be ashamed of. I wrote after intense prayer. My language failed to transmit the love and the greatest goodwill that prompted it. The only regret is that I dared to be familiar. My love would have been as true as now if I had refused to call you by any other name than Miss Slade. I like the English coldness and correctness. But my regret is superficial. The change is good and substantial. I have given the warning. You have no reason to change your course because of any opinion I express. What I did was to suggest your waiting. But you need not since it does not commend itself to you. Yes, time and action will show what we are and what we meant. I have patience.

Yours,
M.K. Gandhi

20. Letter to Mirabehn

As From Kazirkhil, Ramgunj Post,
Noakhali District,
Camp: Chandipur,
January (2/6)[24], 1947

Chi. Mira,

Your registered letter is in front of me. The news will be given to you by Parasuram together with this letter. I simply dictate to say that the position you adumbrate is the correct thing. Everything depends upon one's purity in thought, word and deed, using the word 'purity' in its widest sense. Then there may be no cause for even so much as a headache. Only get hold of this fundamental fact. We often loosely use the word 'purity' and excuse all sorts of lapses. Do not ever worry how I am faring or what I am doing here. If I succeed in emptying myself utterly, God will possess me. Then I know that everything will come true but it is a serious question when I shall have reduced myself to zero. Think of 'I' and 'O' in juxtaposition and you have the whole problem of life in two signs. In this process you have helped me considerably for, though at a distance, you seem to be doing your duty to the fullest extent possible in your field[25] of work. This was dictated four days ago when I was resting in bed. But it remained untyped. Meantime your another letter and samples of *khadi* have been received. Have you any *khadi* to spare for sale ? I make this inquiry for the sake of the refugees. Do not overdo things. Do not overwork. "Be careful for nothing."[26] The pilgrimage on foot commences tomorrow. There may be then no letter to you. A bulletin will be sent to you. This I am scribbling in the early morning. "Blessed are they that expect nothing."

Love,
Bapu

21. Letter to Mirabehn

Birla House, New Delhi,
January 16, 1948

Chi. Mira,

I got your letter yesterday. Evidently when you wrote it, you had no knowledge of this, my greatest fast. Whether it will ultimately prove so or not is neither your concern nor mine. Our concern is the act itself, not the result of the action. The fast was commenced as usual with a service, part of which was singing of "When I survey"[27]. It was well sung by Sushila. There were some good friends at the service. The company was impromptu. No one was invited. I am dictating this immediately after the 3.30 a.m. prayer and while I am taking my meal such as a fasting man with prescribed food can take. Don't be shocked. The food consists of 8 ozs. of hot water sipped with difficulty. You sip it as poison, well knowing that in result it is nectar. It revives me whenever I take it. Strange to say, this time I am able to take about 8 meals of this poison-tasting but nectar-like meal. Yet I claim to be fasting and credulous people accept it. What a strange world !

I shall watch and see how you can keep two typists constantly at their typewriters. If it is only self-deception and the typists a fraud on you, you will succumb and fall ill in the midst of attractive surroundings of your own choice. One man claims that oil-cakes are easier to make, cheaper in the end, and yet as effective as compost which requires a fair amount of technical skill for a *kisan*. Your description of Goswami's Goshala is tragic, if true. It is enough to make one despair of the cow, the mother of prosperity, receiving her due in a country accused of cow worship. There is no *swaraj* in such a land.

Your describing the Ashram as "Pashulok" is a magnificent idea. It is poetic. Don't ever write Pashulok Ashram. Ashram—Pashulok with a dash in between is good. Though now that I am thinking over it a little more deeply, Pashulok Ashram perhaps better represents your idea. Since, however, it is your excellent idea that is to be carried out, your choice is to be final.

I see that you are destined for serving the cow and nothing else. But I seem to see a vital defect in you. You are unable to cling to anything finally. You are a gipsy, never happy unless you are wandering. You will not become an expert in anything and your mother is also likely to perish in your lap. The only person and that a woman who really loves the cow will fail her. Shall I pity you, the cow or me, for I, the originator of the real idea of serving and saving the cow for humanity, have never cared or perhaps never had the time to become even a moderate expert. Satis Babu is better than you and me. He adopted the idea and has become a fair expert, in fact the real source of milk among Muslims, not Hindus in Bengal. It is he who has produced with amazing labour and concentration the only classic we have on (the) cow. He is a genius. I bow my head before him. Correspondence with him will give you something.

Don't rush here because I am fasting. The *yajna,* as I have called it, demands that everyone, wherever he or she is, should perform his or her duty. If an appreciable number do this, I must survive the ordeal. Trust God and be where you are. Pursue Goswami.[28]

NOTES

1. b. 1892; Gandhiji gave her the name Mirabehn; joined Gandhiji's Ashram in November 1925; accompanied Gandhiji to London for Round Table Conference in 1931; suffered several terms of imprisonment during India's struggle for freedom.
2. For the text of the letter, *vide* Appendix "Letter from Madeleine Slade", 29-5-1925.
3. From the postmark.
4. In Devnagari in the source.
5. *ibid.*
6. The name is not quite legible.
7. Of the *Autobiography*; *vide* "Letter to Mirabehn", 6-12-1926.
8. Motilal Nehru.
9. Jamnalal Bajaj's wife.
10. From the postmark.
11. The superscription in this and other letters to Mirabehn is in Devanagari.
12. The superscription in this and other letters to Mirabehn is in Devanagari script.
13. Gandhiji had reproached the addressee for being over-anxious about his health.
14. Ignorant attachment.
15. *Ishopanishad,* 11.
16. The names have been omitted.
17. *ibid.*
18. This and the subsequent names in the letter have been omitted.
19. The specialist at London who had treated Mirabehn for tubercular glands in 1907. *Vide* "Letter to Dr. Arthur Saunders", 5-3-1933.
20. *Vide* "Letter to Mirabehn", 3-6-1933.
21. The reference is to the nine rules of behaviour known as "the nine-fold hedge or wall" for the protection of *brahmacharya.*
22. Massage.
23. In *Bapu's Letters to Mira,* in a note placed before a letter of September 7, 1940, the addressee explains: "The inner struggle had come to a crisis and such bewildering and delusive mists and fogs had enveloped my path that, in my anguish, I went into silence and seclusion that I might the better pray to God for help. The silence, with a few days' breaks for travelling, lasted 15 months. For part of the time my rule was to speak once a day for half an hour, if necessary, and for the rest

of the time when I was in a cottage in the Sevagram fields, I spoke twice a week in the evening when I went to see Bapu."

24. Inferred from the contents; the source, however, has "January 4, 1947".
25. Up to here the letter is typewritten; what follows is in Gandhiji's hand.
26. *Philippians,* iv, 6.
27. A hymn by Isaac Watts.
28. This letter remained undespatched due to oversight and was sent hurriedly, when discovered, without being signed by Gandhiji, on January 19, 1948.

Chapter 6

Lilavati Asar

Lilavati Asar, the long time associate of Gandhi from 1929 to1948 lived in Ashram. She studied at Ashram. Gandhi used to tutor her personally. Gandhi called her by nickname 'a limpet'. Gandhi was her mentor. By nature she was quarrelsome, lonely person. Due to her nature no body loved her. Gandhi was quite concerned about her. She used to acompany Gandhi. She also played an important role in Gandhi's experiment of *brahmacharya*. She used to give service to Gandhi. She dedicated her life in the cause of her mentor Gandhi and libration of India from foreign rule.

She participated in freedom struggle. She also actively participated in Quit India Movement of 1942.

1. Letter to Lilavati

Bareilly,
June 13, 1929

Chi. Lilavati,

I could not reply to your letter earlier; I had absolutely no time. Whatever you would do rests solely on your strength. My only advice could be that you can do whatever you would, after satisfying your uncle who, you say, has such great affection for you. If you wish to take some step in spite of his dissatisfaction, it must be subject to two conditions. It should proceed with restraint and be prompted by the inner voice. The bonds of kinship too slacken before the inner voice. All the same one ought to know that the inner voice is very often wrongly interpreted.

Blessings from
Bapu

2. Letter to Lilavati Asar

Yeravda Mandir,
June 30, 1930

Chi. Lilavati,

I have your letter. From here I cannot send you a letter in a sealed envelope. But what is there to hide for one who has a pure heart ? You should throw away the letter you have received. After having once given up the thought of marriage, why think about the matter again ? Moreover, for you now true marriage lies in clinging to the duty to which you have wedded yourself. It is only in such marriage that true happiness is found. It gives rise to no problem and there is no possibility of widowhood in it. So you should dismiss the thought altogether from your mind. Meditate on the last portion of the second chapter of the *Gita* which we daily recite. If this does not help you to feel at peace you may write to me again and you should have no hesitation in writing freely. Forget the past. Take care of the present, and the future will then take care of itself. This is the meaning, plain and simple, of non-attachment. If we do our duty today, we shall automatically know our duty tomorrow.

Blessings from
Bapu

3. Letter to Lilavati Asar

January 23, 1932

Chi. Lilavati,

I have your letter. We at least could see each other, but what about the other women who could not even see me ? However, I should have realized your eagerness and sent a special slip for you. Have it now. I should advise you not to exert yourself beyond your capacity. However, God will look after you all. Remember the first verse of the women's prayer. It has universal application. You should not think that it is a prayer which was offered by someone thousands of years ago.

All of us are helpless, as Draupadi was. Before God such distinctions as man and woman lose all meaning. The same *atman* dwells in the man's and in the woman's body. In our infatuated state, we are deluded by the different bodily forms and are even overcome by passion. If we know the soul living within and, realizing that all individualselves are essentially one and the same, devote ourselves to the service of all, no disturbing thoughts would attack us and harass us.

Blessings from
Bapu

4. Letter to Lilavati Asar

October 23, 1932

Chi. Lilavati,

I do not wish to improve you by confining you in a cage. I have faith in you. You have refrained from remarrying out of your own volition. You have come to the Ashram on your own. You will rise by your own strength. Therefore, do whatever you think proper. Come to the Ashram and stay there as if it was your father's house. Of course, even in one's father's house rules must be followed. You can consider yourself totally free and leave the Ashram. Whatever you do, do after due consideration. I regard Mridu's company as *satsang* for you. Whatever outward impression she may give, she is saintly girl.

May God bless you.
Bapu

5. Letter to Lilavati Asar

March 22, 1933

Chi. Lilavati[1],

You are a silly girl. Would you feel hurt if I told you that I tolerated you because you were a good girl and that I would take no interest in you if you were a bad girl ? If not, then why should you be hurt by what I said ? My remarks were prompted only by love. I expressed my love by saying that I tolerated you in spite of your unsettled state because your intentions were good, but you misunderstood my remark completely. What is one to do to a person who thus displays his or her ego ? You should know that by learning some work or by studying you may become self-supporting, but you cannot be sure that that will make you good. On the other hand, if you become good, mentally strong, and healthy in body, then your character will be sound and you will become self-supporting also. This does not mean that you should not study further or learn a craft. Do that in the Ashram as much as you can during spare time and be satisfied. Engrave in your heart the golden rule that devotion to duty includes everything else. For the present, only do this much, have full faith in Narandas and follow his advice. Do not look upon your money as your own but regard yourself as a trustee. You should not, therefore, spend it even on buying fruit for me, since I get fruit from the other people. It is the Harijans who need the money most.

Keep it for them.

Bapu

6. Letter to Lilavati Asar

July 6, 1935

Chi. Lilavati,

I got your very strange and sad letter. Only two days ago I had from you a letter full of hope, which gave me an impression that you were now completely composed. But today's letter seems to have been written by another Lilavati as it were. How did such a profound change take place in just two days' time ? You are staying in Rajkot of your own free will. I had even suggested that you might study in Bombay. It has always been my wish that you should not overstrain yourself. What has happend all at once to fill you with such profound despair ? If you find the atmosphere there full of selfishness, it will hardly be different anywhere else. It is in your hands to create and preserve the atmosphere that you desire. Have patience and be calm. But if your patience and endurance are exhausted, leave Rajkot by all means. You are entirely free. The relationship with me does not clip anybody's wings. On the contrary, it gives fresh wings to a person if he has none. Hence, you can fly wherever you want to. Whether you can stay with me here is a different question altogether. We shall think over it if an opportunity occurs. Do not ever give up Narandas's protection. You will repent if you do that. I cannot suggest a better guide for you than he is.

Blessings from
Bapu

7. Letter to Lilavati Asar

Wardha Hospital,
September 10, 1936

Chi. Lilavati,
I understand from Mahadev that you have developed a dislike for Segaon, and whenever you think of the place you become miserable. You have lost your peace of mind. Since you had taken a decision, you want to spend a year somehow with me. I had known this all along. Now it is all the more clear I must consider now what my duty is. For me to seek forgiveness from children is nothing new. The most

recent example is that of Kusum. If you do not know about it ask her. Perhaps even Mahadev can tell you. If I had reason to ask Kusum's forgiveness, I have still more reason to ask your forgiveness. I thought I was protecting you like a flower. Whether you were aware of it or not, despite all the harsh words I threw at you, I was protecting you against attacks from others. But I set no store by it. What has value is the impression made on you. Judging by that standard, I acknowledge my failure. Forgive me for the unhappiness I caused you. I shall not let such a situation be repeated. But now I have lost self-confidence. You do not have to ask your freedom from me. But you have to free yourself of me. Or, say, I have to give you your freedom. Only a few can learn from me by being physically near me.

Countless persons have been able to do that while being away from me. You are one of them. If you wish to learn something from me while being away, I am willing to teach you regularly through letters. Your coming to Segaon is going to benefit neither you nor me. I shall have to be constantly on my guard if I take you with me. You would not like me to be in such a pitiable state. The situation in which parents have to guard themselves from children is always to be avoided. So you should give up your insistence on coming to Segaon. There is no reason to be unhappy about it. There is no reason for you to feel ashamed as you are not giving up Segaon. In despair I am making you give up Segaon. Respect this wish of mine in good cheer. It is my duty and yours to avoid a situation in which you may break down at the end of a year and your heart may be filled with contempt for me. How can I explain this better ? I particularly wish that you should go to Rajkot and help Narandas. You have hardly any place now at Maganwadi. The kitchen is being discontinued. What would you do in that event ? There is no provision at all at Maganwadi to accommodate women. Of course, you may stay in the Mahila Ashram. But Mahadev will guide you in this regard. I urge you once again that you should forget the unhappiness you have suffered at Segaon.

Blessings from
Bapu

8. Letter to Lilavati Asar

September 15, 1936

Chi. Lilavati,

You are still a bad girl. You would not shoulder the little burden placed on you. This shows the stuff you are made of. I have told you that you may give me a pleasant one hour, You should not create a scene with me. Know that the more you persist in your ways, the further you push your coming to Segaon. You know best if all this is but a trick to avoid coming. How heartless of you that even for the sake of my peace you would not agree to stay five miles away !

Blessings from
Bapu

9. Letter to Lilavati Asar

8.25 p.m.,
September 18, 1936

Chi. Lilavati,

I am alarmed by your last sentence. If you think of going to a school after a year, the worthwhile thing is to begin now. One may start one's studies any time, but it ought to be painful to you as well as to me if you have to flee Segaon in disappointment and join a school. Search your heart and shake off your folly. Satisfy your hunger for learning. At Segaon, what can you have except the drudgery and my temper ? I cannot help fearing that you will not find your stay here bearable. I spend a good deal of my time thinking of your welfare. Not that I grudge it. But it should be intolerable for both you and me if in the end you have to give me up in disappointment. If you must come to Segaon, it is for you to determine how soon it can be done. Read my instructions again and again and carry them out cheerfully. Remove all ill-will from your mind. If you resent someone with whom you have to deal everyday, how will you be happy with me ? How shall I be at peace ? Isn't this quite easy to understand ? There is never any shame in doing the right thing.

Blessings from
Bapu

10. Letter to Lilavati Asar

September 20, 1936

Chi. Lilavati,

I have read your letter very carefully. If you could only have some idea of my anxiety about you, you would become straightened as a cane, curb the wild horse of your imagination and become absorbed in the work entrusted to you. I do not trust you and hence you cannot be at Maganwadi. I am anxious about you because I have expectations of you. I am thinking what my duty towards you is. If at Segaon you can mix as sugar does with milk, even if you wanted to I would not let you go. You must admit that you do not have that strength right now. But all will come right in time. Be patient. I have understood the purport of your letter. It contains a few misunderstandings. But I have no time to clear them. It is not ever necessary. Do read *Prithvivallabh* again. And let me know about the effect it has on you.

Blessings from
Bapu

11. Letter to Lilavati Asar

September 22, 1936

Chi. Lilavati,

I have finished *Prithvivallabh*[2]. I am now sending it to you. Read it carefully but quickly, and let me know what you think of it. The book belongs to Kakasaheb. Be careful not to soil it. Don't make any marks in it. The ones you will find in it are not made by me. We should never make any marks in other people's books. I got your letter yesterday and the *slokas* you have copied out. How can the *slokas* convey any meaning to you unless you spend some time to understand them ? Shouldn't we exercise the mind a little ? The work I have given you so far is the least and the easiest. Today also I dreamt of you. What a sorry state. How nice it would be if I did not have to worry on your account !

Blessings from
Bapu

12. Letter to Lilavati Asar

October 6, 1936

Chi. Lila,

Is it any less *lila* that from Lila you have become Lilavati again ? What would have been my plight had you become Lili ?[3] I like your decision. It was beyond your capacity to remain with me. I hope you will always carry my blessings with you wherever you are. You may certainly stay away from me but don't forget me altogether. Your reason for leaving me is unusual. What do you ask to be forgiven for ? Have you committed any fault ? If you have, the proper atonement would be not to abandon me but to cling to me with greater resolve, to conduct yourself in conformity with it and show greater watchfulness. However, a correct decision, though taken for a wrong reason, is always welcome, and this applies to this decision of yours. Consult Mahadev in taking whatever step you may choose to take. Yesterday you could see my anger, but couldn't you see my unbearable pain—couldn't you read my love ?

Blessings from
Bapu

13. Letter to Lilavati Asar

October 1938

Chi. Lila,

I hope you are bringing credit to me and yourself there. Give no thought to my experiment. I have started the experiment to be able to render greater service to womankind. That includes you. In a note written in jest and a little anger, I called you 'Lila'. You liked it. Your father used to call you 'Lili', and so you demanded that I should also call you 'Lili'. For, you had started showing me the same affection as you did for your father. That alone would make your love for me greater than that for your father. If you cannot understand this, ask Mahadev. Replying to one of his letters, I had told him that I would call you 'Lili' when I had qualified myself to do that. This experiment is also to gain that eligibility because you are also a woman. While being there, think that you are with me not because you have gone there to do your work, but because I have sent you there to do my work. And my work means that you should relieve Mahadev's burden as much as possible. Hence, do not waste Mahadev's time talking about your happiness or unhappiness. Your duty is to go on doing unquestioningly whatever work Mahadev or Durga may entrust to you or what you can carry out yourself. And you will do your work silently because I cannot give you here what you would be able to learn there. It is true that you cannot gain there what you can gain here. But since I have sent you there to do my work, you will easily get the benefit of having stayed with me.

Eat well and build up your body. If you do that you can occasionally come here for a brief visit. But do not keep waiting for opportunities to come here. Devote yourself to putting things in perfect order there. You have got to give time to Bablo. Do write to me whenever you wish. And whenever you write, try to make your handwriting beautiful. Do not write with a pencil. And do not follow Mahadev's example of writing with a fountain-pen. I tolerate Mahadev's fountain-pen because Mahadev is a scribe. You are not a scribe and are not going to be one. So, I shall not, and I should not tolerate the fountain-pen in your case.

Blessings from
Bapu

14. Letter to Lilavati Asar

December 9, 1938

Chi. Lila,

I was very much pained by today's incident. But how could you help your nature ?

However, my purpose in writing this is different. I have noticed that you and Amtul Salaam cannot tolerate S. sleeping with me. Whatever may be the cause, I do not want to carry on my experiment by displeasing you two. I, therefore, want to tell both of you that I have discontinued my experiment for the present. The fault is not yours. I believe it is entirely mine. But I do not wish to discuss the matter with you, nor do I want you to reply. I have simply informed you.

Show this letter to Amtul Salaam.

Blessings from
Bapu

(PS.)

I wanted to write and give this letter in the morning, but I could find no time.

15. Letter to Lilavati Asar

Segaon, Wardha,
August 9, 1939

Chi. Lila,

I have your letter. I see no need for girls to go begging on the Balev Day or on any other occasion. Their services should not be used in this manner. Collecting money is the work of the management. Keep yourself fully absorbed in your study. Do not be restless. Do your best and be content with the outcome.

Why did you take quietly what Dr. Mehta told you ? Suppose he had been only joking ? If there was any sting in it, you could have removed it. You could have asked whether a daughter sleeping by the side of her father and a girl in an institution lying on top of another were the same thing. I think your keeping quiet itself implies your admission of some guilt. Your previous letter, however, suggests some feeling of shame about what is happening. In that case you would of course not be able to say anything. How can you, then, blame Dr. Jivraj ? Even if somebody makes an offensive remark about me, it produces no effect on me whatever. But if I ever do something blameworthy, I would shrink into myself with shame even if nobody criticized me.

Blessings from
Bapu

16. Letter to Lilavati Asar

Mahabaleshwar,
May 13, 1945

Chi. Lili,

I read your letter just now. They handed it to me without opening it. But I am going to give it to Narahari, Pyarelal, Munnalal and Hemantkumar to read. That letter is a mirror of your soul. You have always been, and still are, silly. Remember the verse: "Dwelling in thought on *vishayas*."[4] Here *vishaya* does not mean merely what it does in Gujarati, namely immoral sex-pleasure. All objects of desire are *vishayas*, as for example, desiring what appeals to the eye, hearing with the ear, smelling with the nose, and other similar objects of sense. Your object of desire is to come to the hills. If it didn't materialize you should forget about it. But you would not be Lili if you could forget anything. And that is why you suffer. Otherwise there are few other women as fortunate as you. Though married in the prime of your youth, you have remained a virgin all these years so that all the desire in you for that momentary pleasure has been burnt away. You like service and get opportunities for it. The best service you rendered was to Bhansali, then to Ramprasad and then to Krishnachandra. I will not consider your services to Ba, Mahadev and myself as there was attachment in that.

You are educating yourself to be a doctor entirely with the aim of dedicating yourself to public service. What purer happiness than this could one have ? If you are still discontented, does it not mean that you are silly ?

Hoshiari wishes to come to me, and so does Vina. And there is no limit to the number of men who wish to come. If they cannot come, does it mean that they are unfortunate ? You should completely burn up this desire of yours. Hence, though from one point of view your letter is good, from another point of view it is one that you should withdraw, and that too, cheerfully. You must pass, and do so with credit. Afterwards you will be serving to your heart's content. And you do get opportunities from time to time, such as serving uncle. Sushila is there. Pyarelal is leaving tomorrow.

Blessings from
Bapu

17. Letter to Lilavati Asar

May 25, 1945

Chi. Lili,

Your letter lacks spirit and is worthless. It is only a timetable of your work. I am sending it after signing. You must get rid of your pride. There was nothing to feel shy about in your letter. You explained to me your condition in a simple manner and that is why I used my prerogative. Whatever I think worth keeping confidential, I keep confidential. But a person who has faith in God should never keep his personal matters confidential. Confidential means most personal. "Renounce and enjoy" includes "confidential" also. We may enjoy (a thing) only after renouncing it. If you can't understand this, then I can say that your education has been in vain and without any thinking.

Blessings from
Bapu

18. Letter to Lilavati Asar

November 16, 1945

Chi. Lilavati,

I have your postcard. You must give up the craving for letters in my handwriting. I am dictating this lying down in the evening after the prayers. Sometimes two line suffice, but at times I have to write at length. You had better leave it to me when I should write myself or when and to whom I should dictate.

Now that you have started the exercise4 do not give it up. You can go up to 108 *namaskars*. Many *asanas* can be performed while doing *suryanamaskar*. It is largely for you to see which ones will suit you best. Consider also whether you should go up to 108 *namaskars*. There is no point in losing weight by starving. One has to reduce weight if one has put on any because of some disease, but that too not by starving oneself. If even with regular exercise and balanced diet you put on weight, let it be so. You need not worry about it in the least.

You have used the word 'stunt' in a wrong context. You can translate it as *dhating* in Gujarati. The changes in diet or other methods adopted for reducing weight cannot be called stunt. Those who digest what they have studied keep on pursuing the study in order to acquire more knowledge without even thinking about the examination results. While studying they build up their bodies as best they can because keeping the body healthy, strong and lustrous is also a part of learning. I give you full encouragement to study what you have undertaken not for the sake of getting a degree but for the knowledge that you will acquire while studying for it. Since you have already studied Gray[5] once, it should be a mere child's play to go through it a second time. The oftener you read it, the more knowledge you will gain.

It will be good if you give up the habit of walking about as you read. It spoils the eyesight and sometimes the thoughts also wander. While walking one can think over and digest what one has read or think of the work one has done during the day, and so on. But the eyes have to look around and take note of the surroundings and watch out for any obstruction in one's way. One cannot walk with eyes closed but a person like me who walks with the support of others enjoys the pleasure of doing so. But that is not for you. Stick to your decision not to attend Lakshmidas's wedding. I have signed at two places. That shows how bad my memory is.

Blessings from
Bapu

19. Letter to Lilavati Asar

Kalpatali, East Bengal,
January 12, 1947

Chi. Lili,

Either I must dictate or give up the idea of writing. I do not like to do the latter, and hence I dictate, even though you had only asked for a few lines from Manu. I had you in mind in regard to the Harijan girl. However, consult Lilavati Munshi and if she knows of any educated Harijan girl who would be ready to marry a non-Harijan, ask her to write to me. I am glad that the other girl's problems has been solved and that she will now be able to complete her study. Complete your course, too. Avail yourself fully of the services of the excellent professors you have. That will be as good as your coming to me. You will later get abundant opportunity for service. If you had not taken up the course at all, it would have been a different matter. But having once taken up a project, one must see it through. Yes, if one has made a mistake in taking up something, one may rectify the mistake at any time. But you have committed no mistake in deciding to study. Had you done so, do you think I would have given my consent ? I not only gave my consent, but also arranged for the necessary facilities. For there is no shame in becoming a doctor. You should not, therefore, in the least degree feel bad. Manu will tell you the rest.

Blessings from
Bapu

20. Letter to Lilavati Asar

Patna,
April 24, 1947

Chi. Lili,

I have your letter. I have written to Su. at the hospital address. I did not remember Pya. Gupta's address.

You are silly. I have not forsaken you. When you feel that you can no longer stay away from me, come over. I myself am without any home just now. But come wherever I am. You have served Sushila but that's in your nature. Work hard without being impatient and read carefully and intelligently, and you will pass with good marks. There is no reason at all for you to give up hope or feel defeated. If you lose one year, there will be no harm. You will learn more.

Blessings from
Bapu

NOTES

1. A child widow who had joined Sabarmati Ashram in 1930. She later studied medicine at Bombay, worked in hospitals and took part in the national movement.
2. A Gujarati novel by K.M. Munshi.
3. *Vide* "Letter to Lilavati Asar", 2-10-1936.
4. *Bhagavad Gita.*
5. Henry Gray's *Anatomy of the Human Body.*

Chapter 7
Prema Kantak (1905-1985)

Prema Kantak, an ardent patriot, a scholar, a revolutionary and beautiful was born at Kanwar in 1905 in a Brahmin family. She was a brilliant and charming student with creative mind. She was a student of Wilson College and passed the B.A. examination of the Bombay University in 1928. She was very active in student movement and participated in public demonstrations against Simon Commission. She was elected to the Executive Council of the Bombay Presidency Youth League.

Like other women Prema's life was also full off ups and downs with tragedies. When she was only ten months old her mother died. She was brought up by mother's mother. She spent ten years there. Her father had already married twice. She was alone daughter out of five brothers. Being a only one girl she became attraction of every member of the family. When she reached marriageable age father and brother pressurized her to get marry. She revolted against father and decided not to marry. She was very beautiful and youthful. She decided not to marry.

For the first time she saw Mahatma Gandhi when she was in school. The first sight of Gandhi casted magic spell on the mind of Prema and with the passing of the time attraction towards Gandhi increased. She got an opportunity to see Gandhi in 1924 again. She passed M.A. examination in April 1929. She wrote letter to Mahatma Gandhi. On 25 May, 1929 she met Mahatma Gandhi in Bombay and next day she went with Mahatma Gandhi for Sabarmati Ashram. On 26 May, 1929 from railway station to ashram she went in the same car with Gandhi. She was put in charge of it by Gandhi and she managed it efficiently from 1929 to 1933.

Prema actively participated in Salt Satyagraha and arrested twice. After the release she shifted from Ahmedabad to Pune and was actively associated with the Constructive Programme. She devoted her life in propogation of Khadhi and Swadeshi and emancipation and empowerment of women. She was one of the prominent women *Satyagrahis* during the Individual Satyagraha started by Gandhi for resisting the war-effort of the British Government. Prema was arrested four times and sentenced to three months imprisonment each time. For some time she worked for Congress Seva Dal.

Gandhi had a high respect for Prema Kantak due to her courage, commitment and devotion. She was a scholar par excellence. She was a reputed literary figure in Maharashtra. Her correspondence with Gandhi on *brahmacharya* published in book form in Marathi, Prasad Diksha in 1938. This was followed by her next book *Kama* and *Kamini*.

She participated in Quit India Movement of 1942 and jailed for one and half years. In jail, she realized that the young women detenues were attracted more by militant. After the release she joined Shankarerrao Deo's Ashram at Saswad. Prema worked for Women Committee for Constructive Work till 1952. When she realized that women preferred active politics to constructive work, she then, observed a fact for seven days, blaming herself for this change in the attitude of women, and went to Himalayas, detaching herself from worldly things for peace of mind.

After return from Himalaya she return to Pune and took responsibility of Kasturba Ashram at Saswad. She successfully organized a movement for prohibition of liquor and succeeded in declaring four months in a year as dry-months. She led Matkabandi movement. She actively involved in bringing awakening among the women in rural areas and helps them to become self-dependant.

Prema left legacy and died in 1985 in Independent India as unsung heroin.

1. Letter to Premabehn Kantak

Yeravada Mandir,
August 29, 1930

Chi. Prema,

I got your letter. No one should be amused at my writing on slips of paper or be angry with me for that reason. That is the proper thing for me to do. Though I write on such slips, I try to make each letter as interesting as I can in the time I get.

Why are you alarmed by the suspicion that you have got some disease in your body ? What would it matter even if you had a disease and that too a grave one ? "The body may live or perish, what should endure is one's devotion to God."[1] We have learnt at least this in the Ashram, if nothing more. If you fast for a few days, the body will be cleansed. You require Kuhne baths, hip-baths and particularly friction sitz-baths. If you do not know about them, ask Kanta or Radha. I think they know. You may also read about them in Kuhne's book. Whenever women suffer from any disease, it becomes necessary to know the facts about their monthly periods. Are they normal with you ? Are they regular in appearance and duration ? Are they painful ? If necessary, consult a doctor.

I have not read Arvind Babu's book. I alone know how limited is my reading. My main interest is in reading the book of nature. I shall never finish reading it.

You should have enough sleep. You should observe the rule of sleeping from 9 to 4.

Blessings from
Bapu

2. Letter to Premabehn Kantak

Yeravada Mandir,
October 2, 1930

Chi. Prema,

If you wish, you may certainly keep the wooden sandals. But what will you do with those bits of wood ? Keep them if you think that they will add an inch or two to your stature. I would condemn your action as smacking of idolatry. I used to keep with me a photograph of my father. I had hung his photographs in the drawing-room and the bedroom when I was in South Africa. When I used to wear a chain, it had a locket which contained small photographs of my father and elder brother. I have now put them away. That does not mean that I feel less reverence for them now. In fact they are more deeply engraved in my heart today. I think of their virtues and try to cultivate them. I can worship countless gods in this manner. If I tried to keep with me photographs of them all, I would have no room to put them in. And if I tried to keep their wooden sandals, I should have to acquire a piece of land for the purpose. As a man of experience, I advise you, therefore, to follow me when I am walking on the right path. That will be a thousand times better than keeping my wooden sandals, and if anybody follows your example, I would welcome that. On the contrary, if anybody saw the sandals with you and followed your example blindly, would he not fall into a pit ? Think on this and then do what you wish.

He who understands and does his duty, his cravings have already left him. A person whose cravings have not left him has no sense of duty. Our cravings are like a huge mountain which no man can cross over by climbing. The only course for us is to raze the mountain to the ground. To give up our cravings is to become conscious of our duty. Suppose that I wish to go to Kashi. I even know the path which I should follow to reach it. What other craving, then, will force me to stray from that path ? I have no other craving but to reach Kashi, and that is satisfied. What more do I want then ? You have an opportunity for service which has come to you unsought. You should get fullest satisfaction in doing that service with single-minded devotion. Whatever opportunities for human company and for reading you get while doing that duty, may be availed of. Apart from that, you should desire nothing. This, according to me is yoga, "skill in works", "equimindedness" and *samadhi.*

If, however, all this seems idle preaching to you and you thirst for reading, by all means satisfy your craving. Reduce the burden of work on you and take rest. How you may do this, you can decide only in consultation with Narandas. He is a man of profound understanding, patience and goodness. He will certainly help you. What more can I say to cheer you ? A person like me can only suggest the direction which you should follow. It is on oneself, however, that you and everyone else should depend for peace of mind. I understand what you say about Sushila. In future, let her send her good wishes in Marathi. My blessings to her. I understand that after having enjoyed Panditji's music, a person like you will not enjoy music by anybody else. But why should you not, yourself, lead the *bhajans* ? If you have the courage to do so, ask them to let you do it. If you wish, I will write. You certainly know how to sing. I have not forgotten that you used to sing *bhajans* almost every night. How are your tonsils ? Did you get them examined by Dr. Haribhai ?

Blessings from
Bapu

3. Letter to Premabehn Kantak

Bardoli,
July 26, 1931

Chi. Prema,

I got your letter. You did not say how many years you had completed. I admit that I ought to know. But I am stupid in such matters. Instead of saying, 'May you live long', I will say, 'May you soon become free from the sway of passion, become pure in heart and an ideal worker. May you succeed in your striving.'

You have made your letter rich in both colours. It breathes frankness. I like it. But it is also full of anger and pride. I will not, however, comment on it in detail. I beg this of you. If you have not been writing up your diary, start doing so. With whom did you get angry during the day, whether it was a child or a grown up person whom did you beat, whom did you abuse ? I will be satisfied if you note down these details for my information. As for the rest, you and Narandas may do what you think best. I don't wish to interfere with what you do. It lies outside my sphere. For one thing, I would not be able to judge about it; I would not be able to do justice to the parties concerned, nor have I the means of doing so. I have assumed the role of your father and mother and, therefore, I can give you but one-sided advice. A *satyagrahi*, moreover, never demands justice. Justice means "measure for measure". Satyagraha means truth even against cunning, nonviolence against violence, forbearance against anger and love against hatred. Where, in such satyagraha, is room for dealing out justice ?

Blessings from
Bapu

(PS.)

I reach Borsad on Tuesday.
(From Gujarati)
Bapuna Patro—5: Ku. Premabehn Kantakne, p. 52. Also C.W. 6708.
Courtesy: Premabehn Kantak.

4. Letter to Premabehn Kantak

January 25, 1932

Chi. Prema,

I got your letter. I don't know whether I shall be able to describe to you all that you want to know.[2] I didn't know that Dhurandhar had become the King's guest. I very much enjoyed seeing the paintings in Rome, but what opinion can I give after a visit of two hours ? What is my competence to Judge ? And what is my experience in these matters ? I liked some of the pictures very much indeed. If I could spend two or three months there, I would go and see the paintings and sculptures everyday and study them attentively. I saw the sculpture of Jesus on the cross. I have already written and told you that it was this that attracted me most. I didn't feel, however, that the art of that country excelled that of India. The two have developed along different lines. Indian art is entirely a product of the imagination. European art is imitation of Nature. Probably this makes Western art easier to understand. But, maybe, after we have understood it, it keeps us glued to the earth, whereas the more we understand Indian art the more it lifts us above the earth. I have stated these views simply because I must say something to you. I put no great value on them. It is likely that my unconscious partiality for India makes me say this, or my ignorance makes me ride the horse of fancy. But anyone who rides such a horse is sure to fall ultimately.

Even so, if you can learn anything from these views you may. If you have risen beyond such things, leave them aside. Parents can freely tell their children, who know less than they, stories from the *Ramayana* and the *Mahabharata* in the manner they know best; I am in a similar position in this matter.

You will be able to see from this that I do take interest in art. But I have renounced, have had to renounce, many such interests. I have relished to my heart's content the joy which everything connected with the search for truth gives me, and I would be ready still to relish it in more of such things. Tasks come unsought to a votary of truth. That is why by nature he is equipped to follow the teaching of the third chapter (of the *Gita*). I believe I had been practising *karmayoga* even before I had read that chapter.

But I am straying, I am afraid, from the path. You have done well in putting me questions[3] about the Ashram. Work is given the chief place in the Ashram life, because it is man's duty to do body labour. Anyone who shirks it, eats stolen food. Moreover, the work which we do in the Ashram is as much for service as it is for one's own benefit. We have put the spinning-wheel in the centre of our activities, because for the millions in the country spinning is the only work we can think of as a universal supplementary occupation to agriculture. It subserves moral and economic ends alike.

The Ashram exists not only for the service of the country but, through it, for the service of the world and to help us to attain *moksha*, to see God, through such service.

Not everyone can join the Ashram. It is not an infirmary, not an orphanage. It is meant for men and women who have dedicated themselves to service, to the realization of a spiritual goal. Hence it is not meant for people who cannot do body labour. However, we may admit persons who are filled with the spirit of service but who are disabled in body. Of course, we can admit only a small number of such persons. And we certainly cannot ask those who joined the Ashram as regular members but who may have become disabled afterwards, to leave the Ashram. Outwardly, many of our actions in the Ashram may seem inconsistent but they will cease to appear so when examined more deeply. If you do not understand any point in this, you may ask me again. You may also express any other doubts which you may feel.

It was only rarely that I posed for a photograph while in England. I believe I have not violated my vow in doing that. It is certainly not my wish, nor is it desirable, that everyone who comes close to me should be like me in every respect. That would mean mechanical imitation. If anybody wishes to take from me what may seem good to him, it will help him only if he takes what he can assimilate. In any case, who can prevail upon Sardar to stop taking tea ?[4] And may it not be that tea serves as medicine to him ? Some persons who are close to me, who are my co-workers, are even meat-eaters ! What do you say to that ?

Only those with whom tea does not agree or who refrain from it because they have considered how it is grown will never take it. Though Ba lives with me, she does take tea. She takes coffee too. I would even offer them lovingly to her. Why ? I know, of course, that your question was good-humoured joking, but some false ideas and a degree of intolerance prevail among us in such matters and it is necessary to get rid of them. I don't know if you have this weakness, but it is desirable that you should know my views on this subject. There is much else in my other letters of this week; if you get an opportunity, read them and ponder over them.

Blessings from
Bapu

5. Letter to Premabehn Kantak

June 17, 1932

Chi. Prema,

What else am I to believe but that you are a fool ? If children have no interest in asking questions and still write, they waste their time. If they write with interest, though merely as a formality, there is some meaning in that. Children may not expect letters from parents, but are bound to be glad when they get one. There will be no trace of selfishness in this. In any case, you cannot see in this evidence of hysteria. I have explained to you in one of my letters what your hysteria is.[5]

I have not opposed contemplation of a personal form at the time of prayers, but have given a higher place to the formless. Perhaps it is not right to make such a distinction. What suits one person will not suit another. Comparison is out of place in this matter. For me worship of the formless has greater appeal. Your explanation regarding Sankara and Ramanuja does not seem correct.[6] Personal experience is more important than the influence of external circumstances. The latter should have no effect on a votary of truth. He ought to see beyond them. We often see that opinions formed on the basis of external circumstances are afterwards discovered to be wrong. The connection between the *atman*[7] and the body is a well-known instance of this. Because the *atman* is intimately connected with the body in this life, we cannot easily think of it as distinct from the body. No one has equalled the power of vision of the person who saw beyond this outward fact and first uttered: "Not this". You will be able to think of any number of such instances. It is not at all proper to take literally the utterances of Tukaram and other saints. Recently I read one such utterance of Tukaram. I quote it for your benefit. An image of Lord Pashupati is made out of clay: what, then, would clay called ?

The worship of the Lord reaches unto Him, the clay remains clay. An image of Vishnu is carved out of stone, yet the stone does not become Vishnu.

The devotion is offered to Vishnu, the stone remains a stone. From this, I draw the lesson that we should pay attention only to the idea behind the words of such saints. They may describe personal God and yet worship the formless. We ordinary human beings cannot do that and, therefore, we would come to grief if we do not try to understand their real meaning and guide ourselves by it. If a person who can read Urdu goes to Imam Saheb's house, he will soon find the books. You have there Mirabehn's Urdu-English and English-Urdu Dictionary. Send that, too, along with the other books. Does anyone clean Imam Saheb's house periodically ? Every unoccupied house should be cleaned once a week or a fortnight. You will find it difficult to keep an account of time only till it has become a habit with you to do so. Afterwards, it shouldn't take any time. Such things have a value and bear fruit only if they are done in the right spirit.

I cite the example of children in South Africa in order to encourage the children in the Ashram and not to find fault with them. These children, too, are capable of working, if we have anyone among us who knows how to take work from them. Aren't you there ? For the pain in your back, you should sit in warm water. You should do that for fifteen to twenty minutes. At the same time you should massage the back with your palm. If you do this, your pain will be cured and there will also be a beneficial effect on menstruation. Let me know what the doctor says. Such diseases should be effectively treated at the very first appearance of their symptoms. I carefully examined your daily programme of work. It is much too heavy. You can easily make a few cuts in it. From 12.30 to 5.40 you run a class and give instruction in crafts. That comes to five hours and ten minutes. If you reduce this period by one hour, you will get the free time which you need. You may retire into privacy and have a nap or simply lie down for one hour, or do some work which makes you feel that you are resting. You should not, however, spend the time in talking or in any serious work. If you do not wish to utilize the free hour just then, you may advance the time of those items of the programme for which it is convenient to do so and get an hour in the evening. Anyone who feels completely absorbed in his or her work does not feel it a burden or a strain, but to one who feels no interest in his work even a small task seems heavy, as a day seems as long as a year to a prisoner. To a person given to worldly enjoyments, a year seems as short as a day !

In the past, I used to get bored when listening to European music. It is only now that I can understand and enjoy it a little. You are not right when you say that "one should not hope to do any reading here."

It is quite true that you cannot do much reading. It is equally true that reading is given less importance in the Ashram. Even so, many persons in the Ashram have been able to do some reading. I do not like your expressions of despair. Try to perfect what you find imperfect. If, however, on the balance you feel that things are unsatisfactory, if, that is, after weighing the good points against the shortcomings, you feel that the latter exceed, you should leave the Ashram. Justice to oneself and to society requires that. You need not apologize for your long letters. They don't bore me; on the contrary, I like them. I learn something from them, for each of them mirrors the state of your heart at the time of writing it.

Bapu

6. Letter to Premabehn Kantak

June 23, 1932

Chi. Prema,

Among the Urdu books, are there two volumes by Nadvi ? He wrote something in continuation of Shibli's work. Perhaps the author's name on the cover of the book will be Maulana Sulaiman Nadvi.

About fish, I have not made an exception in your favour. Though cod-liver oil is forbidden for us, I have allowed it in the Ashram. Meat and fish are forbidden in the Ashram itself, but they are not forbidden to individuals, cannot be. I at any rate have never forbidden them to anyone. That is why Imam Saheb was permitted to at them outside the Ashram. Suppose it was Narandas and not you. He was never touched meat etc., in all his life. But suppose he fell seriously ill and his life was in danger, and he wished to save it by eating meat. I would certainly not prevent him from eating it. Today he knows my views and also what dharma teaches. But the approach of death may change one's ideas. If at such a time, anyone wishes to eat meat, it would be my dharma not to prevent him from doing so. But suppose it is a child and I have to decide for it. I would let it die but not give it meat. Do you know that Ba once passed through such an ordeal ? Most probably the incident is described in the *Autobiography*.[8] If you do not know about it, nor does anybody else, write to me and I will narrate it. It was a blessed occasion for both Ba and me. Do you now understand my meaning ? I don't wish to urge you to eat fish. If by not taking it you are likely to die and you are ready for that, I am ready to let you die. Even if eating fish enables you to live longer, will not the end be death ? But, then, dharma is for one who has faith in it and is ready to follow it. Do I follow such dharma in my own life in regard to milk ? I do not, though it is clear to me as daylight that one should not drink the milk of any animal. Such principles of dharma however are not meant to be enforced in the lives of others. One should follow them in one's own life. I think I have said enough. Let me know what your present diet includes, with the quantity of each item. If I feel like suggesting a change, I will.

Your questions about men and women are good. We should explain to a child any matter about which it shows curiosity, if we know the answer. Otherwise, we should admit our ignorance. If we think the child's question should not be answered, we should restrain it and also tell it not to ask others. In any case, we should never give an evasive reply. Children know more about these things than we think they do. If we refuse to tell them what they do not know, they learn to satisfy their curiosity in improper ways. We should, however, take that risk and not tell them what we think they ought not to be told. There are, of course, very few such things. If they want to know about the obscene act, we should certainly not satisfy their curiosity. Don't mind if they learn the facts in a clandestine manner despite our forbidding it. If children see birds engaged in the sex-act and want to understand what it means, I would certainly satisfy their curiosity and use the opportunity to teach them the lesson of *brahmacharya.* I would teach them the distinction between man on the one hand and birds and beasts on the other. All the men and women who act in the same manner are, despite their human form, like birds and beasts in that particular respect. There is no condemnation of anyone in this; it is only a statement of fact. We have been granted the human form and our intelligence so that we may rise above our animal nature. All the facts about menstruation should be explained to a girl who has reached puberty; if a younger girl comes to know about the phenomenon and asks you about it, you may explain to her, too, as many facts as she can understand.

Despite all our precautions, children will not always remain ignorant about these facts. Hence, it would be better to impart that knowledge to them at the proper time. If *brahmacharya* is so frail a thing that a person who know the facts about sex cannot observe it, we have no use for such *brahmacharya.* The knowledge of these facts should strengthen one's *brahmacharya.* That is what happened in my case.

The motives for seeking or imparting this knowledge differ from person to person. One person may seek it in order to gratify his lust. Another may learn the facts without his showing any curiosity about the subject. A third person may seek the knowledge in order to calm his passions and to help others. One should impart this knowledge to others only if one is fit for the job. You should have that ability, and also the confidence that by imprating it to the girls you will not awaken sex-thoughts in them. You should remember all the time that you impart this knowledge to the girls in order that they may not be disturbed by such thoughts. If you yourself are not free from them you should take care that they do not disturb you while you are imparting this knowledge to the girls. The primany aim behind the partnership in life of man and woman as husband and wife is physical enjoyment. Hinduism has tried to teach in its place the practice of self-control, or say, rather that all religions have done so.

If the husband is Brahma, Vishnu and Maheshwar, so is the wife. A wife is not a servant; she is a friend with equal rights, a partner in dharma. Each is the guru of the other.

A daughter's share should be equal to a son's.

A husband and a wife have equal rights in what either earns. The husband earns with the wife's help, even if she does no more than cook for the family. She is not a servant, but is an equal partner. A wife has the right to live separately from her husband if he ill-treats her. The two have equal rights over the children. After the children have grown up, neither of them has any. If the wife is unfit to exercise her right, she loses it. And so does the husband.

In sum, I do not admit any differences between men and women except those created by Nature which all of us can see. I don't think now that I have left any of your questions on this subject unanswered. I have the fullest trust in Narandas. When he says that his mind is at peace, I would not believe that it is not so. I have cautioned him again and again. I will harass him no more from this distance. He has great capacity for working in a spirit of non-attachment. Such a person always works much more than another who is attached to his work, and yet seems to be doing no work. He is the last person to tire. Realy speaking, he should never feel tired, but that is only an ideal. Since you are on the spot, your duty will be different from mine if you observe that his mind is not at peace and that he is deceiving himself. In that case you ought to caution him. I, too, would do that if I were there and found that the evidence of my eyes contradicted what he said. If he disagrees with you and rejects your advice, you should accept what he says, so long as you believe that he is a truthful man. Very often our eyes, too, deceive us. If I think that you feel depressed but you contradict me, I must believe you. If I have reason to fear or suspect that you are trying to hide the fact from me, then it would be a different matter. In that case, I should not ask you. I would have to seek other means of discovering the truth. The Ashram life, however, cannot go on thus. Truth is the very foundation of that life. There even with a good motive one cannot deceive others. You will read about *khadi* either in my letter[9] to Narandas or in the letter to children.

Ask Narandas and know from him why he does not try an oil massage. By all means wait for 4th July[10]. But, then, 4th July of which year is a matter for speculation. It doesn't matter which year, though. It is much even if only the month and the date are known for certain. We won't have to wait, then, for some other month or date. After 4th July has passed, we shall wait in patience for the July of 1933.

Bapu

(PS.)

Vidya seems to require attention. I think she is dull. She does not even know how to ask questions. Look into this.

7. Letter to Premabehn Kantak

July 30, 1932

Chi. Prema,

I got your letter. There seems to be no limit to your foolishness. When you get angry, you lose all sense. In the very letter in which you write about having taken a vow to overcome anger, you get angry and that too without reason. You did not understand the reason for my gentle rebuke. I had complained that there was no beauty or art in the slips with zigzag edges which you had pasted on the envelope.[11] I would not find fault with anyone for spending time on art. But in this case there was no art at all. What art can there be in pasting slips on an envelope ? And, moreover, you had pasted them so carelessly that they had half come off. Your anger, therefore, was without reason. It only amused me. If I were with you, I would have slapped you. But your having erred is a more serious matter. You spent so much time on the thing. You entered into unnecessary argument about it and harmed your health, for scientists have discovered by experiments that anger has a very bad effect on health. Our people have always held that belief. Besides, you violated your vow. Don't get angry like this again. My criticism, moreover, was gentle and you did not show even sense enough to understand it.

About letters, follow the example of the child who eats up the carrot when he finds that he cannot blow with it as with a pipe. That is, you should not feel unhappy if the letters stop. In any case, you should go on writing from your end. If I decide to stop writing, I will let you know. Even if I cannot write to you to tell you about that, your writing to me will not be a waste of effort.

Greet the new flowers on my behalf. Try to cheer them by telling them that I hope to sleep in their midst one day. You are very difficult to persuade. If you grow tomatoes and some *bhajis* round the flower plants, you will get them all the year round and your health will benefit. If the body is not yours, but is a trust given to you by God, you should certainly give some time for keeping it fit. Growing tomatoes and *bhajis* does not require much time. They don't cover up much plot either.

An English friend of mine who lived with me in South Africa used to grow, in a few days and with little trouble, a *bhaji* named cress which is eaten uncooked. I have already written to you in regard to the bad health of the girls. Inquire into the matter carefully and find out the facts. I was certainly afraid that it was so about Rambhau. Since he has told you everything, try and win him over.

If your weight has gone down, you must eat fruit. Don't mind a little additional expense. What is the good of trying to save money and injuring your health ? What is true about food is also true about rest. You must make it a rule to take some rest in the afternoon. It is not for me to show how you can spare time for that. If you are determined to find it, you will succeed.

Now about your questions:

(1) Instead of worshipping an individual, one should worship virtues. An individual may turn out to be unworthy of our worship, and in any case he is bound to die. Virtues, on the other hand, never perish.

(2) If you do not like most of those who run the Ashram, this is a golden opportunity to learn to tolerate their defects. No human being is without defects. If we wish to regard others as our ownselves, we should have no likes and dislikes.

(3) If you accept the principles on which the Ashram is founded, differences of opinion regarding its outward form should not matter. We should be concerned with the principle of a thing and not with its form.

(4) It is your duty to remain in the Ashram so that you may overcome the defects of your temper.

(5) If you cannot realize your ideals in the Ashram, the fault is yours. Everyone enjoys perfect freedom in the Ashram.

(6) Why should the attraction of those whom you love force you to leave the Ashram ? Their love should draw them to the Ashram whenever they feel the need to see you. Love never requires the physical presence of the person loved. Love which requires such presence must be momentary attraction. The purity of one's love is tested by separation from the loved one after his or her

> death. But all this is mere intellectual exercise. You will live only where your heart is. What can I do or you either, if your heart cannot accept the Ashram ? The yarn spun by me ought to be converted into *saris*. It belongs to a time before I expressed my views about yarn[12]. It was in fact earmarked for Ba. Hence it is for her to renounce her claim over it. I cannot say that it is not for her. She will never be able to wear very coarse *saris*. Even the *saris*, therefore, supplied to her by the Ashram will usually be fine. For that reason, too, she may wear *saris* made from the yarn spun by me. But we should be very strict about the yarn spun in future, though even with regard to that I will not exercise compulsion on Ba. I certainly wish that she should, of her own free will, refuse to use it and be content with whatever she gets as her share. But this is about the future. As yet all the yarn spun by me recently is here. In any case, my yarn should not lie unused. In fact no one's yarn should lie unused. As soon as a person has spun enough quantity of yarn to be used for weaving, it should be processed for the purpose.

You know about Dhurandhar. If none else, Lilavati, I believe, spins. What you say, however, is correct. Most women will prefer embroidery to spinning. What is true about eating is also true about work. The mind will run after *bhajiyan*[13] in preference to *rotli*. There is self-control and renunciation in continuing to eat *rotli*, whereas it is self-indulgence to start eating *bhajiyan*. Similarly, there is self-control in keeping to spinning and self-indulgence (relatively) in taking up other work.

Your comments on my advice "Judge not lest ye be judged"[14] are unworthy of you. You have not understood the meaning of the statement at all. There is much pride behind your comments."Lest ye be judged" means that we should not do anything for which we should be judged by others. We should not be insolent towards the world. Why should we say, "Let the world say or do what it will" ? We should be humble before the world, that is, even when we follow the right path we should not use violence against it or sit in judgment over it. On the contrary, we should endure its punishment and its condemnation. This is humility or nonviolence. I should not like you to write what you did, though you probably wrote it sarcastically or in anger. I don't mind your being angry with me. I can laugh it away. But this other remark rankles in my mind. You should never be prompted to pen such a remark, that is, you should not even have such a thought. Since you had it, I don't mind your expressing it to me. It is because you expressed it that I am able to explain to you how it is wrong. I have not written this paragraph so that you may keep back your thoughts from me. I wish to see you as you are, whether foolish or insolent or humble. But what I ask of you is that you should not even let such a thought enter your mind.

If the girls cannot massage with sufficient pressure, you should teach them how to do so. That requires not physical strength but skill. Now about what you have been reading. The belief which you refer to was held once. It is no longer held now. People have not understood some of Malthus's theories, and some others are faulty. The law which applies to lower animals does not apply to man. Lower animals live on one another. Man strives to grow out of that condition. It is the spirit of nonviolence which prompts him to do so. So long as one's body endures, one cannot realize perfect nonviolence. If, however, a person cherishes the ideal of nonviolence, he will live so as to commit the minimum violence. Man's excellence lies in his readiness to let others live and lay down his own life. As he progresses, his food also changes for the better. He has capacity to grow still further. There have been many more discoveries after Darwin's. The book which you have been reading seems to be an old one. Whether it is old or new, the principle of "the greatest good of the greatest number" or "survival of the fittest" is false.

Nonviolence aims at the good of all. The divine law cannot be any other but the good of all. It is our duty to discover how to bring that about and what man's duty is under such a law, and not to oppose that law by another. But this is a vast subject. I have dealt with a few points in brief. If you want me to discuss the subject further, put me some questions.

Bapu

8. Letter to Premabehn Kantak

August 3, 1932

Chi. Prema,

I got your letter of the 1st. I hope you are not getting frightened at the crowing in the hostel. If the girls are well behaved, there will be no difficulty. There will be none, either if we have perfectly learnt the lesson of non-attachment. Others can suggest mostly external remedies for tour health. About internal remedies, you alone can judge. I do not have much faith in psychologists. How much can even the best trained psychologist know about the human mind ? Hence, you yourself should try and know what connection your ill-health has with your mind and adopt the proper remedies. In this very letter, however, you say that heavy or light work and proper sleep or its absence do have an effect on health. Thus the truth is that both internal and external factors have a bearing on one's health. No one has been able to maintain good health with the help of mind alone, neglecting external measures. You should, therefore, listen to Narandas's advice in regard to sleep, rest and work, and examine the mental cause yourself. Take any measure you think necessary but make your body as strong as steel. I should have told you at the very beginning that you should not take Kuhne-bath in warm water during the period of your monthly course.

The inner voice is something which cannot be described in words. But sometimes we have a positive feeling that something in us prompts us to do a certain thing. The time when I learnt to recognize this voice was, I may say, the time when I started praying regularly. That is, it was about 1906. I searched my memory and tell you this because you asked the question. In fact, however, there was no moment when I suddenly felt that I had some new experience. I think my spiritual life has grown without my being conscious of the fact in the same way as hair grows on our body.

This is how repetition of God's name wipes out one's sins. Anyone who sincerely follows that practice is bound to have faith. He starts with the conviction that such repetition will wipe out his sins. Wiping out of sins means self-purification. One who repeats God's name daily with faith will never grow tired of doing so, and, therefore, the name which he repeats with his lips to start with sinks ultimately into his heart, and that purifies him. This is a universal experience. Psychologists also believe that man becomes what he thinks. Ramanama follows this law. I have unshakable faith in the virtue of repeating God's name. I am convinced that the person who discovered it had first-hand experience (of spiritual life) and that his discovery is of the utmost value. The door of purification should open even for the illiterate. Repetition of God's name opens it for them. (See *Gita* IX. 22, X.10.) Telling beads and similar practices help one to concentrate and to count the number of times the name has been repeated.

Studies should be undertaken only with the aim of equipping oneself for service. Since, however, service of others gives one the highest joy, one may say that studies are for joy. I have not heard of anyone, however, who found unbroken joy in life through literary pursuits alone without devoting himself to service. Art cannot be the monopoly of any country or individual. That which requires secrecy is no art.

It is the right and the duty of every country to protect its industries. It is the duty of a person who follows the path of nonviolence to give shelter to the homeless. Who should be treated as homeless can be decided only by reference to the circumstances of each case.

What seems bad in its outward appearance is not always so in its substance. The unattractive appearance of Urdu books indicates their publishers' lack of means. But cannot their contents be excellent ? In fact the contents of some of them are so. In making the list, however, how does the question of the work being or not being interesting arise ? Since the list has to be made, the work must be interesting because there is interest in doing one's duty. If you take the trouble some time of learning a little Urdu, you will find the study interesting in itself.

Bapu

9. Letter to Premabehn Kantak

August 12, 1932

Chi. Prema,

The following books are required for Parachure Shastri. Send those from among them which you have there. I will get the others from elsewhere. See if you can send them soon. Give them to Manibehn or to Nandubehn[15]. Either will send them to Dahyabhai. Parachure Shastri was in the Ashram once. He is a man of great learning. He is in this jail just now. He has been suffering from leprosy. That is why I am in a hurry to send the books to him. He spins daily. I am not permitted to see him, but can write to him. His wife, too, is ill and confined to bed. She is outside. The books are: (1) *Imitation of Christ*, (2) *Works of Swami Vivekananda* (whichever volumes we have), (3) *Works of Sister Nivedita* (whichever volumes we have), (4) *Essays of Tolstoy*, (5) *Vyakarana Mahabhashya*, (6) *Yajurveda Bhashya*, (7) *Dispensations of Keshab Chandra Sen*.

Since Parachure Shastri has lived in the Ashram, he informs me that the last three are available there. He seems to have read them while he was there.

I got your letter. You seem to believe that I could write an interesting letter whenever I wished to. But you see now that that is not true. I cannot even judge which letter is interesting and which is dull. I am telling the truth. Moreover, who can say that the letter which you think interesting is in fact so ? If there is an independent yardstick for judging whether or not a thing is interesting, God seems to have kept it under lock and key. On this earth, therefore, everyone has his or her own yardstick for this purpose. If I tried to come up to your standard, wouldn't I be in a miserable plight ? All my time would be taken up in trying to succeed in the effort. Should I start writing a letter all over again, or a third time, for fear that what I had written might be uninteresting ? And if I must write interesting letters to you, I must write similar letters to others. And the result, bankruptcy ! ! ! Instead of that, I follow a simple rule. Without considering whether the letter will be interesting or not, I should write what I think in such language as I can command. But you are foolish, and proud too. How can you ever appreciate this simple reasoning ? And now I see that you claim to be omniscient. Any wise thing I try to explain to you, you seem to know it. But pause a little. One who believes in an idea or knows it to be true but cannot act on it does not in fact know it, or knows it in a sense and yet does not know it. Hence, as long as you go on writing foolish things, get angry and feel proud, you will remain foolish in my eyes. This does not mean that you should not let your pride, anger and foolishness be seen in your letters. As long as you have them in you, you must express them. The value of your letters lies in letting yourself be seen as you are. I don't mind your remaining foolish. But you must overcome your anger and be a little less proud. It is impossible to get rid of pride altogether. You cite the instance of Narada. But do you know the real significance of his statement ?[16] By all means worship a personal form in the manner in which he did. Such worship is proper. His Krishna is as historical as the God in Vaikuntha[17]. Narada's God dwelt in the temple of his imagination. That Narada is alive today, and so is his Krishna, for both live for ever in our imagination. According to me, imagination is superior to historical fact. This is the only possible meaning of Tulsidas's statement that the name Rama is more potent than the person Rama.

Is it not because you are caught in the whirlpool of worship of the individual that you worry me again and again ? You have not been able to free me from worries regarding the Ashram. Narandas has succeeded in doing so. I can cite instances of other persons too. They also worship persons, who doesn't ? But, ultimately, they go beyond the person and learn to worship his virtues, that is, his creations. We forgot this priceless truth and, in our ignorance, we taught women to burn themselves on the pyre of their husbands. That is worship of the person taken to its extreme !! The real duty of a loyal wife is to immortalize in herself her husband's life-work. If we purify the relationship of husband and wife of sex and banish from it the distinction of gender, this ideal will apply to every woman in the world, whatever her state may be. In other words, love for the husband merges in love of God. But I leave this subject now.

Why are you upset by the news that Dhiru is arriving ? Have confidence that you will be able to control him too; have that much faith in yourself. Let the immortal statement, "Love conquers all", sink into your heart. We should be pleased whoever may arrive. Our only wish is to serve everyone as best as we can. Why don't you have faith that, if the other children have become well-behaved, under their influence Dhiru also will become like them ? It is also possible that Dhiru has become a wise boy now. Personally, I have always hoped much from him.

You should dedicate your whole life to the service of the girls. If they do not talk frankly about themselves to anyone, they are bound to fall ill. Read my letter to Anandi. If she lets you have that letter, all the other girls who have grown up should be asked to read it. I have never observed from my own experience that bananas give rise to gas. I have consumed more bananas than anybody else is likely to have done. For many years they were my chief food. I neither took milk nor ate bread. My diet consisted of bananas, olive oil, ground-nut and lemon. However, I never suffered from gas. After many years, I have started eating them again. I observe no ill effects. You must, of course, observe one rule in eating them. Either bananas should be cooked or they should be completely ripe. An unripe banana is pure starch, and I saw in Gopal Rao's experiment that starch should not be eaten uncooked. Hence, one should not eat bananas which have not become soft or ripe. They will become ripe if kept aside for two or three days. If you want to eat bananas before they have become ripe, you should either roast them or boil them in water. The book which you read may have been published in 1924, but the theory which it mentions has become outdated.

I had opponents in the past and have them even today. But I have never felt angry with them. I have not wished them ill even in my dreams. The result has been that many opponents have become friends. No one's opposition has had any effect on me. On three occasions they sought to take my very life, but I am still alive. This does not mean that no opponent would ever succeed against me in his plan. Whether he succeeds or does not is no concern of mine. My dharma lies in wishing well even to them, and serving them whenever an opportunity offers itself. I have tried to live up to this principle to the best of my ability. I think this thing is part of my nature. I get physically tired by the worship of vast crowds. It has never made me happy, nor have I ever felt that I was worthy of it. On the contrary, I have always been conscious of my unworthiness. I do not remember to have ever hungered for honour. I always want work. I have tried my best to make people who honour me do work, and, when they refused to work, I have run away from their honour. I will feel myself blessed only when I reach my goal. But, as the saying goes, will that day ever dawn ?

It is not necessary to cultivate pride or contempt in order that one may be able to stand against the world. Jesus stood against the world, Buddha stood against his times and Prahlada also acted in the same way. All of them were humility incarnate. To have such humility, one must have faith in oneself and in God. Those who have opposed the world with pride have ultimately fallen. Sometimes your pride and your anger are only pretended. But even such pretence in an evil thing. It may ultimately become a habit and often gives cause for unnecessary misunderstanding. One should be very careful in one's conduct so as to guard against such possibilities. I think it impossible for anyone to have the strength to stand alone against the world at a critical hour unless he or she has the utmost humility. And it is such strength which has any value at all. It is tested only at such a time. Many of those whom the world has believed to be brave, it had no opportunity of judging whether they were really so. Now read my letter to Amtulbehn too.

Bapu

10. Letter to Premabehn Kantak

August 18, 1932

Chi. Prema,

I got your letter.

I got the *rakhdi,* but late by two days. I had, however, taken it that I had received it on Monday. If bananas do not agree with you and yet you go on eating them, they will not benefit you. Every stomach has its own peculiarity. I have fully understood your analysis of the reasons why you get angry. Try to overcome your weakness. I know that you will succeed in overcoming it. I understood your meaning in that part of your letter which you had decided not to leave out. You did right in not leaving it out. There is great pride in not explaining one's need to a person whom one loves, it does him injustice and puts a heavy burden on him. Civility and humility on our part save him from the trouble of ascertaining our need. This is the first lesson in civility.

Learn it now.

Write to Krishnan Nair and tell him that I often think about him. You did very well in going to Rajkot. It seems your health requires such rest.

Public opinion means the opinion of that section of society for which we care. It is our duty to respect it so long as it is not against morality.

It is difficult to come to a just conclusion on the basis of the incident about the *dhobi*. Such conduct would certainly not meet with our approval in this age. Anyone who abandons his wife because of such criticism would be regarded as a cruel and unjust man. But I am not in a position to say what the poet's intention was in the *Ramayana* in narrating that incident. We need not bother about that problem. I would not. I do not read even works like the *Ramayana* from that point of view.

I believe that I must stop taking the freedom which I do with the girls if that shocks the inmates of the Ashram. There is no reason which makes it a moral duty for me to take such freedom, nor does my taking it violate morality. If, however, my refraining from it was likely to have an undesirable effect on the girls, I would reason with the inmates of the Ashram and continue to behave as I have been doing. If the girls themselves do not leave me, I would have to consider how to meet the situation. In any case, no one should follow my example and take similar freedom with them. The freedom one takes should be spontaneous. No one should consciously and deliberately decide to take such freedom from one fine morning and behave unnaturally; it would be quite improper if anyone did so. Narandas is free to act as he thinks proper. I would not wish even to criticize him. The truth is that anyone who takes even the most innocent freedom with impure feelings falls into a pit and also drags others behind him. As long as the relations of men and women have not become natural in our society, one should certainly be careful in one's behaviour. There is no royal road in such matters which all can follow. There is a good deal of clumsiness in your own behaviour. Your innocence saves you, but it is certainly not proper for you to be proud of it and obstinately to persist in your behaviour. There is thoughtlessness in doing so. You do not see today the harm which such behaviour may do. But you way have to repent one day. No one's pride has endured for ever. One should not deliberately try to shock society, arguing that all conventional restrictions are bad. Have you now some idea of what public opinion means ? Write to Dhurandhar and tell him that he should bear in mind what the Major told him. He will himself have to become a walking advertisement for *asanas.*[18]

Bapu

11. Letter to Premabehn Kantak

August 26, 1932

Chi. Prema,

I got your letter. I hope you do not exhibit different virtues from time to time in order to win from me the praise which they deserve. If you do that my praise will lose all its value[19]. You will not see anywhere else the fierce hatreds which you see in Kathiawar. I am not, therefore, surprised that you saw an exhibition of them too. Such exhibitions take place there without any preparation. A person like . . . is likely to get frozen by an exhibition of such hatreds, but it is strange that though . . . . lives in Rajkot she could not remove . . . 's depression. I am sure she must have tied on his wrist the customary *raksha* on the Balev Day. But were they satisfied with a *raksha* of hand-spun yarn ? It ought not to be beyond . . .'s strength to discover the cause of. .'s unhappiness and remove it . . . used to adore his wife, . . . My belief is that, though married, they observed *brahmacharya*. . .'s passing away was a great shock to. . . . Perhaps deep down in his heart . . . wishes to marry. He cannot understand his own condition. But. . . should have as wife a girl with the same ideals as his own. Failing to get such a wife, if he gets a sister with strong idealism in her character, . . . may perhaps blossom out. I have supposed. . . .to be a perfect *brahmacharini.* She cherishes friendship for. . ., and has idealism in her character. Since you wrote about. . .'s depression, I have been tempted to write this. If you think that I have understood . . .'s character correctly and that what I have suggested is not beyond her strength, you may safely send this letter to her. If you feel that this is beyond her strength or that it is not her work, you may ignore this part of the letter. . . . craves for pure love. But. . . is full of likes and dislikes. He can love very few persons and so remains discontented within himself all the time. Such a person feels little need for a wife. But (,if married,) he can remain absorbed in his wife. He must get the sisterly love of a woman who is free from passion. If . . . gets such a sister, his life will take a new turn. Women in our society do not try to cultivate this virtue. They know how to be good wives, but do not know how to be good sisters. In order to be a good sister, one requires great capacity for renunciation. It seems self-evident to me that a wife can never be a perfect sister. A woman can be a true sister to the whole world. A wife can surrender herself only to one person. The capacity to be a good wife is a useful virtue, but it does not have to be cultivated, for a wife's relation to her husband permits the satisfaction of physical desire. It is extremely difficult to cultivate the virtue required in one who would be a sister to the whole world. Only a woman for whom *brahmacharya* is a natural state and in whom the spirit of service has become the strongest impulse of her life can become that . . . . has not given me the impression that she has risen so far, but I certainly believe that she has the capacity to rise so high. Maybe you have been instrumental in creating this impression in me. I have now said everything which I felt about this matter. I have indeed been striving to make you such a sister. It is a difficult task. Let the result be as God wills it.

You have given a good description of the exhibition. Your You have given a good description of the exhibition. Your descriptions are always interesting to read and make one think. You did right in returning to the Ashram for the Janmashtami festival. See that you overcome your anger. Do you know that Dhiru was simply not ready to go with you ? Don't get angry with him at any time. He is a child; you are not. If you win over Dhiru, it will be your victory; if you fail to do so, it will be your defeat. Is there any test by which to judge whether a father and a mother are cultured ? Who can say what the parents' state of mind was at the time of conception ? I think, therefore, that it is best to cling to the rule that what is good bears good fruit. If we cannot prove the truth of this rule in every individual case, the reason may be our ignorance and not the inadequacy of the rule.

Even if I did[20] believe in Fate, its decrees could not be altered. Fate means the effect of past *karma*.

For saving the prostitutes from their profession, it is necessary that men should cease to be beasts. As long as we have beast-like men in the world, so long shall we have prostitutes. If any prostitutes give up their profession and turn a new leaf in their lives, the so-called "respectable" men will certainly come forward to marry them. It is not true that once a prostitute, always a prostitute. The belief that in every country girls are abducted for the army seems exaggerated to me. In a well-governed country this cannot happen. It is not correct to believe that residents of the Malabar coast can digest coconut even after they have left the air of that place. By mixing coconut with *tandalja,* you weakened the effect of *tandalja.* I have often included coconut in my diet. It didn't agree with me. But it is highly probable that it is essential with other articles of food in regions where it grows.

Bapu

12. Letter to Premabehn Kantak

September 11, 1932

Chi. Prema,

If you have patience and faith, all the pages of the "book of nature" will be open to you. It is the promise of the God of Truth that "to those who worship Me (Truth) with love, I grant the yoga of understanding".[21] Meditation on this verse opens up to me all the pages of my nature. When the book is lying before you, whose fault is it if you cannot read it or do not take the trouble to read it ? But I think I have said too much. In any case, I have explained to you the method of reading that book. You will say that you knew it. If you do, would it not prove me right in describing you as omniscient ? I can have no objection at all to your sending all my letter to . . . The last letter was about her and, therefore, I particularly wished that you should send it to her. You may now write and tell me how the matter stands. . . .[22] says that I could not find the correct remedy for . . . and she is right, but only partly. I have discovered the remedy, but I am not in a position to apply it. How can I help that ? The remedy which he needs is a woman—either a woman whom he could love and would marry, or one who would be more than a sister to him. I had my eyes on . . . ever since I saw her and . . .'s affection for her and hers for him. I have always believed in the innocence of their love. But how could I burden . . . with a responsibility till an opportunity arose ? Your letter gave me the required opportunity. I do not know whether my diagnosis is correct and whether . . . is the remedy for him. Perhaps . . . herself does not know it. We can discover the truth only if we try the remedy which I have suggested. All that I desire is . . .'s peace of mind. In the absence of such peace, his abilities remain unused and his health is wasting away. He does not even know whether he feels interested in the work which he does. You seem to have collected from somewhere a good many stories about my childhood.

Do you know that Ramabehn is ill ? You should at least go and talk to her. In actual fact there is often no cause for the fear which we entertain in our imagination. The saying, "A ghost is the projection of our fancies and a witch of our fears" is literally true. It is a hundred per cent true. I hope you are properly looking after the new arrivals among women. You may reduce your other work, but attend to this carefully. I read about Kisan[23] in the paper. Dhurandhar has been doing fine work. But he should take care and make his body strong. What is his weight ?

What did I write about you in my letter to Anandi[24] ? What did I tell Lilavati[25] ? I don't remember. I have no doubt at all about your observing *brahmacharya* at present. I don't know what may happen in the future. If you can tell, you know more than Narad and Rama did. However, I have always admired your resolution. I don't believe that anyone can easily tempt you. But I have seen women as determined as you get married. How can anyone blame them for that ? Hence, at present I can only wish that you will remain faithful to your resolution, and bless you that you may. I may help you as much as I can, and give you blows as often as necessary. The result lies in God's hands.

I want your letters to be in no way different from what they are. If you cease to be natural, I will take no interest in you. You are full of complexes. I can try to remove them only as and when I observe them. However, who am I to remove them ? It does not lie in man's power to do so. I should like to be an instrument in removing them to the extent that He permits me to be so. It is in my interest to do this, since I hope to take much work from you. If I believed that what I was trying to inculcate in you would bear no fruit, do you think I would take the trouble to write these long letters ?

I do not know any instance of the cause of an individual's or society's fall having been discovered. Many guesses, of course, have been made. The immediate cause is sometimes discovered, but in all cases there is not one such cause only. Generally speaking, however, it may be said that a fall can be traced to lack of dharma. Political subjection can never be the root cause, for it is itself the result of other causes, other weaknesses.

One's duty as a neighbour is always to help a neighbour in a manner consistent with dharma.

The seed of ego is destroyed only when one feels oneself to be a cipher. If anyone looks inward and ponders deeply over the matter, he cannot but realize his total insignificance. As we count an insect insignificant relatively to the earth, so is man insignificant in relation to this universe which is millions of times vaster than the earth. That he is endowed with reason makes no difference to this fact. His greatness lies in realizing his insignificance, for simultaneously with such realization, he realizes that, insignificant in himself, he is an insignificant aspect of God and that, when he merges in Him, he becomes God, that this microscopic atom which he is contains the infinite power of God.

I believe in the theory of *maya* in my own way. In the cycle of Time this universe is *maya,* but, during the moment of time it exists, it is real enough. I believe in the theory of the many-sidedness of truth. If there is anything in this world which faces man as a certainty, it is death. And yet we fear that inescapable certainty; that is the greatest wonder of life, that is real attachment and that is atheism. It is possibe only for man to rise above it.

One's good and evil deeds do accompany the soul after the death of the body. The soul, as soul, suffers their consequences, whether in another physical body or in a subtle body. Isn't this enough ?

Bapu

13. Letter to Premabehn Kantak

December 18, 1932

Chi. Prema,

I wrote to you some letters in the course of the week. This one is in reply to your weekly letter.

I have decided to obey your order forbidding me to show your letters to Chhaganlal. Of course I had to show him your order. I think you, too, would not wish that he should remain ignorant of what you wrote about him. I showed him the relevant part of the letter and asked him not to read the rest. All the same, I did not like your order. Why should any person in the Ashram hide anything from another inmate ?

I can understand a child or a grown-up who knows no better feeling thus. But what can you have to hide from anybody ? The fact that others read your letters doesn't lessen, but rather increases, the sanctity of your letters. You should not at all feel embarrassed if the whole world knows your thoughts. We have no right to think any thought which others may not know. If we follow this as a fixed rule in our life, we automatically learn to control our thoughts. Every human being is God's representative on the earth. He knows all our thoughts, but we do not know that He does, because we do not see Him face to face. If, however, we look upon human beings as God's representatives on the earth, we should not mind others knowing our thoughts. Moreover, since we see a representative bodily, it becomes easy for us to acquire control over our thoughts. I wish that you should voluntarily withdraw your order. I had hoped that I would be able to write with my right hand, but I see that I ought not to use it and, therefore, I shall not perhaps be able to write all that I wished to say. I don't mind your writing about Ramabehn whatever comes to your mind. She does know indeed that you will write nothing out of ill-will for her. So you may write anything you may wish to. I will carry out any suggestion you may make.

You seem to have left the hospital much too soon. If you are carrying out the doctor's instructions faithfully, there will be no difficulty. It will be fine indeed if the operation succeeds in its purpose.

. . . 's[26] story is a sad one. I am not ready to blame . . .[27] without knowing his side of the case. . . .[28] is man of pure heart; he is not cruel. He knows his duty. If I had more time at my disposal, I would have explained the matter in greater detail. You should serve . . .[29] as well as you can. If she feels lonely, she is not altogether blameless in the matter. But she should not be left uncared for because of that. . . .[30] has quite a few good qualities too.

Indu is of course careless. He is a simple-hearted boy and loves play a little too much. I have written to his father and told him that he should take the boy under his loving care.

Take milk and fruit for some time and think that they are medicines. Don't eat *kanji* etc., for a while. If you wish to eat rice, you can. See the doctor regularly.

A letter for Sushila is enclosed.

Bapu

14. Letter to Premabehn Kantak

January 7, 1933

Chi. Prema,

You are as sensitive and obstinate in nursing resentment as you are quick to get angry. How long should a daughter nurse resentment against her father ? Her love will melt away her pride. How long do you intend to nurse your resentment ? Probably you repented immediately after writing the letter.[31] Do you know that by writing that note you have sprinkled salt on my wound, so to say ? But probably I know you better than you do yourself. At first I felt extremely unhappy. But afterwards laughed. You are not as bad as you seem to be in your letter[32]. I immediately reassured myself that, as you had sulked for some time once before and afterwards, felt unhappy for that, so you would feel sorry this time, too, and apologize. If I was wrong in thinking so, well I should like you to apologize now. You may then write any kind of letters. I had rebuked you only for nursing hatred in your heart. However, so long as it is there, you can relieve yourself of it only before me. And if I don't show your shortcomings to you, who else will ? So long as the poison of hatred is there in your heart, you must let me drink it. Probably you do not think that it is poison. Rarely does a person know his or her own nature. I want you to know yours and wake up.

Bapu

15. Letter to Premabehn Kantak

January 15, 1933

Chi. Prema,

Your continued sulking shows that you have a good measure of childishness in you. If you do not tolerate my criticizing you, you are not at all likely to tolerate anybody else doing so. Instead of thanking me for (telling you) the impression you produce on me, you get angry with me. Your duty is to try to ask me again to explain my charge against you, if you have not understood it. You may also quarrel with me. But all your education and wisdom seem to have disappeared on this occasion. You cannot even see that behind your sulking lies your extreme pride. Let me tell you that this is not freedom but self-will. I wish that you should open your eyes and understand my love, and not falsify my estimate of you. It is not right for you to sulk; on the contrary, you should feel sorry and weep for having made me suffer. Why don't you realize that, if I say anything harsh to you, it is for your own good ? If I am making any mistake in doing so, it is your duty to point it out humbly to me. If you are sure that you are innocent, you should be confident of being able to prove it to me. Instead, you resent my criticism and sulk, and thereby seem to aggravate your guilt. I had never expected this from you. Wake up and express sorrow for nursing resentment against me.

Blessings from
Bapu

16. Letter to Premabehn Kantak

January 22, 1933

Chi. Prema,

I was relieved to get your letter. Even worry is a child of imagination. Why should I worry if I do not get a letter from you, and why should I feel relieved on getting one ? If you ask me this question, I would not be able to reply to it, or would only say: "This is what ignorant attachment means."

A foolish letter from you would not upset me. If, however, I see your error or shortcoming and do not point it out to you, I would not be doing my duty as your well-wisher, co-worker, friend or father. What I find strange is that you should get angry with me and sulk for telling you something with a sincere motive, instead of thanking me for it. Should we not thank a person for telling us frankly what he feels ? I learnt this in my very childhood. I do want you to learn it from me. If my understanding of a situation is wrong, I deserve to be pitied, and, if it is correct, I would be doing you good. In either case, you gain something, in that you come to know better the person with whom you have thrown in your lot. I want that all of you should know my shortcomings and deficiencies and it is always my effort to show them myself. I don't wish to hide even my thoughts. I would even write them down if I had the necessary gift. But I know I cannot do that. I don't think there can be any power in the world which can penetrate all the secrets of thought. Probably we shall be able to know them if somebody invents a machine to reveal them. Even while I was writing these few sentences, my imagination traversed the universe many times over.

You will admit that everybody cannot understand whether or not he has the poison in his heart. Because one does not consciously wish to nurse hatred, it does not mean that there is no hatred in one's heart. It takes hold of us against our will. You will probably not admit that anybody whose heart is full of anger is also full of hatred. If you do not, then the word "poison" does not have the same meaning for you and me. I remember that Ba often charged me with having poison in my heart. How can I deny that charge ? I may not have believed that there was any poison in my words. But that is beside the point. What should matter to me is that she felt the poison. Words which are perfectly truthful and spoken with perfect love will never hurt anybody. They may sometimes hurt one in the beginning, but such a person himself will afterwards admit their beneficial effect on him. I should like you not to be your own judge in all matters. It is possible that others judge you better than you do yourself. I will now end this tale of "poison".

The question of your leaving the Ashram does not arise just now. It will arise only after I am released and return to the Ashram to stay there. That is how I read your letter. Morally speaking, it can arise only then, if at all, for, so long as I cannot return to the Ashram to stay in it, in the eyes of the inmates of the Ashram I will remain a prisoner. All of you who decided to stay on when I bade good-bye to the Ashram bound yourselves thereby to remain there till I returned. If I am right in believing this, it is a waste of time and energy to think now what should be done when I return to stay there. The news you have given about happenings in the Ashram is very useful to me. You should discuss the problem of Lakshmi with Narandas, and if both of you decide that she should be married, it should be done soon. Her restlessness also is likely to be the result of an unconscious desire to get married. She is now of marriageable age, and she does intend to marry. The desire to wait till I am released should be regarded as nothing but ignorant attachment to me. You should try and understand her heart properly, and not wait for her emphatic consent. It seems to me desirable to take the advice of Lakshmibehn and Durgabehn in this matter. They would understand the problem better than you can. I understand from what you yourself have said that you have no experience of how a girl feels when she desires to marry. In other words, you have never felt the desire to marry. I also know some other unmarried women who have never felt it. Some other women remain unmarried with an effort of will. They know what marriage means.

What advice should I give you about your health ? Ghee seems to be absolutely necessary for it. Whenever you leave the Ashram, your weight increases, and as soon as you return to the Ashram you lose the weight you had gained. You must get over this weakness. How it can be done, you alone know. I hope you experience no difficulty now in speaking.

I don't wish to catch anybody in my snare. What would be my plight if all people became my slaves ? And, moreover, I am sure that any such effort would be doomed to failure. Even if it is true that I try to catch people in my snare, why should you lose confidence in yourself for that reason ? Your letters are sufficient evidence that you are vigilant and not likely to succumb. It does seem, however, that you are perpetually afraid that you will let yourself be caught. That is a bad sign. Having resolved that you will not let yourself be caught, why should you feel afraid ? But may it also not be possible that you and I do not mean the same thing by "getting caught" ?

Bapu

17. Letter to Premabehn Kantak

February 13, 1933

Chi. Prema,

It is the morning of the silence day. I got up at three and have taken up your letter to reply to it. I liked it very much indeed. You have given me in it all that I wanted. It fully answers to my imagination of what women can give me. What it gives seems small and unspectacular, but is very useful to a seeker after truth. I learn something from an objective letter like this one, and it helps me to guide you and others.

The Ashram is indeed a dharmashala. But the word has two meanings. It means a place where people can stay free, but it also means a place where one can learn dharma and try to follow it. The Ashram is a dharmashala in this second sense of the word. But dharma means truth. The Ashram, therefore, is a place where one may know the truth and try to follow it, that is, show *agraha*[33] for it, and hence it is

Satyagraha Ashram. In our quest for truth, we wish to cultivate unity with all living creatures. The Ashram, therefore, is an ever-growing family. But it is something more even than that, for it is the means and dharma is the end, and not *vice versa*. It is also a big school, and yet it is not so; for, since it is a family, we cannot mechanically apply there rules of outward behaviour such as are followed for other types of training. The letter of the rule has to be sacrificed in order to save the spirit of the rule.

I will now apply these observations to some specific cases. In bringing up and educating Lakshmi, we, including you, are being tested. What would we do to children in our own family ? What would you do to your own sister ? If Lakshmi does not observe the rules, the fault is chiefly mine, and then yours. I leave out the others. I leave out Narandas, too, for if we hold him responsible for the behaviour of every person in the Ashram, he will not be able to attend to his own duties. Looking after Lakshmi is a woman's job, and particularly of the woman to whom it is entrusted. The fault is chiefly mine because I am her adopted father and also mother. I did my duty as a father but not as a mother, because I remained away from the Ashram most of the time. I feel now that I should not have accepted Lakshmi at all. But who was I to decide ? I am but a servant of God. I did not seek Lakshmi. God sent her. Let Him, then, look after her. She was under the charge of Ba first, then of Santok, then of Gangabehn, and now she is under your charge. None of you asked to have charge of her. It was time and circumstances which put her under the charge of these persons one after another. You should now do the best that you can. Whenever necessary, you may consult me. Do not get tired of your charge or despair. Have faith and bathe her with your love. God will ultimately solve the problem. She has come to us as a representative of Harijans to claim payment of the debt which we owe to them. If she is full of shortcomings and is indolent, the responsibility for that lies on you, me and on the caste Hindus. We reap as we sow. I am trying to get her married off. I have written to Lakshmidas and inquired about Maruti. I have also written to Dudabhai. You need not get upset because more boys and girls are coming to the Ashram. They will benefit to the extent that they observe the rules. We may let them stay as long as we tolerate their laxity, and ask them to leave when we can do so no longer. People do not stay in a dharmashala permanently. Even near relations do not stay permanently. Those of them who can accommodate themselves to the discipline of the Ashram will stay, and the others will leave. Why should we care either way ? Moreover, we cannot adopt any other policy in the present circumstances. As long as we can do so, we should admit people who come unasked and who seem deserving. Most of them will leave on their own. Our rules themselves will drive them away. Everybody who comes must do physical work. They should clean lavatories and eat simple food in the same manner as we swallow medicine. They will not get jaggery, nor wheat as often as they might wish. If we can daily demonstrate more and more clearly by our manner of life that the Ashram is a representative of the starving poor, we shall always be safe and happy. This means that there should be increasing simplicity in our life in the Ashram and the rules should be observed more and more strictly. If fire preserves its nature, creatures which cannot endure it simply cannot live near it. That is the virtue of fire and not its defect. It is because, unlike fire, we are not true to ourselves that all the problems arise. My suggestion about simplicity and strictness in observing the rules concerns ourselves. We should cultivate them in ever greater degree. We seek,protection for ourselves in our inner selves and not outside of us "we" here means all of us who voluntarily stay in the Ashram, you, I and everybody else. And one should not observe only as many rules as the other inmates do. One must observe every rule as strictly as one can. In this lies the secret of the progress of the Ashram. The rule should be, a liberal attitude towards others and strictness towards oneself. Even so, we shall preserve some minimum decency in our attitude to ourselves, for very often our liberal attitude towards others will not be sincere and our strictness towards ourselves will be so only in appearance.

The ideal for girls is a life of inviolate *brahmacharya*. Training for it includes training for ideal married life. Boys and girls do not require to be instructed as to what married life means. That relation is a part of the animal nature of men and women. The institution of marriage was devised as a means of exercising some control on that nature. Its perfect control means *brahmacharya*. Anybody who can observe this perfect control will also be able to observe the limited control of marriage. But those who regard marriage itself as their ideal will not understand the real purpose even of marriage. What training does one require for lust ? It will grow of itself. However, the girl who has accepted complete *brahmacharya* as her ideal must learn how to manage a home. She must learn something about child-care. She will not be a nun living in a cave. An unmarried woman marries the whole world, makes herself a mother and a daughter to all people and thereby becomes fit to manage the affairs of the whole society. Maybe there has been no such unmarried woman. Nevertheless that is the ideal. For all girls, therefore, the training should be the same. I think I have explained the idea clearly. If I have not done so, ask me to explain it again.

This will explain your duty towards that Muslim woman. The real cause of fainting fits and similar ailments in girls lies in our own shortcomings. If we have made fairly satisfactory progress, even the presence of young people among us will not be dangerous to the Ashram. But whenever we see such danger, we should ask the young man or woman to leave. If you wish to stop admitting other young men or women, you may do so.

All my hopes rest on Narandas. If Narandas, who is the secretary of the Ashram, is the Narandas as I imagine him to be, everything will be well. My faith in him is daily increasing. If he is defeated, some other old inmate of the Ashram will grow and advance, and I am sure, therefore, that everything will be well. There are many residents in the Ashram but only a few inmates. That is why we do not get sufficient workers. In these very imperfect conditions, all of you should do the best that you can.

The Ashram is the measuring rod by which people can judge me. I take it with me wherever I go. Wherever my body may be, my soul is always in the Ashram. All the shortcomings found in the Ashram must be present, visibly or invisibly, in me too. If I have made a mistake in understanding you all, the blame must be mine and nobody else's. If, however, I do not know myself, how can I sit in judgment over all of you ? When I think of particular persons, I see that I did not invite anybody except Chhaganlal and Maganlal. All the others were sent to me by God to test me or to help me. And now another matter. You made a mistake in not going to Dr. Patel yourself. You cannot ask a doctor's advice through a note. Observe complete silence. Show your throat to the doctor and follow his advice. You should not be obstinate in this matter.

Bapu

18. Letter to Premabehn Kantak

Yeravada Mandir,[34]
March 6, 1933

Chi. Prema,

I am starting on this letter at five sharp (Silence Day). Yours was the last letter I read from the Ashram post. I have not been able to go beyond 75 counts with the slivers which you sent. Yarn of 75 counts should be regarded as very much below the mark. I have calculated the count on the basis of the figure you give for weight. The scales here are not good enough for weighing with any minute accuracy. I do believe, however, that if my hand was all right I would be able to go up to 100 counts. What you write to me regarding Sushila is simply incomprehensible to me. I am not aware of having ignored her in the least. She herself made me feel that there was no need to inquire after her or advise her. So I did not ask her any detailed questions. Tell her this. How could I know that like you she also craved for a show of love and for compliments ? I ought to have known that your friend would be like you. Isn't that what you suggest ? But probably Sushila herself will not admit this. Isn't one Prema enough for me ? There are other Premas, of course, but they are all different from one another and from you. However, I will be more careful in future. How old is Vijaya ? How does she behave ? Train Lakshmi thoroughly.

I also suspect something from the fact that Durga's boils cannot still be cured. She used to write to me regularly, but she never writes now. From that, too, I suspect that she is hiding something. Inquire and find out if she is suffering from some other disease. A diet of raw vegetables and dates is bound to help you to reduce your weight. You should also include in it two and a half ounces of unboiled milk. Among raw vegetables, you may eat tomatoes, radishes, carrots, lettuce, etc. You should exclude salt. You should take two or three lemons with water or with dates. Probably it will be better to take it with water. If, however, it sours your teeth you may not take it. You can also mix soda bicarb with it. I cannot discuss the question asked by Rajaji and others. That would be violating truth. It can be done when a suitable opportunity arises. My writings, however, contain a reply to every doubt. I will admit all the shortcomings of the Ashram which you may point out. But you will help me better if you also suggest suitable remedies at the same time. Even if, however, you cannot do that, I must have your criticism. I use my brain as much as I can. I know this: the Ashram's shortcomings are not its own, but mine. If the potter makes an ill-shaped pot, is that the fault of the pot or of the potter ? I literally believe what I have said, and the shortcomings of the Ashram, therefore, are a measure of my ignorance. But notwithstanding its shortcomings, I like the Ashram, for I am not ready to say positively that I do not like myself. I like myself in the measure that I do not feel the sense of "I", and ceaselessly strive to overcome what still remains of that sense.

Bapu

19. Letter to Premabehn Kantak

March 12, 1933

Chi. Prema,

Your argument is worthy of an M.A. "If someone can hang himself upside down, why can I not play music ?" Many other questions like this can be framed. The only reply is that no reason can be given why you may not. If one person can do one thing, why may another person not do something else ?

But it is certainly possible that someone who hangs himself upside down may be able to give a valid reason even for such an action, while a person like me who then starts playing music may not be able to give a convincing reason for doing so. But let that pass. You should now put your proposal before the other inmates of the Ashram and, if a majority supports it, by all means go ahead and make the necessary preparations. Being a prisoner, I myself will not be able to join that marriage procession. And a prisoner has no vote either, so you need not consult me. Q.E.D.

I will patiently wait for Dhurandhar's letter. Whether you reply to my question or not, I will keep on inquiring about your health. Tell me, therefore, is it all right ? Is the throat all right and can you speak ? How is the backache ? Is your weight increasing ?

When the time comes for giving away the yarn which I am spinning with the slivers sent by you, I will certainly give it to you if you continue to deserve it even then. I hope you will be satisfied with this answer. The count of the yarn will not exceed 75. There are fairly numerous rough particles in the slivers. It is possible that even Keshu's machine is not good enough for *devkapas.* I hope you know that this variety of cotton cannot be carded with the ordinary bow. I don't know anything about Mahadev having been offended. Nor did I know that he had written to anybody about the matter. I knew something from Narandas's letter. I knew about disrespect only from your letter. Mahadev has told me nothing. Nor did I know, when I asked him to spin (with your slivers), that he found himself in a moral dilemma[35]. In this matter your case seems to be perfectly correct. I did not feel disrespect to anybody in your remark or your request. I don't know why Mahadev felt it. I am observing silence just now, otherwise I would have asked him. I did feel, however, that your request sprang from ignorant attachment. Why should you have such attachment for me ? One should eschew attachment for a person who cannot belong to any one individual but daily strives to belong to all. Such attachment can avail nothing. But this is one thing. To deduce from it a dislike for others is a different thing. Sardar, I believe, was only joking, as is his wont.

And now see how I valued your love. Surely you will agree that I should make what I believe to be the best use of the slivers sent by you. Wouldn't that be the best way of showing how I valued your love ? If a vaid, out of his great love for me, sends me gold *bhasma*[36], would it not be right to give it to my neighbour to whom it might be more useful than to me ? Or, if somebody sends me a carriage to drive and if my neighbour can drive it more safely than I can, would I not show better appreciation of the donor's love by letting that neighbour drive it for me ? The same argument applies to slivers. Among us here, Mahadev can make the best use of such fine slivers, and so I gave half the quantity to him. This will test his skill and increase national wealth and I also will feel happier. You should, therefore, change your nature which makes you wish that your gift should be used only by the person to whom it is given. If you make a gift, you should do so unconditionally. Sushila's description of you was correct. If Kisan was not likely to get in time the fruit which were brought for her, you would have served both Sushila and Kisan by eating it yourself. It was foolish of you to have let them rot. Q.E.D. again. I am sorry I cannot reply to your last question.

I hope you have had long talks with Lakshmi.

Bapu

20. Letter to Premabehn Kantak

March 26, 1933

Chi. Prema,

I got your beautiful letter. I hope you will always keep up this attitude. Haven't I promised to preserve the yarn for you ? I will keep my promise. You need not refuse it. You certainly have a right to ask anything from me. Your request for the yarn was blameless. It was the manner in which you made it that was wrong. You have now rectified your mistake, and so I have nothing to say. You see how my hopes are being reduced to ashes. How much I thought of. . . and of. . . ? I could never suspect them. I had built high hopes on them, but they were like a house built on sand. What should we do to realize the ideal which the Ashram has placed before itself ? It can be done only if everybody tries to do what he can independently of others. Do you do that ? I hope you know my definition of *brahmacharya.* Do you think you can observe such *brahmacharya* ? Likes and dislikes have no place in it at all. I don't wish to criticize you, nor to lecture to you. I only beg. Till my begging bowl is filled, the Ashram will never become a true Ashram. I am glad that you wrote about your health. If you eat crushed cabbage, uncooked, it may possibly do you no harm, but it will certainly do no harm if you eat it boiled. It is not necessary to eat all vegetables uncooked. It will be enough if you eat a few raw vegetables. But the main thing is that you should speak as little as possible. The delay in following this rule may lead to such serious consequences that subsequent self-control will not avail you. Everything should be done at the right time. The throat requires rest exactly when it is sensitive.

I am glad that you became acquainted with Maruti. Write to the couple from time to time. Lakshmi wants a companion from the Ashram. Is there anybody whom you can send ? Also write to Lakshmidas and find out if she can stay there.

Jamnalalji told me that there were many Maharashtrian ladies in the Ashram whom he had sent there. It is his desire, which he wanted me to convey to you, that you should train some of them for the Mahila Ashram. Is there anybody whom you can train ? She should be a mature woman. Let me know if there is any such. Jamnalalji wants this to be conveyed to Narandas also. I will not mention this message separately in my letter to him. I reserve for it some further explanation in connection with it. I cannot say anything about the White Paper[37]. Moreover, the matter is out of my sphere while I am in jail, and so I have not even read it.

Bapu

21. Letter to Premabehn Kantak

April 2, 1933

Chi. Prema,

I have your letter. You did well in writing it. It is a good one. I cannot reply to you in detail today. Though the letter is good, it shows a pride unworthy of a woman who claims to be a *brahmacharini*. Remember the story of Narad. The moment he felt proud of his *brahmacharya*, he fell. One who aspires to observe *brahmacharya* relies only on God, and hence he is always humble. He never trusts himself. Anybody who is incapable from birth of feeling passion is not a human being. Such a person is either God, or lacks the power which makes a man a man or a woman a woman. In other words, he or she is an incomplete human being, is diseased. How can God be proud ? Is a stone proud of being a stone ? A diseased person should not be proud of being so. A man or a woman can cultivate the strength to control his or her passion and put the power so conserved to better use. But as soon as he or she becomes proud of such strength, it will be lost. How do you know to what extent the power of *brahmacharya* which you may have in you is being wasted ? Your *brahmacharya* is certainly not perfect. Find out the natural truth about you. If you never feel passion, are you a goddess ? A goddess would be a different kind of being from what you are. You are no goddess, and I don't think that you are diseased, since you get monthly periods. Examine yourself and write to me again.

Bapu

22. Letter to Premabehn Kantak

April 2, 1933

Chi. Prema,

I wrote one letter[38] to you today morning. You will probably get it before this. What you write about . . .[39] and . . .[40] is a half-truth. Everybody makes mistakes. We should not be upset if somebody makes one, but we are bound to feel unhappy when a person hides his mistake and it is brought to light in spite of him, and then he puts up an unworthy defence. If we do not feel unhappy, we shall never find a way of preventing such incidents. If we assume that such things will always happen and do nothing to prevent them, that will mean destruction of society. We must, therefore, do what we can to prevent them. We will do so only if we are shocked by such incidents. We can say that one should not feel pain or get angry for things which don't matter, and I think you also mean only that. If you mean anything more, I am sure that you are wrong. If some other word is suggested in place of "pain" or "shock", I might accept it. But your letter seems to spring from *moha*[41], I cannot explain how. I cannot say whether the word *moha* is correct. I will be satisfied if you understand what I mean.

I have already admitted the mistake which I made. What I want you to show is simplicity of heart, tenderness, humility, patience, forbearance and generosity towards others. You can show these things only if you come down from the sky to the earth. When will you begin to feel that you are nothing ? Is it proper to bow down to Mother Earth everyday and then kick her everyday ? If our prayer to her is sincere, we should make ourselves mere particles of dust and learn to suffer the kicks of the world. Mother Earth then will not feel our feet, as we shall have become ash, though still alive. "Scatter the dust of separateness", as the poet says. I have still a stock of the slivers sent by you. It was not your fault that they contain rough particles. The fault was partly that of the carding-bow and partly of the cotton. If you had carded the cotton still further, the fibres would have become weak. Other slivers do not yield very fine yarn, but they contain fewer particles. I am very glad that you have taken Parachure Shastri's son in your hand.

You advised Shanta well. She may now do whatever she likes.

Bapu

23. Letter to Premabehn Kantak

April 12, 1933

Chi. Prema,

I have your letter. It is enough that I have cautioned you. Your belief that I do not read your letters carefully is not correct. I had fully understood what you had said. Such cock-sureness is itself a sign of pride. The pride shows in your language. This does not mean that I want you to hide your thoughts or express them in carefully chosen words. I like you to write as you feel. According to me it is your virtue that you let me see you as you are both inwardly and outwardly. If you were to write with unnatural self-control, I would be helpless and unable to advise or admonish you. I cannot teach you to become humble as a dust particle. If one understands what God is, one naturally feels like that. That understanding will come to you in its own time. Nor do I mean that you do not have to endure many things from others. But the fact that you can wipe out all that in a moment makes me unhappy.

You believe that an atmosphere of prejudice against you has been created around me. You are mistaken in this. Sardar is certainly not against you. Do not take his humour as a sign of his being against you. I do not at all feel that Mahadev is against you either. What Chhaganlal has said against you is nothing new. He knows your worth, but says that till you can control your tongue you should be entrusted with no responsibility. This is his old complaint. You should know that I rarely talk with my three companions. There is, except for a little joking at meal times or during walks, no time for any discussion. We rarely talk about anybody unless there is an occasion to do so. With all my work, I never feel in a mood for talking about other things, nor could I waste my time in idle discussions. I have hardly been able to discuss even the painful episode of . . .[42] and . . .[43]. I have contented myself with the briefest exchange of views. There is no atmosphere of prejudice against you around me, nor is there any such prejudice in my mind. If I admonish you rather harshly, it is because I regard you as my daughter and want to see you perfect. Why, then, do you feel hurt by my criticism ? You may accept such of it as you think worth accepting and forget the rest. For it is perfectly possible that my criticism may be based on ignorance and that I may not have correctly understood what you said.

It is quite true that different people may see the same thing differently. We daily observe that the same energy or strength is used in different ways.

I do feel that no woman should be asked by others to do any routine work during her menses. Nobody can know when she may be having a pain. It would be best not to burden a woman with any work during such a period. She may do of her own free will whatever work she feels inclined to do. Some women feel nothing during menstruation and go on doing their work as usual. Some others feel unbearable pain. Some don't feel any pain, but can do no physical work. A woman who spends the period in the right manner gains fresh energy every month. Those three or four days are for getting back lost strength, and for that the woman should be left free from all responsibility. She should be free to lie down if she wants to. Some ignorant women do not lay aside their hectic domestic work even during that period, not knowing the harm which they do themselves. They should be properly advised. On the whole, therefore, I like Lakshmidas's suggestion.

What you say about Kisan is possible. I was very glad to learn that she had recovered. She seems to have waited for my reply to her letter. But I do not remember having not replied to any of her letters. I have already written to you about your slivers.

You will not lose weight by living on unboiled milk. If you eat boiled vegetables once a day, I am sure you will benefit. Probably your throat needs them; I think it does unboiled milk. Why not try ?

Bapu

24. Letter to Premabehn Kantak

May 1, 1933

Chi. Prema,

My fast will be for all the inmates of the Ashram, including you. You should, therefore, get rid of all your diseases.

I assume that you have kept a copy of your questions[44] and so I give here only brief replies to them. I am hard pressed for time today.

1. If persuasion does not succeed, you may become silent and pray in your heart for that person, whether she is a girl or a grown-up woman. This will help you to overcome your impatience.
2. We should know what is meant by 'necessity' in this question. Suppose that I am reciting Sanskrit verses and leading a prayer, and just then I see a snake. It is necessary that I should catch it, and I may, therefore, stop reciting the verses and violate a rule. I may also do that if I feel an immediate call of nature at that time. If, however, I feel thirsty, I should control my desire for some time and go on reciting the verses. You felt something in the throat and yet continued. That was worse than foolishness.
3. We may disregard any social practice or custom which obstructs our quest for truth.
4. If you have absolute faith in me, you should believe that what you regard as the voice of your conscience may not be so. If, however, that voice is so direct as to be more powerful even than your faith in me, you should follow it whatever the cost.

5. It is not possible to reply to this question categorically.
6. I do not follow this question.
7. If a person is often found telling lies or shirking work, even a lover of truth will suspect him of doing the same on another occasion, but will, despite his suspicion, love him and continue to give him opportunities.
8. There can be no one rule for all people in this matter. It depends on one's attitude. However, simplicity should not be sacrificed for the sake of art.
9. Mutual fault-finding is always bad. It is petty-mindedness to retort, 'You are no better'.
10. This is implied in *ahimsa.*

Thinking that you may have had no time to keep a copy of your questions, I return them with this.

I am sending two women[45] to the Ashram. I hesitate very much to do so, but I send them because I feel that I ought to. I do hope that they will not increase your work but will help you. Make some arrangement to help them to learn Hindi.

I should like Sushila[46] to spend this vacation in the Ashram. That is likely to give rest to both of you. I hope you know the English saying that change of occupation is rest. There is a good deal of truth in it. Treat this only as brain-wave which I got while writing this letter.

If Sushila has made some other plan, I certainly don't want her to abandon it to please me.

Bapu

25. Letter to Premabehn Kantak

May 17, 1934

Chi. Prema,

Kisan stayed with me for so many months, and now Sushila is with me. It should be enough for you to know how often and what precisely we must have talked about you. That being so, where was the need to send any message to you ? There are two reasons why I am writing this letter today. One is that Sushila has been urging me to do so. And the second reason is the news given by her. I am told that you cried for three days because of my decision. I had thought that you would feel unhappy on hearing of it, but I had also expected that you would at the same time dance and sing with joy because you would not fail to see its significance and importance and its absolute conformity with truth. Experience is daily proving the correctness of the decision. There is no question here of the unworthiness of co-workers. Nobody has proved himself unworthy. But the facts which had come to light were significant and prompted me to take the decision which I did. When the time comes— and it will certainly come—those very co-workers will fight again. The chief thing is to cultivate more strength and self-control. My weapons cannot be said to be wrong because they are ineffective at present. Maybe they require sharpening or the time is not ripe for their use. I cannot write more on this subject. When you are released, come straight to me and, if you are not convinced even then, contend with me as much as you please and understand my reasons. This decision will test everybody, myself included. With God's grace, I am sure all of us will emerge successful. I think this should be enough.

Blessings from
Bapu

(PS.)
I wrote this letter in the train which is taking me to Patna. Trains on the E.I. Rly. run so smoothly that one has no difficulty in a moving train.

26. Letter to Premabehn Kantak

August 1, 1934

Chi. Prema,

I got your fairly long and frank letter. Parents don't think or talk about their children's good health. They think and talk about their diseases, which are not of the body only. I am not surprised to learn that you are observing the Ashram rules. I would have been surprised indeed had you not observed them.

May you succeed in your noble aims.

Everyday is one's birthday. We are born everyday and we die everyday and are born again. But, following convention, we regard a particular day of the year as our bithday. You certainly have my blessings for that day and for all other days of the year. I am sending this reply through Narandas and thereby saving five pice. Narandas also will write to you. I have to write to him today and so, instead of sending the letter through Dhurandhar, I am sending it through him.

Please keep writing to me. Your description of that place was good. This letter is being written before the morning prayer.

Blessings from
Bapu

27. Letter to Premabehn Kantak

Unrevised
December 4, 1934

Chi. Prema,

I got your letter. If I gave wise replies to your questions, would they necessarily be a sign of real wisdom in me ?

None of you would know the (strength of) anger in me. I alone can know it. I wouldn't describe as anger what Lilavati or Gangabehn may have observed in me.[47] I suppress most of the anger which I feel. Gangabehn and others could have seen only what remained of it. If I did not let them see even that, I would be a hypocrite or ruin my health and become a mere skeleton. That does not happen because I make a conscious effort to control my anger and tread my way through the problems. Because I don't think it necessary to be careful with people who are intimate with me they occasionally get a glimpse of the anger in me, but, being kind to me, they forget it.

Prabhavati will send to you whatever yarn is still lying with me.[48] My calculation has turned out to be wrong. Prabhavati is in Bombay at present. She has gone there to be of help to Swaruprani and to meet Jayaprakash.

What you believe about . . .[49] is probably not correct. Be extremely careful about believing any story against a person. It would be better not to listen to such a story at all.

What can be done about a worker like Dr. Hardikar ?[50] His views and aims are different from ours. The Government will not permit him to carry on the activity which is dear to his heart, and he cannot take interest in the other activities which are going on. A person can participate in popular activities only if he can adjust himself within their framework. A person like Dr. Hardikar should take up some occupation and do what service he can while engaged in it. I have been advising many people to do this. People who follow an occupation honestly also serve the country. Those who claim to be servants of the people may in fact be a burden on them whereas people who earn a livelihood by following an occupation may be true servants.

You are right in what you say regarding your letters. You can write "Private" on letters intended exclusively for me. As regards letters which you leave to me to deal with, I shall dispose of them as I like. I rarely preserve the letters which I receive. You may do what is possible regarding crafts.

I hope Deo will not change your place of work too frequently.[51] You can do some work only if you remain steady in one place. If the place where you are living now is but a suburb of Poona' you will not be able to do much useful work there. However, since you have been working there, I hope you will not be asked to leave it too soon. But don't attach much importance to my advice in this matter. If you think that it was a mistake to have gone there, you certainly need not cling to the place. A mistake must be rectified when it is realized. Who am I to secure swaraj for the country through *ahimsa* ? If I have real *ahimsa* in me it cannot but prove infectious. I have little faith in myself, but my faith in *ahimsa* is unshakable. The world has recognized it as a great principle, but it has rarely been acted upon. I daily get a fresh experience of its sweetness, for to me it is the only wish-fulfilling tree. No other way is possible for me, for I have found no other means of attaining Satyanarayana[52] and life without the prospect of attaining Him has no meaning for me. Hence the path of *ahimsa*, whether difficult or easy, is the only one that I can follow. If violence breaks out after my death, you may conclude that my *ahimsa* was very imperfect or was not real at all—but not that the principle of *ahimsa* was wrong. or it may also be that we shall have to cross the river of blood in which the wicked suffer for their sins before we reach the goal of *ahimsa. Ahimsa* came into politics in the 1920s. But didn't the Chauri Chaura[53] and other outrages occur after that, and hasn't the Government gone to extreme lengths of repression ? I am sure, however, that despite all this violence, *ahimsa* has had a profound effect on people. But it has been no more than a drop in the ocean. My experiment continues and is ever growing in its scope. May your faith never waver !

Our senses do not always perceive the truth. Very often what they perceive is utterly false. That is why the path of non-attachment was discovered. To cultivate non-attachment means to rise above the senses. one can do that only by overcoming one's attachment to objects of the senses. If we believe the evidence of the eyes, would it not prove that the earth was flat ? And doesn't the sun seem to be only a golden disc ? If the Prema that my eyes see was the true Prema, what a wretch would I be ! And suppose you believed all that you heard against me !

I think I have written enough. Mirabehn's alarm has sounded. The bell for prayer will soon be given. You may draw from this whatever picture you can (of my state of mind). I am thinking of going to Delhi after the 15th. I intend to stay there for a few days in the Harijan Ashram.

So far as I can see at present, I think I shall be in jail at last.

Blessings from
Bapu

28. Letter to Premabehn Kantak

December 16, 1934

Chi. Prema,

Your letters I shall send on to Narandas. Today also I got up at 1.45 a.m. and started writing letters. It has become a habit with me now to wake up at about 2. I go to bed before 9 p.m. During the day, I take a nap once or twice and get half an hour to one hour. That seems to be enough for me.

By writing "not revised" I ensure—and do—justice to myself and to the person to whom the letter is addressed. If by chance I have written *"aaj mar gaya"* instead of "Ajmer *gaya*", the other party may correct the mistake or, in case of doubt, ask me. A letter which has not been revised should always be regarded as incomplete. But I would prefer, and so would you, that I write an incomplete letter to you rather than not write any.

Most probably I shall be going to Delhi on or about the 27th. Continue to write to me at the Wardha address till you hear from me or you read in the papers.

The atonement for any violation of a vow in a dream is generally greater vigilance and Ramanama on waking up from the dream. Such violations of vows or moral rules in dreams are signs of our imperfection. Unconsciously we harbour deep in our hearts the desires which we gratify in dreams. We should not despair because of such dreams, but should become more and more vigilant. Despair may be a sign of the person being attached to the senses; it is certainly a sign of his lack of faith. If a person tires of repeating Ramanama— despairs about its usefulness—shouldn't we say that he has lost faith in it ? When Columbus's companions lost faith, they wanted to kill him. But with his eyes of faith Columbus could clearly see the coast and he asked his companions to give him some more time, and he reached America ! ! ! If a person dreams that he is eating forbidden food, such a dream also means what I have explained above. There may be external causes for such dreams and, whenever we discover any, we should remove them. "I am the spotless Brahman that is witness of all the states." This is what we sing. We can sing thus only if we strive ceaselessly to be that. The dreams that we get are a signth at we have not succeeded in becoming spotless. They are a warning light for us.

Not a leaf can stir without God's grace, but we cannot dispense with human effort either, which is the means through which God's grace works. Realization means nothing but pure and selfless service of all living creatures.

It is very good indeed that Kisan has decided to stay with you.

Blessings from
Bapu

29. Letter to Premabehn Kantak

February 3, 1935

Chi. Prema,

I am very late this time in replying to your letter. I get no time at all.

I have been writing so much today that the right hand feels tired and I am now writing with the left hand.

The body must have lost some strength but I have no such feeling. The fast[54] has not in the least led to an increase of weakness. Fasting never does if one knows how to return to normal diet afterwards. I believe that the effect of my diet on my health has been nothing but beneficial. But I cannot give reasons for this belief. I am very glad that Father, Mother and others came and saw you.

There is certainly a remedy for the frequent pimples which you get. For a few days live only on fruit and uncooked *bhaji.* Take steam treatment and the pimples will then immediately shrink. Having done this, bathe in cold water. The skin will probably clear up in three or four days. Then start taking milk or curd which is not sour along with fruit and uncooked *bhaji.* Among the different *bhajis,* fenugreek leaves, spinach, *luni* and lettuce are the best. I eat even the leaves and twigs of mustard.

To pray to God for anything means to aspire for it intensely. God is both different and not different from us. He is different because He is perfect, and He is not different because we are portion of Him. If a drop of water separated from the sea may not pray to the sea, to whom else may it pray ? But does the sea have to do anything to answer the prayer ? Prayer is the anguished cry of one who cannot bear separation. The embodied soul cannot help uttering such a cry. The key to the nation's progress both is and is not in our hands. We can help in its progress if we reduce ourselves to a cipher. It is in our hands to do that. But the progress itself is not in our hands, because our reducing ourselves to a cipher means leaving ourselves entirely in the hands of God who alone is the digit of unity. "O Udho, the secret of *karma* is beyond human understanding" is an absolute truth. We can know that there is a law of *karma,* but we do not know how it works. That is

God's mercy. We do not know the laws of even an earthly king. How then can we know the laws of God who is Law personified ?

The appearance of victory in the early part of this struggle was an illusion, and the appearance of defeat also is nothing but an illusion. In the lexicon of one who has unshakable faith in the ultimate victory of truth, there is no such word as "defeat".

Blessings from
Bapu

30. Letter to Premabehn Kantak

April 5, 1935

Chi. Prema,

I have taken up for reply both your letters of 8-2-'35 and 30-3-'35. How is Kisan now ? Is she doing anything ? How does she keep herself occupied ?

Do you still go on with your self-chosen occupation of ploughing the fields and working the water-lift ? You should try and persuade those over whom you have influence to save the expenditure on births and deaths. All may not listen to you, but a few certainly will.

You had a good discussion with Nariman. It is true that most people follow *ahimsa* only as a policy.[55] But there are a few at least like you who strive their utmost to follow it as a dharma. Ultimately it is such *ahimsa* that will work.

There will be an army even after the country has become free. I don't feel that my *ahimsa* is sufficiently strong to convince the people that there will be no necessity for an army. If the army remains, military training also will remain. But this is only speculation. It is not inconceivable that, if we really and truly win freedom through *ahimsa*, we may not need an army afterwards. There is no limit to the power of *ahimsa*, as there is none to that of the votary of *ahimsa*. The latter does nothing of his own will. All his actions are prompted by God. That being so, how can he say in advance what God will prompt him to do at a future time ? There is thus no question of compromise in this matter. It is only a question of recognizing the limit of one's strength. My killing a snake through fear is no compromise but merely an exhibition of my lack of strength. One might say that God has given me only so much strength and no more, or that I have not purified myself sufficiently—have not adequate *tapascharya*—to make myself fit for greater strength. A compromise, on the other hand, is a deliberate and voluntary act.

A perfect *satyagrahi* means a perfect *avatar* of God. Do you doubt that such a perfect *avatar* can shake the whole world ? It is no exaggeration to say that this world is a laboratory for preparing the ground for such an *avatar*. If all of us prepare overselves for a partial manifestation of the Divine, we may rest assured that the perfect *avatar* will come some day. If you have such faith, you will not need to ask about the necessity or otherwise of an army.

The Government may indeed be a machine, but is not the machine controlled by an engineer ? There is no harm in attending a music or dance performance, provided there is nothing obscene in it. But I would certainly mind going when somebody else pays for us. It may be possible to pay for one person, but who will pay for the millions ? We are among the millions. In this matter, however, everyone should act according to his or her own strength. Preserve carefully Mahadev's article about bread. The problem of keeping the wells clean is a big one. It will be a great achievement if you can persuade the people to stop using the steps on wells wherever they exist.

Write to me in detail the method of straining oil so that I may try it.

Don't mind if your weight is increasing. Acid things are necessary in one's food. I have introduced here both tamarind and onions.

If Sushila has been appointed an Examiner, she should share her fees and set a question paper that will be easy to answer and that will test originality.

My remark about menstruation is correct. Such freedom from passion takes a very long time to acquire. Passion is so subtle a thing that we are not always able to recognize it. It would be proper for Europe to carry on an agitation for the release of Jawaharlal.

The disregard of the Assembly voting does not fill me with disappointment. This contingency was taken into account. Entering the Assembly was necessary and remains so. I keep silent about Hindu-Muslim unity because I can do nothing about it. When the Elephant King had realized his helplessness, he started praying and his prayer was answered. My condition is like his. My prayer continues. Let deliverance come when it will. Why should an *anasakta*[56] be impatient to know its exact time ? We have a large number of newcomers here. Cooking has been drastically simplified. Everything is cooked in steam. Containers for all the three articles of food are put into the cooker at the same time. This saves a lot of time. Cooking now practically means only making *rotlis*. I am trying to discover some method of simplifying this work too.

The oil-press is still working. We continue the cleaning of the neighbouring village everyday. I visited it only once. Mahadev goes there daily.

You can come when you get time and wish to do so. You may come to Indore, too, if you wish. I think this is enough.

Blessings from
Bapu

31. Letter to Premabehn Kantak

Unrevised
May 28, 1935

Chi. Prema,

Why did you have to keep waiting for forty-five minutes ? In any case, I didn't think you would run away. Since you were meeting me after a long time, I was eager to ask you a few questions and have a careful look at you. Of course, you did well to go back to your place of work. But I was eager because on that day you had stayed on. I am unable to say anything about Aurobindobabu. If a man with a flabby body cannot have pure wisdom, what can one say of one who is slim ? I can only say that my path has borne fruit for me. Let us not make ourselves judges of the whole world. We should admit that among the slim ? I can only say that my path has borne fruit for me. Let us not make ourselves judges of the whole world. We should admit that among the two hundred persons living under his wing there are several whose lives have undergone a great transformation through his influence.

Everybody follows his own natural bent.

It is not quite correct to say that in the West they do not recognize the necessity of purity in private life, nor is it correct to say that here everybody recognizes it. We ourselves not only recognize it, but go further and believe that the actions prompted by a reason not purified inwardly will not endure, however attractive they may appear. Such actions cannot be judged from their immediate results. It is true, of course, that actions which have no connection with morality do not require inward purity. A dissolute carpenter will be able to make a right-angled table. But a person lacking in purity will not be able to eradicate untouchability or turn the people to the spinning-wheel, for both these tasks require qualities of the heart. In such activities calculations of time count for little. We should have no doubt at all that actions performed with sincere and truthful motives are bound to have certain results. If we do not have such faith, we shall never be able to adhere to moral principles. God is beyond the reach of human thought. The God, therefore, whom we worship is a creation of our imagination. Nobody has seen the real God. If anybody has seen Him, he has not been able to describe Him. It is difficult to say which Form of Him is dearest to me. The Form, however, which I worship is known as Truth. He both has a manifest form and has none. He manifests Himself in innumerable ways. How can imperfect man see perfect truth ? I don't intend to write anything about the jewellery though I have alreay made a note of the point in my diary. The additional note which will appear after your letter will be for my information. Isn't that what you desire ?

I will use the *khadi* when it is received. Lilavati has arrived here from Rajkot. This time her health is excellent. She has gained weight, too, and seems to be quite happy.

I intend to leave on the 31st and reach Wardha on the 2nd.

Blessings from
Bapu

32. Letter to Premabehn Kantak

June 21, 1935

Chi. Prema,

I was not in a position to reply immediately to your excellent letter. When the right hand demands rest, it becomes impossible to cope with the work.

All my questions are not such as can be asked in a letter. I must of course have asked you such questions. Questions which occur to me at any moment belong only to that moment.

My aim in taking you to Borsad was that you might be able to do such work more easily in future, and to show you that I had taken a share in anti-plague work also.

I have already written in *Harijan* and explained the connection between our sin and the earthquake.[57] Read that article. Nobody was angered in Bihar. On the contrary, everybody realized that it was the result of our sin. All this follows from the principle of oneness. I have written an article[58] in *Harijan* about snakes etc. Read it. If you are not reading the articles which I have been writing recently in *Harijan,* I would advise you to read them carefully. I hope you get copies of it.

I wouldn't see any sin in ending the life of the husband who was lingering in pain and to whom no relief could be given even by careful nursing.[59] If, however, the husband is conscious, his wishes should be ascertained. If he wishes to live despite the pain, he should be allowed to live.

The owners becoming trustees means their handing over to the poor, that is, to the State or any other public welfare institution, all income in excess of a certain percentage.

If everybody handed over all their possessions to the State, the spirit of enterprise would disappear and everybody would become an automaton.

My relations with the rich will continue. I don't look upon the rich as wicked and upon the poor as angels. Both in the East and the West there are a great many rich who earn money with philanthropic motives. They deserve to be honoured. I know numbers of poor people whose company should be shunned. In the swaraj of my dream, the tiger and the goat should be able to drink water together from the same pool. What will it matter if this remains for ever a dream ? If I didn't know what I wanted, what would I strive for ? It is certainly true that I cannot understand people correctly, but do those who claim to understand them really do so ? I, therefore, do not regret my ignorance. Since I cannot know human beings, I trust them.

Is it necessary for you to answer every time somebody asks you a question about me ? Why don't you say, "I cannot answer your question. I like the man's work and his ideas. Does one always give reasons for what one likes ? You should, therefore, address your questions to the man himself ?" If you replied thus, you would be saved from a great deal of unpleasant argument. However, you may certainly impart to others what you have learnt from me and fully digested. But then what one has digested doesn't remain somebody else's but becomes one's own. One entertains no doubt about what is one's own and is always ready with answers to any questions about it.

Let this suffice for today.

Blessings from
Bapu

33. Letter to Premabehn Kantak

September 10, 1935

Chi. Prema,

I had received the *rakhadi* in time. I got the (hand-made) paper made in Junnar. It was good. I have given the whole bulk to Khurshedbehn whose need was greater than mine. The yarn being kept aside. It attracts a good many people's eyes. And what will be the payment for my labour of spinning ? Whenever I can spin 160 rounds during a day, it is Diwali for me.

I have all along been under the impression that indigenous reedpens are available in plenty. The one with which I am writing is believed to be Indian. I will inquire. Among the Socialists there are many good people, and some have the spirit of self-sacrifice in them; there are some who possess a powerful intellect and some who are rogues. Almost all of them have Westernized minds. None of them knows the real conditions in Indian villages or perhaps even cares to know them. Be thankful that your food was appreciated. I do not recollect the name Lakshmibai Thunse[60]. It is all right if Kaka has invited you. Your duty, however, lies where you are.[61] I have not changed my views. Deo seems to be upset by the attempt to entice you. Reassure him on my behalf. He needs no such reassurance from you of course.

I also feel about Hitler nearly the same way as you. If one points regarding my attitude is borne in mind, everything else will be clear. I am indifferent about the time when the goal will be reached, but not at all about the work to be done and the good to be reached. I say that I do not care whether the rich do or do not give up their wealth not because I am unconcerned whether or not they do so but because I have no fear that they will not do so. If the steps we are taking are right, sooner or later they will lead to only one end.

The theory about man having descended from the ape does not convince me. There is no doubt, however, that the soul which lives in the human body now has lived in the bodies of an ape and other animals in the past.

I do not like the argument that the *atatayi*[62] may be killed. Who should be regarded as an *atatayi ?* For the present I do believe that murderers and other criminals will have to be imprisoned. But I do not remember even having said that that is *ahimsa*. I certainly do not believe that it is. I have said that in the existing circumstances such action may be unavoidable. This only means that my *ahimsa* is still far from perfect and that, therefore, I have not yet been able to discover a remedy for this kind of violence. Truth lies in recognizing a fall from an ideal as what it is.

If we win power by any means other than *ahimsa*, the swaraj will most certainly not be the swaraj of the poor. They will profit only in proportion to the degree of *ahimsa* we observe in winning swaraj. Perfect *ahimsa* neither you nor I nor anybody else can claim. But one who believes in *ahimsa* will become more and more nonviolent day by day and in consequence his field of service will keep ever expanding. The field of service of the votary of violence will become narrower day by day and will ultimately become restricted to himself. You have done well in inviting Kelkar.

Blessings from
Bapu

(PS.)
Ba has taken Devdas to Simla. His illness was fairly serious. We have a good many sick-beds here these days. Mira is ill. Amutussalaam also is practically ill. Nimu and her children are with me. Lakshmi is arriving from Delhi today. She is going to Madras. Prabha is here.

34. Letter to Premabehn Kantak

May 6, 1936

Chi. Prema,

You can write to me now. We are leaving on the 8th for Nandi Durg.

You seem to have gathered good experience. Merely because we doubt a man's sincerity we cannot reject his application if he is prepared to sign the Congress Pledge. There will always be men who will wangle admission under one or the other pretext. If the majority of the members are sincere, ultimately all will be well. The report of the Maharashtrian's letter is perfectly correct.[63] But his supposition was completely wrong. The correspondent's letter could be interpreted to mean that by resting my hands on girls' shoulders I used to gratify my sensual desire. His words of course were different.

But the truth is that my discontinuing the practice of resting my hands on the shoulders of girls has nothing to do with my sensual desire. It had its origin in my pampering the body with food while doing no work. I had a discharge, but I was awake and the mind was under control. I understood the cause and from that time stopped taking rest as prescribed by the doctors. And my state now is better than it was, if such a state could be imagined. If you wish to ask me more questions about this you may, for I have cherished high hopes of you. You may, therefore, know from me anything concerning myself that you wish to.

The articles I have written recently deserve careful pondering over. If you have understood them, the practice of *brahmacharya* will become very easy. If one is convinced that the genital organs are not intended for sex-gratification, wouldn't one's attitude change completely ? As a man happening to see on the road the blood-stained sputum of a consumptive may take it to be a gem and long to pick it up, but will come to his senses as soon as he realizes his error, so is the case in regard to the function of the genital organs. The truth is that this belief has never been held with sufficient conviction and clarity.

And now the new education denounces it, teaches that moderate sex gratification is a good thing and asserts its necessity. Think over all this.

The experience of your friends that you have described is excellent.

Let this suffice for the present.

Probably Lilavati will join you.

Blessings from
Bapu

35. Letter to Premabehn Kantak

May 21, 1936

Chi. Prema,

Here in Nandi Durg, I may claim, I am able to dispose of each day's mail practically on the same day. I read your letter of the 18th last evening, and am replying to it today.

It matters little what hopes I cherish about you. You may go on striving according to what you think these hopes are and according to your ability.[64]

You have put the question very well. You could have put it still more plainly.[65] I have always had involuntary discharges. In South Africa they occurred at intervals of several years. I do not remember exactly. Here in India they have been of months. I have mentioned the fact of my getting discharges in a few articles of mine. If my *brahmacharya* had been completely free from discharges, I would have been able to place before the world very much more than I have succeeded in doing. But it seems practically impossible that a person who has indulged in sex gratification from the age of 15 to 30, maybe with his own wife only, can, on taking a vow of *brahmacharya* control the discharge of his vital fluid completely. One whose capacity for retention has progressively weakened from day-to-day for fifteen years cannot recover it fully all at once. Both his body and mind will have become too weak for that. I, therefore, consider myself a very imperfect *brahmachari*. But my position is like that of the castor oil plant which looks big on a heath where there are no trees. People know this shortcoming of mine.

The experience which tormented me in Bombay was a strange and painful one. All my discharges so far had occurred in dreams and they never troubled me. I could forget them. But the experience in Bombay occurred while I was fully awaken and had a sudden desire for intercourse. I felt of course no urge to gratify the craving, there was no self-forgetfulness whatever. I was completely master of my body. But despite my best efforts the organ remained aroused. This was an altogether strange and shameful experience. I have already explained the cause.[66] As soon as that cause was removed the state of remaining aroused came to a stop, that is, waking state.

Despite my imperfection, one thing has always come easily to me, viz. that thousands of women have remained safe in my company. There have been occasions in my life when certain women, though aroused, were saved by God, or say, I was saved. I am a hundred per cent certain that it was God who saved us and, therefore, take no pride in the fact. It is my unceasing prayer to God that I might remain in the same condition till the very end of my life. I have been striving to attain to Shukadeva's[67] condition. I have not succeeded in that aim. If I succeed, I would become a eunuch[68] though possessed of the vital fluid and discharges would become impossible.

However, the views which I have recently expressed[69] regarding *brahmacharya* have no flaw in them and contain no exaggeration.

With effort, any man or woman can attain that ideal. This does not mean that the whole world or thousands will realize, it in my own lifetime. Let it take centuries to be realized, but the ideal is correct, is realizable and must be realized.

Man has a long way to travel yet. His instincts are still those of a beast. Only his frame is human. Violence seems to reign all round. Untruth fills the world. And yet we do not doubt the rightness of the path of truth and nonviolence. Know that the same is the case with regard to *bramacharya.*

Those who strive but continue to burn inwardly are in fact not striving. They nurse lust in their minds and only wish to control loss of the vital fluid, to refrain from the physical act of intercourse. Such persons are correctly described in Chapter II[70] (of the *Gita*). They may be regarded as hypocrites.

What I am at present striving to achieve is purification of thought.

Modern thought regards *brahmacharya* as *adharma* and recommends the 'dharma' of self-indulgence and control of progeny by artificial means. My soul rebels against this. Sex-craving will always remain in the world, but its moral basis rests and will ever rest on *brahmacharya.*

Blessings from
Bapu

(CWMG: V. 69; p. 23)

36. Letter to Premabehn Kantak

August 10, 1936

Chi. Prema,

I had a reason for not being content with a three-pice postcard.[71] I didn't get your *rakhdi*[72]. I would certainly have worn it had I received it. Since you sent one, however, you have had the joy and earned the merit of sending it.

You seem to be picking up knowledge of a good many subjects. I shall at any rate glance through the book sent by you. I can certainly enlarge the area of experience in Segaon, but not just now. I have neither the time nor the inclination. The experiences don't seem to me worth communicating to anybody. Man's speech has a conventional meaning but in addition each utterance also has a specific meaning intenc.ed by the speaker which can be known from the context.

Nobody has known truth in its perfection and, therefore, each person describes a thing as he sees it and that is the truth for him, even though as a matter of fact his view might be false.

In like manner man's view of a thing changes from age to age and the view held in a particular age is the truth for that age. This is the meaning or idea in *asato ma sadgamaya*[73]. Where the notion of high and low has disappeared I see no harm in the Shudras serving the other three *varnas*.[74] (Nobody)[75] is compelled to be a Shudra. (If, then, service is the natural bent of mind of a Shudra,)[76] why should he change that calling for another ? If the Brahmin and the Bhangi both get just enough for their sustenance, what is the difference between the two ? Nobody will prevent a Bhangi from becoming a *jnani*[77]. In the *varna* system of my conception, no *varna* will have the monopoly of knowledge. Think over the verses in the women's prayer.[78] What are the common dharmas of the four *varnas* ? Maybe you will find some utterances of Jnanadeva[79] and others which seem to support the distinction of high and low. But nobody should be judged in this way by a few isolated sayings of his. I know what you wish to say regarding Ramdas[80]. Even if those examples could be shown to be inapplicable, my argument remains untouched. I cannot accede to your request, for you have given no thought as to its propriety. You have just been carried away by the present tide. You, I and all others are cast in the moulds inherited from our parents. There is as much sense, or lack of sense, in rejecting it as there is in forgetting the fact and claiming ourselves to be different. We can remain in the old mould and still make many changes. That is growth or progress. To assume a completely new appearance will mean a total revolution or a new religion altogether. Does Hinduism have no definite mould in any respect ? Children daily trace new letters in water which disappear the moment they are formed, but they enjoy the game. It seems you wish to do the same. But do you think you can lure an old man of 67 who has grown up in the old mould, and interest him in drawing circles in water ? Standing on the bank, I watch the play of such as you. In the next issue of *Harijan*, you will see something having a bearing on this in my comments on a letter.[81] You have discovered my ignorance all right. If you search more, you will discover still grosser ignorance. But I hope you will not desert me when you have discovered all my ignorance. If you promise me that, I will confess that I don't know anything at all, for I have not made such a study.

I have read enough about communism to satisfy me. What we shall need in swaraj I can tell only when I see the swaraj. Any opposition from me that you may notice will be concerning the question of truth-untruth and violence-nonviolence.

Blessings from
Bapu

(CWMG: V. 69; p. 293).

37. Letter to Premabehn Kantak

Unnrevised Segaon,
February 5, 1937

Chi. Prema,

My right hand needs rest and it takes time to write with the left hand. How can I spare that much time ? The burden of work has increased considerably and so I dictate most of the things I have to write. On Mondays I make full use of my right hand. The amanuenses are Vijaya and Manu, and also sometimes Prabhavati. Probably you do not know Vijaya. She is a Patel woman and hails from Bardoli. She has, so to say, forced herself on us, for we had made a firm rule not to make any fresh admission. Vijaya prevailed upon us to break that rule. She put her case in such a manner that I could not send her away. So far I have not regretted admitting her. She goes on doing her work silently and makes up for Lilavati's absence.

Shankarrao must be all right now. I have asked Haribhau Phatak to give me news about his health. But I think you will be able to give detailed news.

I had told Patwardhan that he could come whenever he wished. But, then, don't the hills seem beautiful only from a distance, as they say ?

You seem to be going through a fairly severe test. It is at once easy and difficult to put more money in villagers' pockets. If they follow our advice, we can, without any capital or with a minimum of it, double the earnings of all villages. I am not including in this the money earned from villages by those who exploit the villagers. If, however, they do not follow our advice, that is, refuse to do the work suggested by us or to learn the crafts we try to teach them, it is not only difficult but impossible to increase their earnings. Another big difficulty is this. Only a handful of workers are willing to go to villages, and they, too, are inexperienced. Their bodies are not accustomed to the hardships of village life. They don't know the villagers' nature and are ignorant of their needs. They cannot use their hands or their intelligence. The knowledge acquired by them in schools and colleges is of little use to them. In these circumstances we have to be patient. We should have faith in ourselves. If the villagers possess sound health, even without Government help we can improve the economic condition of villages considerably, say, to the extent of 50 per cent. I mention 50 per cent as the minimum. My belief is that we can improve it to the extent of 90 per cent. Improvement in physical health, social reform and moral uplift, these are the three main things. They require no Government help at all. If we get a little Government help only in economic improvement, our task would be very much easier. But in the absence of progress in respect of the foregoing three things, Government help will be of little use. If, therefore, you become a real expert in the science of *khadi* and refuse to leave the village despite all temptations, you will realize from first-hand experience the truth of all that I have said above.

You are not doing right in not insisting on cow's milk. Whenever you go out, you can carry with you ghee and *pendas* made from cow's milk. The *pendas* should be without sugar, i.e. made from *mava* only. If you wish, you may eat jaggery with it. This keeps down the expense and fully meets one's requirement of milk. Instead of eating dry *pendas* you can turn them into powder and mix them in warm water to make milk. Such milk lacks only vitamins, but absence of vitamins from the diet for a few days does no harm.

Narmada is Narmada Rana. This whole episode is a pitiable one. It is perfectly easy to understand that everybody cannot observe lifelong *brahmacharya*. Those who cannot curb their physical senses may by all means marry. But I cannot tolerate secret indulgence. Man falls through such secret indulgence for no restraints are observed then. I have no prejudice at all against *grihasthashrama*. It is a necessary state, and a beautiful one. But, being an ashram, it has dharma at its heart. *Grihasthadharma* is a fine thing, but self-indulgence is reprehensible. My opposition is solely to self-indulgence. Jamnalal's question to you was perfectly right. He wanted to know your point of view as a woman. Whatever Vinoba, I or others may say, it is very necessary to know what a mature and pure woman feels. And ultimately the real contribution has to be made by the woman. The burden of demonstrating the importance and necessity of *brahmacharya* should not be on man alone. Till now it has been mostly shouldered by him, and in consequence it has become his right. This has earned a bad name for *Brahmacharya*. What is more, though it should have been easy to observe, it has proved so difficult that most people find it impossible to observe. In this, too, I blame mostly man. He has done his best to keep woman his inferior. Flattery and brute force have played an equal part in this. Be that as it may, one half of man's body became and has remained weak. The result has been that man has failed in most of his endeavours, as he deserved to do. There is some awakening among women now. But at present it is assuming a perverted form. Man has been indulging her whims and feeding her ego under the pretext of respecting her freedom and woman has taken freedom to mean self-indulgence. Let those men and women who can save themselves from this do so. Save yourself.

Blessings from
Bapu

38. Letter to Premabehn Kantak

Tithal, Bulsar,
May 13, 1937

Chi. Prema,

Only today I got your letter and I am replying to it immediately. Your previous letter is still lying in my file. But let me dispose of this. I will see about the other later. Tell Sushila that, if all of you had come here, I could have accommodated you but wouldn't have been able to give you the privacy you had there. Nor the cold of that place, if your description of it is correct. Here we do feel the heat.

I don't know if injustice has been done to Nariman.[82] Why should it be assumed that the leader of Bombay should become the leader of the whole Presidency ? And can anybody misguide or coerce all the representatives of three Provinces ? If injustice has been done, why do all those representatives, who are still alive, put up with it ? I, therefore, don't understand this talk about injustice. I don't even understand what Sardar is believed to have done. I felt that the whole agitation was got up. But if I don't understand this matter properly, you may reason with me and convince me. I have no antipathy to Nariman. My attitude has nothing to do with the charges which have been levelled against him. The truth or falsehood of these charges can be inquired into whenever Nariman wishes. I learnt only today that he is your friend. I have expressed my opinion in a perfectly objective spirit.

I was pained to read about . . . [83] I have published only what both of them told me and that, too, because she wanted me to publish it. It seems to me that . . . [84] makes no distinction between truth and falsehood. You may show her this.

I had written to Dev. I have received his reply. I did not write immediately.

I was glad to learn that the work in Saswad has not been given up. I believe in the saying, "Not to embark upon a thing in the first instance." If you take up any other work now, cling to it. It would have been better if you four had asked me to give you an appointment. I accept your argument that I wouldn't have been able to say much without knowing the position at Saswad. You are also right in saying that this is only the beginning of my experience of village life, and that, therefore, all of us are equal in that respect.

Even so, my ideas have an element of originality in them, and the power behind them comes from *ahimsa*. I think, therefore, that all four of you would have learnt something from me. I like your effort to learn the art of thinking for I had found your speech[85] at Hudli lacking in thought. Your ideas there seemed to me like so much smoke emitted by your brain. They were not outpourings of the heart. I wanted to spare some time and discuss them with you and convince you, as clearly as two and two make four, that there was no real thinking behind them. But you left in a great hurry and so I did not get any opportunity. Since I was in no hurry to prove to you your lack of thought, I didn't hold you back. I was sure that you yourself would sooner or later see this deficiency in you. And now I see your admission of it in this very letter of yours. It is understandable that you do not see this deficiency in the ideas you expressed at Hudli. But if you really learn how to think, you are bound to see the deficiency in those ideas.

I, therefore, like you having given up the thought of asking for my views regarding principles. I will like it better still if you resolve to make no speeches till you have mastered the art of thinking, and you will acquire the art the sooner if you make no speeches.

Blessings to you all,
Bapu

39. Letter to Premabehn Kantak

May 29, 1937

Chi. Prema,

I shall not probably be able to reply to the whole of your letter. I will try, though. I have certainly issued no order forbidding you to make speeches. And even if I have issued any, I withdraw it. I wish to order no one. What can I have to say if your views change ? You will follow your nature, as everybody should do.[86]

The fact that pure love doesn't care for touch certainly doesn't mean that all touch is impure. I had pure love for my mother, but Iused to massage her legs when they ached. There was no impurity in that touch. Touch prompted by lust is evil. I would, therefore, say that anybody who says that pure love is impossible without touch doesn't know what pure love is.

I still do not understand what you wish to suggest regarding Nariman. Who did him injustice and how ? At least for the sake of truth you should come out frankly with what you have in mind. I find it intolerable that there should be a difference of opinion between us in a matter like this. If you are convinced that injustice has been done to Nariman, you should prove that to me, for, though unwillingly, I had to interest myself in the affair. I have, moreover, assured Nariman that I shall be ready to study his case whenever he wishes. But whether or not he comes, your duty is clear.

What you have assumed regarding . . .[87] is not correct. The evidence which you have got is of no value. Before believing in such a thing you should ask the person concerned. I don't wish to suggest that no such untruth has been practised. But the matter should be carefully investigated. If somebody tells me that Prema did a certain thing, should I believe it without asking you whether it is correct ? Maybe what you said at Hudli came from your heart. But what you said in your speech was different from what you say now. Will you admit this much ? Be that as it may, I have told you that my experience was different from your reasoning. You are certainly entitled to attach more importance to your reasoning than to my experience. But what should I do ?

Blessings from
Bapu

40. Letter to Premabehn Kantak

Segaon, Wardha,
August 25, 1937

Chi. Prema,

You must have heard about my ill-health. I have been ordered minimum mental exertion and maximum rest. Since both the brain and the right hand demand complete rest, I will content myself with writing what you want immediately. I did tie your *raksha*[88] which I received in time. I have completely re-written the reply to your question.[89] The old replies are not incorrect, but being incomplete they may lend themselves to misinterpretation. I am returning them. Cancel them. See that they are not published at all. If the new reply is useful you may publish it. I have preserved your letters and will reply to them when I am all right. You may even receive my reply sooner if I am permitted to dictate. There is no cause for worry about me. However, I have to be extremely careful.

Blessings from
Bapu

Question: A professor who is married wants to observe *brahmacharya*. The wife doesn't agree. What is the professor friend's dharma in these circumstances ?

Answer: This question could have arisen only if the idea of observing *brahmacharya* came to the husband after marriage. What I mean by marriage as a part of dharma is that intercourse between husband and wife is resorted to only when they desire children, and never for sex-gratification. Those who do not look upon marriage as a holy bond will of course respect each other's wishes. Intercourse without the consent of the other party is nothing but rape. Let us now deal with the above mentioned question. In a case in which it is only the husband who wishes to observe *brahmacharya* but the wife does not, if the husband has become completely free from passion, that is, has, in the language of the *Gita*, Ch. II, v. 59, realized the Supreme, intercourse will be physically impossible. The wife will realize the husband's condition and her passion will subside. But the question refers to a man's striving for *brahmacharya*. A husband or wife can strive for any aim which was not present in the minds of both at the time of marriage, only with the consent of the other partner. In other words, a husband cannot take the vow of *brahmacharya* without the consent of his wife. Of course, everybody should try to practise ordinary self-control. When either party is aroused, generally the other party also is agreeable or becomes so after a little persuasion. When this does not happen, bitterness results. I have, therefore, come to the conclusion, from the experiences of many people and after careful reflection over them, that practice of self-control depends on mutual consent. I should therefore say that the question is defective. Where *brahmacharya* has become a natural condition, the question does not arise. And it has no room when passion is present and the person only wants to strive for *brahmacharya*.

41. Letter to Premabehn Kantak

New Delhi,
April 22, 1946

Chi. Prema,

Your silly letter in Marathi addressed to Sushila was read out and translated to me. It is good to be clear about one's goal. Forget the person who has become the symbol of your goal. But the difficulty is that the person himself has become your goal. That happens to many and they suffer in consequence. When we make the person symbolizing our goal himself our goal, the result is that we feel happy when his actions and words are such as please us, but get offended when they are otherwise. One should, therefore, keep one's goal independent. Until you can do that, you will suffer, and so will your work. You have been educated, but learnt no wisdom !!! Learn it now. Learn it from me if you don't have it. In doing this there will be no conflict at all between your goal and the syambol of your goal, for learning wisdom means acquiring knowledge of practical affairs. But remember that practical affairs may be conducted either truthfully or untruthfully. Wake up.

Blessings from
Bapu

42. Letter to Premabehn Kantak

New Delhi,
October 16, 1946

Chi. Prema,

Two letters of yours are lying in front of me. I started writing a reply as soon as I received the second one, but laid it aside when the people for whose sake I am here came in. I am, therefore, writing the reply today.

I will say nothing about Nuremberg. In barbarity there are no comparisons. Whether it is here or there, it is all "here". It is not correct to say that I have abandoned constructive work to come here, nor that I have yielded to the temptation of politics. In fact life cannot be divided into compartments. The organs of the body are called by different names, but the body is one. The same is true about life. But since you think that it is an error on my part, you should believe it to be so. One day you will realize your error and see the unity of my life, or reform me. I have never laboured under the delusion that what I believe is true. Yes, what I believe is true for myself, otherwise I would cease to be a *satyagrahi*. The same rule applies to all.

And now your particular question. I should like the girls to remain unmarried, but they cannot be forced to do so. We must, therefore, help those who wish to get married. It was, and is, Acharya Bhagawat's duty to plead with you and other co-workers and carry them with him in whatever he did.[90] He made a mistake in doing what he did without consulting you. You also should not tolerate his improper conduct through your desire for gaining something from him. But you did that. In this matter, too, the final decision must be yours. For occasions do arise when one has to swallow such bitter draughts. I have merely explained a general principle to you. Please understand that I have no time to write more than this. If Sushila, who is here, has understood the situation better, she will write to you. I am observing silence. It is doing me good. I was afraid that I might break down. More when we meet. I was not happy that the meeting of the Agents did not take place.

Blessings from
Bapu

43. Letter to Premabehn Kantak

Patna,
May 19, 1947

Chi. . . .,

I got your letter yesterday. Today is silence day and I am, therefore, able to reply immediately. Why need you thank me for having sent you the shawl[91] ? Does it mean that, when you send me something, I also should thank you ?

That is no true love which expects formal courtesy from the person loved.

I did not understand your point regarding Karnataka[92]. Write to me again about it. Did a large number of girls come under bad influence ?

You seem to be doing good work in Maharashtra.[93] If I do have to fast, I should certainly like you to be with me at the time. But should I fast merely for that reason ? If a fast does come about, we shall think then what your and my dharma should be. We need not even think about the matter just now. It was with some hesitation that I gave even the hint you refer to. It would not have seemed right if I had not given it.

The news which Gadgil gave you is not correct. I cannot conceive of any circumstances in which I might have to fast against women. Banish from your mind all thoughts about a fast and go on with your work.

As a doctor, Dr. Gilder will only say that my point of view is clear. A man who becomes a *sthitaprajna* in the sense described in the verses which we recite every evening, from the second chapter of the *Gita* cannot but live for 125 years. The word *shatam* used in the *Ishopanishad*[94] does not mean 99+1. It means 120, 125 or 130. I mentioned 125 on August (8)[95], 1942, in Bombay,[96] and have been mentioning the same figure since then. If, however, I cannot overcome my passion and anger, I cannot live to be 125. In the case I ought to give up such an aspiration. My desire, thus, is conditional.

Blessings from
Bapu

44. Letter to Premabehn Kantak

New Delhi,
June 15, 1947

Chi. Prema,

It is 4.30 just now. I am writing this after the prayer. Others around me are sleeping. The nib of the pen is broken and I don't wish to get up and get a new one. Meanwhile Chi. Manu came in with a glass of fruit juice and I asked her to bring me a nib. And now I am writing with a new nib, and it won't move smoothly till the grease on it has gone. This is how the old man's work goes on. What place does a man like me have in the midst of you all who are soaring in the sky in the refreshing breeze of the coming independence ? I am now waiting to see where God will lead me next. I cannot permit you to publish my letter. It will do me no harm. But I am afraid lest my imperfect memory harm somebody else.[97] General Shah Nawaz told me that he would not be able to do full justice to the job unless its control was entirely in his hands. I replied that, if it was so he should resign. This is all so far as I am concerned.

I accepted . . .'s[98] offer because she wanted to work under me in Bihar. She is a great help to me indeed. It is perfectly true that she has no faith in truth and nonviolence. But, then, how many others like her have been doing such fine work ! Who cares for truth and nonviolence these days ? You look at the matter from one point of view only. Go on doing your work to the best of your ability and bring credit to yourself.

Blessings from
Bapu

(From Gujarati)
Bapuna Patro–5: Kumari Premabehn Kantakne, pp. 325-26.

45. Letter to Premabehn Kantak

New Delhi,
June 25, 1947

Chi. Prema,

I have your letter. I understand about your birthday. How is it that all of you wish to leave before I do ? What will be my condition then ? What selfishness is this ? Thank God, living or dying is not in our hands. All our efforts to that end are in vain. As the saying is, that which we do alone keeps us company.

My future plans are wholly uncertain.

What public statement can I make in connection with the Gen. Shah Nawaz affair ?[98] How am I responsible for what someone else may say ? I am certainly responsible for what I do or say, but for nothing else.

Publication of the correspondence with you will serve no useful purpose. If Deo wishes to publish anything, he will ask me. If what you say regarding Mridula is true, that is to say, if I have correctly followed your meaning, then you make too subtle distinctions. Reflect over this.

This much is true. If you come and spend a few days with me, you will probably understand the position better. That is, you should come and stay for three or four days at a time at short intervals. Alternatively, go on doing whatever work falls to your share and let the world go its own way.

You are doing your work well.

Sushila Pai has left.

Blessings from
Bapu

NOTES

1. From the Marathi saint Namdev.
2. The addressee had asked for an account of Gandhiji's visits to places of artistic interest in Rome and elsewhere.
3. The addressee had asked what the ideals of the Ashram were and, quoting instances of apparently contradictory approaches to life, sought Gandhiji's opinion.
4. The addressee had asked how Vallabhbhai could take tea while staying with Gandhiji in the jail.
5. *Vide* "Letter to Premabehn Kantak", 3-8-1932 and "Letter to Premabehn Kantak", 18-8-1932.
6. According to *Mahadevbhaini Diary*, the addressee had argued that our attitude towards God had changed with the change in social and political conditions. Sankara lived in an age of freedom when people talked of equality with God; Ramanuja lived in an age of slavery when people talked of being the slaves of the slaves of God. In the book *Bapuna Patro-5: Ku. Premabehn Kantakne*, pp. 99-101, however, the addressee, presumably relying on her memory, says that she had argued that both Sankara and Ramanuja could attain greater heights of spirituality because they lived in an age of freedom whereas the

later saints, being born in slavery, worshipped personal gods and not the abstract Brahman.

7. Sel.
8. *Vide* "An Autobiography".
9. *Vide* "Letter to Narandas Gandhi", 22/26-6-1932.
10. It had been predicted at that time that Gandhiji would be released on this date.
11. *Vide* "Letter to Premabehn Kantak", 6-7-1932.
12. Gandhiji had said that those who took part in the spinning *yajna* should not keep back the yarn for their own use; *vide* "Letter to Narandas Gandhi", 31-5/3-6-1932. The addressee had argued that the yarn spun by Gandhiji should be kept for Kasturba's use.
13. Fried delicacy.
14. *Vide* "Letter to Premabehn Kantak", 6-7-1932. Commenting on it the addressee had said : "I would only be a coward if I hesitated to criticize others lest they should criticize me. Why should I be afraid of the world and refrain from telling people what I regard as truth, since I do not care ?"
15. Wife of Dr. Balawantrai Kanugo of Ahmedabad.
16. "Devotion means profound love for God."—*Narada Bhaktisutra.*
17. Abode of Vishnu.
18. Dhurandhar practised the yogic *asanas* and propagated them wherever he went.
19. The names in the following two paragraphs have been omitted.
20. The addressee explains in *Bapuna Patro—5: Ku. Premabehn Kantakne* that she had asked Gandhiji whether he believed in Fate, and thinks that the reply should read: 'Even if I did not believe in Fate . . .' .
21. *Bhagavad* Gita, x, 10.
22. The names have been omitted.
23. Daughters of Lakshmidas P. Asar.
24. *Ibid.*
25. Addressee's friend, Kisan Ghumatkar.
26. The names have been omitted.
27. *Ibid.*
28. *Ibid.*
29. *Ibid.*
30. *Ibid.*
31. Gandhiji's letter to the addressee, dated December 25, 1932, had offended her. She had got it on her return to Ahmedabad from her visit to Gandhiji and written back to say that she would never write to him again.

32. Presumably the one to which Gandhiji had replied on December 25, 1932.
33. Firmness.
34. Literally, 'Yeravda Temple', that is, Yeravda Central Prison, where Gandhiji was imprisoned from January 4, 1932 to May 8, 1933. This place-line is not reproduced in subsequent letters.
35. The addressee had inscribed on a gift parcel of slivers to Gandhiji: "To revered dear Mahatmaji". Mahadev Desai, therefore, had felt that it would not be proper for him to spin them.
36. Gold oxide used as medicine in Ayurveda, the Hindu system of medicine.
37. The names have been omitted.
38. *Vide* "Letter to Premabehn Kantak", 2-4-1933.
39. The names have been omitted.
40. *Ibid.*
41. Attachment.
42. The names have been omitted.
43. *Ibid.*
44. Which read: (I) What should one do and how should one overcome one's impatience if someone older, younger or of the same age misbehaves despite persuasion and thereby creates a bad impression on others and time is wasted and work delayed ? (2) How would it affect others if a person violated Ashram rule or discipline under some necessity while doing one's duty ? (3) How far should we pay regard to social practice or custom in the path of satyagraha ? (4) What would be my duty as a *satyagrahi* when I disagree with a renowned mahatma like you on a certain step which I find to be right according to the voice of my conscience and which might violate the rules of the institution ? (5) Should one love the individual for the sake of the institution or the institution for the individual ? (6) By what test can one find out that one has bad thoughts about others ? (7) If a person is found on every occasion telling lies, or shirking work or being selfish, and others too have complained about it, would it be proper for a *satyagrahi* to have doubts about him ? (8) What is the limit for simple living ? To embroider one's *sari*, to wear fashionable blouses, to adorn the hands and neck with flowers, wear chappals —should this be considered as love for art or breaking the Ashram principles ? (9) Would it be slander or violence if in the Ashram one person finds fault with another and commits the same fault himself, i.e., indulges in mutual fault-finding ? (10) As those who join the Ashram do so

with different motives, should we judge each of them from his own standpoint ?

45. Margarete Spiegel and N.; *vide* also "Letter to Narandas Gandhi", 29-4-1933.
46. Sushila Pai.
47. Gandhiji had refused both of them permission to attend the Congress session.
48. The addressee had asked for yarn spun by Gandhiji in Yeravda Mandir from the slivers supplied by her.
49. The name has been omitted.
50. Dr. Hardikar's co-workers who had given up their professions etc., at the time of the Civil Disobedience Movement were in a miserable plight when the movement was withdrawn and Hardikar himself could be of no help.
51. Shankarrao Deo wanted to move his Ashram to a small village as Saswad where it was established was the headquarters of a taluk.
52. God in the form of Truth.
53. *Vide* "The crime of Chauri Chaura", 16-2-1922 and "divine warning", 19-2-1922.
54. This is in Hindi.
55. Nariman had argued that the Congress had adopted *ahimsa* only as a policy and not as a creed and that, therefore, when the country became free it would have to maintain an army.
56. One who remains unattached to fruits of action.
57. *Vide* "Implications of Prayer", 15-6-1935.
58. *Vide* "All Life is One", 22-6-1935.
59. The reference is to a news item in a newspaper that an actress had shot her husband, who was suffering from cancer, to save him from a painful death.
60. An old Congress worker of Poona.
61. In *Bapuna Patro—5: Kum. Premabehn Kantakne*, the addressee explains that she was asked by Kalelkar to take charge of Mahila Ashram at Wardha leaving the village work at Sasvad to Shankarrao Deo.
62. Akiller.
63. A Maharashtrian professor from Poona had written to Gandhiji in connection with his article "Nothing Without Grace" ; *vide* "Nothing Without Grace", 29-2-1936.
64. The addressee had pleaded lack of confidence in her own capacity to grow into an illustrious *brahmacharini,* as hoped for by Gandhiji. *Vide* "Letter to Premabehn Kantak", 13-2-1933.

65. The addressee could not readily believe Gandhiji's confession of involuntary violation of *brahmacharya*. *Vide* "Nothing without Grace", and letter to the addressee, "Letter to Premabehn Kantak", 6-5-1933. After an inconclusive discussion with and at the instance of Acharaya Bhagavat the addressee had hesitantly sought clarification from him.
66. *Vide* "Letter to Premabehn Kantak", 6-5-1936.
67. Son of Vyasa and the ideal *brahmachari* described in the *Bhagavata.*
68. *Vide New Testament, St. Matthew,* XIX, 12.
69. *Vide* "For Contraceptives", 4-4-1936 and "For Women Reformers", 2-5-1936.
70. In fact Chapter III. 6.
71. The addressee had enquired why Gandhiji had used an envelope for his letter dated July 22, 1936, when the matter could have been fitted in a postcard.
72. The thread tied by a sister to her brother's wrist symbolizing the brother's obligation to protect her.
73. Lead me from untruth to truth.
74. The addressee had maintained that the whole tradition of the saint-poets of Maharashtra had more or less acknowledged the idea of high and low as inherent in the *varna* system; how then could they look upon all with equality ?
75. This sentence is incomplete in the source.
76. *Ibid.*
77. A spiritually enlightened person.
78. *Vide* "Letter to Prabhavati", 15-12-1930.
79. Jnaneshwara, saint-poet of Maharashtra.
80. Samartha Ramdas Swami, Shivaji's guru.
81. *Vide* " *Varna v* . Caste," 15-8-1936.
82. K.F. Nariman, President, Bombay Provincial Congress Committee, who was defeated in the Bombay Legislature leadership election, had charged Vallabhbhai Patel with bringing about his defeat. This led to a prolonged controversy which was finally settled by arbitrators, who declared Vallabhbhai Patel free from blame.
83. The names have been omitted.
84. *Ibid.*
85. *Vide* footnote 3, "Speech at Gandhi Seva Sangh Meeting Hudli-II", 17-4-1937.
86. *Vide* also "Letter to Premabehn Kantak", 13-5-1937.
87. The name has been omitted.

88. A thread tied on *Shravana Shukla* 15 by a sister to the wrist of her brother or a person regarded as such implying that he would protect her.
89. The addressee had written a novel based on a discussion Gandhiji had with a friend about the case of a married professor aspiring to observe *brahmacharya*. The addressee included Gandhiji's answer in her novel, a Gujarati translation of which appeared under the title *Kama ane Kamini.*
90. Acharya Bhagawat had persuaded women workers of the Kasturba Trust to get married and even arranged their marriages.
91. For which the addressee had asked as a token of Gandhiji's Love.
92. At a meeting of the Kasturba Gandhi National Memorial Trust, the Karnataka Agent had mentioned certain lapses on the part of some women workers.
93. As Agent of the Kasturba Gandhi National Memorial Trust.
94. Verse 2 which reads: "Doing verily works in this world one should wish to live a hundred years."
95. The source has "7".
96. Gandhiji, however, had mentioned "120". *Vide* "Speech at A.I.C.C. Meeting", 8-8-1942.
97. *Vide* the preceding item; both letters are written on the same sheet of paper.
98. Omission as in the source.

Chapter 8
Sushila Nayyar (1914-2000)

Dr. Sushila Nayyar born on 26th December, 1914, Kunjah, Gujarat, (now in Pakistan), was the younger sister of Pyarelal Nayyar, personal secretary to Mahatma Gandhi. She graduated from erstwhile Punjab University. From Punjab she came to Delhi to study medicine at Lady Hardinge Medical College. In the same institution where she studies later worked for some time as Registrar and Assistant Professor.

After getting medical degree she came to Sevagram to join her brother, and became a close associate of the Mahatma Gandhi in 1939. Shortly after her arrival, cholera broke out in Wardha, and being young medical graduate she tackled the outbreak single-handedly with dedication to service needy people. Gandhi praised her dedication to service and appointed her as personal physician. She was one of the circles of young women who followed Gandhi and were deeply impressed by his charisma and magnetism. She never married. In 1942 she was awarded an MD. She took part in the Quit India Movement and she was imprisoned along with others at the Aga Khan Palace in Poona.

In 1944 she set up a dispensary at Sevagram, but soon grew so large that it disturbed the peace of the ashram, and she shifted it to a guesthouse donated by the Birlas, in Wardha. In 1945 this little clinic formally became the Kasturba Hospital and later on it grew and became famous the Mahatma Gandhi Institute of Medical Sciences in 1969 (Institute of Medical Sciences at Sevagram, which was founded by her in 1969) where she was Professor of Community Medicine.

Several attempts were made on Gandhi's life and Sushila Nayyar testified on several occasions to the attacks. In 1948 she appeared before the Kapur Commission regarding the incident in Panchgani in 1944 when Nathuram Godse allegedly tried to attack Gandhi with a dagger.

After Gandhi's assassination in 1948 at Birla House in Delhi, Sushila Nayyar went to the USA where she took two degrees in public health from the Johns Hopkins School of Public Health. After receiving degree from USA she return to India in 1950 and set up a tuberculosis sanatorium in Faridabad. Dr. Nayyar was instrumental in blocking a bill for compulsory sterilization of leprosy patients. Dr. Nayyar and her colleagues established the Gandhi Memorial Leprosy Foundation in 1951, and the Foundation conducted trials of chemotherapy in leprosy in 10 endemic states. The National Leprosy Programme in India was based on the results of these early trials. She also headed the Gandhi Memorial Leprosy Foundation.

In 1952 she entered in politics and was elected to the Legislative Assembly of Delhi. From 1952 to 1955 she served as Health Minister in Nehru's cabinet. She was Speaker of the Delhi Vidhan Sabha from 1955 to 1956. In 1957 she was elected to the Lok Sabha and served till 1971. She was Union Health Minister again from 1962 to 1967. She strongly believed in the need for prohibition and linked this to the degeneration of women. She was a staunch campaigner for family planning because it is essential for empowerment of the women.

She fell out with Indira Gandhi and was member of the opposition Janata Party. She briefly held a position when it was voted to power by overthrowing Indira Gandhi's government. Thereafter she retired from politics to devote herself to the Gandhian ideal. She had set up the Mahatma Gandhi Institute of Medical Sciences in 1969, and remained committed to confine her energies to developing and extending it. She became Chancellor of Gujarat Vidyapeeth in 1994. She died on 3rd January, 2001 at the age of 87 years at Sevagram, Wardha.

1. Letter to Sushila Nayyar

On the Train,
April 16, 1938

Chi. Sushila,

Lately you have been figuring in my dreams. Shall I call it attachment or love ? Be that as it may, you have become a big question-mark for me. "You have already taken one; you want to take the other one too ?" These words of Mother still echo in my ears. Her concern was justified. My duty is clear. At least today your place is not with me. If Pyarelal finds his moorings, it will be well. But if that does not happen I shall consider myself worthless. And what can a girl like you do by living with a worthless person ? There is no strong reason for you to leave your mother's lap. I failed in my duty when I let you ignore the letter from Delhi. You should have accepted one of the jobs offered. Even now if the posts have not been filled, you may still write, 'It so happens that I can now entertain one of the pro-positions, if the posts or any of them be still open.'[1] Your duty is to be near Mother and earn. And even while you earn, increase your knowledge as much as you wish. This is my considered view. Mahadev will say the same. I shall convey this to Pyarelal. If he has anything else to say, I shall write again.

Stop worrying about me. The night passed well. In the morning the blood-pressure was 164/102. Even otherwise I am feeling fine. How can I forget the service I had from you ? How can I reward it ? How and why should a father reward a daughter ? God will reward you. It will be reward enough if Pyarelal's mind becomes quiet. If that does not happen, what good will be a reward ? You did your duty. Why should you be concerned with the fruits of it ? You must go on writing to me. God will show you the right path.

Blessings from
Bapu

2. Letter to Sushila Nayyar

Bombay,
May 10, 1938

Chi. Sushila,

I had been awaiting your letter. I had it yesterday. I found nothing in it that would do any harm if Mahadev read it. Mahadev read all the letters. What was there in it to add fuel to the fire ? Stupid girl ! You are indeed stupid. For that reason I love you all the more. Your obstinacy does not hurt me. I will not let you remain stupid for ever. You are not a goddess, nor is Mahadev a god. The future is bright if this illusion has been dispelled. I consider both of you simple-hearted. The only difference is that you have not experienced lust. Mahadev has done so in full measure. He is a married man after all. But the god of love is subtle. You were both unaware of his attack. You needlessly blame yourself. Desire had certainly taken possession of you. But you were not aware of it at all. For that matter even Mahadev was not aware of it. Mahadev was not careful. But he was not aware even of that.

Neither you nor Mahadev has given me any unhappiness. So long as your reason does not accept something, you must never accept it, however much it may hurt me or anybody else. My advice is that you should now forget the past, and remaining cheerful by doing your present duty, free my mind from anxiety. Let me know your programme.

Dr. Gilder was here. The blood-pressure was 180/108. The climate is lovely. We expect to go to Wardha from here on the 17th. I return your letter to Mahadev. I shall tear up the remaining letters. There is a churning going on in my heart. I am happy. God alone knows what the outcome will be. Massages etc., have been stopped. I bathe alone.

Blessings from
Bapu

(PS.)
Are you laughing ? I have not revised this letter. I have torn up all the letters.

3. Letter to Sushila Nayyar

May 18, 1938

Stupid Daughter,

You have been proving your stupidity in every letter. Yes, I did say that if you were tired of Segaon then I had not been entitled to receive service from you. This could not in any way imply that you should not come to me. It did imply that you should hasten your return. If your mind cannot grasp such a simple thing, ask me again. In this context let me describe to you my condition. These two day's have not passed well. Yesterday I worked for 12 hours. I was mentally exhausted. I had a terrible backache. I slept well. I was alert again. But the mental condition is not good. In such a situation I do feel your absence. But how can I send for you, how can I ask you to come so long as you do not feel drawn to this place ? Would I have been able to work so much if you had been near me ? Now do you understand what I want ? But this certainly does not mean that you should come here at once under any circumstances.

Now your second question. I accept your version of what happened on the 9th night. There is no question of your account being incorrect. Those who see silver in a sea-shell are right at all times. But he who knows a sea-shell will see it only as a sea-shell, will he not ? Oh, the things that sexual impulse makes us do ! This does not even mean that I am in the right and what you thought was merely imagination. Believe me, I admit I may have been a prey to illusion; so you can stick to your own position. Indeed it is your duty to do so. Ponder that verse in the *Bhajanavali*. Only that is dharma which is followed by the learned and practised by the saintly and by people free from attachment and hatred, and which your heart accepts as dharma. What the learned, the saintly and people free from attachment etc., believe can never be acceptable to us if our heart does not accept it. I am neither a learned man, nor a saint; nor am I free from attachment etc. I have only appointed myself your godfather. The words of such a man must be rejected unless your heart and mind accept them. Whatever you do, your position with me will always remain the same. In no way have you fallen in my estimation.

Yes, a man's words should be taken at their face value. But even so, one must consider their context. That is to say, while it is necessary to exercise discretion, we must take it that if the reasons which dictate avoidance of physical contact are applicable to any other behaviour or gestures, such gestures, too must be avoided. So much for the literal interpretation. But even this much is not sufficient. To know the meaning of words it is also necessary to know their deeper significance. When you recite the *Gita* everyday, you know the literal meaning of the words. But so long as you do not understand their deeper significance, going by the literal meaning of the words would be futile and burdensome. Does this fully answer your letter ? We shall probably leave here on the 20th. I have torn up your letter. Mahadev does not read your letters these days. He sees what I write. He continues to be miserable. That is in his nature. Time will do its work. Is not *Kaala* one of the names for God ?

Blessings from
Bapu

4. Letter to Sushila Nayyar

Segaon,
May 23, 1938

Chi. Sushila,

I have received two of your envelopes together. Mahadev appears calm. But if his calm is genuine, he will not be distressed by your letters. I send him all your letters. You certainly are stupid, but certainly not unfortunate and undeserving. And why unfortunate ? Have you lost my love ? Have you lost Mahadev's love ? Why undeserving ? What have you done to make you undeserving ? You certainly are stupid because you could not understand some simple things about the world. But it is I who make you stupid. What if I should be seeing my stupidity in you ? Now about the 9th night. Why are you suffering so much ? Can it not be that my affliction is the result of my latent lust ? Maybe it is not. Can it not be that it is the result of my delusions ? I have not claimed divinity. If you can be in the wrong, why can I not be in the wrong too ? Both are a matter of imagination, are they not

? You have not experienced anything and I cannot know your heart. God alone is the ruler of the hearts of both of us. He alone knows our hearts. That is why as your godfather I command you to regard your conduct as having been absolutely innocent and to forget your anguish. My misconceptions are the cause of your anguish. Forget it; that you forgive me I can hardly ask.

Blessings from
Bapu

5. Letter to Sushila Nayyar

Sevagram, Wardha,
June 1, 1938

Chi. Sushila,

I received your two letters together. Now everything is changed, is it not ? My letters of yesterday and the day before will have made this clear. Now I have more or less decided that with the exception of Ba I will not accept from any other woman any service involving physical contact. After that, there is no question at all of an affectionate touch. I have made another discovery. In saying that I alone might touch women and that no one else might do so, I was guilty of a terrible error—and for how many years I persisted in the error ! I should have known that I could claim no scientific sanction for the experiment. I was impelled solely by my terrible arrogance. Among all my colleagues I considered only myself entitled to break the restrictions of *brahmacharya*. As long as I am not willing to accept my colleagues touching women I have not the slightest right to touch a woman. I hope to settle everything in a day or two. I have only your firmness to thank for making me see my error. In my view the restrictions I had laid down for you and Mahadev are no longer justified. What qualifies me to lay down such restrictions ? When I admit that my accusing you was merely the reflection of my own failing, not yours or Mahadev's, where is the place for the restrictions set by me ? To the extent I am involved in this affair, I am the guilty person, not you, nor Mahadev.

I am writing all this dispassionately. And what reward I gave you for your services ! Now for Pyarelal. Mother's words were like nectar to me: "You have already taken away Pyare. Now you want to take away Sushila too ?" She was right. I did not do you any good. What good have I done to Pyarelal ? Pyarelal's future would be the test whether my acts were good or evil. As for you, I still consider you stupid. You have worked for me like a benign spirit. But for your resolute stand, my eyes would not have been opened. I would have still been in the slumber of my illusions. Mirabehn has rightly said that I would have died repenting. God has alerted me only through you. Even though you came to me as a daughter, you have acted like a mother. Not my merit but may be yours will save your brother.

It is good that you are helping Brijkrishna. My advice is that you should take the place for the hospital. You must be fully recovered. But who am I to guide you ? You have got a brother like Pyarelal. He is with you. Do only what he says. After all, how can God give you up ? Who will be left for Him if He gives you up ? You will always prosper. Do not worry about me. I am well.

Blessings from
Bapu

6. Letter to Sushila Nayyar

(After June 2, 1938)[2]

Stupid Girl,

Are you trying to prove your stupidity ? What did I know of your purity before Mahadev told me ? Since then I have been taking service from you. If you too have experienced desire, it is as well. For then we are both in the same plight and we both ought to be on our guard. For me it is sufficient that I am on my guard. The day I have to save myself from you, you will only see my dead body, you will not see me alive. After my 69 years, the *vikara*[3] in you cannot affect me. I burn with my own *vikara*. Because of my *vikara* I regard myself unfit to take service from any woman. For that reason, you are free to abandon me, but you are always telling me that you do not want to leave me under any circumstances, so I must accept your services in all humility.

Have you read the letters of others ? No one has any complaint to make. Mirabehn had only imagined things. Even then there was no complaint against you. Only I have a complaint. But that is a different story altogether. You should forget these people.

You have to consider two questions. I must not take you away from your duty to Mother. Deep in your heart you desire to study. It is a good desire too. Should I make you give up that desire and continue taking service from you ? These two questions are very pertinent. About my experiment later. I can write now, but you must show pity for my hand.

Bapu

7. Letter to Sushila Nayyar

June 5, 1938

Stupid Sushila,

How stupid you are ! Sitting there, you cry and make me cry !!! You are unnecessarily taking the blame upon your self. I have not given up taking service from Ba. Other women feel a little unhappy, but they are cheerful. They have also understood the point. A.S. does feel miserable. But I am also making her laugh quite a bit. She is more stupid than you. She too will calm down in a few days. I hope that abiding by my order, both of you will have arrived here. It is impossible to start today. I am writing this letter so that the day does not pass without communication in case you are unable to leave. Stop crying now. I am eager to see you laugh. You have committed no sin.

Blessings from
Bapu

8. Letter to Sushila Nayyar

June 6, 1938

Stupid Girl,

Is there any limit to your stupidity ? How could I abandon you for ever ? Why are you raising me so high ? The place you assign to me is not my place, though I certainly wish it was. My experience on the night of the 7th could not in any way have been influenced by the prurience of any of you. As for the incident of the 14th, I find only my own sensuality reflected in it. I shall explain it further when we meet. Why do you presume the existence of something in your heart which was not there ? Your saying such a thing is a matter of shame for me. I constantly see that I am sensual. In that case why should we ignore what is evident and look for what is not evident ? But you both will have left before this letter reaches Delhi.

Blessing from
Bapu

9. Letter to Sushila Nayyar

September 10, 1938

Chi. Sushila,

What must I do to please you ? I gave you the cutting to make you laugh. It only hurt you. I showed you Mahadev's letter to make you see what I feel. Even that hurt you.

Why are you so sensitive ? If Mother does not see your good the way I see it, how can I keep you ? Even you agree that Mother should be kept happy.

Now be calm. Whatever has to happen will happen. If you cannot have peace by staying with me, then leave me. If you think it is in your interest to stay with me, what does it matter to you. . .[4]

4

Blessings from
Bapu

10. Letter to Sushila Nayyar

September 17, 1938

Chi. Sushila,

Where did you learn all this cunning ? There are criticisms on three heads and still you say it was only for my information. What a way of putting things ! But you have the right to write whatever you like. Chimanlal had asked me whether or not to give you the figure. The expenses here are certainly on a royal scale. I could not preserve my health without that. The experiments in ghee etc., also mean some expense. So the expenses here are not a standard for anybody to follow. If anyone were to tell me that friends give me money and I squander it I would listen and laugh. No doubt there is scope for improvement but it can be effected only if I get a wise manager like you. But you are not going to stay here for ever. The figure was not given you so that you might pay the amount. You may pay only according to your capacity. I have already told you that I will not mind even if you do not pay. It would be better, however, to pay as long as you can afford.

It would be more accurate if you described me as lazy. Would you consider Chimanlal, Munnalal, Nanavati, Balwantsinha, Parnerkar, Kanu, Sharda and Shakaribehn lazy ? The others are only staying there. Bhansalibhai certainly cannot be considered lazy. Krishnachandra is ill but otherwise he is a saintly person. Shankaran has to be trained up. I make do with whatever work Anand does. Even so, because of my incapacity I put up with some laxity. I have only mentioned the names that occurred to me. You may explain to me in greater detail giving particular names.

You did not reply to me. There is no question of your forcing anything on me. In spite of my being not free from passion, do you and Manudi desire that I should let myself be ministered to by and should touch women ? This question is an important one. Manudi will not understand it but you can. All of you can say: 'So long as Bapu is not free from passion, let him be served only by Sushila and Ba.' Or you can say: 'When he puts the burden on us, we do wish that he would let us touch him. What effect can his passion have on us ?' Either stand can be justified. The first is safer from all points of view. In fine, the experiment which I had commenced with a particular aim can be said to have ended, and I invite the views of you all regarding any new step I may take. I do not want to act in haste. I will do only what I can with objective detachment. I believe you to be wise. You are thoughtful. In such matters you can guide me as a woman. Please, therefore, give me your independent opinion.

Blessings from
Bapu

11. Letter to Sushila Nayyar

Segaon, Wardha,
August 14, 1939

Stupid Girl,

You are really stupid. You sit there and are afraid. You even forget that time is doing its work. And why should you be scared when someone attributes to you a failing you do not have ? Why do you not learn this much from me that we should not allow ourselves to be affected however much we may be criticised or condemned ? Maybe when you come here, you will face neither criticism nor condemnation. The reply to Dr. Young is enclosed. He used to accompany me to the Working Committee meetings. Once Pyarelal and Shirin came along.

It will not do to be careless about food and sleep. It would be good if you did not spoil your eyes by falling to the lure of films. But if the craving is too strong, go and see them.

Nimu left for Bombay yesterday. Krishnachandra will be coming in a day or two. Kundar has gone to Ba.

Blessings from
Bapu

12. Letter to Sushila Nayyar

Segaon, Wardha,
August 24, 1939

Stupid Girl,

Pyarelal has gone to Nagpur with Krishnadas to visit David. Prakash arrived yesterday. He has taken her also with him to show her the clinic etc. I have got two patients here—Durga and Asha Devi—for whose sake I do feel the need of your presence. Durga is afraid she may have appendicitis and Asha Devi has been suffering from fever for the past two months. But what can you do about this ? However, I am so perturbed that twice in my dreams I spoke to you about it, telling you that you had neglected your duty by staying on there—had there not been work enough here ? When I woke up I said to myself 'after all what could you have done ?' Young compelled you and you passed the responsibility on to me ! I could take only one decision. The dream was the expression of my anxiety. Why so much anxiety ? That shows inadequate practice of the *Gita* ! You must be free of all worry and complete your work.

Blessings from
Bapu

13. Letter to Sushila Nayyar

Segaon Ashram,
August 30, 1939

Chi. Sushila,

I read your long letter last night. The scene at Abbottabad rose before my eyes when I had scolded you and you had cried. I cannot forget your face as it looked then. Now when I think of my heartlessness my heart cries. Your answer to D. was correct.

You are faced with three questions: 'coming to me, fear as to what would happen if you came and your duty towards Mother. Your fear is meaningless. If you can learn to be tolerant, what do you have to fear and why ? Can you not be content with serving me, and looking after the sick and working in the mess ?' The problem concerning Mother is very important. It is your duty as well as mine to thin about it independently. But I do not have anything on which to base a decision. Pyarelal can be of little help in the matter. You alone should think calmly over it. You must also assess your own strength. My feeling is that Mother will have to come here and be with you. Not now. Let your dispensary be ready; let me have a room built for you. Then, too, there will be the question whether Mother can leave Mohanlal. You have to carry a great burden. You can decide the matter even after coming here on the 16th. Do not be afraid. God will be your guide. You do not have to get away before the 15th. Complete what you have undertaken.

Blessings from
Bapu

(PS.)
Why are you not writing to Ba ? She is yearning for you.

14. Letter to Sushila Nayyar

On the Train,
February 3, 1940

Chi. Sushila,

What pain you caused me ! And while leaving you threw the barb: "What is the good of letters ?" So much anger ? Consider. If I let you abandon the patients and take you with me for the sake of my health, I would be demeaning myself and lose the dharma I have followed all my life. Why can you not understand that it would not be right for me to take you with me, leaving Kishorelalbhai behind ? Here the question is not of medical knowledge. The question is of my sentiment. But right now, I have lost my place in your eyes. You seem to be under the impression that I am purposely hurting you. What kind of weakness was it that you did not even walk with me ? But I know that at the root of your odd behaviour was your unhappiness. If you leave me, out of obstinacy, you may be sure that I shall not run the dispensary as it is being run now. The instruments will go with you. What good will they be to me ? You are forgetting your duty.

Blessings from
Bapu

(PS.)
Calm down. Think. Listen to me. Give up the idea of going away. Just because you would not be with me for a couple of months in a year, will you give up serving me for the rest of the ten months ? Give some thought to the matter. Have a little pity. What I have done is in your and my interest and in the interest of the Ashram. I shall be happy to receive a telegram that your mind is at peace.

15. Letter to Sushila Nayyar

Sevagram,
May 25, 1940

Chi. Sushila,

Your last sentence was unbecoming of you. "I do not want a relevant truth, I do not want a half-truth, I want the whole truth"— think over its meaning.

So long as you are at Sevagram the question of what your duty and mine is does not arise at all. You may well believe that you are here on my account and I may think that because you are here I should take service from you. When there is an occasion to go out, I am faced with a dilemma, not you. If, thinking otherwise, I act differently, then it is self-deception. That cannot happen in Sevagram because I am already taking service from you. If this distinction is not clear to you, let both of us leave the matter to God. When God reveals to us your or my mistake, you or I shall correct it.

I have told you that so long as the mists have not rolled away, you must stay. If you do not feel certain about it, do as you like. Do nothing under any pressure. Do only what brings you self-satisfaction. Ultimately, only what you think to be your duty would be your duty.

Blessings from
Bapu

16. Letter to Sushila Nayyar

Sevagram,
May 25, 1940

Stupid Girl,

You really are stupidity incarnate. I do not understand your letter at all. How have you become a sinner because I told you an untruth ? I want to keep you with me, but not by making you believe an untruth. It was due to love that I resorted to the untruth. There was attachment in that love. How are you at fault in that ? If at all, it is I who should undertake a fast. But I will not do so because my untruth was not so very sinful. If you undertake a fast, you will cause me pain and add to the wrong which you are doing. If you are keen to see your mistake, abide in peace. So long as I am here, you will continue to serve. Then you will see your mistake. But if you cannot endure it, do go. One day you will discover your mistake and laugh. You have your reason for staying whether I believe in it or not. You can stay out of the Ashram if I go out and do not take you along. Why run away now ? Why are you not ashamed of running away ? What did I write to hurt you ? What should I write ? I am ashamed of your stupidity. I should certainly fast to cure you of your stupidity. This is not tragic. It is comic.

Blessings from
Bapu

17. Letter to Sushila Nayyar

Sevagram,
May 25, 1940

Chi. Sushila,

It was not a question of my being insulted. You insulted yourself. But if you are not able to see it, there is nothing I can do. I have not taken it as an insult to me. Read my words again. I see that there is a vast difference in our outlooks. What should I do to persuade you, how can I persuade you ? I can say nothing more. How is one to prove that red is red ? For you it is sufficient to say that what I see as red appears yellow to you. I have expressed my feelings to you. If you cannot discover any meaning in what I say, how can I find another language to explain it ? Even when I took you along with me it was not the question. I have already explained that. The question was there even then. That is why I said that I resorted to untruth in order to keep you with me.

Blessings from
Bapu

18. Letter to Sushila Nayyar

Sevagram, Wardha,
July 15, 1940

Chi. Sushila,

I have received your letter of complaint. You had a right to hope. In fact I wrote you a letter before I reached Mathura. But Pyarelal did not like it. His argument convinced me, so I cancelled the letter and asked him to tear it up. That is why Mathura was missed. After that I wrote three letters between Itarsi and Wardha. So you did not hope in vain, did you ? Admit it. I would forget writing to you only if I forgot you. You are always before my eyes. Pyarelal does try to make up for your absence, but how can he do it ? Where would he find a hand like yours ? He sleeps even closer to me than you did. But who would be jealous of him ? However, I have not regained that fearlessness I had with you. Pyarelal does almost everything you did. I am looking after my health. Ba is well.

You are free to write to me anything you want. I shall wait for you on the 24th. My order stands. But my order is meaningless. Follow the guidance of God. I can wish for nothing except your well-being.

Take care of yourself, will you ? It will be good both for you and for Mother if you return the food she may bring. Sensible children never succumb to the blind love of their parents. If you return it once, she will not express her love in this undesirable way again. I am personally seeing to it that the articles are sent to you on time. Three are being sent today. Mahadev sent you his Gujarati article yesterday. I shall go through what has come from you today. As you might have guessed, I have written a lot today.

Blessings from
Bapu

19. Letter to Sushila Nayyar

Sevagram, Wardha,
July 25, 1940

Chi. Sushila,

I have your letter. 1 understand about the patients. I see your point about the dispensary too. Even as your view becomes stronger, mine does too. My mind will never accept that I have let you down. I claim to have actually saved you when you felt you were being let down. I have saved you like a mother saves her child. The child would think with irritation that the mother was stopping its progress. But you are and are not a child. Hence, we shall call it a difference of opinion and pull the curtain down over the affair. Moreover, in spite of my explaining it you refuse to be convinced that none of those staying with me have any certainty of tenure. I can let any of them go whenever I like. If any of them assume any such right, it is a mistake on their part. Even though some of them may have been with me from the beginning, it is not by virtue of any such right. I may have acted as though they had this right, but there has been a reason for it. But why go into that discussion now ? I am accepting your decision. Come here when you cannot help it. You do have a place here. I shall welcome you. I do not wish to make you unhappy by dragging you here against your will.

I am not able to send you the English matter early because I have not been able to get it ready. I see from Pyarelal's letter that you wish to have the Tata scholarship (or something) if you can get it. It would be nice if Mahadev could do something. Then why do you not let Mahadev talk straight to you ? You take from me whatever money you need. Or I shall arrange to raise the amount. This should be the easiest way for you.

Your health has deteriorated. It is my wish and demand that you should improve it. It can be easily done.

Blessings from
Bapu

20. Letter to Sushila Nayyar

Sevagram, Wardha,
August 1, 1940

Chi. Sushila,

It would be better if instead of conveying to me your thoughts after amending them, you expressed them as they are. That way I would be able to understand you better. It is only right that you should come only when all your three conditions can be met. But why should you worry about conditions ? You will come only when you cannot help coming. Then there will be no room left for any conditions. At the moment we seem to be going in different directions. So there is no question of your coming. You are required there every moment.

You can live in peace and happiness only where you believe that you are required. You like my company. That is something to be cherished. It cannot be acquired. If we have it, we take it as God's grace. If not, we shall be content with merely desiring it. I always wish to have Manilal's company. But if I call him here, it will be only at the cost of his duty, won't it ?

Blessings from
Bapu

21. Letter to Sushila Nayyar

Sevagram, Wardha,
August 8, 1940

Chi. Sushila,

1. You did take interest in Sevagram, but you did not consider it your duty like your work there. Your heart was not in Sevagram. It was wherever I was.
2. Conflicts do not arise overnight. Nothing would have happened if you had not regarded it as conflict. You made a mountain out of a molehill without seeing or listening and without paying attention to my letters.
3. What I have said is a cruel, stark truth. Your statement that the old do not let the young have their way is far from true. Had your observation been correct, the Ashram would not have continued to grow at such a pace as it is doing.
4. I have not raised you high. Nor have I pulled you down. But you are so touchy that you did not hesitate even being unfair to me. Bapu has not changed but you saw him changed. It is another matter that you forgave him out of generosity.
5. There was jealousy indeed, but it was not of you. Had you understood this much, there would have been no need for you to suffer as you did.
6. Pyarelal says that you have understood it all wrong. But if Pyarelal really believes what you have told him, then he does not know me at all. Bapu's entire life has been spent in coping with opposition—internal and external, never in submitting to it. I have always preferred losing colleagues rather than wrongly submitting.

7. I changed my attitude, when protests were ceasing. Does it not show that it had not been in any way related to the protests ?
8. But I do not agree that I changed my attitude. I have proved to you that I explained the truth. I claim that my attitude has remained unchanged.
9. This is true.
10. But he who regards me as the centre, must consider himself safe. Instead of taking that view, you followed your own mind and then felt puzzled. This much in reply to your letter of 29-7-1940. Now for the letter of 2-8-1940.

1. 2. 3. If your experience till the time of my going to Calcutta was sweet, you must accept that if it turned bitter later you should have put up with it. You could not do so because you never considered Sevagram your field of action and field of duty. Your field of action was only I, which was wrong in itself. I must never become the field of activity for anyone. The cause of envy lay in this fact, not outside it.

4. It is not true that I had raised you high.
5. The reply has been given above.

The rest is nothing new.

I hope you will be able to read this.

How can I expect that my reply will satisfy you ? I shall be content if you can only accept that we are considering the same thing from different points of view. But forget all this; start afresh. Not for my sake but for the sake of my work. Come whenever you can decide to come. Right now you are in your field of duty. You are well trained for it. Go on with it. Later on you can come if you think it proper to come. So long as our view-points are different, you will not find peace even if you come. Pyarelal will explain this better. In your absence I cannot keep the dispensary in its present shape. It is your thing. Now that you have gone, I cannot bear the sight of it. But I cannot bear it either that you should return merely for the sake of the dispensary. I had and have altogether another use for you. It may include the dispensary. But that is a different matter. You need not feel miserable that we had a dispensary and now it may be closed down. I would not hesitate to set up and let go such things for your sake. That is how I am made. I have always incurred such expenses for those I like. All I want is your good, be it anywhere.

Blessings from
Bapu

22. Letter to Sushila Nayyar

August 26, 1920

Chi. Sushila,

I have received no letter from you for a week. Pyarelal says that he has not shown me some of your letters. I did not have the time and since there was no letter from you, I did not write. Today I saw your letter to Pyarelal. There is no limit to your foolishness. I shall not press you to come. If you do come in your present state, you will not feel happy here. What you ask is a thing you should not ask and even if it were possible for me to give it I should not give it. So you may take the chapter as closed. When you find that you cannot help coming to me without laying down preconditions, rush to me and become one with me.

You must live there in total detachment. Then only will you be happy. When you go home you should go as an outsider or as a doctor. Do not involve yourself in the cares of the household. It would be best if you could start earning. You can then satisfy Mother's hunger. You have no special needs. Give up the temptation of sending your savings to me. You can be absorbed in many places if you take up a job. By refusing to accept my help, you are not earning merit but incurring sin. Are you ashamed to be known as my daughter ? Lilavati introduces herself as my daughter. Your false pride is eating me.

Mohanlal and Shakuntala should live away from Mother. Mother's place is here. Parnerkar's mother had been staying here. She will be coming again. Mahadev's mother comes and goes. She is his step-mother. Why should not Pyarelal's mother live with Pyarelal ? I am prepared to provide a separate kitchen for her. Thereby, the question of expenses will be solved. Arguments will come to an end. And the meanness resulting from lack of money will disappear. This is a natural arrangement. Mother will be able to pay occasional visits to Mohanlal as a guest. You will be relieved of a heavy burden. If you become calm, everything will be well soon. If I remain alive, in course of time you are bound to become one with me. I am in no hurry about it. You should not be in a hurry either.

Enclosed is a list of mistakes in *Harijan Sevak* prepared by Munnalal. The first mistake is obvious and it is bad. I have hurriedly glanced through other errors. Some of them may not be errors. The rest are insignificant.

Harijan Sevak will probably be shifted to Poona next week. Chandrashankar[5] will arrive there on Saturday to make arrangements. Rest assured that my decisions are likely to have more knowledge behind them than yours. You will feel calm if you have such confidence. This does not mean that you should rush here. But it means that you should become humble. If you have humility in you, you should never have any doubts concerning my decisions. You are free to ask questions. But you must have trust in my answers. Think over this.

Blessings from
Bapu

23. Letter to Sushila Nayyar

May 8, 1941

Chi. Sushila,

I have sent you a telegram. I had been waiting for your reply and so did not write to you yesterday. I do hope that Ba is really all right. So that is not the reason why I have sent the telegram. I feel perturbed that just when you are having your examination you have to be worrying about Ba. But I know God will save you.

I am doing very well. Doctor and Sankaran together had removed Lilavati, Rajkumari and Amtul Salaam from the proximity of my bed. Das slept on one side and Sankaran on the other. This went on for five or six days. Lilavati created a row and so she came back last night. Rajkumari and Amtul Salaam were in agreement with the plan. Lilavati was not aware of it. Even so she slept at some distance. She did not even protest when Dr. Das made other suggestions. The whole change was with a view to giving me rest. I forgot to write to you that I had read your article in *Hardonian*. I thought it was good.

Blessings from
Bapu

24. Letter to Sushila Nayyar

Before July 16, 1941

You cannot return the (present) like this. It is gift of love. It will always be so. You can pass it on to others.

What is all this you have written ? You are stupid and will remain so.

Why harbour such thoughts in your mind ? What does it matter even if I get annoyed ? But since I know you, you may take it that my anger is already gone. You may not reform yourself, old as you have grown ! ! ! But I am reforming myself and shall keep on reforming till I die. Why have any doubt at all ? Why do you not listen ? There is no question at all of your moving from here. How can you leave what you have built yourself ? You are not going to stay anywhere else at all. I am beginning to believe that whatever is to be done by you will be done only from here. After me some at least will carry on my work. One of them would be of course you. Now drive away all doubt. Pass your examination soon and come and sit in my lap.

Bapu

25. Letter to Sushila Nayyar

October 9, 1941

Chi. Sushila,

I have your letter. You are filled with anxiety about your studies. Content yourself with as much as you can do. Your aim is not to pass an examination but to enhance your knowledge. Of course, you have to appear for the examination but that should be when you feel fully confident. Do not worry about the delay. Let it take as long as it may. Pyarelal had spoken to me about the idea of your staying in Lahore. I had told him that I would keep myself ready to make the arrangements later. I forgot to write to you about the matter. I can make arrangements quickly if you will allow me to do so. Kanu having left, A.S. is doing the massage. Dhiren has his class at 8, so A.S. has to do it. You should take it that all talk about my taking service from you has now ceased. Of course, I want you to rise above all such talk. Why should it affect us whether somebody praises us or blames us ?

My teaching was only with regard to the duty of a *satyagrahi*. A *satyagrahi* will not court imprisonment to forget his pain or to escape from it. He will do so in the faith that to offer satyagraha is his duty. As for A.S., I would only say that one should forget about her. One should accept whatever services she offers, but not expect anything from her.

It seems Pyarelal's statement has been well received. It is brief but to the point.

Do not worry about my weight. Increasing it only gradually may be the best thing. I have again increased the quota of butter.

Blessings from
Bapu

(P.S.)
Rajkumari has again fallen ill. She is coughing more. She writes in her letter today that it is reduced. Thus, it is sometimes better, at other times, worse.

NOTES

1. In English in the source.
2. This letter is written on the reverse side of the addressee's letter to Gandhiji dated June 2, 1938.
3. Meaning here lustfulness.
4. Illegible in the source.
5. Chandrashankar Shukla.

Chapter 9
Bibi Amutussalaam (1907-1985)

Bibi Amtussalam hailed from prominent Muslim family of Patiala. She was born in Zamindar Pathan family of Patiala, Punjab in 1907. She was influenced by Gandhi. In 1930-31, she visited him for the spiritual guidance. She worked with Gandhi for Hindu-Muslim unity. She was well-versed in the Sikh religious scripture and could recite Guru Granth Sahib. She was closely associated with Gandhi from 1931 to 1948. She was, a nationalist par excellence from core of her heart, and was with Mahatma Gandhi in Noakhali in 1946 when the worst riots took place in Bengal. Gandhi treated her like her own daughter and affectionately called her 'the crazy daughter'.

Gandhi was concerned about her because she (Amutussalaam) suffered from delicate health. She was thin, pale and sickly, suffering from Tuberculosis, piles, asthma, pleurisy, tonsillitis, pneumonia, migraine and other diseases. Despite these diseases she actively participated in freedom struggle and bold enough to tackle Pir Pagaro in persuading him to end communal riots in Sind.

When her brothers and other family members left for Pakistan, she was enraged and expressed her disappointment to Gandhi, who had arranged for the safe journey of her brothers to West Pakistan. She wanted to return to Patiala (from Noakhali where she was coordinating Gandhi's work of re-establishing communal harmony) from where the Muslims, including her family, had been evacuated to Pakistan. She wanted to demonstrate by living there, all by herself as a young Muslim woman, that she could dare the worst, perhaps even die, by way of exemplifying her absolute commitment to the cause of peace and communal amity.

Gandhi wrote to her on August 26, 1947: "You are needlessly finding fault with your brothers. When all others lost courage there, they too decided not to risk their life. It is enough if we ourselves stand firm. Let us not sit in judgement on others though they may be our own relatives." He further wrote, "You are fickle-minded in wanting to go to Patiala. It is one and the same, whether you are in Noakhali or in Punjab. It is not that your place is only in the Punjab. Your place is everywhere."

She was undergoing great agony at the divide between Hindus and Muslims. To assuage her feelings, Gandhi wrote to her, "I have never felt that you are a Muslim and that I am a Hindu. The only feeling I have is that you are A.S. and I am Gandhi, where our *atmans* are concerned, we are one. In my view, you are the moving spirit behind whatever peace has been achieved in Noakhali. It was and still is your most significant work. Only you can sustain it. Wherever you stand, you stand in the capacity of my daughter, do you not ? What can be done if you hold a different view, despite my opinion that you should forget all about Patiala ? ..."

Despite that Bibi did not forget Patiala the native place. Between 1947 and 1948, she along with Lajjawati Hooja (a prominent Congress worker of All-India Women's Congress), evacuated thousands of kidnapped Hindu and Muslim women from their respective homes in India and Pakistan. Lajjawati Hooja, who was very active in Jalandhar and associated with K.M.V. College, worked in three districts of Pakistan, including her native place Dera Ghazi Khan, while Bibi worked in Bahawalpur district. Both worked under the guidance of Rameshwari Nehru, a close relative of Jawaharlal Nehru, to mitigate the sufferings of thousands of innocent women.

Son of the soil, Amutussalaam worked at the grassroots level and set up many institutions to serve the people and country. She had her maternal relations near Rajpura. So, she established the Kasturba Seva Mandir and other institutions in Rajpura, where she helped Hindu migrants from Bahawalpur, Pakistan, to settle down. A dedicated, self-sacrificing, a quiet worker who never sought the limelight died on September 29, 1985.

1. Letter to Amutussalaam

August 12, 1932

My Dear Amtul,

I have your letter. There was nothing to hide from anyone in your letter. I would like all girls and women to shed this false shame about the monthly sickness. There may be a sense of shame on the part of those who want to indulge their animal passions and treat the monthly business in terms of sexuality. But those who want to lead a life of continence should discuss this sickness as any other sickness. Now for the remedy. In the first place you should take perfect rest as soon as there is any symptom of the sickness coming and rest should be continued whilst there is the slightest discharge. During the free days of the month regular sitz-baths should be taken as also hip-baths in order to avoid undue discharge or a discharge beyond three days in pains. There should (be) no pains during the sickness. If there the treatment does not answer, you should allow the womb to be examined by a doctor. On this matter you should consult Mrs. Lazarus and be guided by her. She is likely to be able to tell you what to do.

You should take Premabehn into your confidence. She does not know much about this. But you two can put your heads together and read up the literature on the subject. If you don't know what sitz-baths are and if Prema also does not, you should read up Kuhne's book. If you master the secret of this illness, you can impart it to the other girls. It is the most fruitful source of the diseases of women. A false sense of shame prevents girls from understanding the sickness and regulating it in the proper manner. It is sinful to hide this thing and then suffer untold miseries. Herewith letter[1] for Dr. Sharma.

Love,
Bapu

(PS.)
Your Urdu letter is good. I will reply to it in another letter. Today the time is up.[2]

2. Letter to Amutussalaam

September 11, 1932

Dear Daughter Amutussalaam,

Explain to me why I should not call you only 'Amtul'[3]. It is well if you receive the money you are expecting but you should be content even if it is not forthcoming. Your letters are quite good, only you must write more legibly. Anyway, after I have read a few of your letters I shall be able to follow everything. It is astonishing to learn that there is no arrangement in Bombay for the education of girls; I had an idea that the Anjuman had pretty good provision. Consult Narandas about Dr. Sharma I think there is no harm in his coming to the Ashram if he conforms to its rules.

I understand about Kudsia[4]. How nice it would be if the girl gained her health in the Ashram ! As for you rest is the most important consideration.

Blessings from
Bapu

3. Letter to Amutussalaam

July 7, 1933

Dear Daughter Amutussalaam,

I have received your letter after a long interval; it gave me immense pleasure. If the word 'dear' has been missed in some letters, it does not mean that you are no longer dear to me. I was very happy to learn that all is well with you. No other letter from you has reached me. You are, of course, getting all the news about me.

Blessings from
Bapu

4. Letter to Amutussalaam

On or after February 11, 1934

Dear Daughter,

You are stupid. Who told you I was displeased ? Do you not see I have put myself in front of you ? I came up to you twice and you were asleep. I do not come to you often, for I am busy. But I direct everything from here. But you are stupid, obstinate and sensitive. No silence today or tomorrow. You must learn to obey cheerfully. Your peace lies in obedience not in willful silence or anything else. That is the meaning of discipline and faith.

Did you understand ?

Bapu

5. Letter to Amutussalaam

After May 9, 1934[5]

Dear Daughter Amutussalaam,

I have read all your letters carefully. You are grieved over nothing. On the one hand you await my orders, on the other you imagine all sorts of things. The obedient never indulge in melancholy. You must not even think of undertaking jobs which your health cannot stand. You must visit your mother. You have also to undergo the operation for piles. You must relinquish the temptation of coming to me. Travelling on foot is beyond you. Even the requisite food is not available in the villages. Doing work is as good as living with me. Patience is indispensable for you and your place is in the Ashram. Why do you take it that going to jail has been totally put off ? You have to prepare for it. And the preparation consists in being calm, giving up temptation, refraining from obstinacy etc. Your worrying the doctor is also not good. What more can I write now ?

Blessings from
Bapu

6. Letter to Amutussalaam

May 28, 1934

Dear Daughter Amutussalaam,

You are right in saying that only the rich and educated people can live with me. I have to turn the rich into poor and place a broom in the hands of the educated. Why should I have you with me ? To make you poorer still or to place a broom in your hands ? What was there to do in Patna ? Did you have to deliver lectures there ?[6] If you wish to serve you must calm yourself. I got your telegram. Why was the operation postponed ? I shall learn that from your letter. Yes, the best course for you would be to listen to your mother and get married. Where is the single-mindedness in you that is required for remaining a virgin ? You are prone to all kinds of thoughts. You cannot concentrate on any one thing. Therefore attain tranquillity if you wish to remain unmarried. When will you learn Hindi ? By now you ought to know Gujarati too. Tell me now your plan. I shall arrive in Bombay on the 14th and remain there till the 18th; afterwards, Poona. I shall be in Poona for six days and then on to Ahmedabad. Make yourself well and give up all childishness.

Blessings from
Bapu

7. Letter to Amutussalaam

February 10, 1935

Dear Amutussalaam,

I read both your letters and was distressed. I have not done a thing for you and what could I have possibly done ? It was not right to go (and live) in the jungle. If you will but listen to me, you will come here. All your troubles will disappear. I have written to Devdas to send you here. It will be a great favour to me if you comply with my suggestion. You can go back when all the rest have shifted to Harijan Colony. What can you do by living there at present except cause me anxiety ? If you are not agreeable to my suggestion, you may live with Devdas. But you must leave Harijan Colony whether or not you agree even to the latter course. And I reiterate that I cannot compel Sharma. Please come away, do come away. I repeat it. And if that is not possible for you, for God's sake, let us part company. The stock of dates is exhausted.

Blessings from
Bapu

8. Letter to Amutussalaam

After September 12, 1935)[7]

Dear Daughter,[8]

All your efforts are invain until you have been able to win over Kanam.[9]

I don't think it will affect me, if anyone touches my feet. But I want to put down this idolatry. I do not regard myself so pure. I see no benefit in cutting off the hair but you can certainly have it trimmed by someone if it comes in the way of your doing your work.

I do not accuse you of harbouring any impurity. There can be no fear on my part if you find nothing wrong with yourself. It is a matter of your own choice whether or no to go to Kanpur or any other place.

Bapu

9. Letter to Amutussalaam

April 3, 1936

Daughter Amutussalaam,

I have your long letter and have read it carefully. Bapa's letter has not at all pained me. I know you are not the one to take defeat and I believe the taunting words of Rukminibehn[10] will not affect you.

However, Bapa's letter suggests that you are not really needed there. It is a different matter that you are sure to be of service wherever you may be. I wish to put you where they need your services, and you are indeed needed elsewhere. Hence I have written to Bapa to send you to me if you are not really needed there. Now do what Bapa says. It is not true that people find fault with you because you are a Muslim. But do not mind if they do so because you are a woman and an unmarried one. Even in such a case, however, be assured that they are just a few, if any, whereas there are countless people who respect you and love you for your purity. But you never care for praise or censure, do you ? You may start worrying when I entertain any suspicion of you. Go to Segaon. Get away from Bapa.

Blessings from
Bapu

10. Letter to Amutussalaam

May 28, 1936

Chi. Amutussalaam,

I have a letter from you after a long time. Nowadays I am afraid of writing to you. You see in my words what was not intended because you have grown very suspicious. I am even considering whether I should stop writing in Urdu. You were hurt by an innocent letter containing nothing offensive because you put a contrary interpretation on it. I was only jesting when I worte to you not to quarrel with Thakkar Bapa[11]. I know that you are not one to quarrel with anybody, and hence it can be only a jest if I talk of a quarrel with reference to you. I made the joke only after I had Thakkar Bapa's loving letter and understood that it was all over. Why should you then feel unhappy and not be glad about it ?

Shall I henceforth give up all joking with you ? What if there are all kinds of stories about you ? Are you sure it is not your suspicious nature that is at work here again ? You are concerned with your work alone. Tell me what other work can be better than cooking for the Harijan children, feeding them and keeping all things clean. Moreover, you have Tyagi and Rajkishori with you and you should therefore experience no difficulty. It will pain me greatly if you ruin your health. You ought to forget the grief over Dr. Ansari's death and take up the work he has left behind.

The talk you had with your brothers at Patiala was not right. It was nothing but your foolishness and it evoked the response it deserved. What else would an unhappy member of the family say ? All have to bend before your obstinacy.

I had already sent for Saraswati and her mother even before you made the suggestion. I believe they will come to Bangalore. Have no anxiety on Kanti's account.

The reply should now be addressed: Bangalore City. I am writing to Sukirti and Raj. Write about your health. Tell me whether you can correctly read this letter. Have I not answered all your questions now ?

Blessings from
Bapu

11. Letter to Amutussalaam

June 26, 1936

Chi. Amutussalaam,

What do you want me to withdraw ? You say, "You should not have sent Sharma at all. I am not going to follow his instructions." But I committed the mistake of sending him. Should I not now ask to be forgiven for my mistake ? I wrote[12] "You used to revere Sharma"; and you say, "I worship no man." Now tell me how we should manage to agree with each other. I, on my part, revere everyone, including you. I thought you revered Kanti, you worshipped Draupadi. What will the worshipper of God do if he does not worship His creation ? Will not one holding me in reverence revere my Kanti ? But how can I cope with you ? You presume to be a veritable storehouse of knowledge. What do you care for my grace or anybody's ? It is doubtful if you would care for His grace.

To be stubborn means 'to refuse to be persuaded'. Neither by the mother, nor by the brother, nor by a companion, nor even by a poor adopted father like me. Now tell me, who is merciless ? You or I ? You do not discard your own pride and kiss Bapu's feet. Only when you sincerely reduce yourself to zero and think that not you but God is the Doer of all things, will your self reveal itself to you. At present, however, your pride has been leading you away. Why don't you persuade yourself that the work you have is enough and be content ? Why should you take up any new work that Bapa might entrust to you ? Your agreement with me is that you will do only what I tell you to do. When did you have my permission to take up new work ? Give the enclosed letter1 to Lilavati when she returns from Badri-Kedar. Krishnan Nair will learn in due course. The letter for the students accompanies this. Saraswati has gone to the Mahila Ashram.

Blessings from
Bapu

12. Letter to Amutussalaam

September 25, 1936

Chi. Amutussalaam,

Not only are you foolish, but you are also silly. Your letter is full of nonsense. It appears that in your view no man is good. I got your letter regarding Dr. Gilder. He did not open any of your Urdu letters nor has he read any. I read out your last letter to Mahadev as it contained nothing confidential. Doesn't a parent have that freedom ? I had replied immediately to your letter regarding Dr. Gilder saying that if you needed to be examined by Dr. Gilder it could be arranged. Did you get my letter addressed c/o Bari, the Theosophical Lodge ? I have not failed to reply to any of your letters. What can I do if letters fail to reach you ? If you wish, I shall obtain a certificate of posting. Why do you make yourself unhappy for nothing ? Zohra and Shaukat are getting married today in Delhi. The ceremony will be entirely private.

Write to me regularly. You should write only in Urdu.

Blessings from
Bapu

13. Letter to Amutussalaam

September 7, 1938

My Daughter Amutussalaam,

I do not know what I should say; you repeat the same question which I have answered again and again. Bhansalibhai writes to me; but does he complain ? Whatever I say reaches his head and heart. Whatever I say to you does not satisfy you— I cannot discuss your food. If I ask you to strain less, you will exert more. If I ask you to sleep, you will not listen. Even if you try to sleep, your heart will protest that it is not correct advice. How can I know what was said to the Maulana ? Tell me, how can I make you understand.

Blessings from
Bapu

14. Letter to Amutussalaam[13]

Before December 12, 1940[14]

Daughter,

Your letter is very bad. I have never entertained any suspicion. If that is your sin, call it a sin. You do not understand your guilt. I tell you, you will not succeed so long as you are not cleansed. This is bare truth. It is futile to go to Maulana. Whether you approve or not, I shall write to Jairamdas. If you permit, I am prepared to talk to Sophia and Kafi. If you want to fast, you cannot do it here. Fasting is not the remedy for cleansing yourself.

Bapu

15. Letter to Amutussalaam

Silence Day,
December 16, 1940

Daughter,

If you wish to act on principles, where is the room for service to me ? In that case, all your time should be devoted to the service of Shastriji. I do everything in the capacity of a father, not of a mother, although I aspire to be a mother. The status of a father sets its own restrictions on a man.

Bapu

16. Letter to Amutussalaam[15]

Before January 14, 1941[16]

Daughter,

Why should you write a letter to me ? If you keep well I shall value it more than a letter from you. I received Wahid's angry letter. If you saw it you would be able to judge his pain. I have not felt hurt on account of his anger. He has a right to be angry. I would now advise you to make all arrangements for Mother and return only after getting well yourself.

I am all right. Kanchan sleeps on one side and Abha on the other. Khan Saheb has written about you.

Blessings from
Bapu

17. Letter to Amutussalaam

Sevagram,
August 31, 1944

Dear Daughter Amutussalaam,

Seven annas had to be paid for your unstamped letter. Why are you in such a great hurry ? Such waste is not a sign of our poverty. I do not remember that I failed to address you as 'Daughter'. I allowed the pen free play. I do not see any difference between 'Daughter' and 'Chi.'. It might have made some difference if I had written 'Behn'. But is there any cure for suspicion ?

You can do any work without seeking my consent. Then the question of my displeasure will not arise at all. When you had asked me earlier, I had told you what was proper work for you. The work which you are doing covers the Hindu-Muslim problem too. I waited for the Maulvi you mention. But he never turned up. It was clear you had made a mistake. In spite of it, I had sent word to the Maulvi that he could certainly come.

You must have received the letter I sent through Bhagirathji. You can certainly draw Rs. 75 a month for your expenses. Do not ask your brothers for it. If they send anything of their own accord, pass it on to the Ashram.

Blessings from
Bapu

18. Letter to Amutussalaam

Sevagram,
January 10, 1945

Chi. Daughter A.S.,

I have read your letter to Sushilabehn.

If you must come here, come when you find the time. Your falling ill is not good and is contrary to our pact. Dying is not an ideal. Indulging in such things is false attachment. You must free yourself from that.

Do preside over the meeting if you wish. But your giving a lecture on the basis of a note sent from here is pointless. You should give to the meeting what you have digested.

If the officer has sent you the money without attaching any conditions, I see no harm in your accepting it. It is different that having gone into the matter further I may suggest something else. Your worrying about my health shows that you know neither God nor me. If you knew God, you would realize that you, I and everyone else are solely in His hands. If you knew me, you would know that I take every possible precaution. There are lapses nonetheless, but what can one do about it. However, I am maintaining good health. Under any circumstances you need not worry.

I repeat you may come any time you wish.

You have nothing to do with the 26th of January. You are all the time doing that work.

Blessings from
Bapu

19. Letter to Amutussalaam

Mussoorie,
May 30, 1946

Chi. Amutussalaam,

I have your letter written from Indore before you left for Bombay. As long as you rely on anybody except God, there will be nothing but darkness around you. We have not heard of the blind leading the blind. It is an error and ignorant attachment to say that a particular person guides one. That all of us let ourselves be guided, up to a point, by somebody is one thing and to rely upon one person in all matters is another. I see this every moment, and more clearly in your case. My test has no meaning at all. I do not test anybody, nor do I wish to do so. Really speaking I do not know how to test anybody. You can, therefore, stay in Bombay. Kafi Khan can guide you best and you can guide him. After all you are brother and sister and there would be nothing unusual in your guiding each other. Nor is there anything unusual in your trying to help Rashid Khan's widow. If your advice is not accepted in all matters, you should not feel offended. However, how can I fully know the position in your family and its affairs ? I am sure, therefore, that you should do what seems best to you. What I have said above concerns the members of the same family. But you have looked upon the Ashram as your family. You may draw from it whatever consolation you can. You need not ask me even for that. You know all the members of that family. You may, therefore, take from each, whatever service you can easily get from him or her. You need not ask me to help you in that matter. You may go to the Ashram whenever you wish to and leave it whenever you feel inclined to do so. When you go to the Ashram, observe its rules during the time you remain there. After leaving it you may follow whichever you can. The others do the same. There is no benefit in carrying with oneself wherever one goes what one finds a burden.

In Borkamata you have created your own family. I did not know about it. Whether to go there or not also rests with you. If I have forbidden you, I withdraw my prohibition. If anything happens there or somebody does not respect your wishes, do not seek my help. I do not even know everybody there.

You have by now written a good many letters. Since you had lost a dear brother, I felt that I should share your sorrow and, therefore, wrote to you despite pressure of other work. You should not take improper advantage of that now. If you need to write to me on some special business, that would be a different matter. Make your way in life truthfully and with ease and do everything with God alone as witness. Give up your attachment to me. To rely on one human being in all one's affairs is nothing but attachment.

Blessings from
Bapu

20. Letter to Amutussalaam

December 17, 1946

Daughter,

I have your letter. What shall I say to you ? I have already said that you do not understand me and still call me your guide. You caused pain to Kanu also. Now what shall I say ? It is a crime even to talk to you. I shall be satisfied if you act according to what you have gained and be happy. I am afraid to talk to you about anything. You misinterpreted what I told you with great affection and caused pain to Kanu by giving him your interpretation. Neither you nor I will lose anything if you do not come here. Lose yourself in whatever service you like to take up.

Blessings from
Bapu

21. Letter to Amutussalaam

January 6, 1947

Dear Daughter,

I have your long letter. Did you get my yesterday's letter ? I had written two letters. Why do you wish to die in my lap ? Have you decided to die ! All this is against dharma. I cannot go there specially (to see you). I do whatever I can from here. You have to die or live as God wills. Give up any other thought. Your village is also there in my itinerary. If you are alive till then, we shall certainly meet.

Blessings from
Bapu

22. Letter to Amutussalaam

January 8, 1947

Dear Daughter,

I was glad to have your letter. Nothing but dharma can help you. If it is God's will that we should meet in person while doing our duty, we shall certainly meet. Not otherwise. How does it matter even if we don't ? We have never been separate spiritually nor shall we ever be. Whatever happens, remain happy.

Blessings from
Bapu

23. Letter to Amutussalaam

Foolish Daughter,

You read the opposite meaning of what I write. It is no atonement to do something which gives you pleasure. Your massage gave me pleasure . . . . [17] A man does not display love when he is angry. I showered so much love on you because my anger had cooled down. Do you get me now ?

Kanu does not undertake a fast. Apply ointment to the piles. The question of accompanying me remains. There should be no promise to keep you always with me. This insistence has to be abandoned.

Bapu

NOTES

1. *Vide* the following item.
2. The postscript is in Urdu.
3. In some previous letters, Gandhiji had addressed her as 'Amtul' to which she seems to have objected; *Vide* "Letter to Narandas Gandhi", 7-11-1932 Her full name consisted of two words 'Amtul', meaning 'servant', and 'salaam' meaning 'peace'.
4. Addressee's niece.
5. According to the editorial note in *Bapuke Patra-8: Bibi Amutussalaam ke Nam*, this was written during Gandhiji's walking tour in Orissa which commenced on this date.
6. The addressee, wishing to be in Gandhiji's company, had said in her letter that he had no place for an uneducated person like herself.
7. Inferred from the sentence : "I don't think it will affect me, if anyone touches my feet." On September 12, 1935, Gandhiji had renounced the practice of placing his hand on a girl's shoulder for support while walking. *Vide* also "A Renunciation", 21-9-1935.
8. The source has this in Urdu.
9. In *Bapuke Patra—8 : Bibi Amtussalamake Nam,* the addressee explains that she was asked to take care of Kanam, son of Ramdas Gandhi, as Ba was in Simla.
10. Wife of N.R. Malkani.
11. *Vide* "Letter to Amutussalaam", 18-5-1936.
12. *Vide* "Letter to Amutussalaam",19-6-1936.

13. Gandhiji did not allow the addressee to go to Sind; thereupon she asked him what suspicions he had and what sins she had committed.
14. From the reference to the letter to Jairamdas Doulatram; *vide* "Letter to Jairamdas Doulatram", 12-12-1940.
15. This was in reply to a letter from the addressee's brother, Abdul Wahid Khan, asking Gandhiji to send the addressee to look after her ailing mother.
16. Inferred from the reference to ailing mother in this and the following item.
17. A sentence here is illegible.

Chapter 10
Margarete Spiegel

Margarete Spiegel became part of history for her association with Gandhi. She was interested in India since a very young age. Living in Germany during the First World War, she was drawn towards pacifism. Gurudev Rabindranath Tagore was her favourite author. She came to know of Gandhi through Romain Rolland's book. After wards she then read all the books by Gandhi and about him which were available in the State Library at Berlin, where she was a teacher at a Government college.

In Germany there used to be no prescribed text-books for higher classes, so she chose a German school-edition of Gandhi's speeches and writings for a class she was preparing in English for the University entrance examination. In order to study the Gandhi's movement she got leave to visit India for two months in 1932. After travelling over several parts of India she stayed as a guest at the Sabarmati Ashram for three days, taking part in all Ashram activities from morning to night. In December 1932 she saw Gandhi for the first time sitting under a mango tree in the Yeravada jail. Gandhi scolded her for having given up vegetarianism because it was troublesome during his journeys. She again became a vegetarian. She returned back to Germany.

She was constantly in touch with Gandhi through letters and Gandhi used to reply her promptly. The constant touch with Gandhi made her to believe nonviolence and she finally became vegetarian by conviction and beliefs. On 1st April, 1933, she was dismissed from the Government College in Berlin for being a Jewess. As the Jews were deprived of their passports, she left for Venice on 2nd April, 1933 and waited there for twelve days for the next boat to India. From Venice she wrote to Bapu (Gandhi) that she was coming, and after landing in Bombay she went straight to Yeravda jail, and stayed in Poona for some time, seeing him almost daily in the prison.

In May1933 Gandhi began a fast for 21 days. To understand the science of satyagraha she also started fast but after two days on May10, 1933 she gave up the fast on Gandhi's advice. On the same day (10th May) she got the following little note from Gandhi: "I am glad you have broken your fast. You were too decent to persist in your folly. Now be good. You are forgiven. You should come and see me when you feel like it Love." Gandhi then sent her to the Ashram at Sabarmati, and Gandhi named her Amla. Gandhi becomes her spiritual guru. Gandhi was being gallant when he told her, "I shall love you in spite of your faults."

After his release from prison in August 1933, Gandhi went from Poona to Wardha in the last week of September, and she had the good fortune to stay with him there till he started on the Harijan tour. She was also a teacher at Shantiniketan.

1. Letter to Margarete Spiegel

January 14, 1933

My Dear Margarete,

I must continue to dictate. You are entitled to call yourself an Indian since you have felt like one from your childhood, but that is not a substitute for your German birth. The adoption should be an addition both to your name and to your strength, and what can be finer than that we should all add on the virtues of our own nations to those of the others !

Why was there a struggle to choose between Gurudev and myself ? We are no competitors. Gurudev occupies a throne which belongs to him by sheer merit. I have none of the gifts that he has, and what is more, we dearly love each other, and as years roll on, our love becomes stronger, and we understand also each other better and better. I would have you therefore to say that you like us both equally for whatever gifts God has bestowed upon us. No more therefore of choice-making, if you would be a real daughter like Mira. I hope you got my previous letter in which I acknowledged your letter written from Aden. The registered packet addressed to Mahadev was also duly received.

Love from us both.

Bapu

2. Letter to Margarete Spiegel

February 24, 1933

I had your beautiful letter. I prize your love. Of course I was not angry with you and therefore there is nothing to forgive. On the contrary, it is a matter of joy to me that I have friends to whom I can write without reserve and without any fear of being misunderstood. However, I am glad that you have resolved upon not spending money on love cables. Love need not express itself in words, but if it must, love-letters ought to be quite enough. Immediately we realize that we have nothing of our own, that all we have is held in trust for those in greater need, we have to spend it like misers. I hope you are getting your copy of *Harijan* every week.

Bapu

3. Letter to Margarete Spiegel

March 2, 1933

My Dear Margarete,

You are sending me letters regularly. But you are telling me nothing except about myself. You must now begin to tell me something about your children, and the many things that you teach them and how you teach them. You don't think that those things will not interest me. They will, because they might be of use for the Ashram children. You should tell me also as a teacher what you would do to and for the Ashram children if you had them under your charge.

Love from us both.

Bapu

4. Letter to Margarete Spiegel

March 24, 1933

My Dear Margarete,

Your letters continue to come with clock-work regularity. Of course you are not going to be upset if you are turned out as a Jewess. I shall be now eagerly waiting for your letters to know your fate. If you will have it so, you can take the palm for economy, though you must remember the old proverb that "One swallow does not make a summer", and for that reason your summary dismissal of the question of food does not mean that the solution is as easy as you fancy it is for you. Whilst it need not be given undue importance, it is a gross error to think that food has nothing to do with a person's moral or even physical growth. The experience of the sages of the world shows that they have given importance, some more and some less, to it, and the majority have admitted that a bloodless diet is necessary for full spiritual enlightenment.

You need not worry over the poor comprehension that your girls have shown of *ahimsa*.[1] I do not wonder. There is no response to *ahimsa* from the atmosphere. They have never been taught to attach the slightest value to it, and probably they have been taught to despise it. You can not expect them all of a sudden to understand the value of *ahimsa* in an atmosphere so hostile as yours.

Mahadev has been receiving your letters and he has got your booklet too. As I have heard of *Parsifal* and as it was quite a booklet I read it during odd moments in two days and I liked it very much. Yes, Mr. Kodanda Rao also got your letter.

Yours sincerely,
Bapu

5. Letter to Margarete Spiegel

'Parnakuti', Poona,
June 22, 1933

My Dear Amala,

I have your two stupid and silly letters. I never knew that you were so unbalanced, suspicious and hypersensitive. What led you to think that I regarded you as a stranger ? Or that you were less than a daughter to me ? You, nowadays, sign yourself as a disciple. But do you not know that I claim nobody as my disciple ? I have one disciple, too many, and that is myself. You suppose I would take additional burden and make my life a misery ? I delight in owning sons and daughters, sisters and brothers. Therefore, you are either a daughter or nothing; certainly not a disciple, and what a disciple suspecting her own master at every step ! Are you now surprised that I called you mad ! And why do you worry about my food ? Can you not have trust enough in me and feel that I would not take any risk with myself ? In any case, now that I am taking milk and fruit, after my own style, perhaps you will cease to worry. Anyway I am flourishing, gaining weight and strength. Are you flourishing as well as I am ?

Love,
Bapu

6. Letter to Margarete Spiegel

July 2, 1933

My Dear Amala,

You have done well in reminding me of my two promises. The letter to your mother I had in mind but I could not reach it when I had it in mind. Then it slipped my memory. I knew that I had to send you something. Herewith you will find that letter. As to the yarn necklace I thought that Mahadev had given it to you. You will find it herewith. It is made out of my own yarn.

If you are wearing what Mira wears, surely it is a petticoat. Is it not the petticoat the Ashram women wear ? You should remember that Mira's *sari* is a mere scarf thrown round her body. It is perhaps not even three yards in length. It simply covers her naked back and head and abdomen.

If your Ashram ideal is not there, you are doomed to disappointment some day. Better watch yourself. Your letters betray lack of ballast and responsibility. Take care and be humble. I have already written[2] to you about your passport.

Love,
Bapu

7. Letter to Margarete Spiegel

'Parnakuti', Poona,
July 4, 1933

Chi. Amala,

I have your letter. There is no occasion to stop writing to me. But I would like you always, whether I am busy or otherwise, to write sense and not nonsense, as you almost invariably do. But when you write sensibly and have to say much, I do not mind how long your letters are. But a senseless letter is too long even when it contains only one sentence or one word. Do you know how much senseless stuff you have written in your letter under reply ? That is why I called you a baby, 35 years old.

Your question about your future is too curious. You have hardly yet commenced your training, in my opinion. After all it is the trainers who have to give the certificate that you have been sufficiently trained. You would not give it yourself. When you are sufficiently trained you will find your work cut out for you, and of course you are being trained for Harijan service. What shape that service will take, it is difficult to say now, but before you can do that you have got to be well-versed in Hindi, well-versed in all the processes through which cotton goes before being turned into cloth. I have mentioned only two things, but there are many other things which you should know in order to be able to render Harijan service efficiently. I hope you received my letter of yesterday together with the chain and my letter to your mother.

Love,
Bapu

8. Letter to Margarete Spiegel

July 8, 1933

Dear "Grand Mother",

Your old age does not permit you to master the simple Hindi alphabet.

For your sake I have looked up the word 'petticoat' in the Oxford Dictionary and it was properly used by me.[3] The Indian woman's skirt is part of her *sari* which hangs from the waist and covers the petticoat.

The word ballast was properly used. Look up the dictionary. I have not the time just now to give you instances of what I mean. It would be better if you will discover them yourself. The necklace sent to you is strong enough to last for months. Another can be easily made. Do you want me to send you a spare one ?

Love.

Bapu
Amalabehn

9. Letter to Margarete Spiegel

'Parnakuti', Poona,
August 26, 1933

Chi. Amala,

I have now got all the letters from the jail. Yes, you may write as often as you like, only handing your letters to someone who is writing to me so that the postage may be saved. As a rule, there is a regular post from Wardha for me. The best thing for you, therefore, is to hand over your letters to Dwarkanathji[4] or Lakshmibehn[5].

I wonder what you mean when you say you read the *Gita* everyday. You read it to understand and act accordingly. You must now forget the past and look after the present, never mind how you behaved. I have forgotten all about it and I know that it was all out of excess of love. There was nothing immoral about it. Your letter to Mira has not been received. Vinoba is quite right in asking you to learn cooking, Hindi, and cotton processes well, if you are to do real work amongst Harijans.

I hope you are keeping quite well and fit.

Love,
Bapu

10. Letter to Margarete Spiegel

December 1, 1933

Chi. Amala,

I have your letter. I call it good because it is truthful. I knew you were deceiving yourself and me. Will you now tell me what your nature demands ? If it demands simply being in my presence, it cannot be satisfied. If it demands more teaching work and a life natural to most Europeans, I shall try to help you with hope of success. You should confer with Jamnalalji when he returns. Meanwhile do so with Dwarakanathji. You ought to be steady and brave. To desire to die is cowardice. There is nobody about you who has any wish to repress you. You have built in front of you a mountain of difficulties. Make your choice resolutely and act.

It is nearing 3.30 a.m. now. I get up always as usual, at 3 a.m. Just after washing I read your letter and began this. You must be wise and sure.

Love,
Bapu

(CWMG: 62: 245).

11. Letter to Margarete Spiegel

December 5, 1933

Chi. Amala,

This is being written before morning prayer time. I have your further letter. You must not conceal things from me or act unnaturally to please me. That would be a wrong way to go about it. You will please me most by being quite natural. Your own room is quite untidy. You are not taking care of your finger. It is high time you got well. You should go to a hill, if you cannot be better there.

Love,
Bapu

12. Letter to Margarete Spiegel

December 30, 1933

Chi. Amala,

Let us be natural. You should write when you feel like writing and let me write when I can spare a moment. Not a day passes when I do not think of you. I am glad you are making steady progress. I would like you to feel perfectly safe and free from nervousness. You should tell me all about your pupils. Do you see Ramdas and his wife often ?

Love,
Bapu

(PS.)
I am keeping excellent health, diet remaining the same.

13. Letter to Margarete Spiegel

February 2, 1934

Chi. Amala,

I have your unbalanced letter. You are morbid. Why should you continually think of yourself and brood over the wrongs done to you by other people ? Why can you not think of the wrongs other people are suffering from ? Brooding over our own wrongs makes us unbalanced. Identification with other people's wrongs makes us stronger. But now that I have received permission to send you to Sabarmati, I hope your grief will be over. I have sent a wire just now to send you to Sabarmati. It is likely therefore that this will be sent to you there. You will share all your thoughts freely with me and let me know how you feel in the new surroundings. You may choose your work. Do not overstrain yourself and you should take the food that suits you.

Love,
Bapu

14. Letter to Margarete Spiegel

February 19, 1934

Chi. Amala,

Your two letters came the same time. I am glad you like the place and the people. You should arrange your hours as you think proper in consultation with the manager. For the girls, you should do as the manager advises. When you have acquired sufficient control you may make drastic changes. For the lice, rub spirit into the roots of the hair and wash them with carbolic soap and the lice will disappear. The hair should be combed daily with a clean comb. Let the girls take for the time being the food that is cooked for them. There can be no harm whatsoever in your being interested in natural scenery and Islamic architecture.

Love,
Bapu

15. Letter to Margarete Spiegel

April 16, 1934

Chi. Amala,

I have your letter. Mira has been keeping you in touch with things concerning me.

You may take the vows, if you feel the confidence. Your things will be disposed of. Why do you think I doubt you or that you are less than Mira ? Mira has come in for rebukes and reproaches to which you are an utter stranger. But that is nothing. You should simply lose yourself in your work and you will find me truly.

Love,
Bapu

16. Letter to Margarete Spiegel

May 15, 1934

Chi. Amala,

Your Hindi transcription is quite good. You are certainly making more rapid progress than Mira in Hindi. The latter has never tried Gujarati. Nor was it necessary for her to do so. The accident produced no effect on any of us and there was nothing more to say about it. Of the attack on the car, I had said so much in public. Instead of thinking of me as a god, why not think that I am more man and less beast ? We have only the form of the human being but in manners we are often even less than beasts. Hence it is something to be human in substance as we are in form. Are you well ?

Love,
Bapu

17. Letter to Margarete Spiegel

June 4, 1934

Chi. Amala,

You did well in writing the letters. I want to know you as you are and not as you would be. I shall love you in spite of your faults. You have no cause to fear me. You must dismiss from your mind the thought that I hate you. I hate nobody in the world. You never gave me any cause for hating you. On the contrary you have given me many reasons for loving you. You must not therefore let your imagination run away with you.

I have read your letter to Mira. I think you should go to a cool place. I could easily send you somewhere. Why should you swear by German medicine ? There are competent doctors enough in Ahmedabad. Tell Parikshitlal and he will take you to one. You should be sane in these matters. You will be a cause of great anxiety to me, if you become ill and your body is undermined. Why do you want to be like Mira ? She is not perfect. No one is perfect. You should strive to be good according to the gifts God has given you. No two persons are alike in the world. But all can be good if they choose to.

We shall soon meet. I would like you to be fit when we meet. And this you will be, if you won't brood over you illness and take the necessary measures for getting well.

I enclose herewith some letters to be handed to those concerned.

Love,
Bapu

18. Letter to Margarete Spiegel

July 20, 1934

Chi. Amala,

I have your letters. You are unnecessarily alarmed over my fast. Nobody else is. Seven days' fast can't kill me. But if my end is to come, it will come, fast or no fast. Therefore I would ask you to give up all anxiety about me.

It betrays gross neglect of duty to want to come to Wardha. You are living with me when you are doing my work, even though you may be physically miles away from me. And you are not living with me though you may be physically in the same place, if you are not doing my work. When God will it you will be physically near me. But as I have said, if you simply cannot live in the Ashram you must do as you like. In that case there is no question of permission. I cannot surmount my nature and do the impossible. Will you go and live with Narandas in Rajkot ?

Dwarkanath has not yet left Wardha. I am quite well. Blood pressure normal.

Love,
Bapu

19. Letter to Margarete Spiegel

Segaon, Wardha,
September 16, 1936

Chi. Amala,

You seem to have deserted me. How so ? Do tell me all about yourself.

Love,
Bapu

20. Letter to Margaret Sanger

Wardha,
November 27, 1936

Dear Sister,

It was very thoughtful of you to send me an assortment of your choice dried fruit. Agatha Harrison is here just now and I remarked to her, "Whilst Mrs. Sanger went away from me without taking anything, you see how much I am taking from her even though she is so many miles away." You may judge who is the better of us two, of course apart from the natural superiority of the sex to which you belong. I have gone through your reproduction of the interview[6] in *Asia*. My hurried reading left on me the impression that it was a faithful reproduction.

Blessings from
Bapu

Mrs. Margaret Sanger
Birth Control Clinical Research Bureau
17, West 16th Street
New York City

NOTES

1. The addressee had said, "For two months I have been studying your works with my girls: a German school edition, excerpts from *Young India* . . . The result is miserable. Out of 20 girls, I have not converted a single one to *ahimsa*."
2. *Vide* "Letter to Margarete Spiegel", 30-6-1933.
3. *Vide* "Letter to Margarete Spiegel", 2-7-1933.
4. Dwarkanath Harkare, an Ashram inmate.
5. Laksmibehn N. Khare.
6. *Vide* "Interview to Margaret Sanger", 3/4-12-1935.

Chapter 11 Rajkumari Amrit Kaur (1889-1964)

An eminent Gandhian, a freedom fighter, and a social activist Rajkumari Amrit Kaur was born on 2nd February, 1889 in Lucknow. She was the daughter of Raja Sir Harnam Singh of the Kapurthala royal family. Her mother Râni Harnam Singh was the daughter of a Bengali Presbyterian mother and an Anglican father. The Rajkumari had her early education in Sherborne School for Girls in Dorset, England, and had her college education at Oxford University. After completing her education in England, she returned to India.

Amrit Kaur's father was connected with Gopal Krishna Gokhale and many other party leaders of Indian National Congress. After her return to India from England, Rajkumari got interested in India's freedom struggle through the occasional visits of those leaders to her father's home. On her return to India she came in touch with Gopal Krishna Gokhale and later with Mahatma Gandhi. This was a turning point in her life, which had initiated her in freedom struggle. She came under the influence of Mahatma Gandhi and became one of his close associates.

She for the first time met Mahatma Gandhi in 1919 in Bombay. She felt drawn to Gandhi's thoughts and vision for the country. The Jallianwala Bagh massacre in the same year had deep impact on Young Kaur and convinced her of the necessity of India's gaining its freedom from the British yoke. She became member of Indian National Congress and began to participate in India's struggle for freedom. She also started taking part in social reform activities.

Rajkumari co-founded the All India Women's Conference in 1927, became its secretary in 1930, and president in 1933. She participated in Dandi March in 1930 and was imprisoned by British authorities. Rajkumari went to live at Gandhi's ashram in 1934, and took up the austere life there despite her royal family background. She served as one of Gandhi's secretaries for sixteen years. In 1937 she went on a goodwill mission and to advocate the cause of the Congress to Bannu in Northwest Frontier Province (in the present day Khyber-Pakhtunkhwa) as a representative of the INC and she was arrested on the charges of sedition. In 1942, she participated in the Quit India Movement, and the British Government imprisoned her again.

Rajkumari served as the Chairperson of the All India Women's Education Fund Association. She was a member of the Executive Committee of Lady Irwin College in New Delhi. The British Raj appointed her as a member of the Advisory Board of Education; (she resigned from that Board during the Quit India Movement). She was sent as a member of the Indian delegation to UNESCO conferences in London and Paris in 1945 and 1946, respectively. She also served as a member of the Board of Trustees of the All India Spinners' Association. She was also the first woman member of Hindustani Talimi Sangh.

Rajkumari championed the cause of universal suffrage, and testified before the Lothian Committee of Parliament (1932) on Indian franchise and constitutional reforms, and before the Joint Select Committee of British Parliament on Indian constitutional reforms. She worked to reduce illiteracy, and eradicate the custom of child marriages and the *purdah* system for women, which were prevalent in India.

In independent India she became first Women Cabinet Minister in the Jawaharlal Nehru's first Cabinet in 1947 and was assigned the Ministry of Health. In 1950, she was elected the president of World Health Organization, becoming the first woman and the first Asian to hold that post. She was a strong moving force behind the establishment of the All India Institute of Medical Sciences in New Delhi, and became its first president.

She and one of her brothers donated their ancestral property and house (named Manorville) in Shimla, Himachal Pradesh to serve as a holiday home for the staff and nurses of the Institute.

She served as the Chairperson of the Indian Red Cross society for fourteen years. Under her chairpersonship, the Indian Red Cross did a number of pioneering works in the hinterlands of India. She initiated the Tuberculosis Association of India and the Central Leprosy Teaching and Research Institute in Madras. She started the Rajkumari Amrit Kaur College of Nursing and the National Sports Club of India. Between 1958 and 1963 Kaur was the president of the All-India Motor Transport Congress in Delhi.

She spent most of her time for the uplift of women and the eradication of social evils. She was a strong champion of female education and equally concerned with the upliftment of Harijans. She was a spinster all through her life.

From 1957 until her death on 2nd Febuary.1964, she remained a member of Rajya Sabha.

1. Letter to Amrit Kaur

Wardha,
July 4, 1935

My Dear Amrit,

I have your letter. Your letters to me are love letters, each time I suppose not less than an hour's effort even for you—a ready and fast writer. Now that we know each other so well, you can certainly save your time by writing only when you must. Though I treasure your long letters, I would be satisfied with a mere postcard telling me of important events.

You have your work cut out for you at Poona. Are you coming to Wardha on your way to Poona or on your way back or both ways ? The weather is much cooler just now.

I have shared your letter with Kumarappa[1]. If you can establish contact with rickshaw-pullers, it would be a great thing. They can easily spin, weave and add to their meagre earnings.

I am sorry Krishnarao is leaving you. Of course, ultimately you will have to rely upon yourself. Though your arms may not be strong enough to work at the bow, it is good that you will know the process of carding. That would enable you to regulate and control carding by others. If your girls learn spinning, you will insist upon their carding. Unless they do, they will never spin regularly. And it is a bad job to depend upon others for slivers. If they form a kind of spinning-club, they can have a division of labour. Some may gin, some others may do the carding, many can make slivers and all will spin. The clothes you have for Quetta relief, may be sent to Dr. Gopichand for the refugees in the Punjab, unless of course there are refugees in Simla itself, in which case you can distribute your clothes among them. Only I fancy that in Simla you will have the most well-to-do refugees, whereas in Lahore the poorest must have congregated. I shall hold on the money. It can be sent where they have spent what is being collected now. There is always in such calamities an ample fund in the beginning stages.

You need not get out of your 'Ville' to sell those paper sheets and envelopes I have sent you. I am in no hurry to have the price of them. And ultimately even if they could not be sold there, there would not be any difficulty in selling them here, without any loss. I know we cannot make the profits that you can, but you must not give undue labour to their sale.

The slivers I have sent you, should give you at least 25 counts, as they are capable of giving 30 counts. Please hand over the enclosed letter to Andrews.

Love,
Bapu

Shri Rajkumari Amrit Kunvar Behn
Manorville
Simla

2. Letter to Amrit Kaur

Wardha,
August 23, 1935

My Dear Amrit,

The promised wire has come. And I am glad your place remains vacant. Whenever I take my seat, I miss you. You had become a fixture. Then you have left so many reminders behind. The thermos is a perpetual reminder. The citronel (la) bottle, too, I found lying on the table. I suppose you left that, too, by design. The baskets are still there. The beet never ends. I must try it again. So you see what you have done !

I hope Shummy was able to issue the certificate I wanted. You have invited Kumarappa to be your guest whenever he could go to Simla. The Civil Surgeon examined him yesterday and regard being had to the slight temperature, he wants him to go to a hill for a month or two. I am sending him to Bombay for further examination and then he may be ready to go to Simla, if you really can take him in without any inconvenience to you at all. If you can, please wire to me. But you must not hesitate to say no, if you will be inconvenienced in any way whatsoever.

Love to you both.

Bapu

3. Letter to Amrit Kaur

Wardha,
August 27, 1935

My Dear Amrit,

Don't be alarmed. I am writing with the left hand to keep the right fit for Monday.

Your two letters and wire came in duly. Perhaps you will have to receive Devdas, too, if you have room for him. Poor boy ! He is in danger of being attacked by paralysis. Jamnalalji wired yesterday saying Ansari had advised change to Simla. Simla must have come to his lips because of you. What other special recommendation could Simla have ? I am simply preparing you for the application. If it comes, you will know what to do with it. Once more I warn you. Never hesitate to say 'No' when you mean 'No'. That is the only way to preserve friendships. You have become dearer to me than a friend. But if you are to remain a dear daughter, I must not put undue strain on your loyalty. And yet my life is so full of companionships that everyone intimately connected with me is taxed to the uttermost. May God give you the strength to carry the burden you have imposed on yourself.

Shummy won't now regulate Kumarappa's life from the heights of Simla. For he is having Kumarappa under his own observation. Tell him I am religiously eating daily the beet he sent. Amutussalaam has found out the way of cooking it well. I did not have much talk about Puri with Gopichandji. I see from Pyarelal's letter sent by you that his heart is not in Simla. Is there no local man there who would take it up ? I am writing to G. How did you find the paper that was given to you by Choudhury ? You should send me samples of the sizes and the colours you want.

The meetings of the Board[2] were quite good. I wish you had been present. But I know it was right for you to go. Of course, you will come and resume your work here whenever you can come. Give my love to your two faithful attendants and tell them I was sorry I was not able to know more of them as I would have liked to do. But my activities leave me no time for such amenities.

Love from us all.

Bapu

4. Letter to Amrit Kaur

Wardha,
April 22, 1936

My Dear Idiot,

Only idiots can think of idiotic interpretation[3] and because you are such a brilliant specimen and agent of the A.I.V.I.A., naturally you will like the rest to belong to your species. Heaven help poor me—their guide ! ! !

Do you think anything on earth can be done without trouble ? You can't do even your unpacking without trouble. Then what is the use of your saying that I should redeem my promise to send you honey if it can be done without trouble ? I tell you that it cannot be done without some trouble. But that trouble is going to be taken and honey is being sent. You will cover the expense when you next send your cheque. The parcels to follow will be sent to you direct from Calcutta or Shillong, V.P.P. if you like. You will tell me when you will want the next parcel. Let all eat this honey, if they prefer it to the Australian. I am sure the Shillong honey is any way better than the foreign stuff, if only because it is fresher.

Your lace, mattress and the reversible *sari* must be in the box that was being packed for you. You must receive it by this time. I know there was some bungling about it. You are not the only idiot. You may be the princess among them !! Are you ?

I go tomorrow to Nagpur, probably return on 25th, 27th for certain. I go to Segaon, 5 miles from here, on 29th or 30th, returning when required. I go with Sardar on 9th May or about the date on Nandi Hill, Mysore. Mahadev and others accompany me. Or else I would have insisted on Mahadev going to you for a month. We descend to Bangalore about 1st June and leave it about 10th June. This outing is necessary because Dr. A(nsari) wants Sardar to go to a hill-station. He would not go without me. If I had not to go to Mysore, I would have passed a fortnight with the sister at Panchgani. I am sorry to disappoint them.

Of course I inflict myself on you, if I have to come to Simla. I do not think I shall have to just yet. As for you, I shall hold you to the three winter months with me and then you will diet yourself under supervision. What would Shummy say about it ?

Love,
Bapu

5. Letter to Amrit Kaur

Nandi Hill,
May 11, 1936

My Dear Idiot,

I have just got your letter. We reached here yesterday safe and sound. It was Sunday and so though I thought of you, I dismissed the talk of a wire. Those who try to approach the villagers have to forget that there is such a thing as telegrams. A weekly post is all they have and often not even that. In Segaon there is supposed to be a weekly delivery but I am told the postman in Wardha hands the letters to any Segaon man whom he comes across and whom *he* trusts ! ! ! Your letters are all torn (up) after I have read and answered them.

I hope you got my letter[4] written on the train in pencil hand. It was posted at Madras.

I walked up the hill from the base. It took me 2½ hours, the distance covered was over 5 miles. I walked very slow. Hence there was no fatigue. It was Dr. Ansari who wanted the Sardar to pass the summer on a hill. And he himself is no more. Evidently his death was quite sudden. For me it is a very personal loss. I relied upon his advice in so many matters.

The pressure put upon you not to resist your nomination to the Jullunder Municipality, I quite understand. Idiots being honest people and therefore impartial, are always in demand. How could it be otherwise—you, a princess among them—not the hereditary one but by right of merit.

I do not mind your trying to make Simla less insanitary. Only don't you catch the infection. Why don't you move the Municipal Committee ? Of course, what is true of Segaon and Sindi must be true of the black town of Simla. I suppose you know that the old Indian part of Madras is to this day called black town. It has not occurred to any of the city fathers to change that name, though they give patriotic names to some of their streets. We cannot all of a sudden develop sanitary habits because we heave up to Simla heights. But the M. Committee can, if it will, enforce proper sanitation. Many things are enforced over there. Sanitary enforcement will be least open to objection.

Well, Nandi Hill is really a model of sanitation, of course, enforced from above. The air is beautiful. The calmness is divine. No1 cars or carts or even rickshaws. Only 30 families can live here comfortably. More are not allowed. I do not know a more secluded, cleaner, quieter hill. Sardar is in raptures over the stillness. I know you will love it, if you were here.

Ku. reaches Wednesday.

Love,
Tyrant

6. Letter to Amrit Kaur

May 28, 1936

My Dear Rebel,

Your letter came in yesterday. The post comes after the closing of the outgoing mail.

You are a proper family party—Judge, Government Member, Doctor, with rebellious sister in their midst and you want the Collector Brother in your midst to finish your happiness. Remember that feeding up an exhausted brother is not the only manner of expressing a sister's love. She has to know the food that is required for a given constitution. I know cases where rich and nutritious food has resulted in harm But you have lived with me in vain if you do not know how to choose the correct articles. The manner of preparing them must be your very own.

When I read the sentence in your letter, attributed to me as having ever said to Kallenbach, I couldn't believe it. I re-read the thing and then I laughed. I never lay down the law like that even for little children. Though K. had immense faith in me, he would not tolerate the autocracy and arrogance attributed to me. And faith like his would not require such assertions of infallibility. You must now fill in the gap and tell me who regaled you with the precious information and I might be able to throw some more light on the grave problem ! But my denial should not be taken to mean that I won't lay down the law for rebels and idiots and require obedience because it is given by me. I must live up to the title given to me if only to give you the satisfaction of proving your rebellious spirit ! And then heaven help me, if such assertion being heard by somebody is quoted as an authentic example of my arrogance ! ! ! When we descend to Bangalore I shan't have time to give you such nonsense. Here there is quiet and therefore comparative leisure for giving you senseless things.

I do hope this hospitality even of nearest and dearest is not proving a strain on your weak body. I know what closest attention to the tiniest details, of which you are capable when it is a matter of loving service, means to the person giving such love. Happily Shummy is there to prevent you from overdoing it. Mira was badly ill but she is better now. She was taken to J.'s bungalow. She must have returned to Segaon. Rameshwari Nehru comes here today for three days. She had a very successful tour in the Harijan cause in Travancore. There was no indication in your note on Lucknow Exhibition that you did not want it published. I read it carefully, made alterations to hide your identity and let it go. You will tell me how it reads. And why did you not want it published ? Next time you will mark all such things suitably so as to indicate your wishes. That note had little value if it was not meant to tell me people what a town-bred woman had felt about the Exhibiton.

Here is a note received from Mr. Marsden which speaks for itself.

Love,
Tyrant

(PS.)
Remember we descend to Bangalore City on 31st and stay there not beyond 15th June.

7. Letter to Amrit Kaur

Segaon, Wardha,
July 12, 1936

My Dear Idiot,

I have your letter. *Do not* strain to write to me. You must not thin away. Do not waste your energy. Your letters to me must be a pleasure and a recreation or they must not be written at all. We shall not come closer by reason of letters. Absence of them can't separate us or create coolness. Why should you become a chronic invalid ? Your sense though of an idiot evidently led you aright. For your Simla *khadi* experiment seems to be succeeding beyond expectations. I suppose I must call it a mere accident. Idiots can't design good things !

The cottage here is a picture. I have just now a young sadhu.[5] He is a great *bhajani*, singer of bhajans of his own composition. He will be with me for a month. I occupy one corner, he occupies another, the third is occupied by Munnalal, a co-worker. The first accommodates a plank bedstead which you have seen. That corner will be taken up by Ba, if she comes, *and* you. So, you will prepare yourself for the proper village life. No privacy except in the bathroom which you will share with me. You must shudder to think of the fate that awaits you. You will enjoy the newness. There is no noise in spite of the seemingly crowded state of the room. All round is open and beautiful. Fresh breeze blowing throughout the day. It is quite cool. Perfect walks all over. When you come for two nights you will tell me what changes you will want.

You are there perhaps much more crowded than you are likely to feel here. All of us sleep under the sky without a roof separating us from it. Nevertheless you should bring your mosquito net and the cork for your thermos which you have made mine. I am managing with the one which is now almost all eaten away.

Agatha[6] expects to attend the Ceylon Conference which you have tabooed for yourself.

This is the newest sample of Maganwadi paper. You will have this in an envelope of Maganwadi make.

Love,
Tyrant

8. Letter to Amrit Kaur

Segaon, Wardha,
August 29, 1936

My Dear Amrit,

I hope you got my letter of yesterday. I am writing this in Segaon; therefore this can't go by late fee post. Your daily telegrams and letters giving cent per cent truth are absolutely necessary for the peace of my mind. Why must you send vegetables too ? Surely that is repugnant to the village sense. Trust me to ask for what I need from you.

There is no hurry about the surgical instruments. I can wait till Shummy is himself again. *Y*ou have to make up your mind to win him back. It is sheer nonsense for you to talk of running away from the home. It is so unlike you. 'Love is patient and long suffering.' And what are you if not embodiment of love ? Your precious association with me is not going to make you less loving and less lovable. If you have not been able to give satisfaction to the family by showing better health, surely it is within your power to show an equable mind and a love that will quench the fieriest anger. Do wire to me that you have reconquered Shummy. I tell you the thought of his pain over your illness haunts me all the day long. I do not know how I can appease him except by your unmistakably showing him that you have not lost, but if possible gained by your contact with me, in all that counts. Mira came back yesterday. The appointments in Betul were too dirty for her.

Love to both of you.

Bapu

9. Letter to Amrit Kaur

Segaon, Wardha,
August 30, 1936

My Dear Amrit,

You are good. You are sending me full letters and wires. I needed them all. Your letters are also cheerful. But whilst I do not worry in the sense you do. I must confess that your illness has given me a rude shock and

Shummy's estrangement has proved unbearable. You must walk to his room and stoop to conquer. Bathe him with your tears. I want his wire that he has forgiven me from his heart. It hurts me to think that I should be the cause of estrangement between you and him.

Here you were perfect in your obedience. I want you to obey me in this from your heart. Voluntary obedience always carries its own conviction. And I know that your obedience will restore the harmony of the household. The exact, method of winning over Shummy I must leave to you.

When you are entirely restored, I shall discuss with you and Shummy, if he is then composed, my own opinion about the cause of your painful collapse.

It may be well for you to reduce the quantity of milk rather than giving up eggs. The heaviness need not be looked for in that direction first. And if the doctor agrees, you should take a little garlic always. I cannot vouch for it but I am inclined to think that onion oil should be good for eczema.

I was not amused over Subhas's fear. There is much truth in what he says. If you were feigning strength however unwittingly, under the impulse of your enthusiasm and your intense love for me, naturally the separation would produce a collapse. You alone could be the judge of the condition, which (you) can fathom by introspection. No more tonight.

Love,
Bapu

10. Letter to Amrit Kaur

Segaon, Wardha,
September 29, 1936

My Dear Idiot,

Your two letters at the same time.

Khan Saheb is delighted that you are giving all that attention to the girls.

You should yield to Shummy now and take what meat he wants you to. There will be grace in your yielding now. There will be little or none if you yield when you are driven to it. And there will be no restraint possible. That you took very little meat when you did is no argument to prove that it will produce no effect in your case. Since you have no religious objection, I would like you to listen to me and straightway tell Shummy to prescribe what he likes. You must get rid of the eczema before you begin to move about. I see that you can't come to me in December. Let us see what is possible in January and February. Of course you are to be in Faizpur at the time of the Congress if you are able to go to Ahmedabad. When do you descend to Jullundur ?

The idea of building a separate cottage for yourself in Simla is a chimera. If you had one, you would be torn to pieces. You are physically unfit to have an eternal round of guests. Mira is free from fever but is not herself still. But she will be quite well in a few days. I am getting stronger though slowly. You will persevere with the hip-baths and try the sitzbath too. I have described the latter to you. Sit on a stool with the legs outside the water which should be level with the stool and then gently wash the genitals with a smooth towel. It is supposed to work wonders. You should take this separately.

Love,
Tyrant

11. Letter to Amrit Kaur

Segaon, Wardha,
October 10, 1936

My Dear Rebel,

I have been obliged to neglect you these few days. My only comfort is that the correspondence has been practically suspended—all my time being given to the sick ones. I can't say they are yet on the mend. The temperature is slowly rising daily. There is no danger as yet. But both are very weak. They will be all right if they have enough vitality. Anyway neither they nor I have any anxiety. The C.S.[7] was here today to examine them. They are having only watercure. I have just finished your broadcast.[8] Your experience of the village is excellently reproduced. The other part is not well balanced.

You say "old systems... have perished." If they have, where is the cause for revival ? But you yourself show later that they have at most decayed, not perished.

And then you begin at the wrong end—build roads and houses !! Who can do the thing ? Surely sanitation comes first. We were agreed upon it too !! And *you* began with it. But how should (you) be Idiot, if you remembered such a very simple fact ? And then you have not made a sharp division between what people can and should do themselves and what the State can and should. You do not want more than this, do you ? And you are in no need of praise. Of that you must have had a surfeit.

If you are only permitted to pass two months with me, I should hope to reconstruct your body. This eczema is certainly a source of anxiety from the medical standpoint. But I do not despair. Of course you won't go to Ahmedabad, if you are not quite fit. The apples of late have been quite hardy and all in a good condi(tion). You should tell me what the fruit costs each time and what the railage costs. The honey too came in quite safely. I finished the whole yesterday. It was quite nice. I have not yet heard from Lionel.

Khan Saheb has all the fruit he can eat. I get apples from you and Ambujam—more than I need—*mosambis* from Bombay and oranges locally.

Love,
Tyrant

(PS.)
Khan Saheb leaves for Delhi on 14th.

12. Letter to Amrit Kaur

Segaon, Wardha,
October 21, 1936

My Dear Rebel,

You have certainly provided me with excellent material for *Harijan*.[9] Mahadev will see your letter. I shall make judicious use of portions of it. You must then do a little propaganda work, even write to the papers and invite other women to do likewise. If you women would only realize your dignity and privilege, and make full use of it for mankind, you will make it much better than it is. But man has delighted in enslaving you and you have proved willing slaves till the slaves and the slave-holders have become one in the crime of degrading humanity. My special function from childhood, you might say, has been to make woman realize her dignity. I was once slaveholder myself but Ba proved an unwilling slave and thus opened my eyes to my mission. Her task was finished. Now I am in search of a woman who would realize her mission. Are you that woman, will you be one ?

If Shummy will be happy and healthy going to Europe and won't go without you, why should you not accompany him ? No time for more. Gave you a long letter yesterday.[10]

Love,
Tyrant

(PS.)
Yes, you should write to Natesan without doubt.

13. Letter to Amrit Kaur

November 19, 1936

My Dear Idiot,

I write never to make you weep but always to make you laugh. After your letter I realized the meaning you gave to your previous letter. At the same time your paragraph did bear the meaning I put upon it. But why should my play make you weep ? Why don't you weep over the many choice adjectives I apply to you ? You must develop a thick skin, if you will be well, both physically and mentally, and will take up the task for which you seem to be cut out. I am not going to Faizpur on 1st December but I may on 10th or 11th, certainly about 20th. If you come after 27th it will be very late. Why not come earlier and go from there to Ahmedabad. Then you may be a little late, if you like. But you will see what is possible. I am not touring after the Congress. My destination is Segaon. I shall have to go to Belgaum in March or April, whenever Gandhi Seva Sangh meets. This gives you all the information you need and ask for. The session begins on 27th and ends 29th.

I shall certainly read your article if it comes to me in time for suggestions.

Love,
Tyrant

14. Letter to Amrit Kaur

Segaon, Wardha,
December 18, 1936

My Dear Idiot,

So you will receive this in Ahmedabad. You will go to the Harijan Ashram and speak to the girls, the cattle and the trees of which there was not a trace when I took the land. There was a solitary *neem* tree, I think. You will see old Ramji, the Harijan, and his tall wife. And you will see also some familiar faces. Anandi, I think you know. And you must see the Vidyapith and the labour work of Anasuyabai. You should see her indigenous kindergarten for the Harijan brats. Of course, you will see Mridula's Jyoti Sangh. The other things will be shown to you in the usual manner. Don't bury yourself in the routine work, though that can't be neglected, I know. But you *must* learn the art of doing things without fretting and feeling the strain. What a long-drawn-out sermon this letter has become ? You will be quite comfortable with me in Faizpur. Only don't come there in a dilapidated condition.

You have all the love you may be in need of therefrom.

Tyrant

(PS.)
I reach Faizpur on 20th.

15. Letter to Amrit Kaur

Unrevised Segaon, Wardha,
March 8, 1937

My Dear Rebel,

I have an excuse for writing to you. You have left a small blue bottle. It contains a white powder resembling epsom salt. What is it ? I do hope you had no trouble in the train. The moral is no onion, no sweet potatoes, a fair quanity of garlic. Bowels ought not to be loose. Hip and friction sitz baths and garlic ought to set the bowels right and eradicate eczema. You must take at least 3 lb. of milk per day. Try unboiled fresh milk twice a day. It must be taken whilst it is yet warm from the udder.

Your place is vacant and looks dismal. Fancy doing without one's Secretary ever at your side ! But such is life, everything fleeting, only God is, nothing else is.

ईश्वास्यम् इदम् सर्वम् यत् किन जगत्याम् जगत्।
तेन त्यतेन भुज्जीया मा गृधः कस्यस्वित् धनम्।।

I have written it breaking up the *sandhi.*

Love,
Bapu

(PS.)
Forgot to give you Hindi *Anasaktiyoga.* I am writing to Delhi.[11]

16. Letter to Amrit Kaur

Segaon, Wardha,
May 8, 1937

My Dear Rebel,

This is being written on paper prepared by Prabhu Dayal. He has brought a fair lot of paper and has been showing it to me with great pride. I thought therefore that I should let you see his handiwork. This is not the best specimen but it was a convenient size for me to cut.

Well, normal men are just as good and as bad as normal women. You have been known to have behaved just as badly as if not worse than Lionel. And I see from your letter to Mira that you do not give me any news about your health thus leaving me to infer that you are keeping quite well. But now I understand you are not keeping extra well. Why should I not know all this ? And you have been taking medicines too ! You *must* let me know accurately what the matter is with you.

Balkrishna[12] is just as you left him. I thought I had told you as much.

I am glad you are giving so much time to Sanskrit. Your Hindi writing is a trifle too large but you are erring on the safe side; when the hand has settled you will soon begin to write the natural size. I have not had a bill from Mehta. He was given the full address. But an evil fate hangs about your address which no one but I would write correctly. I hope you had to pay nothing extra. I hope it will be of use. You should write to Dinsha Mehta to send you the bill for the kettle.

Love,

17. Letter to Amrit Kaur

June 26, 1937

I forgot to write to you about one thing. You referred to Devdas's third child. I agree with you that he should stop now. I must not write, you can, perhaps, must. I have no doubt he knows. I do not know who is greater sinner. They passionately love each other. And then love expresses itself in the painful fashion. I suppose they cannot help themselves. I know what an effort it is to exercise self-restraint when physical love is let loose. Duty separated us for long intervals. That gave me time for thinking and disciplining myself. After the appearance of Devdas I had fairly conquered the animal in me. Intense public activity of an exacting nature cast upon me a burden which I could not carry at the some time as making additions to the family. Thus did nature help me. And my greatest good luck was that in Ba I had a companion who never tempted me, so far as I can recall. Such is not the case with the present generation. I do not know that it was better in my generation. Ba is perhaps an exceptional woman. So you see I have boundless charity for Devdas. And yet how I wish the terrible burden on Lakshmi could be removed. Devdas and Lakshmi almost make out a case for the use of contraceptives. And yet I know that it will be a fatal conclusion to draw from this hard case. If they cannot restrain themselves Lakshmi must suffer. Now you have all the data, if you have self-confidence enough, to write to Devdas.

18. Letter to Amrit Kaur

Segaon,
September 8, 1937

My Dear Idiot,

This is being written after the evening walk. No cause for any worry about me. You must not be shocked to learn that I am taking that specialist's ampules. He has given me full details. It is a simple herb treated with the sun's rays. He says it has never failed to give lasting relief. It can do no harm. Of course, it deprives me of one food substance.[13] But that does not matter. It would be wrong not to try this drug.

Khan Saheb's letter is worthy of him.

I am glad you are taking ice and steam. You must add the earth bandage. What had Shummy[14] to say to your health ? I would like his opinion. Tell him this with my love.

I understand what S. and J. have to say about Charlie.[15] You should not only regulate his food whilst he is with you but you should also draw his attention to his weakness.

I was looking at that note on education. Do you still want me to study it and give you my opinion on it ?

Mira is getting on. She is doing some writing work. A(mtul) Salaam is fairly happy just now. Sharda[16] is flourishing. Lilavati has left in a huff because I lost my temper with her. I can become an ass. Sometimes, I doubt the reality of my *ahimsa*. Why can I not curb my temper for ever ? If my *ahimsa* is worth anything, surely it ought to resist all temptation and provocation. Please don't defend me but go for me. If Lilavati is lost to me, I shall be largely to blame. She is too good not to return to me. If she does, the credit will be hers.

Love,
Tyrant

(PS.)
J. is due tomorrow.

19. Letter to Amrit Kaur

Mardan,
May 7, 1938

My Dear Idiot,

Sushila has been keeping you informed about me. I have not therefore worried to write to you. It has been an anxious time here. Your analysis is good. Of course, the experience was due to my "weakness, lack of faith".

Let us all hope that I shall come out of the well of despair stronger and purer. There is as yet no sign of the end of the crisis. Darkness is still there. There is still an unaccountable dissatisfaction with myself. Moodiness is wholly unnatural to me. it creeps over me now and again. I suppress it by constant work. But the body does not respond to it as readily as I want it to. But I have not lost faith. There are signs that I shall get out of the slough. I may be deceived. I have patience. I do not fret over the delay. If it is to be a new birth, a regeneration all-round, it must be preceded by adequate travail. You are not to worry over my present condition. The sexual sense is the hardest to over come in my case. It has been an incessant struggle. It is for me a miracle how I have survived it. The one I am engaged in may be, ought to be, the final struggle.

Love,
Robber

20. Letter to Amrit Kaur[17]

About June 11, 1938[18]

Your argument is welcome. I haven't the time for long argument with you.

S.[19] is out of the picture. She must be an exception being a doctor. But your objection is sound in that even one woman vitiated the experiment. I am struggling to exclude Ba, too. S. has put herself out. She wouldn't have what others can't. Therefore, she is training a male nurse.

You are again right in saying that even a woman's proximity, speech, look, letter etc., may work the evil as her touch might. But I had to think of myself. If I scented danger then I must put out my eyes, rather than have the animal in me be aroused.

You miss the crucial point. It is not the woman who is to blame. I am the culprit. I must attain the required purity. This experiment is but a way to be tried.

The article has not gone to the press. It may never go though the prohibition is in force. You will put yourself wholly in the wrong if you avoid me because of my decision. If you were here I would convince you of the necessity of the decision, in spite of your finding flaws.

21. Letter to Amrit Kaur

Segaon,
July 8, 1938

My Dear Idiot,

What a question ? Of course you pass through Wardha on your way to B[20]. That means you may be here when the W.C. meets. And here you will find yourself in a crowded room. But that you don't mind.

How you manage to lose your voice from time to time ! You must go to a place where you can't be pestered. Is it not Segaon (?) And now I can build for you also to your design !

J.'s[21] letter to S.[22] You have now, I hope. The talks have stopped of course. The reply has to go from W.C.

Yes, Jawaharlal is having a grand time. He is raising India in the estimation of the West.

It is perhaps as well that you will be the only member of your Peace Brigade. This work does not need thousands. True immolation of a few will do the trick.

You are wrong. I began work among women when I was not even thirty years old. There is not a woman in S.A. who does not know me. But my work was among the poorest. The intellectuals I could not draw. My appeals have always been from heart to hearts. I have felt like fish out of water in the company of intellectuals. Hence you are wrong in laying down the sweeping proposition you have. You can't blame me for not having organized the intellectuals among women. I have not the gift. And then my method of organizing is out of the ordinary, not necessarily superior. All I mean is that I have nothing to show on paper. But just as I never fear coldness on the part of the poor when I approach them, I never fear it when I approach poor women. There is invisible bond between them and me. And why do you miss the agony I am passing through ? Is it not for woman kind ? I am wringing my soul for adequate purity, to enable me (to) render greater service to them and through them to the whole of humanity. *Ahimsa*, which is my sheet-anchor, demands all this. I expect your next letter to tell me you are well.

Love,
Bapu

22. Letter to Amrit Kaur

Unrevised Segaon,
July 11, 1938

My Dear Idiot,

I write this just as I got your letter and before destroying it. You must not allow your imagination to destroy your sanity. I have taken no drastic step. I shifted to Pyarelal's hole for giving Hanna the privacy she needed. She is wholly unaccustomed to our ways. I have now come back and you will occupy your usual corner. Sharda is my constant attendant. Amtul Salaam sleeps by my side, fans me and covers me when I need more covering. She feeds me. Lilavati is helping Mahadev, Shanta having gone back to England. You must not be quite so idiotic as you seem to have become over my travail. It is there. But my faith in my original conception is not shattered. Only I must learn how to realize it. Bad dreams must be avoided. There must be no repetition of 14th April.

Hanna has been sent by Kallenbach to gain experience and to know me personally as she has known me through him for years. She is most lovable but I fear she is too delicate to be able to stay here long.

I shall expect you on 23rd, the day of the meeting of the W.C. It is quite cool just now but the road is fearfully muddy. You will feel a little crowded. But that you won't mind.

You are criminally wasting your body. There is no occasion for all the neglect of which you are guilty. Some people deem it a merit to neglect their bodies. I wish you would have your name removed from the register of these illustrious criminals.

Love,
Tyrant

(PS.)
You inquire about my health. I assure you that it is in good order and condition. Hakumatrai was here yesterday. You can ask him. It is true I have lost weight. But that is of no consequence in blood-pressure cases. I must not attempt to regain it in this weather. If I keep well otherwise, the weight will be regained, at any rate most of it. T.

23. Letter to Amrit Kaur

July 15, 1938[23]

My Dear Idiot,

What a sad and wretched letter, yours of 11th. I am enjoying myself and you are sorrowing for nothing. When you come here, you will laugh at your own folly. My misery is superficial if there is any yet left. My peace cannot be permanently taken away by anything or anybody. You simply do not know me if you think that my experiences have undone me. If there is real attempt at purification, it must strengthen me and make me more joyful. But how can I help you if you must allow your imagination to run riot ?

You have to apologize about women. I could not organize intellectual women as such. I have not organized intellectual men as such. But this thing does not lend itself to argument. I simply cannot subscribe to the charge that there has been any neglect on my part about organizing women. It may be that I have not had the qualifications for doing better. But that would (be) no charge against me. However, I do not mind your complaint. I rather like it. It shows that there are things in which we look at things differently. And why not ? True affection does not demand identity of outlook. But I do not even on this point despair of convincing you that I could not have done better than I have. My passion for *brahmacharya* has that meaning. I must be wholly pure if I have true love for womankind.

Love,
Tyrant

(PS.)
I believe apricots did arrive—all rotten. Apples have come. I shall certainly eat them. You must be well quickly.

24. Letter to Amrit Kaur

Peshawar,
October 8, 1938

My Dear Idiot,

I am glad my wire went to you before your letter and wire came into my hands.

I offer no apology for not telling you anything about the closing of the experiment[24]. I had prepared you for it. And then I wrote a note[25] announcing the termination. There was no desire to keep it from you. A copy of the note herewith. Mahadev may not have it handy. He must read it to you, if you can't. It is Kanu's hand. No apology either for suppressing Mahadev's letter. Mahadev had guessed (wrongly) that something which I forget had happened on the basis of your talk with him. As it had not, and as Mahadev had told me not to deliver it to you if his guess was wrong, I did the right thing. It would have been wrong on my part even to have mentioned the thing to you and taken your time (and) my time for nothing. Supposing somebody swears at you thinking that you had been painting your face everyday, I would correct the person but would certainly not feel the call (*sic*) that that person had done you an unintentional wrong. Now you understand, I hope. I won't ask for your apology.

I have never enjoyed so much rest as Khan Saheb gives me. No visitors, no talks practically even on slips of paper. The result is I have been able without effort to write five articles for *Harijan*. You will give me your reaction to the articles on the European situation.

Your estimate of N.N. Joshi is correct. He prevaricates without knowing that he is doing so. But he is a good worker.

This tour has taught me one lesson. I must not put such heavy burdens on you. What I had hoped would be a light thing evidently was a serious drain on your energy. I hope that you will soon regain your lost health such as it is.

I know that Mahadev & Co. will flourish under your grandmotherly care. I was anxious for M. to accept your invitation. And Shummy is there—first class for such occasions. I shall look forward to your daily bulletin.

We are flourishing. There is no cold yet. I have never been so fit as I have felt latterly. There is an interruption because the old devil in the shape of animal passion is at me. When he assails me, I do feel worried. But the thing will wear away. So you see the most relevant thing I do share with you. But you are not to disturb yourself over this. It worries without disturbing me or making me morose. I seek the presence of God.

Love,
Tyrant

25. Letter to Amrit Kaur

Bannu,
October 24, 1938

My Dear Idiot,

You must do with the pencil hand and on mill-made paper—the pencil does not move well on the glazed hand-made. Your two letters were awaiting me when we reached Bannu. 'A Woman's Letter'[26] I may use for *Harijan.* Your Kathiawar thing[27] will go in this week with the last paragraph or two cut out. It is not likely that my articles on the European situation will bear fruit immediately. But they will, if India develops nonviolence. There are grave doubts about its possibility. My own impurity is probably the chief stumbling-block. My word has lost its power as it appears to me. It should, according to my views of purity. However, I push on in faith. I must detach myself from the results of my thought, word or deed. I am not going to judge myself and condemn me to inactivity because I cannot get rid of the impurity in spite of incessant effort. Now perhaps you will understand my disbelief in my power to reach the woman's heart. But this is a long story. So much has come in spontaneously. You won't worry because I do not worry at all. I do not brood over my impurity. I see the snake is there. I know his fangs worse than a krait's. I am therefore on my guard. The best test of no worry is my uniformly steady b.p.

I wish you would show this to Mahadev. When I began the letter I did not know that it would be a serious business. It is good in a way. I have simply given you a few lines for love's sake.

Love,
Tyrant

Otherwise Warrior
According to the
Latest Honours' List

26. Letter to Amrit Kaur

Delhi,
November 10, 1938

My Dear Idiot,

This is Satis Babu's latest production. He is making vast strides in this direction.

Your two letters came in today, the first without anything from M.

What could I say but from the heart about your pathetic appeal ? If the message comes to me nothing on earth would deter me. I have told you, perhaps, I have not the requisite purity to penetrate the woman heart. There must be a distance between her and me so long as I have the snake in me. You can but pray. But the effort has to be mine. Therefore don't feel angry or sorrowful if I can't answer your expectations.

Love,
Bapu

27. Letter to Amrit Kaur

Rajkot,
May 26, 1939

My Dear Idiot,

Of course I will give you the time you may need for explaining all you wish. But you must cease grieving. Weeping and brooding over injustices done to oneself is no virtue, it is definitely a vice. It is better cheerfully to submit to injustices than even unwittingly to do any injustice to anyone.

I forgot to tell you that P. was better after my severe talking to him. Only boundless love can cure him of his malady. I lack it. I lose patience with him as with no one. Have I ever told you that somehow or other I never spoke to Chhotelal or Pyarelal without losing temper ? The wonder to me is that Ch. never resented my explosions. He is gone. I feel responsible for his suicide. My harsh treatment of P. when I discovered his love for Y. must be held to be unforgivable. Had I treated him sympathetically things would have taken a different turn. As it was, I had practically banished him to Orissa. My *ahimsa* failed me. But neither Ch. nor P. ever complained. On the contrary they read love in every act of mine. If Mahadev has time he must tell you what I mean.

Love,
Tyrant

28. Letter to Amrit Kaur

Rajkot,
6.20 a.m., May 28, 1939

My Dear Idiot,

This is the fourth letter I am writing without the break of a day. I can't feel happy till I have convinced you that we are all authors of our own misery. If we have imbibed the first principle of *ahimsa* we must learn to put up even with real injustices from dear ones and that without grief. We do nothing strange when we require felt love. But our love becomes potent when we rejoicingly suffer felt injustice. This really resolves itself into what I started this letter with, that justice and injustice have no existence apart from our feeling. I want you therefore to imbibe this first lesson of *ahimsa* and assure me that there will be no more of weeping or harbouring secret and silent sorrow and grief. If you cannot learn this from me, you will learn nothing.

Love,
Tyrant

(PS.)
7.30 a.m.
Khurshed has written to you about Women's Congress. I would favour the idea, if it appeals to you.

29. Letter to Amrit Kaur

Segaon, Wardha,
June 12, 1939

My Dear Amrit,

I have your letter. Of course everything is forgiven you. The fact is I have not felt offended against you. My love burns as bright as ever. It is little worth if it cannot stand the heart pourings of loved ones. I simply gave you my reactions[28] to your letters. You are as much wanted here as ever. You will find me not in the least altered or if altered, it will be for the better. I shall know how much more tender you are than I had believed you to be. Navin is in Bombay tending his sister. His address is care Dr. Shah, Polyclinic, Queen's Road, Bombay.

Love,
Bapu

30. Letter to Amrit Kaur

Patna,
March 18, 1947

Chi. Amrit,

I had your letter. I wanted to write to you at once but never got the chance. It is a very strenuous time I am having here. But do not worry.

You remember those two notebooks containing rich treasures from the Bible and other Christian literature. If they have not taught you and me to be anxious for nothing and nobody, they have taught nothing worth learning, for our faith in the living God is to be measured by the extent of freedom from anxiety of any kind whatsoever and full faith in God requires an accurate knowledge of His laws and corresponding obedience thereto. This is the sum total of nature cure. The supreme law, making others superfluous, is heart assimilation of Ramanama in every fibre of our being. The truth of this is verified in everyday experience.

I note what you say about your suffering and about Dr. Jacob's treatment. I hope to be able to learn some day that you have shed all your illnesses.

Tell Shummy[29] that he belies the teaching of the Bible which among our company he seems to know best. Sardar[30] must not have any swelling whatsoever. But his obstinacy is very great.

I have asked you to pay me a brief visit. You might be of some use in the work that is being done here. That means your sparing a fortnight at the most. But I do not want you to neglect the duty you have undertaken, of course with my full consent.

Who told you that I had consented to take some rest ? That rest must certainly come some day. Meantime I am learning day by day, though little by little, that all work, without any the slightest trace of anxiety, is true and living rest.

Jajuji[31] has sent me a copy of your letter about the Secretaryship. I want you to give me a full and accurate account of the big tragedy that is going on in the Punjab.

Surely you cannot be called "Her Highness" as Catlin calls you.

Lastly about myself. I had an affectionate but mournful visit from Nathji and Swami Anand. I gave them as much time as I was capable of giving. Our discussions were full, frank and cordial. You will have no difficulty in accepting at its face value my statement that not one of our company knows the full value and implications of *brahmacharya*, and that among these ignoramuses I am the least ignorant and the most experienced. With one solitary exception I have never looked upon a woman with a lustful eye. I have touched perhaps thousands upon thousands. But my touch has never carried the meaning of lustfulness. I have lain with some naked, never with the intention of having any lustful satisfaction. My touch has been for our mutual uplift. I would like those who have felt otherwise, if there are any, truly to testify against me. Even the one solitary instance referred to by me was never with the intention of despoiling her. Nevertheless my confession stands that in that case my touch had lustfulness about it. I was carried away in spite of myself and but for God's intervention I might have become a wreck.

My meaning of *brahmacharya* is this:

> One who never has any lustful intention, who by constant attendance upon God has become proof against conscious or unconscious emissions, who is capable of lying naked with naked women, however beautiful they may be, without being in any manner whatsoever sexually excited. Such a person should be incapable of lying, incapable of intending or doing harm to a single man or woman in the whole world, is free from anger and malice and detached in the sense of the *Bhagavadgita*. Such a person is a full *brahmachari*. *Brahmachari* literally means a person who is making daily and steady progress towards God and whose every act is done in pursuance of that end and no other.

You say K.[32] and N.[33] had agreed to withdraw their boycott. From the letters I have, such is not my impression. Nor did I gather that impression from N(athji) and S(wami).

Love,
Bapu

NOTES

1. J.C. Kumarappa, Secretary of the All-India Village Industries' Association founded in October 1934.
2. *Vide* "Discussion on Minimum Living Wage-I", 22/23-8-1935.
3. The addressee had interpreted A.I.V.I.A. as 'All-India Village Idiots' Association'.
4. *Vide* "Letter to Amrit Kaur", 9-5-1936.
5. Tukdoji Maharaj: *vide* the following item.
6. Agatha Harrison.
7. Civil Surgeon.

8. To village women.
9. *Vide* "Obscene Advertisements", 14-11-1936.
10. The letter is not traceable.
11. *Vide* "Letter to Viyogi Hari", *infra.*
12. Balkrishna Bhave, Vinoba Bhave's younger brother.
13. Since 1915 Gandhiji had been observing a vow of restricting his meals to five substances of food; *vide* "An Autobiography", sub-title "Lakshman Jhula".
14. The addressee's brother, Kunwar Shamshere Singh, a retired surgeon.
15. C.F. Andrews was convalescing in Simla after a serious illness.
16. Daughter of Chimanlal N. Shah.
17. She had written to Gandhiji regarding his decision to give up touching women.
18. There is a reference in the text to the article not having gone to the press. There is a similar reference in the "Letter to Jamnalal Bajaj",11-6-1938, where Gandhiji says: "I won't publish the statement in a hurry." This letter therefore could have been written about June 11.
19. Dr. Sushila Nayyar.
20. Bangalore.
21. Jinnah's.
22. Subhas Chandra Bose.
23. According to the addressee the postmark on the envelope bears the date 16-7-1938.
24. Involving physical contact with women.
25. *Vide* "A note", 19-9-1938.
26. *Vide* "Woman's Special Mission", 5-11-1938.
27. *Vide* "Kathiawar Notes", 4-11-1938.
28. Vide "Letter to Amrit Kaur", 26-5-1939, 28-5-1939 and 10-6-1939.
29. Shumshere Singh, addressee's brother.
30. Vallabhbhai Patel.
31. Shrikrishnadas Jaju, Secretary, A.I.S.A.
32. Kishorelal Mashruwala and Narahari Parikh; *vide* "Telegram to Kishorelal G. Mashruwala", 9-2-1947.
33. *Ibid.*

Chapter 12
Kanchan M. Shah

Kanchan Shah married to Munnalal G. Shah. Kanchan's husband was a lawyer by profession. Her husband was manager of the ashram which was the hub of the political activities of the country. Kanchan was staying in the ashram with her husband. Kanchan Shah taken married *brahmacharya* vow. Kanchan and her husband was the role model couple for practicing married *brahmacharya*. Kanchan used to accompany Gandhi during tours.

Kanchan broke the vow and blessed with daughter. She also sacrificed her life for the cause of Gandhi. She was part of inner circle of Gandhi. She played an important part in the Gandhi's experiment on *brahmacharya*.

1. Letter to Kanchan M. Shah

September 7, 1941[1]

Chi. Kanchan,

I do not know what truth there is in the accompanying. Mu(nnalal) claims that it is the plain unvarnished truth. Even if it is not so, there is an agreement between us that you should take no offence.

Blessings from
Bapu

(PS.)
Will you let yourself be medically examined by Manjulabehn ?

2. Letter to Kanchan M. Shah

June 25, 1942

Chi. Kanchan,

I got your letter. It is good that you wrote. I am pleased that you saw your error. Improve now.

I believe that your good lies in living with Munnalal, but only after Munnalal is more properly settled. Then also you must watch what happens to me. You should, therefore, work with Manjubehn for the present, and become proficient in work. If you engross yourself in work, no matter what it is, it will do you good. It will be desirable for you to spend at least a year there. Keep writing to me from time to time.

Blessings from
Bapu

3. Letter to Kanchan M. Shah

Poona,
June 22, 1944

Chi. Kanchan,

I waited for you in Bombay. If you had met me there, you could have travelled with me up to Poona. Now I cannot send for you here. If I send for you, why not Amtul Salaam ? Why not the other women also who wish to come ? Vasumati is pining to come. Even the present number in Panchagani is too large. When I go there you all can have the pleasure of my company to your hearts' content. I am impatient to go there just for that reason. I hope that you will understand my position and have patience. There are lots of people here to attend on me.

Blessings from
Bapu

4. Letter to Kanchan M. Shah

Bombay,
April 3, 1945

Chi. Kanchan,

What a woman you are ! If I write something for you in a letter to Amtul Salaam, is it not as good as a letter to you ? Now have this and write to your heart's content. Hope you are keeping good health. I do not think we can pay A.S.'s doctor's bill. Was the doctor sent for ? I hope A.S. is in fine condition. Live there in peace and help A.S. For the present I am here.

Blessings from
Bapu

Shri Kanchanbehn
C/o Amutussalaambehn
Kasturba Seva Mandir
Burkamata, District Tripura
Bengal

5. Letter to Kanchan M. Shah

May 20, 1945

Chi. Kanchan,

I do not like it at all that you have really fallen ill. You have become restless too. So run away from there without delay. I have written to Munnalal. He should go there and fetch you or send somebody. Or ask somebody there to accompany you. Write to me after you reach the Ashram. It will be better still if you write before leaving.

Blessings from
Bapu

6. Letter to Amutussalaam and Kanchan M. Shah

Mahabaleshwar,
May 24, 1945

Daughter,

I have your letter. How wonderful Kanchan was so ill all of a sudden, and is now recovered and does not want to leave the place. I am happy that she is well and wants to stay there. You want to know when I shall be going there. Your wish and mine are the same in this matter. But I cannot go over on my own. If God wills it, I shall certainly do so.[2]

Chi. Kanchan,

Amutussalaam's second letter is very good. Be firm. I wish that both of you sisters should return only after finishing your work. How nice it would be if you were fully restored to health.

Blessings to both of you from
Bapu

Bibi Amutussalaam
Kasturba Seva Mandir
Borkamata, Bengal

7. Letter to Kanchan M. Shah

June 13, 1945

Kanchan,

It is good that you have come. Now get well completely.

Blessings from
Bapu

June 14, 1945

Chi. Amrit,

Your letter. You must not write when you have run down to the extent you have. I can never misunderstand absence of letters from you.

The restrictions are bad. But nothing to be done till you are with me.

Hope all things will go well regarding family affairs. I hope to go to Sevagram in the beginning of July. The weather there may be too trying for you then.

I am well.

Love,
Bapu

(PS.)
You must not allow Gope or his wife to be a load on you.

8. Letter to Kanchan M. Shah

August 29, 1945

Chi. Kanchan,

How are you getting along ? Do not lose heart. Make your body strong.

Your work is different from that of the other women and, therefore, requires a different approach.

Do you give any time to study ?

Blessings from
Bapu

9. Letter to Kanchan M. Shah

Poona
October 31, 1945

Chi. Kanchan,

I do not like your recent letters. Ask me about Madras when I arrive there. I hope to reach there on November 21. I have written a short letter to Munnalal and am daily awaiting his reply. Ask him why he has not sent it till now.

When will you improve your health ?

Blessings from
Bapu

10. Letter to Kanchan M. Shah

November 3, 1945

Chi. Kanchan,

I have your letter. I feel sorry for you, and equally sorry for Munnalal. I have written to him and told him in so many words that he should set up house with you and that, if the two of you cannot voluntarily observe self-control, you may have children. However, if he cannot bring himself to agree to this I cannot force him against his will. You should, therefore, remain calm. Show this to Munnalal. If he refuses to change his mind you should leave the matter to God and engross yourself in work. For the present I should like you, if your health permits, to look after Gomatibehn, as also the others who are ill. We shall discuss the question of your accompanying me when I come. You had wanted to accompany me to Madras. Now you suggest both Madras and Bengal. That will have to be thought over. We shall do so when I arrive there. Meanwhile you should remain calm, get well and serve as much as you can. You are a fine worker. Let service be your husband, your hobby, your all. But if that cannot be, it does not matter. In any case do not think one thing and speak another.

Blessings from
Bapu

11. Letter to Kanchan M. Shah

Poona,
November 11, 1945

Chi. Kanchan,

I got your letter. I wrote to you on the basis of what you had told me. Nobody has been able to achieve what you aspire for. If you can, I would consider that you have made great progress. My blessings to Raihana and Sarojbehn. More when we meet.

Blessings from
Bapu

Chi. Kanchanbehn
C/o Raihanabehn
Rastrabhasha Prachar Samiti
Wardha

12. Letter to Kanchan M. Shah

Simla,
May 6, 1946

Chi. Kanchan[3],

You are now left alone. I do not worry about that. You are brave. But I do worry about your health. If you can become mistress of your health in the atmosphere there, I would consider it a great achievement.

I have deliberately isolated myself. The others understood my need and have returned to Delhi. I need to be left alone at the present moment. Rajkumari, however, is here and so is Dr. Mehta[4]. Hence I am not having as much solitude as I should have. But is it not true that we can do only what God permits us to do ? Munnalal also will remain in Delhi. I think I shall meet them within a fortnight. It is not possible to say anything about the position here. Please convey the contents of this letter to all.

Write to me a detailed letter. I left Amutussalaam and Sohra at Delhi but they were to go to Sevagram with Sushilabehn.

Blessings from
Bapu

13. Letter to Kanchan M. Shah

New Delhi,
May 23, 1946

Chi. Kanchan,

Munnalal is now prepared to have a separate establishment and live with you. What is your wish now ? Would you like to start as soon as possible or are you content that you have the promise ? If you keep good health there and the work is going on well you should not mind waiting a little longer. Don't think of what I would like but state your own independent view.

I am not writing separately to Zohra. I hope she is all right. Look after the women there carefully.

Blessings from
Bapu

14. Letter to Kanchan M. Shah

Delhi,
June 9, 1946

Chi. Kanchan,

I have your two letters. The first frightened me. The second is good. I presume that the latter is final. We are sweating in the heat here. You are breathing cool air there. We shall now shortly reach Poona. So be patient and go on doing your work. I shall be happy only when you start living with Munnalal. I shall go there first if Manibhai so desires; otherwise I shall arrive *via* Panchgani. If this is not possible, you may come to Poona where we can talk. Others do not give the news which you have conveyed in your letter.

Blessings from
Bapu

15. Letter to Kanchan M. Shah

N[ew] D[elhi],
Silence Day, October 7, 1946

Chi. Kanchan,

I got both your letters. I do not at all like your having fallen ill. Now that your yearning has been satisfied, you should get well soon at least for the sake of the baby that will be born. You will do so not by overeating but by eating moderately, taking sunbaths, living in the open air, drinking clean water, taking fruit juice, eating steamed or boiled vegetables and avoiding sweets and spicy foods. If you take friction-baths and hip-baths, you will get well soon.

Why need you feel ashamed of being pregnant ? That is what you were yearning for. Why need one feel ashamed of what one yearns for and of what happens to everybody ? You must now overcome your sexual urge for three years at least. And that for the sake of the child.

Yes, Munnalal has reason to be ashamed of himself, for it was his ambition to observe *brahmacharya* though he had no capacity for it at all. I had cautioned him sufficiently. But what could even he do ?

Could he have helped following whither nature led him ? If he humbly admits his weaknesses, they will disappear.

I advise you to have the confinement in Vyara itself. If you wish, you may go to Sevagram for it. But there are difficulties in that. To ensure easy delivery, Munnalal should be told to stay away from you. Moreover, he should now earn enough for a living. Nobody need hesitate to ask for his market-price.

I told Munnalal that, even if you two satisfied your passion, you could continue to do my work. If, therefore, he is ready to take up a regular job, I am prepared to give him one and pay him for it. Whatever may have happened from my point of view, Munnalal has committed on sin. He should, therefore, humbly admit what has happened without feeling guilty about it and take up whatever work is available. He should earn a modest living and do whatever other service is possible in the time he can spare from his duties as a householder. He should do nothing that will heighten sexual craving; he should try to control it. The birth of a baby is a reminder. You may show this letter to everybody without feeling the least embarrassment. Neither of you has committed a sin. If any party is guilty, generally it is the man. For the present I am here.

Blessings from
Bapu

16. Letter to Kanchan M. Shah

New Delhi,
4.30 a.m., June 19, 1947

Chi. Kanchan,

I have your letter. I hope you are now content. Munnalal is in your hands, and so certainly are you in his. If you understand this, it will be more than enough. If the Ashram does not improve, how can Sevagram improve ? If Sevagram does not, how can India ? May all of you keep well.

Blessings from
Bapu

17. Letter to Kanchan M. Shah

New Delhi,
November 19, 1947

Chi. Kanchan,

I have your letter. I see that you have still not learnt to write letters. My cart is jogging along, but it seems to have got stuck here just now. I don't see any chance of my going over to that side in the immediate future.

Blessings from
Bapu

NOTES

1. From the postmark.
2. What follows is in Gujarati.
3. Wife of Munnalal G. Shah.
4. Dr. Dinshaw Mehta.

Chapter 13
Prabhavati Devi (1906-1973)

Prabhavati was born in June 1906 in Shrinagar, Saran (now in Siwan district) in Bihar in a reputed and well to do Kayastha family. She was the eldest among the four children of Brajkishore Prasad and Phool Devi. Her father was a top most lawyer, an ardent Gandhian and a renowned Congress leader of Bihar who had given up a lucrative legal practice for the sake of the country. He was the President of the Bihar Provincial Congress Committee for several years. He also managed Champaran Campaign of Gandhi very effectively with devotion and dedication. Prabhavati inherited the legacy from father. Prabhavati was a social worker par excellence. She dedicated her life for the cause of poor women and children. She was a courageous and self-determined woman who lived her entire life for the upliftment of poor and downtrodden people.

Prabhavati received her primary education at home. But she often went to public meetings and listened to the speeches of prominent Indian leaders attentavely. These speeches made impact on Prabhavati and she developed great respect for her ancient heritage.But at the same time she discarded old customs and accepted modern ideas.

She married with Jayaprakash Narayan at the age of fourteen and J.P. was eighteen, without any dowry or ostentations.The marriage was solemnised in October1920. As per tradition, the newly-wed bride slept in the bedroom of her mother-in-law. Soon she return to her parents to stay with them. Her *gauna* (second marriage) ceremony took place in 1921. After the marriage, breaking the tradition, she entered her husband's village home at Sitabdira unvelled on foot without the '*doli*'. She was a teenage so after a few days of stay with her in-laws, she went back to her parents and her husband left to pursue his second year science course at the Patna College. One can see the determination of Prabhvati and her husband that the marrige was not to be comsummated in the beginning and it was not consummated until her death. Inspired by the spirit of the non-cooperation movement. young Jayaprakash left college with a vow never to return to it until India attained freedom.

On 16 May, 1922 her husband left Patna for U.S. to pursue higher studies.Gandhi had stayed at the residence of her father during his Champaran Satyagraha. Gandhi requested her father to send Prabhavati to stay at Sabarmati Ashram as his adopted daughter.

As JP's stay in the United States got prolonged, Prabhavati's father sent her to the Gandhi Ashram where she devoted herself completely to Mahatma Gandhi and Kasturba Gandhi. Both Gandhi and Kasturba treated her like their own daughter. Gandhi became her father, teacher, guide and guru. She, on her part, took keen interest in the ashram life. Bapu gave her regular lessions in Sanskrit, Gujarati, English, Mathematics, Health and Food Sciences. She studied the *Ramayan* and the *Gita* and tried to acquire knowledge of English.

After studying seven year in USA her husband Jayaprakash returned to India towards the end of 1929 and went straight to Gandhi's Ashram at Sabarmati where her wife was staying. Gandhi discussed with Jayaprakash about the Prabhavati's vow of *Brahmacharya*. Gandhi presented to Jayaprakash the option of marrying again. He was very annoyed to hear this from Gandhi. But Jayaprakash respected Prabhavati's vow.

At ashram Japrakash met Jawaharlal Nehru and travelled together to Lahore, where Nehru presided over the historic Congress Session.

Jayaprakash helped Nehru with party work at Allahabad and was given the charge of the Labour Research Department.

Prabhavati accompanied her husband to Allahabad. As a result of shared political commitments a deep friendship developed between Prabhavati and Nehru's wife, Kamala and became her confidante. When Prabhavati moved to Patna with her husband, she was always in touch with Kamala through correspondence. Kamala Nehru wrote several letters to her when she was having problems with the Nehru family.

Prabhavati intered actively in freedom Movement in 1932. At the annual Congress session at Ramgarh in Bihar, she was made the leader of women volunteers. She was appreciated for the role she played in 1942. She was imprisoned and spent time in gaol on several occasions.

When her husband returned, he was regarded a revolutionary and this led to several differences with her because of her Gandhian orientation. Nevertheless they respected each other and jointly decided not to have any children until the country was free from foreign yoke.

It was under her influence that her husband by now a cult figure in India joined the Sarvodaya movement and actively participated in peace overtures in the North East India and the Middle East.

After independence she established two institutions, Mahila Charkha Samiti and 'Kamala Nehru Shishu Vihar'. She established Mahila Charkha Samiti in Patna to involve deserted and abandoned women in the charkha or the spinning wheel movement on the Gandhian model.

J.P started Sampoorna Kranti to save Indian democracy was arrested and sent to prison. After J.P. was released from prison, Prabhavati, paid attention in looking after him. She moved with him wherever he went like a shadow. J.P. too was deeply attached to her. J.P. found in her a good cook, a nurse, a secretary and indeed a true friend.

Towards the end of his life J.P. publicly approved that it was Prabhavati who had transformed him from Marxism to Gandhism. She died of cancer of the uterus on 15 April, 1973.

1. Letter to Prabhavati

Friday, November 23, 1928

Chi. Prabhavati,

I can understand your misery. Physical separation will however always be there. Shake off anxiety and be firm and devoted to your duty.

Keep writing to me. Go to Dwarka only if you want to, otherwise don't.

Blessings from
Bapu

2. Letter to Prabhavati

November 27, 1928

Chi. Prabhavati,

I have both your letters. Do go to Dwarka if you wish to. Do not at all take to heart my absence. Some day this body is bound to leave for ever. Why be distressed over separation from it ? We should find happiness in devotion to a cause for which our passing away would have a meaning.

Blessings from
Bapu

3. Letter to Prabhavati

Not Revised
December 12, 1928

Chi. Prabhavati,

I have your letter. There is no reason for panic. Write thus to your father-in-law:

"Your wish ought to be a command for me. My father wants me to act in accordance with your command. I am faced with a conflict of loyalties since your son keeps writing from America telling me to live in the Ashram and study. He also wants me to study English too very well. I am quite comfortable in the Ashram. Bapuji treats me like a daughter. Ba too is good to me. Arrangements have been made for my stay in the women's section after Rajbanshi Deviji[1] leaves this place. I am quite safe in the women's section. I therefore wish to stay in the Ashram as your son bids. But then I shall do as you say. And I may assure you that you need not worry on my account. While I live here I am quite alert, there are many women in the Ashram and I am on good terms with them all."

You may, if necessary, improve upon the language. Inform your father also regarding the developments. Give all details to Mrityunjaya and send him a copy of your husband's letter.

Whatever happens you should be unperturbed. Remember the *shloka:* "Hold alike pleasure and pain"[2] etc. Be courageous and recite Ramanama.

Blessings from
Bapu

4. Letter to Prabhavati

July 20, 1929

Chi. Prabhavati,

Herewith find the letter from Rajendrababu. Under these circumstances you should, for the present, remain at the Sadaqat Ashram and learn what you can, and in the month of August go to your in-laws' with courage. Having reached there you should serve your elders but observe your own discipline steadfastly. After all you have but to go there. Having pleased your parents-in-law with your humanity, you may come back. If you do not hear from Jayaprakash in the meanwhile, I think it would be a mistake not to go to them when they are insistent. You should go there but should not observe *purdah*. You should speak to your father-in-law with courage. If he is cross you should patiently bear with it. His anger will subside when he sees your purity. Even after going there you should insist on continuing your studies. You should speak about Jayaprakash's insistence on English. You should explain that the *Gita* is essential for inner satisfaction. You may, if you want to, visit me at Allahabad.

Ask me if you fail to understand anything. I shall reach Allahabad on the 25th morning.

Blessings from
Bapu

5. Letter to Prabhavati

Etawah,
November 24, 1929

Chi. Prabhavati,

Though I did feel sorry when you left, I immediately controlled the feeling as your real duty required that you should go. I got your letter. God will certainly give you the strength to follow the path you have chosen for yourself. I have faith in Jayaprakash too. Tell him that he should write to me, that he should accompany you to Wardha and that even if he is unable to come for some reason, he should make it easy for you to go.

Take care of your health. Recite the *Gita* verses regularly with attention to their meaning. In reciting the chapter for the day . . .

6. Letter to Prabhavati

September 1, 1930[3]

Chi. Prabhavati,

You are too greedy. However long my letter, you will think it too short. I send between 50 and 60 letters to the Ashram every week, and I must write them during whatever time I can spare from spinning. Hence, and also because I don't have much to write about from here every time, I write short letters in which, however, I say all that I wish to say. If I had to write only one or two letters, I could fill them with long description of conditions here. The letter meant for the whole Ashram is always long. Since Mirabehn cannot read Gujarati, I write a long letter to her. All other letters are short and to the point. Look; I have filled half this letter explaining why I write short letters. Kakasaheb and I were weighed on Friday; my weight came to 104 and Kakasaheb's to 114. This is a fairly good increase. We pray regularly everyday. The *Gita* is also read daily. Recently I have given up raisins and dates and, instead, eat boiled vegetables. Generally I eat sweet potatoes and uncooked tomatoes everyday or some other vegetables like cabbage. This diet has done me no harm. The weight has increased and constipation has been relieved. You must have read the reports about the negotiations with the Government. There was no truth in them at all. Let me know your future programme, and also Jayaprakash's. Has your mother-in-law recovered now ? I am sure you will nurse her with the utmost love.

Blessings from
Bapu

7. Letter to Prabhavati

October 27, 1930

Chi. Prabhavati,

You have become very nervous. But you have no reason for it. If now the burden of running the home has fallen on you, you are strong enough for that. If the responsibility is yours, you ought to have the corresponding rights too. You can manage your home as it seems best to you. Jayaprakash will certainly help you in that. You may talk about everything with your father-in-law with the freedom of a daughter. At first he will feel embarrassed but by and by you will see that he, too, will talk freely with you and remove the difficulties from your path. Moreover, you have servants to help you. You should take due care of your health while looking after the affairs of the home. Do not work beyond your strength. Save some time for reading, for going out for a walk and resting, and make yours a model home. It will be a problem for you only if you do not have full authority to do what you wish to do. But I simply cannot believe at the moment that you will not get such authority. Have confidence in yourself. Learn to be firm. God will save you and lead you. In any case, do not be cast down by grief. You may write to me more often if you wish to. You can write to me even directly, without thinking whether or not I shall get your letters. May God protect you.

Blessings from
Bapu

8. Letter to Prabhavati

Borsad,
Friday, May 8, 1931

Chi. Prabhavati,

I got your letter. I feel like writing to Jayaprakash about you. It will be good if you have a frank talk with him once. As long as you have not completely recovered, you ought to stay with me. The state of your health from time to time is closely connected with that of your mind. If you stay with me, probably both your body and mind will grow strong and then you may be fit enough to live with self-confidence anywhere. Do what seems best to you.

I will leave this place on Monday and proceed to Simla. You don't require my address while I am there. If you write only my name on the letter, it will reach me the soonest. If you address it C/o the Congress Committee, the letter may be delayed a little. I am likely to stay in Simla for five days.

Blessings from
Bapu

9. Letter to Prabhavati

May 28, 1931

Chi. Prabha,

I got your letter. If the marriage cannot be celebrated before the end of June, you should come away just now and return afterwards for a week for the marriage. According to me, everyday should be treated as an auspicious day on which a marriage can be celebrated. If, however, the marriage cannot be celebrated soon and if Father and Mother willingly permit you to come away, you should do so immediately. But you may stay on for the whole of June if they are likely to feel hurt. You may go to Sitabadiyara, too, and stay there for some time and do your duty to the family. If you have to stay on, you should write to uncle[4], Babaji and Vinoba about it and get their permission. I, on my part, will also speak to them. You alone know all the relevant circumstances for deciding whether you should stay on there; you should, therefore, do what seems best to you in the light of the circumstances there.

Write a strong letter to Jayaprakash in regard to the pain from which he suffers. If you stay on there, take an opportunity to meet him.

Keep up some study.

Gangabehn gave birth to a daughter. The child lived for a day and died. Amutussalaam feels rather unhappy. I cannot say whether she will continue to stay here till you return. Why have you asked for slivers to be sent to you from here ? Of course I will send them, but you yourself ought to card cotton. If the effort gives you pain in your hand, you should teach some others to card. Is there no one even in Chhapra who spins ? And if a person spins, cannot he card ? Wherever we stay, we should do our best to obtain slivers locally.

What is your weight ?

Blessings from
Bapu

(PS.)
I will leave on the 29th and return on June 3.

10. Letter to Prabhavati

Delhi,
December 12, 1933

Chi. Prabhavati,

I got your letter, as also Jayaprakash's. If both of you come to a firm decision that you would dedicate yourselves to service, I shall have nothing to say. I only explained to you both that it was not morally wrong to do one's duty towards one's own family, but that, if one wished to follow the path of service, one must renounce such private duties.[5]

If you try to do both, you will probably fail in both. There will be no difficulty in sending Rs. 50 every month for Rajeshwar.[6] But that does not satisfy me. What arrangement have you made for your own expenses ? What have you decided regarding the debt ? By solving these problems anyhow, you will not have solved the basic problem. But I will not dwell further on this matter. I don't wish to discourage Jayaprakash. We should hope that, since his motive is pure, everything will be all right.

You have not yet gone and seen Mother. You should do so now. Since your visit to me has been delayed so long, I shall now be far away. If you do not wish to get arrested there, you may come and see me during my Andhra tour, and then from Wardha you may go wherever you like. I think it would be best to go to Bihar. If you decide to go to Bihar, it is not very necessary for you to come and see me. If, however, you are very keen to come, by all means do come. I leave it entirely to your own wish. I shall be in Madras on 20, 21 and 22. I will start from here on the 14th. From the 16th to the 19th, I shall be around Bezwada. I shall be back in Andhra from 23rd to 31st, and the headquarters will be at Bezwada. You may now decide as you like.

Vidya felt bored and has come here. She has brought Kanta with her. I have not decided yet whether to let Vidya go to Multan or ask her to return to Wardha.

Om has been with me. I continue the same diet. The quantity of milk varies from three pounds to one pound. The cold which I had has gone. The weight was 108 pounds when I was weighed in Jabalpur. I have not been weighed after that. You need not worry about me at all. God will keep me in whatever condition. He wishes and get work done through me as He wills.

Could you see Rajendrababu ? Did you see Father ? How is he ? I hear from Ba from time to time. Mani is still with her. Sushila, Pyarelal's sister, is here. Her mother also is here. I have not met her yet.

Blessings from
Bapu

11. Letter to Prabhavati

June 5, 1935

Chi. Prabhavati,

I got your letter. I am writing to Jayaprakash. Send on the letter to him. You have done your best. You should still go on writing to him. If he doesn't take care of his health, what can you do ? When your one year is over, we shall certainly have to think about your future. It will probably be desirable then that you should stay with Jayaprakash. Cook for him and take care of his health. But it is too early to think about that just now. My weight has remained steady. It is extremely hot here.

See that your health is not affected there. It will indeed be good if you can go to Sitabadiyara for three or four days. It was indeed good that you went and stayed with Jayaprakash for a few days. Your leave has been sanctioned. Return on the next day after the wedding. Make the wedding as simple as possible.

The only newcomer here is Chitre. Amutussalaam will remain here for the present. She is working very hard. Devraj[7] has arrived.

Blessings from
Bapu

12. Letter to Prabhavati

Savli,
March 3, 1936

Chi. Prabha,

I got your letter this morning. I read it immediately after having my meal, had a few rounds and am now writing this reply at 8.30. I tore up your letter soon after reading it. What was so confidential in it that you had to doubly reassure yourself ? Indeed, there was nothing private at all. And how could you have so private a thing as that ? I shall, however, carry out your wish so long as you mark your letter confidential and ask me to tear it up. Your going has of course lessened my anxiety because the going meant following the law of truth, and not to go would have been, I feared, its violation. But that had no relation to the blood Pressure, which had already been going down and so went down by itself. I was not so much worried about your staying on, as I knew all the time that you would at last do the right thing only, and you did so quite promptly. As for the bloodpressure, however, things will go on as they have been going. It had reached 188/110 at Wardha and once it went up to as high as 212/120, but the same day again it fell to 188/108. I don't know what it now is. It cannot, therefore, be said at all that the blood-pressure went down because of your going. You may come when you can, after staying there as long as you have the duty to stay on. Happiness ever goes with dharma. And there alone lies peace of mind. Never have any doubt that there can be no happiness in the violation of dharma. Why do you want to be exempted from taking milk ? Your good lies only in taking it. Of course, you have freedom to reduce its quantity when you cannot digest four lb. of it.

There will be no difficulty in digesting four lb. of milk as long as you have regular exercise and sleep. As for fruit, take what is easily to be had. It will be good if Jayaprakash follows the same diet as yours. Keep your diary day after day. I follow your point about studies. You may do what you can. Study Hindi grammar. Send for anything you need from here. I shall leave here on the 6th, hoping to reach Delhi on the 8th. I shall be spending at least a fortnight there. You must have written, I think, to Swaruprani and others about Kamala. Ba is in Bombay, Rajaji, who has gone to Bombay, may perhaps come here.

We have a fairly good gathering here. The weather is fair and they see that I get good peace and rest.

It seems one of your letters has been lost in transit. I have noted that. I know it is unlikely that you would avoid writing out of laziness. The fear is you might grow melancholy, but you ought not to under any circumstances. Doesn't Mother *Gita* teach us to endure cheerfully the situation that we happen to be in ?

Blessings from
Bapu

13. Letter to Prabhavati

Savli,
March 5, 1936

Chi. Prabha,

I got your letter, read it and tore it up. I see that you have been going through mental strain. You should, however, remember that happiness and unhappiness are passing fancies of the mind, and know that pain is no pain, the only real pain being unmindful of God. Yes, you may stay or move about with Jayaprakash as long as he wishes and you can serve him in some useful way. Giving him medicine regularly, cooking for him, looking after his personal belongings—all this is service, of course, and so doing you should gain whatever experience you can. You should certainly keep seeming relatives and acquaintances if you go to a place like Patna. Do all such acts with interest and yet without attachment. I shall of course be pained if you spoil your health. Be careful of your diet. Write to me the experiences you gather.

We shall leave Savli tomorrow. The marriage of Krishnadas was celebrated here today. Both being in every way plain and simple, they had put on nothing more than their usual dress, and there were no presents etc. I have never seen so simple a wedding as this.

Blessings from
Bapu

(PS.)
We shall reach Delhi on the 8th.

14. Letter to Prabhavati

March 8, 1936

I see something troubles your mind, though you may try to conceal it. You may certainly come according to your wish, provided you get the permission. It will be the greatest service you render to Jayaprakash if you lay before him your correct position with the utmost firmness and calm of mind. I am afraid you have not fully stated your case to Jayaprakash and if you have, it did not make any impression on him, that is, he does not take the statement to be correct. He will calm down without doubt, if he is convinced that you have in you no such thing as sexual desire. Your freedom from desire should put out the fire of his, just as water puts out any fire. Why should you be afraid and lose peace of mind, when you do have faith in God ? At the time of going you made me a promise not to get disturbed, and you ought to keep it. Keep writing to me . . . . Take care to be true to the promise, remain calm and undisturbed, preserve your health, come if and when you can. We shall be here for about fifteen days.

(From Gujarati)

15. Letter to Prabhavati

May 13, 1936

Chi. Prabha,

I got your telegram last night. How am I to prevent your unhappiness ? I have of course written to you in the matter of Jayaprakash's visit to me and the proposal to send you to Banaras. Do not be impatient. It is not likely that I won't write to you at all. It is another matter that you may get the letters at irregular intervals. As I understand from your telegram that you will reach Srinagar on the 15th, I am sending this to that place. I expect you are in good health now and are taking milk regularly. What about the Banaras proposal ? Write to me frankly whatever you have to say without any reserve. I shall deal with your letter according as you wish. We reached here on Sunday. It is an excellent place. We have here peace and solitude. There are very few residents as the hill is a small one. I would have been happy to have you here with us. Ba, too, remembers you. Our party comprises Sardar, Mani, Kusum Gandhi, Tara Mashruwala, Navin, Kanti, Kanu, Ba and me. Kumarappa and Shanta are arriving today and Kakasaheb in about four days. Sardar is keeping well. As for Tara one doesn't know when she will get well, though she is sure to. Even Kusum who has been weak is expected to recover here. Our stay here will, it seems, last till the 15th June, part of the time having to be spent at Bangalore.

Blessings from
Bapu

16. Letter to Prabhavati

October 3, 1936

Chi. Prabha,

Your letter brings tears to my eyes. On the one hand, I think that what you say about milk and fruit is true, while on the other hand, we cannot afford your falling ill for want of that kind of food. What is more, any saving thus effected would be spent in paying the expenses of the doctor and the medicines in case you fell ill. So difficult is dharma. It is not proper for me to send you the extra money nor proper for you thus to take more milk and fruit. I must keep my peace having said that you should, if somehow it is possible, take more milk and fruit. God will protect you. Who am I to worry on your account ?

You are quite right in saying that you do everything after consulting me. You are also right in saying that you do it in obedience to my command. If your dharma to do what you have been doing is clear to me, how can I give you an order to the contrary ? And, how can I arrange to pay you Rs. 25 as long as you remain occupied with your own family ? Hence, I have decided to obtain another Rs. 25 also for Jayaprakash and have even given instructions to send it. You should of course take full rest, and also do a little walking. I expect you are not taking oils and spices, and that you take whole-wheat flour. What leafy vegetable can you get ? Is the jaggery that you get good ?

I have written to you about myself earlier. I am on milk, fruit and vegetables. I have not started taking *chapatis* for fear of fever. I have not been weighed recently, as the necessary arrangements do not yet exist. Ba is still with Devdas, and Manu too. What else would I tell Father about you ? He praised your nature and was pleased with you. Yes, I shall reach Kashi[7] on the 24th and leave it on the 26th for Rajkot. After paying my respects to Narandas's parents, I shall go to Ahmedabad and after staying there for three days, to Segaon. You aren't likely to come to Kashi, are you ?

Blessings from
Bapu

17. Letter to Prabhavati

June 7, 1937

Chi. Prabha,

This time you made me wait long enough, but never mind. Pressure of work may cause such delay occasionally. If you get time, don't forget to put in some reading. And you must not in any case neglect spinning. It is indeed very good that you are able to serve Father. How far is Sitab Diara from Srinagar ? Isn't it right on the banks of the Ganga ? How is it hot even then ? Why don't you grow some greens and other vegetables in the garden ? There must be some open land around the bungalow.

Vasumati is here. She will now go to Rajkot. Ba will stay in Maroli at present. In Segaon, therefore, in addition to those who are already there, there will be Babu (Sharda), Kallenbach, Mehrtaj, Lali, Khan Saheb, Lila, Vijaya, Munnalal, Balvantsinha and Anna. Nanavati of course is already there. We shall start from here at 3 in the morning of the 10th and shall reach Wardha at 7 a.m. on the 11th. Tithal is beautifully cool indeed. A cool and gentle breeze blows all the time. Most of us sleep in the open under the sky. There is no dew. If you could have come here, I would have helped you to increase your weight and the quantity of milk, too.

I hope you are getting *Harijanbandhu* etc.

Blessings from
Bapu

18. Letter to Prabhavati

Segaon, Wardha,
October 1, 1937

Chi. Prabha,

I have your letter. You shouldn't have stopped taking milk. To observe mourning[8] one may give up eating delicacies, but one must eat whatever is essential. If one who has taken the vow of *aswada*[9] is observing it properly, he would be eating nothing to please the palate and, therefore, would have no need to give up anything. Moreover, if birth and death are the same thing, and indeed they are, why mourn the death of the dear ones ? Or why rejoice at their birth ? Please, therefore, start taking milk immediately you get this letter. If you wish, you can make use of this letter. Moreover, our duty to the departed consists in taking up and carrying on their work, and that all of you are doing to the best of your abilities. The burden cannot be borne by you alone, even if you wished. And if you give up milk and become weak, your capacity for work will diminish, and one may say that you will to that extent be less able to carry your share of the burden. Reason with yourself thus and resume taking milk and fruit. Come here when you can stir out. And let it not be so late that I may not be here when you come. Never mind, however, if your coming is delayed by work. We shall meet if and when God wills. I am not as weak as you suppose. I am able, more or less, to attend to all my usual work. I can eat sufficiently well, too. I do less physical work. We are having two fairly serious patients here these days. There are other minor illnesses, too, from time to time.

Parnerkar and Chimanlal are in bed. Parnerkar is better and will leave bed in a few days. But Chimanlal's ship is in mid-sea. He has typhoid. Today is the fourteenth day. The temperature has still not come to normal. That means it will last for 21 days at least. He is being looked after chiefly by Sharda and Bhansalibhai.

One cannot yet say that Ba's leg is completely healed. Lilavati keeps indifferent health. She will most probably be operated upon tomorrow for tonsils.

Amutussalaam is, as you know, a permanent patient.

Blessings from
Bapu

19. Letter to Prabhavati

December 29, 1937

Chi. Prabha,

You seem to be quite a cunning woman. What excuses you offer for not writing ! You are like a thief turning round and accusing the police. You went on your own, and now say that you had to leave and, therefore, feel no inclination to write. You had definitely promised me that you would write. You went alone. And even then no letter saying that you had arrived safe ! And even if you don't care about me, what about poor Amtul Salaam ? She inquires everyday whether there has been a letter from you. She writes to you almost daily and you don't write even a few lines on a slip of paper in reply ! What discourtesy ? And what hard-heartedness ! Tell me now what punishment you deserve, and in what measure. What do you do about milk there ? You did well in going away, of course. About myself Amtul Salaam will write. You are often in the thoughts of us all. Do some reading and writing while you are there and serve Father in every possible way.

Blessings from
Bapu

(PS.)
Don't be remiss now in writing to me.

20. Letter to Prabhavati

Segaon,
April 25, 1938

Chi. Prabha,

You have become lazy in writing letters. Nowadays I eagerly await your letter. I couldn't bear the news that you had a fainting fit. Moreover, is it not my unworthiness that you couldn't remain calm this time although you were with me ? I am not joking. These days I often feel my unworthiness. That hinders my work, too. You have to rely on your own efforts to attain peace of mind. Why do you want me to tear up your letters ? Is there anything confidential in them ? Since you wish, however, I do tear them up. But you should shake off this shyness. Write to me freely and let me know all your thoughts. I hope Father is keeping good health.

Blessings from
Bapu

21. Letter to Prabhavati

Segaon, Wardha,
After June 20, 1938[10]

Chi. Prabha,

What an angry letter ! Your anger is the result of your suffering. That you are not educated means that I didn't educate you. Isn't that so ? I don't repent of that. It is possible that you may not be useful there. I have not trained you for the work there. I have trained you for public service. I have trained you for work with me. There is no work here for which you are not fit. You can live in the midst of all types of people. I wouldn't hesitate to send you anywhere. I have no fear that you might do something wrong. You have got the strength now even to mount the gallows with a smile on your face. What more would you like to be ? If you wish to learn English, you may do that whenever you like. I can certainly teach you. Do come in September if you can. I cannot bear to see you unhappy. You have no cause for unhappiness at all. It is your duty to stay there for the present and serve Jayaprakash in whatever way you can. When you have no work with Father and when Jayaprakash can let you come, you will certainly come away, your place finally is here. Work is waiting for you here. What more do you wish ? Why do you unnecessarily make yourself unhappy ? I am well. The blood-pressure is under control. Just now I am experimenting with a diet of milk, dates and lemons. I take mangoes when available. I seem to feel better with this. It is only the third day today.

Saraswati is here. Kanti is in Bangalore. Sushila and Pyarelal are still here. Kallenbach's sister-in-law has come. The place is crowded. There is hardly room even to stand. A *takli-yajna* is going on daily and I join in it. I feel very happy doing so.

Blessings from
Bapu

22. Letter to Prabhavati

Segaon,
August 30, 1938

Chi. Prabha,

I got your letter. Who can help one who makes herself unhappy without cause ? Joy and sorrow are mental creations. I experience this every moment. If Jayaprakash does not go to Malabar at all, will it mean that you will not be permitted to come ? When he goes to Malabar he may take you from here, or he may go directly there and you may leave this place at the same time and join him there. My visit to the Frontier Province may perhaps start around the 20th September. In that case you will remain here. I shall have to be back from there around October 20.

Pyarelal has no fever now, but feels weak. The danger is over. My silence is for an indefinite period. God alone knows when it will be over. But you are not concerned with that. You will be able to talk to your heart's content, and I will reply to you by writing. But the truth is that you do not need to talk. It is enough for you to stay with me to have peace of mind. I need not worry about you then. Please, therefore, come if you can. I will see about your studying. I am well.

Blessings from
Bapu

23. Letter to Prabhavati

Segaon, Wardha
November 11, 1939

Chi. Prabha,

I got your letter. I have no intention of courting imprisonment. Nor have you. The future lies with God. Jayaprakash wishes that you should stay with me so that the household expenses may be saved and your studies may continue. This can be arranged in Segaon or Wardha. I would be generally staying in Segaon. Occasionally when I go out for three or four days, I will not take you with me. Your study must remain uninterrupted. I, therefore, feel that you are needlessly wasting your time there. Ba asks: "What ! Prabha will not come to stay with me or will she never come for my sake ? What difference would it make whether or not you are here ? Write to her, 'Ba wants you here'." This is her message. She often inquires, "When is Prabha coming ?" I have to reach Allahabad[11] on the 19th instant. Come there if you can, and accompany me from there.

Blessings from
Bapu

NOTES

1. Wife of Rajendra Prasad and mother of Mrityunjaya.
2. *Bhagavad Gita,* II. 38.
3. The source has only September, as the original seems to have been damaged here. However *Bapuna Patro—10: Shri Prabhavatibehnne,* pp. 33-4, gives this date.
4. Jamnalal Bajaj, according to *Bapuna Patro—10: Shri Prabhavatibehnne.*
5. *Vide* "Letter to Prabhavati", 23-11-1933.
6. Younger brother of Jayaprakash Narayan.
7. Gandhiji was to open there a Bharat Mata Mandir at the invitation of Shivprasad Gupta.
8. The addressee's father-in-law Harsu Dayal had died in July 1937.
9. Control of the palate.
10. From the reference to Saraswati's presence in Segaon, this letter seems o have been written about the same time as the preceding one.
11. To attend the Congress Working Committee meeting.

Chapter 14

Manu Gandhi (1928-1969)

Manu, grandniece of Gandhi born in 1928 was the daughter of Jaisukhlal Gandhi and granddaughter of Amritlal Tulsidas Gandhi, Gandhi's uncle. Manu was a lonely child. She was not well educated. She lost her mother when she was only twelve years of age. After two years of death of the mother at the age of fourteen, she came to live with Gandhi. She was very close to Kasturba. Manu actively participated in Quit India Movement of 1942. She was arrested and placed in Nagpur Jail. At that time Gandhi and Kasturba were in detention in Aga Khan Palace. Kasturba was seriously ill. So, Manu was transferred to Aga Khan Place to look after Kasturba. Kasturba called her father and advised him to take Manu to his residence at Karachi for studies.

Manu became Mahatma Gandhi's closest associate during 1946-48. She was with Gandhi in Noakhali, touring bare foot in a riot affected area for establishing communal harmony and peace. When Gandhi returned to Delhi she was with her. Gandhi was her mentor and she was with Gandhi till he was shot dead on 30th January, 1948 at Birla House (presently known as Gandhi Smriti,) New Delhi.

Manu never married and sacrificed her life for the cause of Gandhi. She was a part of Gandhi's experiment of *brahmacharya*. Gandhi's death left deep impact on her life. She had left a graphic account of her days with Gandhi in books and diaries. She wrote two books, 'The Lonely Pilgrim' (1962) and 'Last Glimpses of Gandhi' (1964). She died leaving behind legacy, at the age of forty one, unknown, unwept and unsung in 1969 without honour and recognition.

1. Letter to Manu Gandhi

Lucknow,
February 5, 1931

Chi. Manudi,

I can now send the pictures which I collected for you. Preserve them all carefully and ask someone who can understand their meaning to explain it to you. We shall now meet some time. Write to me. Where is Ramibehn ? Ask Balibehn and Kamubehn to write to me.

Blessings from
Bapu

2. Letter to Manu Gandhi

November 7, 1932

Chi. Manudi,

You seem to be very lazy and forgetful. After a long interval, you write a letter. You promise that you will not be lazy again, and then forget and break your promise. This is bad. One should always keep one's promise, and should never make a promise which one cannot keep. You should write a letter every Sunday and post it to the Ashram. You should give in it a report of the work done by you during the preceding week, what you studied, what other work you did and how much yarn you spun. I hope you know that we should wear *khadi* even at home.

Blessings from
Bapu

3. Letter to Manu Gandhi

December 29, 1933

Chi. Manudi,

I felt happy after reading your long letter. I daily think about you. Tell Kusum that I cannot help her now. What will it avail her to think of me ? Let her go on repeating Ramanama. It will give her peace of mind. You should teach her to do that. Sing the Ramadhun to her. You can sing many *bhajans.* What can I say to comfort aunt Bali ? If I were free from other duties, I would go to her and help her run her home and free her from her worries. But it is impossible during this life that I can even stand in such relation to her. What you write about death is perfectly true. It will come to all of us sooner or later.

Blessings from
Bapu

4. Letter to Manu Gandhi

April 8, 1935

Chi. Manudi,

How can you say that I have stopped writing to you ? Have I failed to reply to any letter of yours ? How can you charge me when you yourself do not write ? I got your letter today and here I am replying to it. I am glad to learn that you have passed. Instead of trying to speed up progress from form to form and save years, it would be better to try to master what you learn in every form. Write to me regularly from now on. About other things Ba or somebody else will write. I hope you yourself do not feel that you are already nineteen. Write to me frankly.

Blessings to aunties.

Blessings from
Bapu

5. Letter to Manu Gandhi

April 22, 1935

Chi. Manudi,

I got your letter in Indore. You need not ask me whether or not you should go to Bombay. Respect the wishes of your aunt. I did read about your having entered the nineteenth year. But what you write were only fancies of your mind. What made you write it ? I haven't thought even once from that point of view. But now perhaps I may think.

Does all that you write mean that you wish to get married now ? If so, you should say so plainly. We don't regard it as anything to be ashamed of. It is a quite natural desire. Yes, to me you seem to be a girl of twelve or so. But it is possible that your body has changed recently. If you feel that you have grown up, there is nothing more to be said about it. Write to me openly what you wish. We shall return to Indore[1] on Wednesday or Thursday.

Blessings from
Bapu

6. Letter to Manu Gandhi

June 6, 1935

Chi. Manu,

I have sent both your letters to Bhai[2]. His postcard to you was bad. I have written to him about it. This chapter is becoming more and more painful. It is good that you have shed your fear of Bhai. You say that you wish to abide by my advice. Is it in all matters ? If that is so, you should give up your idea of marrying in the Modh caste. I would certainly get you married in a good family where you would be completely happy. Your happiness would be the sole consideration in the selection I would make. Harilal has been writing to me frightful things. Personally, I should like you to be with me just now. I am inquiring about what Harilal has writen to me. I need your help in that too. But I would like you to come only if you would like to stay with me. It is quite clear that if you have grown more fond of luxuries, I cannot satisfy your desires. Therefore, do what will please you. Whatever you write to me, do so frankly. You are a free person.

Blessings from
Bapu

7. Letter to Manu Gandhi

Palm Beach, Juhu,
May 27, 1944

If I were keeping good health, I would not have let you go anywhere but would have given you what I myself could. But I am a broken reed now. After I get well, they will certainly not let me remain free. Your good, therefore, lies in going down to Rajkot as early as you can. I will write to Narandas about your education. The things which Yukti has asked for can be sent to her. You may send for them. In all this overcrowding (in trains) I would not like to send you there even in Abha's company. Please guess what I mean from this. God is sure to look after your well-being. Your services can never go unrewarded. Preserve this.

Blessings from
Bapu

8. Letter to Manu Gandhi[3]

Poona,
June 23, 1944

Chi. Manudi,

Your falling ill as soon as you arrived there has shaken me. If you faithfully carry out all that I have told you, you would never fall ill. The decision to study is a good one. But you must not study just to get through the examination. Study whatever you can without straining your eyes. You are impatient as all young people are. But I expect patience from you. The virtues that I have seen in you are not found in all girls. Having regard to them, when I see the smallest drawback in you it seems to me a mountain and something unbearable.

Blessings from
Bapu

9. Letter to Manu Gandhi

Sevagram,
February 5, 1945

Chi. Manu,

I am very much worried about you. You are always crying and seem restless. You do tell me that you regard me both as your mother and father. Will a child be ever afraid of talking to her parents, or feel shy ? You do both. I, therefore, wonder what your real feelings are. Why should you have any secrets ? You should not object to others reading your letters. Therefore, while I have returned them to you, I did not like doing so. You should have the courage to say whatever you wish in front of everybody. One hides one's guilt even when it is small. He who has acted truthfully hides nothing. If there is any suspicion that truth is being kept back, it comes out.

Tell Sushila whatever you wish to say. Why should you be afraid of her ? Tell her boldly whatever it is. She tells me that she has not stopped you from attending the class because you share the bed with me. She told you for your own convenience that you might take leave if you wished and get well. She will help you to make up for what you miss.

You may show this letter to Pyarelal, Sushila or anyone else you wish. Get well.

Blessings from
Bapu

10. Letter to Manu Gandhi

May 14, 1945

Chi. Manudi,

I can see no difference between your handwriting and Yukti's[4]. Instead of myself telling you not to go to Karachi, I told Sushilabehn to tell you lest you think I was ordering you. If you wish to go either to Karachi or to Porbandar, by all means go. What I am concerned with is that you should become strong in body and mind. If you can do it there, I shall be pleased. Because of your negligent habits, I thought that, if you could overcome your fear, you would be able to benefit fully and for long from the mountain-air. However, I am not enamoured of hill-stations either. Wherever you stay with a free mind, you are bound to benefit. You may, therefore, do what your sisters desire. I give my consent for it.[5]

Why should we observe anybody's face ? We may even make a mistake in judging a person from his face. We are not God. We might even do him injustice. And moreover, when one has made up one's mind not to fear anybody, why need one know the other person's mind ? The rest from Pyarelal.

Blessings from
Bapu

11. Letter to Manu Gandhi

May 22, 1945

Chi. Manudi,

I have your letter. I had got your previous one also. I did not get the time to answer it. I am answering this at once. It is all right that you have gone to Karachi. But you must get rid of the amoeba and hookworm. But how can you manage to do so, if you are returning on the 4th ? In any case, do not take that vaid's treatment. If you decide to stay on there, do so with a firm resolution to get rid of your illness. Do not be anxious to appear for the examination. If you can easily manage to read a little, it will be all right.

I can see from your letter that you are consumed by the fear of the surrounding atmosphere. The world will always frighten those who let themselves be frightened. You would, therefore, do well to cast all fear into the sea. The best medicine for that is Ramanama. Why need he who worships Rama, fear anything else ? But this is only a suggestion from me. You did not regain peace of mind even after meeting your sisters. You may come whenever you wish. You need have no fear on that score.

Blessings from
Bapu

12. Letter to Manu Gandhi

Sevagram,
July 21, 1945

Chi. Manudi,

I have torn up your letter. It was silly. If there was any thing private in it, it was your silliness. You had promised to stay there for a year if required. And now you wish to go back on your word ! Who will trust you then ? There is no harm in accepting money from Bhai. He is your father. If you ask me, I would say that you should stop all other thought and get well there. If the doctor is put to any expense, it is for him and me to worry about. You may ask him for whatever money you need. Your whole letter was silly. I was pained to read it. Try and see if you can become firm in your mind. Ultimately you are your own sovereign.

Blessings from
Bapu

13. Letter to Manu Gandhi

July 22, 1945

Chi. Manudi,

Do you believe that Jaisukhlal refused to send you money because he distrusts you ? If you think so, you are doing a great injustice to your father. I have told Jaisukhlal that he should not send money directly to you, and that is why he mentioned my name. If you want money, write to me. But where is the need ? I can write to Dr. Mehta. If you do not stay there in peace and keep on saying that you wish to run away, it will pain me. How do you know that Rs. 10,000 are to be set (apart) for you ?

Blessings from
Bapu

14. Letter to Manu Gandhi

Simla,
May 11, 1946

Chi. Manudi,

I have your letter after many days. Were you busy or just lazy ? You are again blaming me for your own lack of confidence. If you have grown wise and never cry, if you don't care for what others say, who could stop you from coming here alone ? Have you not yourself put the condition, "Who will teach me, and what ?" If you have confidence in yourself, why need you ask that question ? I do wish, of course, that

Jaisukhlal should be with you. I understand your explanation. It is sad that Jaisukhlal should take this view. Why should a person dedicated to public service care for sweet or bitter experiences ? It is enough if one's heart is clean.

You may now do what seems best to you. I got J.'s letter about rationing. I am thinking of forwarding it to Bhavangar. First send your annual report and then talk about a message.

I am glad that both of you keep good health.

Blessings from
Bapu

15. Letter to Manu Gandhi

Delhi,
June 26, 1946

Chi. Manudi,

I got your letter of the 15th three days ago. But I am able to reply to it only today. After discussing the courage that you had displayed you asked me whether I would call it violence or nonviolence. I should advise you not to bother about that question. If we go on reflecting over the meaning of *ahimsa*, we shall but act nonviolently when the occasion arises. We should not mind whether other people regarded it as nonviolent or not. The effect of such action depends not on what others think about it but on what is in our minds. We do not know our minds ourselves, but, assuming that we do, if the mind says that in abusing or slapping a person we acted nonviolently, it would be for us a nonviolent action. Whether in fact it was nonviolent God alone can know. The other party and the spectators also can judge it from the effect of the action on the former.[5] But why need you go into all such subtleties ? And why should I take you into them ? You did right in not publishing my letter. It ought not to be published. There is no harm in your having shown it to the *Nagarsheth*[6]. The important thing is to watch the effect of the work that you are doing there. If you persevere in it I shall regard it as part of your education.

I am glad that Umiya's suggestion has been accepted. I do not know who is the Principal of the Science College at the Banaras Hindu University. Even if I knew I would not write to him. The Birla brothers have played an important part in establishing the University and they know many persons there. If Shankarlal writes to him the work will be done. If you experience any difficulty regarding the expenses, write to me. I am returning the wire received by you.

Blessings to you both from
Bapu

16. Letter to Manu Gandhi

New Delhi,
September 3, 1946

Chi. Manudi,

You say, "You and your circle have separated me from Father and so thrashing my arms and legs I try to swim on my own." Now is that true ? When did I separate you ? Who is my circle ? You too are my circle. I have written to you that you may come whenever you wish. Yes I have asked for Jaisukhlal also to come with you. If you can find the strength to face the world by yourself I am ready to keep you here by yourself. But you alone know that. I do miss you of course. Many people ask me when you will be coming. The field of service is wide and the means of learning the work are many. Sushila tells me that if I were to send for you, she would make of you an excellent nurse. Chand has passed the examination. Zohra has joined the hospital. If you were to come three would get trained. Now the hospital is quite separate. I suppose you know that it is in the Birla Dharmashala ?

Your problem is difficult. But if you are going to stay there be patient. The fruits of patience are sweet. Wait for a message from me. For you it is already there.

The talk about my going abroad is quite unfounded. Or are you referring to India ? In India of course I have to travel from place to place. If you accompany me your routine of studies will be disrupted.

Jaisukhlal must improve his health. Everything has been fixed about Umia and Pratap. All the expenses on Vilas will be paid by Birla.

There is a separate letter for Atmaram.

Blessings from
Bapu

17. Letter to Manu Gandhi

New Delhi,
October 11, 1946

Chi. Manudi,

I have gone through your letter. I gave it to Sushila Pai, Kanu, Sushila (Dr.) and Pyarelal to read. Here I shall tell you only this, that I liked your letter.

Further, I shall be happy if you come over and have a talk with me. I do not wish to put any pressure on you. It is my earnest desire that you should remain a pure virgin till the end of your life and spend your life in service.

I hope Umiya's son is doing well.

Blessings to all from
Bapu

18. Letter to Manu Gandhi

New Delhi,
October 14, 1946

Chi. Manudi,

You had left a letter here. I sent the reply the very next day. You would not have got it. It went to Udaipur.

I have your letter today. I was sorry to learn about Shankarlal's illness. It is good you two sisters went to Udaipur. Tell Shankarlal that he should quickly get well. It does not behove a scout to fall ill. Whatever the job he may be doing, he cannot cease being a scout. Why is Umia feeling unhappy ? Bring her along with you. It is another matter if you yourself do not come.

I am not calling you to me to make you unhappy. You are not

afraid of me, are you ? It can never be that I would make you do anything against your wishes. I only wish you well. I wish to see you healthy and well.

Now there is no time to write more.

Blessings from
Bapu

19. Letter to Manu Gandhi

December 2, 1946

Chi. Manudi,

The child may misbehave, but can the mother ever do so ? Your letter is a hotch potch. You have assumed things which I never said in the letter. That is why I consider you silly. Jaisukhlal has called you a slovenly girl. You have received education but learnt no wisdom. I do not, however, wish to point out your faults. I will do so and pull your ears when you come here. You will yourself admit that you have made those mistakes. You need not come just to meet me. Come only if you wish to take up some work here. Otherwise you had better stay with Jaisukhlal at present. You will know in a few months what happens to me. The job here is a difficult one. I am not going to leave the place till everything is settled.

I understand about Umiya. So long as we are satisfied with Shankarlal, we need not pay much attention to what sort of people the other family members are. It is Umiya's job to reform the in-laws. She must regard Birla Sheth as filling the place of Jaisukhlal now. The problem about Pratap[7] also will be solved. In your ignorance you are thinking too much about this matter. As long as Umiya is happy with Shankarlal, there is no cause at all for worry. Ask Shankarlal to write to me and explain frankly what the problem is. It is a mistake to suppose that he cannot write to me because I am a big man. I don't regard myself as one, and in any case of what value is my supposed greatness in relation to you, the children ? Since Shankarlal has married Umiya, he also is like a son to me.

Be calm now and do what you believe to be your dharma. If you wish you may come to stay with me.

Blessings from
Bapu

(PS.)
Vinodini[8] is ill. I had, therefore, asked her to come if she wished. But she has left now.

20. Letter to Manu Gandhi

September 22, 1947

Chi. Manudi,

There are two ways in which you can cure my unhappiness.[9] One is immediately to write down a confession and read it out this very day. The other is henceforth to make your life one with God. Then there can be no frivolous laughter. . . .[10] Read out the confession at the public prayer meeting. That will cleanse the heart. The confession should not be forced, nor should it be made out of shame. A public confession is my own innovation. . . [11] cannot understand its significance. It is my suggestion. Stick to your resolve sincerely. Then only will you rise.

(From Gujarati)
Dilhiman Gandhiji—I, pp. 43-44.

NOTES

1. Perhaps Gandhiji meant Wardha where he returned on April 25 which was a Thursday.
2. Harilal Gandhi, addressee's father.
3. Addressee's elder sister Sanyuka's.
4. *Vide* also the following item.
5. The boy who was punished later turned up to apologize and promised to behave. *Vide* "Letter to Manu Gandhi", 6-6-1946.
6. Leader of a town's business community.
7. Umiya's son.
8. Addressee's sister.
9. *Vide* the preceding item.
10. Omissions as in the source.
11. *Ibid.*

Chapter 15
Epilogue

Gandhi, Women and Sexuality: Reflection Through Letters gives a new insight, colour and dimension into Gandhi's relationship with women and on question of sexuality without any distortion and preconceived notion. Facts are facts. Neutrality is a prerequisite for any analysis and good research. In case of this research on Gandhi, it is not only necessary but also desirable, because it will lead to the distortion of facts and misunderstanding about Gandhi. To keep facts as facts, only primary source has been used in the form of letters and are placed before the readers to draw their own conclusion and form real picture on the issue. It will give the readers the space to read between lines.

True, Gandhi is a systems man and unless we see him that way, we cannot understand him. Gandhi's relationship with women must be seen in the broader context of his worldview based on the harmony of four purusharthas—*Dharma*, *Artha*, *Kama* and *Moksha*. The riddle of Gandhi's association with women can only be unfolded with the proper understanding of non-duality of man and woman relationship. There were several instances that reinforced Gandhi's views on inseparability of man and woman to ensure equality between them. Probably, Gandhi wanted to break the mystery surrounding women's body, and this was not possible unless he would have dealt head on with the hidden realities of women's anatomy from where his idea of celibacy emanates.

In that sense sleeping with women was part of his experiment. Gandhi an ordinary man through his thought and action, became Mahatma, the 'great soul' and an extraordinary person, Bapu, Father of the Nation and Mahatma Gandhi. Gandhi was a unique combination of perceptions and values. Gandhi empowered the women and a number of women rose to prominence under his leadership and guidance. His life was full of unique, unparallel and fundamental experiments after experiments, and the experiment of celibacy was one of them. This spiritualized and unique experiment was part of his search for truth which is the ultimate reality.

One must remember the fact that his personality was so mesmerizing that everyone longed to become his close aides and confidants. This is equally true in the case of women. The mere company of Gandhi catapulted a large number of women to name, fame and social recognition of highest order. Some of them became very close while working with him. Women under his tutelage were metamorphosed that ultimately accorded them an altogether new identity and an enduring position in the society. It led them to a voyage to re-exploring their true self that was incongruence with their self-esteem. They were so much swayed by Gandhi that they willingly became the part of Gandhi's experiment of *brahmacharya*. The women, who participated in the experiment, saw in Gandhi, the *matritva. Matritvabodh* make them fearless with Gandhi. In these letters one can find that Gandhi was knowing, minute details of all the women who participated in experiment. This is possible only because of *matritvabodh* nothing else.

Louis Fischer writes that "the women in the Mahatma's entourage... loved Gandhi, and he loved them. It was a father-daughter relationship and more than usual warmth and interdependence... Her [Mirabehn] bond with him was one of the remarkable platonic associations of our age. He often said to her, 'When this body is no more there will not be separation, but I shall be nearer to you. The body is a hindrance.' ..." Women play a vital role in Gandhi's life. No one can get a real picture of Gandhi, unless one knows the women's contribution in Gandhi's life and *vice versa*. Women like Kasturba Gandhi, Millie Graham Polak, Sonja Schlesin, Sarala Devi Chaudhurani, Mirabehn, Lilavati Asar, Prema Kantak, Sushila Nayyar, Bibi Amutussalaam, Margarete Spiegel,

Rajkumari Amrit Kaur, Kanchan Shah, Prabhavati and Manu devoted their life to Gandhi for a cause. These women were what Gandhi calls his "inner circle". Apart from Kasturba, thirteen women whose letters were included in this volume were part of Gandhi's experiment on *brahmacharya*. *Brahmacharya* experiment was a spiritual experiment to attain the higher truth. In Gandhi's leadership, the women of India found a new identity and hope. These letters give us the real picture about his engagement with them. Being educated themselves, they were conscious of their identity, individuality, self-esteem and self-respect. It is the test of one's wisdom, after reading these letters, to find the answer of these women's willing participation in Gandhi's great experimentation on *brahmacharya*. It is naïve to assume that these enlightened women, master of their own persona, were uncritically swayed and persuaded by Gandhi to become a part of the so-called unusual experiment. Besides, I leave the final judgment to the critical readers of these letters.

Gandhi holds his notion of sexuality quite differently where it is exclusively associated with men's or women's lust. Initially, sex for him signifies regeneration and reproduction, that is subsequently followed by its total negation to bring both wife and husband much nearer to each other to elevate them, absolutely eliminating lust. Gandhi referring to his own life observed that he began to enjoy his married life only after he abandoned sex. For him, "the conquest of lust is the highest endeavour of a man's or a woman's existence whereas physical union for the sake of carnal satisfaction is reversion to animality which has to be avoided by both." Gandhi rearticulated a new idea of sexuality that is enjoyed more not through its abundance rather through its timely renunciation. Instead of trivializing his ideas of sexuality that he abandoned in 1906 and stuck to it till his death, one should appreciate its sublime and culture specific values. Moreover, Gandhi was quite explicit and transparent in dealing with the issue of sexuality both with his wife and other women. He wrote and took open public position on it. He saw his experiments as important for testing the vow that would enable him to achieve *moksha*. Thus, his views on sexuality have simultaneously evoked strong reaction and admiration as well that have become the part of unprecedented and unparallel in human history.

Kasturba was part of Gandhi's experiment on women and as such she provides vital clues to Gandhi's view on women. Gandhi stated honestly about Kasturba, "it is because of her that I am today what I am." However, one can get answer from what Rajkumari Amrit Kaur, who was part of *brahmacharya* experiment, herself stated that "We found him [Gandhi] not a "Bapu"—wise father, but what is more precious, a mother, who's all-embracing and understanding love all fear and restraint vanish." Gandhi gave motherly love, affection and care and security to women who were associated with him. Women were never afraid of Gandhi. Instead, they felt secured and unthreatened. Further in a letter written to Rajkumari Amrit Kaur on 20th October, 1936, Gandhi writes, "If you women only realize your dignity and privilege, and make full sense of it for mankind, you will make it much better than it is. But man has delighted in enslaving you and you have proved willing slaves till the slave and holders have become one in the crime on degrading humanity. My special function from childhood, you might say, has been to make women realize her dignity. I was once slave holder myself but Ba proved an unwilling slave and thus opened my eyes to my mission."

It is pertinent to mention that Gandhi not only valued experiment but he also intended to merge it with metaphysical worldview. The tangible aspect of it is reflected through his experiments and adoption of various other means. In line with this thinking, after twenty-three years of happy marital life, Gandhi took a vow of lifelong celibacy in 1906. It is important here to mention that giving up sex is a renunciation and was a well-established practice of Hindu devotion, known as *brahmacharya*. Renunciation of sexuality was part of Gandhi's spiritual discipline and final journey towards *moksha*, that is, salvation which everyone in Indian tradition wants to achieve.

It is crystal clear that Gandhi's notion of '*brahmacharya*' was different from the old Indian ascetic system that abjured all interactions with women. Gandhi presented a counter view to man and woman relation were running from each other would not serve the cause of either of them. In fact, Gandhi had a number of close women associates, many of whom he treated as daughter, sister, mother, and so on. Interestingly, he himself acknowledged Sarala Devi, as his 'spiritual wife'. In a letter written to Sarala Devi, in July, 1920, Gandhi explained being "spiritually" married meant to him that the "physical must be wholly absent". However, he also admitted that he was "too physically attached to" her. His apparently ambivalent views on sexuality reaffirm that renunciation, will be achieved not only by escaping from it but passing through it. Gandhi's life must be seen as a journey from worldly *asakti* (attachment) to *anasakti* (non-attachment) for final liberation.

Gandhi was an extraordinary human being who could have conflated existing practice with utmost ease. This shows Gandhi's daring experiment of sleeping with young women, to test and affirm his own sexual self-control. This was not acceptable in Indian tradition. Despite opposition he did so and explained the ideal he was trying to achieve. Gandhi described his sleeping with Manu as a bold and original experiment, one that required a practicing *brahmachari* such as he was, and a woman such as Manu who was free from passion. Confessing as she even might have done with her own mother, Manu told Gandhi that she had not ever experienced sexual desire. The fact that women felt no unease in his presence was proof to Gandhi that he was approaching perfection as a *brahmachari*. Indeed, Bose contended that Gandhi attempted to conquer sex was by becoming a woman. Gandhi himself stated that his goal was to achieve the state of "complete sexlessness" by prayer. But for Gandhi, the way to conquer desire was to face the temptation head-on with a naked female in his bed. Gandhi has his own definition of *brahmacharya*. He said "My meaning of *brahmacharya* is this: "One who never has any lustful intention, who . . . has become capable of lying naked with naked women . . . without being in any manner whatsoever sexually excited."

One can argue rightly or wrongly that Gandhi's sexual experiments may have been an abuse of personal charismatic power, where questioning Gandhi's act does not arise. Abha's husband, Kanu, once objected to his wife sleeping with Gandhi and instead offered himself as a "bed warmer" to him. Gandhi rejected his proposal by making it clear that *brahmacharya* tests required young women as bedmates. This was nothing but clear deviation from Indian tradition where even the grown-up daughters were not allowed to sleep with their fathers. Gandhi's experiment is replete with many such deviations. In his conversations with Margaret Sanger, Gandhi referred to a "woman with whom I almost fell", and "the thought of my wife kept me from going to perdition." Again, writing to Rajkumari Amrit Kaur, he admitted that, "with one solitary exception", had never "looked upon a woman with lustful eyes."

Gandhi takes the defiant stand and says that he cares nothing for what others think of his practice: "The whole world may forsake me but I dare not leave what I hold is the truth for me ?" Gandhi in a letter to Sushila Nayyar wrote, "I can hurt colleagues and the entire world for the sake of truth." Thus, Gandhi's experiments with truth were highly spiritual and transparent. In fact, Gandhi was honest about his relationships with women. Whatever we know about this relationship, it is because Gandhi himself wrote and spoke about it. His relationship with women is above sex. Gandhi's letters indicate these relationships to be humane in thoughts and not on body or fulfilment of sexual desire. These letters are now placed at one place to enable the readers to appreciate them in totality and remove the misconceptions. In Gandhi's letters to women, one can find a number of issues related to human concern.

My own understanding is that Gandhi's relationship with women can be interpreted by the different interpreters in different ways due to their different ideologies, backgrounds, time and space in which they interpret. Gandhi was a national manifestation and he derived power directly from masses. It is said that the monument Taj Mahal looks different to different people, depending on where they are standing and particularly on what time of day it is. Further, flowers look different in colours in day time but in night all the flowers look only black. Appearance is not reality and reality are not appearance. This is also true in the case of Gandhi. Everyone visualizes Gandhi according to their ideology, perception, research and depth of knowledge.

Gandhi was a great soul and understanding of great soul is very difficult and it requires extensive research and in-depth analysis of a person and his work. Gandhi's work on any subject is extensive and scattered and for any purpose one has to locate it. No one can understand Gandhi unless he understands Gandhi's relationship with women in the right perspective. There exists not one Gandhi but hundreds of Gandhi. Everyone has their own Gandhi. It is like '*Hari Anant, Hari Katha Ananta*'.

Gandhi is above *Satogun, Rajogun* and *Tamogun*. He was above the physical world. I sum up the whole context and debate of Gandhi's celibacy experiment, by a story of *Muni Sukhdev*, son of *Muni Vyas* author of *Vedas*. Noble and enlightened Soul *Sukhdev* had *Brahamgyan* even before coming in the mother's womb. Conscious of *triguni maya* he decided not to come out of the mother's womb and remained there for sixteen years. Thereupon, father, *Ved Vyas* cosmically communicated with his son in mother's womb and requested him to relieve his mother from the pain of pregnancy. After receiving assurance from his father that his parents shall not emotionally or otherwise try to tie him down, he came out leaving his mother's womb and relieving her of pregnancy. After appearing in the world outside, he acquired the normal physique of sixteen years and bid farewell to his parents and he proceeded for *tapsya* in isolation. As young *Sukhdev* proceeded to his isolation abode, *Ved Vyas* under attachment of parental love and affection started following him to get him back in the *ashram*. In the course of passage, there was a pond in which *Apsaras* (courtier women of Lord Indra) were taking bath. When *Sukhdev* passed by the side of pond, the *apsaras* did not take any cognizance and notice of his presence there. But as *Ved Vyas* reached on the same place, following his son, the *apsaras* shied away and hid themselves. On this behaviour of *Apsaras, Vyas* queried as to why they are conscious of the presence of old man like him, whereas they were totally free when his young son of sixteen years passed from the same spot. *Apsaras* very wisely and knowledgably replied: "*Maharshi* your son who went ahead of you is *Gunateet* (above *Sato, Rajo* and *Tamogunas*) whereas you are not yet out of their grip". Perhaps there is a need to see Gandhi with the eyes of *Apsaras*. In Gandhi, woman saw motherhood not manhood.

Glossary

Adharma	Not following duty
Ahimsa	Nonviolence
Anasakti	Non-attachment
Aparigraha	Non-possession
Ashram	Hermitage; Stages of life—Brahmacharya, Grihastha, Banaprastha and Sanaysi
Aashramite	Inmate of ashram
Atman	Soul
Bania	Person of commercial caste
Bhakti	Devotion
Bhangi	Sweeper
Bhakhari	Home-made wheat bread
Behn	Sister
Brahmacharya	Celibacy
Brahmachari	One observing celibacy
Brahman	The ultimate reality
Brahma	The god of creation
Brahmin	The highest caste in Hindu society
Charkha	Spinning wheel
Chapati	Flat bread made of wheat flour; Roti
Chela	Disciple
Daridranarayan	God embodied as the poor
Darshan	The sight of a holy person
Dewan	Prime Minister

Dharma	Duty; one of the four purusharthas—Dharma, Artha, Kama and Moksha
Dharna	A form of sit-down strike
Dhoti	Loin cloth worn by men
Duragraha	Stubborn persistence
Duvidha	Uncertainty
Gram	Village
Gram-Pradhan	Head man of the Village
Goseva Sangh	Cow Protection Society
Guru	Spritual teacher
Harijans	People of God (the name used by Gandhiji for people of the caste of "untouchables")
Hartal	Strike
Kama	Sexual desire
Karma	Action
Kaffir	South African tribe
Karma	The ethical law of causation
Khadi	Hand-spun cloth
Khaddar	Handspun and handwoven cloth
Khilafat	Movement in support of Khalifah
Kisan	Farmer
Mandir	Temple
Mahabharata	A Hindu epic
Moksha	Salvation, release from the cycle of rebirth; one of the four purusharthas—Dharma, Artha, Kama and Moksha
Panchayat	Village council
Purda	The custom of veiling women
Poorna Swaraj	Complete Independence
Praja	People
Ramayana	A Hindu epic
Ramrajya	The rule of Ram, the rule of God
Sanatani	Follower of Vedic dharma (religion)
Sanyasi	One who has renounce from ordinary life for religious meditation
Satyagraha	Truth force; Insistence on Truth
Satyagrahi	Nonviolent resister

Smriti	Oral Knowledge
Swadeshi	Insistence on local products
Swaraj	Self-rule, Home Rule, Self-government
Takli	A portable contrivance for spinning
Tapasya	The practice of austerities
Upanishads	Hindu sacred texts which form the final part of the Vedas
Varna	Caste
*Varna*shrama	Four fold division in Hindu society
Vaishnava	Follower of Lord Vishnu
Yajna	Sacrificial offering to Fire God
Yogi	One who practices yoga
Zamindar	Landlord

Important Events of Gandhi's Life

1869	Born at Porbandar, India, on 2nd October.
1876	Betrothed to Kasturbai.
1883	Married to Kasturbai.
1887	Passed Matriculation Examination; Entered the Sanwaldas College at Bhavnagar.
1888	Proceeded to England on 4th September, to study Law.
1889	First Public Speech in England to a gathering of vegetarians.
1891	Became Barrister on 10th June; Sailed back to India: Reached Bombay on 7th July, where he received news of his mother's death.
1892	Started legal practice at Rajkot and Bombay.
1893	First time left for South Africa in April to appear in a Civil Suit.
1894	Civil suit decided by compromise.
1895	Enrolled as an Advocate of Natal Supreme Court; organised Natal Indian Congress.
1896	Returned from South Africa to India where he remained for six months and met Indian leaders, Tilak, Gokhale and others; went to South Africa again on 28th November.
1897	Anti-Gandhi demonstrations in Durban, which marked the beginning of a great change in his life.

1899 Helped the British in Boer War.

1901 Returned to India; Organised public service in plague affected areas of Rajkot. Participated in Calcutta Congress.

1902 Went to Burma; Started travelling in India in third class Railway Compartment, Opened an office in Bombay in July; Again proceeded after 3 months to South Africa.

1903 Established 'Transvaal British India Association'; Started editing *Indian Opinions.*

1904 Studied *Gita* and Ruskin's *Unto This Last* which led to a revolutionary change in his life; Established 'Phoenix Ashram'.

1906 Zulu Revolt, Rendered service to the injured in the revolt; Took a vow to observe *Brahmacharya*; The word 'satyagraha' was coined for the first time; Proceeded to England as a member of the Indian deputation.

1907 Started Satyagraha against 'Black Act'.

1908 Interim agreement with British; Restarting of Satyagrah, resulting in his arrest.

1909 Wrote his first letter to Tolstoy; Proceeded to England as a member of the second Indian deputation. While returning from England he wrote *'Hind Swaraj'* or *'Indian Home Rule'.*

1910 Established Tolstoy Farm in Johannesburg.

1912 Gokhale arrived in South Africa; The book entitled *Niti Dharma* was published; wrote another book of general information on nature-cure for health.

1913 Restarting of Satyagraha: Arrested and released; observed fast for seven days and thereafter took one meal a day for four and a half months.

1914 Fast for 14 days; Success of Satyagraha, resulting in on agreement; Proceeded to England on 18th July; First World War broke out on 4th August; Meeting with Sarojini Naidu; Service in World War.

1915 Awarded Kaiser-e-Hind medal on return to India; widely travelled in India; Meeting with Kaka Kalelkar and Acharya Kripalani; Death of Gokhale on 19th February; on 25th May Sabarmati Ashram was established.

1916	Historical speech on the occasion of the establishment of Kashi Vishvavidyalaya; First meeting with Jawaharlal Nehru in Lucknow Congress.
1917	First meeting with Dr. Rajendra Prasad; Started Champaran Satyagraha on 10th April; Abolition of Indentured Labour Act on 31st May; First meeting with Mahadev Desai.
1918	Mill Worker's strike in Ahmedabad, followed by three days fast; Khera Satyagraha; Revival of spinning wheel.
1919	Rowlatt Act; observed 6th April as prayer-*cum*-fast day; Jallianwala Bagh massacre on 13th April; Started editing of '*Young India*' and '*Navajivan*'; Khilafat Movement; Amritsar Congress.
1920	Death of Lokmanya Tilak on 1st August; Tilak Swaraj Fund was established on 2nd October; Congress constitution prepared by Gandhi was approved; Started Non-cooperation Movement; Establishment of Gujarat Vidyapeeth.
1921	Establishment of other national educational institutions; Boycott of the visit of Prince of Wales, followed by riots; Five day fast; Ahmedabad Congress.
1922	Revolt of Chauri Chaura on 5th February; Satyagrah suspended, five days fast; Arrested on 10th March; Six years of imprisonment.
1924	Operated for appendicitis; Released from Jail on 5th February; Twenty-one days fast from 24th September; Presided over Belgaum Congress.
1925	Death of Deshbandhu Chittranjan Das on 16th June; One week fast; Kanpur Congress; Establishment of Charkha Sangh.
1927	Extensively toured throughout India for the revival of *Khadi*; Death of Hakim Ajmal Khan on 19th September.
1928	Simon Commission; Bardoli Satyagraha; Death of Manganlal Gandhi in Patna on 22nd April; Death of Lala Lajpat Rai on 17 November; Nehru Report, Compromise resolution in Calcutta Congress.
1929	Resolution for complete Independence passed in Lahore Congress.

1930 Pledge for complete Independence on 26 January; Dandi March on 12th March to break the Salt Law; Arrested on 5th May.

1931 Death of Mohammed Ali in England on 4th January; Gandhiji released from Jail on January 25; Death of Pandit Motilal Nehru on 6th February; Gandhi-Irwin Pact on 4th March; Bhagat Singh hanged on 23rd March; Karachi Congress; Martyrdom of Ganesh Shankar Vidyarthi on 25th March; Participated in the Second Round Table Conference as the sole representative of India, but returned disappointed in December.

1932 Congress declared unlawful organisation; Restarted Satyagrah; Arrested on January 4th, Publication of '*Young India*' and '*Navajivan*' stopped; From September 20 fast unto death against Communal Award; Yarvada Pact on September 24; fast ended on 26th September.

1933 Twenty-one days fast from 8th May; Started '*Harijan*' weekly; Released from jail and again arrested; one year imprisonment; Fast unto death from 16th August, which ended after one week; Released from jail on 23 August; Death of Annie Besant on 30th September; Death of Vitthalbhai Patel on 22nd September; Left Sabarmati Ashram to live at Wardha; Undertook tour from November 7th for 'Harijan' uplift.

1934 Bihar earthquake; Satyagraha suspended on 7th May; Seven days fast; Gram Udyog Sangh established on 26th October; Bombay Congress.

1935 Golden Jubilee of Indian National Congress.

1936 Sewagram Ashram established.

1937 Accepted Congress membership in July; Started 'Nai Talim' programme.

1939 Death of Maulana Shaukat Ali on 4th January; Fast unto death in Rajkot, which ended after 4 days on the intervention of the Viceroy; Tripura Congress; Subhas Chandra Bose resigned from the presidentship of Indian National Congress; Second World War broke out on

September 3; Congress Government in all provinces resigned on 8th November.

1940 Individual Satyagraha started from 11th October, Vinoba offered arrest as first *Satyagrahi*; Publication of '*Harijan*' Weekly suspended.

1941 Death of Rabindranath Tagore on 7th August; Gave up leadership of Indian National Congress; Established 'Go-Seva-Sangh' on September 30.

1942 Again accepted the leadership of Indian National Congress; Death of Shri Jamnalal Bajaj on 11th February; Cripps Mission; established Hindustani Prachar Sabha,; 'Quit India' resolution on 8th August; Collective arrest of Indian leaders all over India on 9th August; Death of Mahadev Desai on 15 August.

1943 Twenty-one days fast in Agha Khan Palace.

1944 Death of Kasturba Gandhi on February 22; Released from Jail on 6th May; Gandhi-Jinnah talks.

1945 Indian leaders released from jail; 1st Simla Conference. 1946 Cabinet Mission; 'Direct Action' Programme of Muslim League from August 16; Communal riots; Padyatra in Noakhali; Death of Madan Mohan Malaviya on 12th November.

1947 India declared independent on 15 August; Seventy three hours fast for peace in Calcutta.

1948 Fast unto death undertaken to establish peace in Delhi, which continued for five days; Martyrdom on January 30, with Last words; 'Hey Ram', 'Hey Ram'.

Select Bibliography

Alexander, Horace, (1969). *Gandhi Through Western Eyes*, Bombay: Asia Publishing House.

Andrews, C.F. (1931). *Mahatma Gandhi at Work Ideas*, London: George Allen & Unwin Ltd.

Bapu's Letter to Mira, 1924-1948 (1949). Ahmedabad, Navajivan Press.

Birla, G.D. (1953). *In the Shadow of the Mahatma*, Bombay: Orient Longmans Ltd.

Bose, N.K. (1962). *Studies in Gandhism*, Ahmedabad, Navajivan Publishing House.

Bose, N.K. (1966). *Gandhiji The Man and His Mission*, Bharatiya Vidya Bhawan, Bombay.

Bose, N.K. (1972). *Selections from Gandhi*, Ahmedabad, Navajivan Publishing House.

Bose, Nirmal Kumar (1953). *My Days with Gandhi*, Calcutta, Nishana.

Brown, M. Judith (1992). *Gandhi Prisoner of Hope*, Oxford University Press, Delhi.

Chopra, Pran (1972). *The Sage in Rivolt : A Remembrance*, Gandhi Peace Foundation, New Delhi.

Choudhuri, Manmohan (1987). *Exploring Gandhi,* New Delhi, The Gandhi Peace Foundation.

Diwakar, R.R. (1969). *Saga of Satyagraha*, New Delhi, Gandhi Peace Foundation.

Doke, J.J. (1909). *M.K. Gandhi: An Indian Patriot*, Madras, Natesan.

Eleanor, Morton (1954). *Women Behind Gandhi*, New York, Rinehart.

Gandhi, Arun (2000). *Kasturba, a Life*, New Delhi, Penguin.

Gandhi, M.K. (1975). *Hind Swaraj or Indian Home Rule*, Ahmedabad, Navajivan Publishing House.

Gandhi, M.K. (1975). *Satyagraha in South Africa*, Ahmedabad, Navajivan Publishing House.

Gandhi, Kanu and Abha (1990). *Bapu Ke Saath*, New Delhi, Publication Division, Ministry of Information and Broadcasting, Government of India.

Gandhi, Manubehn (1960). *My Memorable Moments with Bapu*, Ahmedabad, Navijivan Press.

Gandhi, Prabhudas (1957). *My Childhood With Gandhi*, Ahmedabad, Navajivan Publishing House.

Gandhi, Rajmohan (2006). *Mohandas: A true Story of a Man, his People and an Empire*, New Delhi, Penguin.

Gandhi, Rajmohan (1995). *The Good Boatman: A Portrait of Gandhi*, New Delhi, Penguin Books.

Ghosh, Sudhir (1967). *Gandhi's Emissary*, London.

Hunter, Doris A. and Mallick Krishna (1990). *Nonviolence A Reader in the Ethics of Action*, Gandhi Peace Foundation, New Delhi.

Huttenback, Robert A. (1971). *Gandhi in South Africa : British Imperialism and The Indian Question, 1860-1914*, London, Cornell University Press.

Kakar, Sudhir (2004). *Mira and the Mahatma*, New Delhi, Penguin.

Kripalani, J.B. (1968). *Gandhi: His Life and Thought*, New Delhi, Publications Division, Ministry of Information and Broadcasting, Government of India.

Kumar, Girja (2006). *Brahmachary Gandhi and His Women Associates*, New Delhi,Vitasta.

Mehta, P.J. (1911). *Gandhi and South African Question*, Madras.

Mehta, Ved (1977). *Mahatma and His Apostle*, New Delhi, Indian Book Company.

Mirabehn (1960). *The Sprit's Pilgrimage*, Arlington, Great Ocean Publishers.

Mishra anil Dutta (2012). *Reading Gandhi*, Pearson.

Mishra, Anil Dutta (2012). *Understanding Mahatma Gandhi: Speeches and Writings that Reveal his Mind, Methods and Mission*, New Delhi, Concept Publishing Company Pvt. Ltd.

Mishra, anil Dutta (2010). *Revisiting Hind Swaraj*, New Delhi, Concept Publishing Company Pvt. Ltd.

Nanda, B.R. (1959). *Mahatma Gandhi: A Biography*, London, George Allen and Unwin Ltd.

Narayan, Shriman (1956). *Selected Works of Mahatma Gandhi*, Ahmedabad, Navajivan Publishing House.

Nayyar, Sushila (1996). *Mahatma Gandhi's Last Imprisonment: The Last Story*, New Delhi, Har-Anand.

Nayyar, Sushila and Kamla Mankekar (2002). *Women Pioneers: In India's Renaissance*, New Delhi, National Book Trust.

Ostergaord Geoffrey (1985). *Nonviolent Revolution in India*, New Delhi, Gandhi Peace Foundation.

Parekh, Bhikhu (1989) *Colonialism, Tradition and Reform : An Analysis of Gandhi's Political Discourse*, New Delhi, Sage Publication.

Parikh, Narhari (1953). *Mahadev's Early Life*, Ahmedabad, Navajivan Publishing House.

Polak, H.S.C., H.N. Brailsford and Lord Pethick, Lawrence (1949). *Mahatma Gandhi*, London, Odham Press Limited.

Polak, Millie Graham (1949). *Mr. Gandhi: The Man*, Bombay, Vora.

Pyare Lal (1965). *Mahatma Gandhi: The Early Phase*, Volume 1, Ahmedabad, Navajivan Publishing House.

Pyare Lal (1956, 1958). *Mahatma Gandhi: The Last Phase*, in 2 volumes, Ahmedabad, Navajivan Publishing House.

Pyarelal and Nayar Sushila (1991). *In Gandhiji's Mirror*, Delhi, Oxford University Press.

Pyarelal (1958). *Mahatma Gandhi: The Last Phase*, Ahmedabad, Navajivan Publishing House.

Rolland, Romain. *Mahatma Gandhi, The Man Who Became One With The Universal Being*, (Translated by Catherine D. Groth), Agra, Shiva Lal Aggarwala & Co. Ltd.

Shukla, Chandrashanker (1951). *Reminiscences of Gandhiji*, Bombay, Vora and Company.

Sitaramayya, Pattabhi (1942). *Gandhi and Gandhism*. Allahabad, Kitabistan in 2 volumes.

Tendulkar, D.G. (1952). *Mahatma*, New Delhi, Publications Division, Ministry of Information and Broadcasting, Government of India.

Thomas, Mark (1993). *Gandhi and his Ashram*, Bombay, Popular Prakashan.

The Collected Works of Mahatma Gandhi, New Delhi, Publications Division, Ministry of Information and Broadcasting, Government of India, (Vols. 1-100).

Watson, Francis and Tennyson Hallam (1957). *Talking of Gandhi*, Sangam Books, Bombay.

Weber, Thomas (2004). *Gandhi as Disciple and Mentor*, New Delhi, Cambridge University Press.

Photos

Gandhi at the Age of Seven

M.K. Gandhi, South Africa, 1900

M.K. Gandhi Wearing the London Vegetarian Society's Badge, Johannesburg, 1906

M.K. Gandhi with his secretary Miss Sonja Schlesin and colleague Herman Kallenbach at Johannesburg, 1913

M.K. Gandhi and Kasturba, Johannesburg, July 1914

M.K. Gandhi with Kasturba at the end of the struggle in Johannesburg, 1914

Mahatma Gandhi, 1915

Mahatma Gandhi, 1915

Mahatma Gandhi during the Kheda Satyagraha, 1918

Mahatma Gandhi and Sarojini Naidu with other women leaders during the Round Table Conference, London, 1931

Mahatma Gandhi with women workers during his visit to Lancashire, September 21, 1931

Mahatma Gandhi on his way to a public meeting, Jabalpur, November 1933

Mahatma Gandhi with Mira Behn and others on the way to a public meeting, Jabalpur, November 1933

Mahatma Gandhi with Rajkumari Amrit Kaur on his daily walk, Wardha, Maharashtra, 1934

Mahatma Gandhi swimming in the sea, Cape Comorin, (Kanya Kumari) Tamil Nadu, January 1934

Mahatma Gandhi during the Harijan tour Assam, April 1934

Mahatma Gandhi with Mira Behn on morning walk,
Wardha, Maharashtra, 1935

Mahatma Gandhi with ashramites on the Ashram ground during the morning walk, Segaon, Maharashtra, 1937

Mahatma Gandhi with an ashramite in front of his hut, Sevagram, Maharashtra, 1941

Mahatma Gandhi and Kasturba in discussion with girls from the Mahila Ashram in front of his hut, Sevagram, Maharashtra, 1941

Mahatma Gandhi and Kasturba with ashramites, Sevagram, Maharashtra, 1941

Mahatma Gandhi with Dr. Sushila Nayyar examining a timpiece, Sevagram, 1944

Mahatma Gandhi with others on morning walk, Panchagani, Maharashtra, May 1944

Mahatma Gandhi with Ashadevi and Balawant Singh near goshala, Sevagram, 1944

Mahatma Gandhi with R. D. Birla, Agatha Harrison and Manu Gandhi on a morning walk, Birla House, Mumbai, 1944

Mahatma Gandhi with others on his morning walk, Juhu beach, Mumbai, 1944

Mahatma Gandhi on way to the prayer meeting, Juhu, Mumbai, May 1944

Mahatma Gandhi on way to the prayer meeting, Juhu, Mumbai, May 1944

Mahatma Gandhi with others on morning walk, Juhu beach, Mumbai, May 1944

Mahatma Gandhi with others during the prayer meeting, Gandhigram, Juhu, Mumbai, May 1944

Mahatma Gandhi on way to the prayer meeting, Juhu, Mumbai, May 1944

Mahatma Gandhi with others, Birla House, New Delhi, 1946

Mahatma Gandhi with Rajkumari Amrit Kaur, Manubehn and others on way to prayer meeting, Balmiki Mandir, Bhangi colony, Delhi, 1946

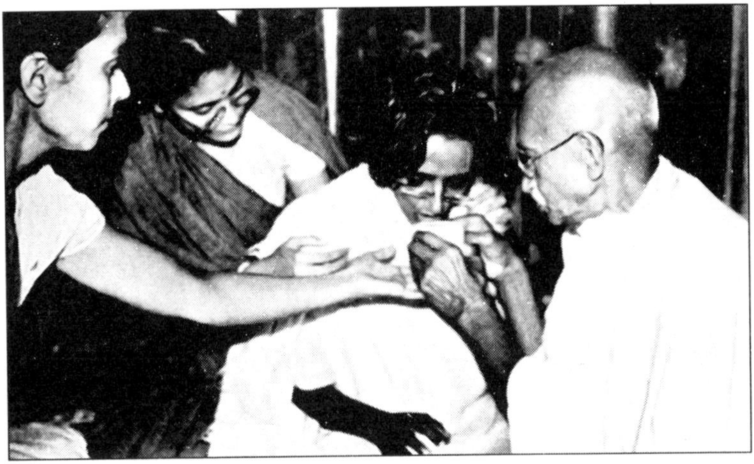

Gandhi and Bibi Amutussalaam

Gandhi and Manu

Gandhi and Mira

Gandhi with Susheela Nayar

Gandhi and Rajkumari Amrit Kaur

Gandhi and Rajkumari Amrit Kaur

Gandhi and Prema Kantak

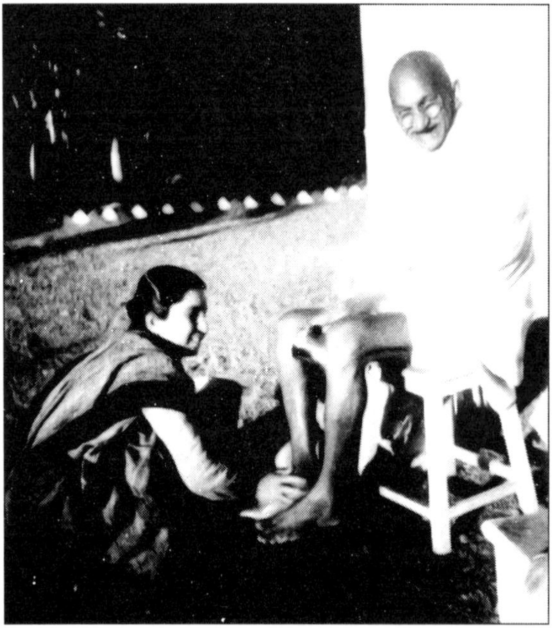

Gandhi and Lilavati Asar

Gandhi and Prabhavati

Index